Queer Anatomies

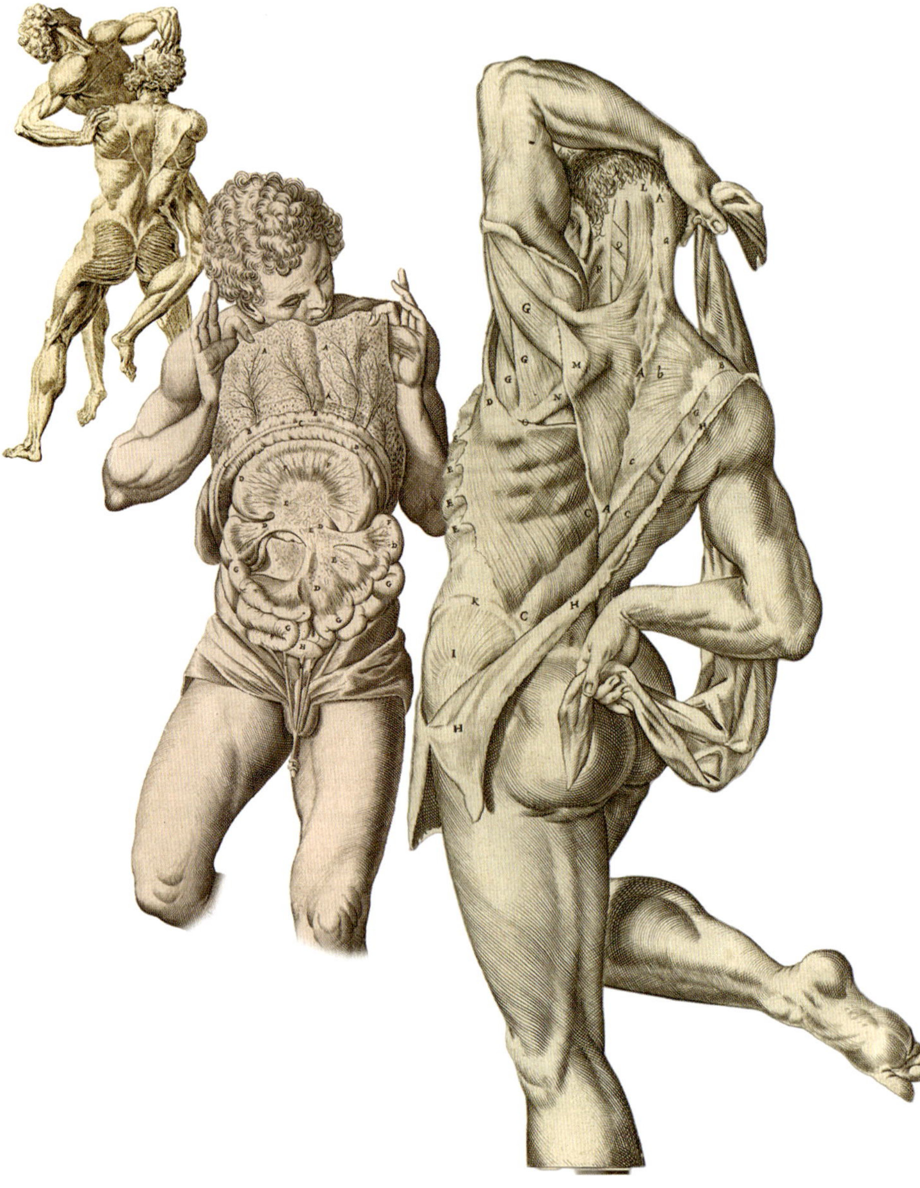

Queer Anatomies

Aesthetics and Desire in the Anatomical Image, 1700–1900

MICHAEL SAPPOL

BLOOMSBURY VISUAL ARTS
LONDON • NEW YORK • OXFORD • NEW DELHI • SYDNEY

BLOOMSBURY VISUAL ARTS
Bloomsbury Publishing Plc
50 Bedford Square, London, WC1B 3DP, UK
1385 Broadway, New York, NY 10018, USA
29 Earlsfort Terrace, Dublin 2, Ireland

BLOOMSBURY, BLOOMSBURY VISUAL ARTS and the Diana logo
are trademarks of Bloomsbury Publishing Plc

First published in Great Britain 2024

Cover design: Elena Durey
Cover image: William Cheselden, *Anatomy of the Human Body*
(London, 1773), tab. 20. Hagströmer Medico-Historical Library.

A catalogue record for this book is available from the British Library.

A catalog record for this book is available from the Library of Congress.

ISBN: HB: 978-1-3504-0086-3
PB: 978-1-3504-0087-0
ePDF: 978-1-3504-0089-4
eBook: 978-1-3504-0088-7

Typeset by Integra Software Services Pvt. Ltd.
Printed and bound in India

To find out more about our authors and books visit www.bloomsbury.com
and sign up for our newsletters.

For Mr X, whose liver was spliced into me, so that years later I could put queer images and queer thoughts before you, dear reader. (Thank you Mr X!)

And for brother Steve, who left us as Queer Anatomies *drifted toward the finish line, and for little Isadora who joined us just the same.*

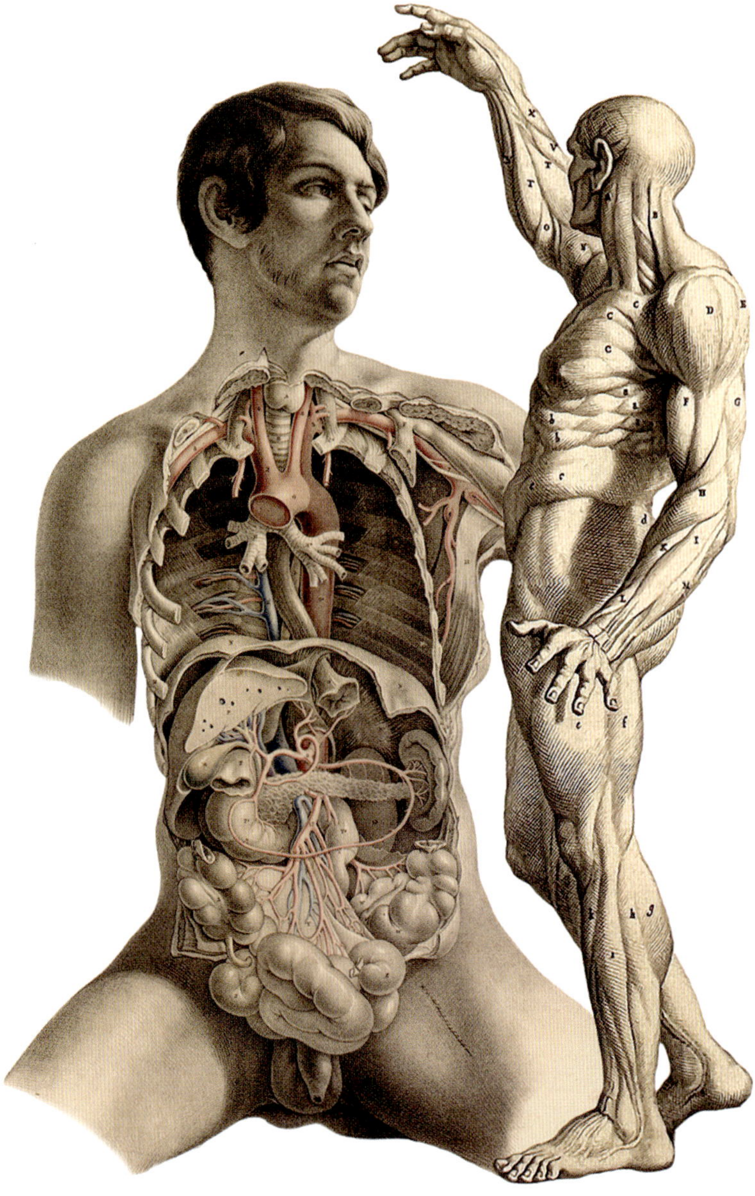

CONTENTS

Part Four Conclusion

LIST OF ILLUSTRATIONS

ACKNOWLEDGMENTS

Many many friends and colleagues have helped and supported this work. I've tried to keep track along the way, but if for some reason, your name is omitted here, please forgive me. I thank you all from the bottom of my heart: Joanne Begiato; Maja Bondestam; Michael Brown; Kelly Caldwell; Anthea Callen; Baillie Card; Sria Chatterjee; Deborah Coltham; Mark Dery; Annelie Drakman; Joanna Ebenstein; Jack Eckert; Emily Evans; Ross Fraser-Smith, Roger Gaskell; Andrew Graciano; Stephen Greenberg; Carrie Greenwood; Anita Guerrini; Mary Hague-Yearl; Petter Hellström; Alexander Highfield; Gertie Johansson; Ludmilla Jordanova; Solveig Jülich; Mark Kessell; Anna Lantz; Christopher Lawrence; Melissa Lo; Sarah Lowengard; Ross MacFarlane; Jessica Murphy; Michael North; Stephen Novak; Holly Peel; Scott Podolsky; Maisoon Rehani; Mary Roach; Elizabeth Savage; William Schupbach; Arlene Shaner; Robin Simon; Ad Stijnman; Paul Theerman; Mike Townend; Sarah Victoria Turner; Aleksandra Urakova; John Harley Warner; Alexander Wragge-Morley; and the anonymous readers of Art History, British Art Studies and Bloomsbury Press, who pushed me on interpretations, arguments and many particulars. Special thanks to Keren Rosa Hammerschlag, who was there at the beginning of *Queer Anatomies*, Ruth Peyser, for all her work on the images, and to Eva Åhrén, Jenny Sundén and Anthea Callen, whose generosity and intellectual comradeship helped get this book over the finish line.

The materials of *Queer Anatomies* come from many wonderful collections. First and foremost, the Hagströmer Medico-Historical Library (Karolinska Institute, Sweden), the Wellcome Library (London), and the National Library of Medicine (USA), but also: the Academy of Fine Arts (Vienna), Painting Gallery; the American Antiquarian Society; August C. Long Health Sciences Library (Columbia University); Birkbeck College, University College London; Bodleian Library (University of Oxford); The British Museum; Consortium for the History of Science, Technology and Medicine (Philadelphia); Francis A. Countway Library of Medicine (Harvard University); Cushing Library (Yale University); La Specola (Florence); Metropolitan Museum of Art; Morbid Anatomy; National Museum, Sweden; New York Academy of Medicine Library; Osler Library, McGill University; The Royal College of Physicians (London); Swedish Collegium for Advanced Study; Towneley Museum and Art Gallery; Truman G. Blocker Jr. History of Medicine Collections,

University of Texas Medical Branch; Uppsala University Libraries; Victoria & Albert Museum; Walker Art Gallery (Liverpool). And a call-out to the indispensable Internet Archive, which put so many obscure and vibrant source materials within reach before, during and after the pandemic.

Over the years, I have presented parts of *Queer Anatomies* as an ongoing work-in-progress at Morbid Anatomy Museum (Brooklyn), the American Association for the History of Medicine annual meeting, Swedish Collegium for Advanced Studies, Birkbeck College (London), Uppsala University Institute for the History of Ideas and Science, and the University of Utrecht.

This book is supported by a Publications Grant from the Paul Mellon Centre for Studies in British Art.

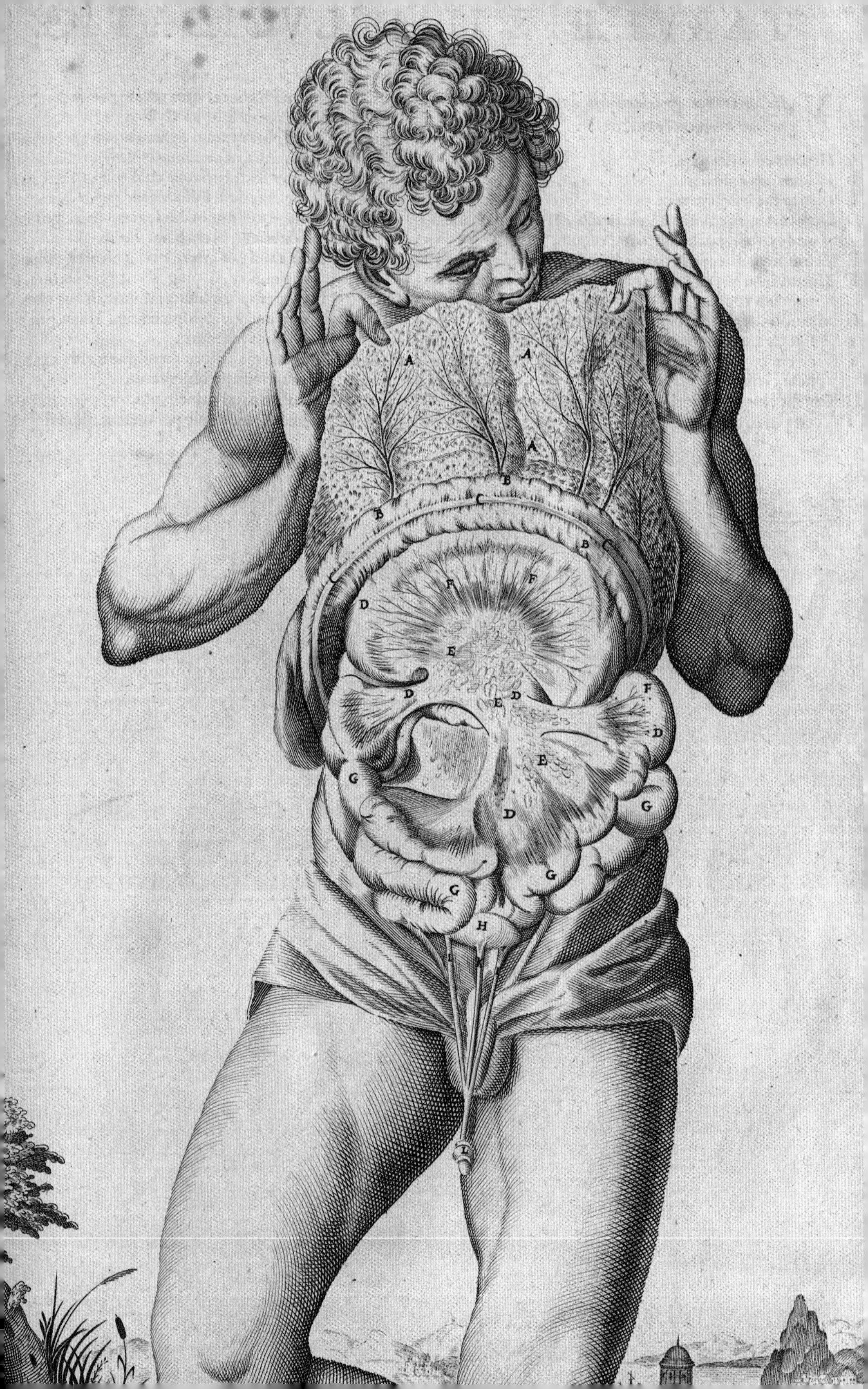
A
B
C
D
E
F
G
H

PART ONE

The unbearable queerness of anatomy

... what is there remaining to be done, if it be not to arrange the facts in hand, with a view to their proper interpretation?

— Joseph Maclise, *Surgical Anatomy* (London, 1856), preface

INTRODUCTION

1.1 A queer ventriloquism act

It's November 6, 1867. Oliver Wendell Holmes Sr., Harvard's renowned Professor of Anatomy and Physiology steps to the podium, amidst thumping cheers, to deliver a lecture to the incoming class. After a few throat-clearing remarks, he announces his subject, "scholastic and bedside teaching."[1] But then leads his audience down an obscure byway of the colonial past, conjuring up "an imaginary clinical lesson from the lips of an historical personage." Which turns out to be Giles Firmin, the preacher-physician who, in the year 1647, is said to have performed the first anatomical dissection in British North America. Holmes is the quintessential modernizer, famous for doubting the value of traditional remedies and tried-and-true therapies like blistering

1.1 *A dissected man lifts up his "lace-like omentum." Adrianus Spigelius,* De humani corporis fabrica libri... *(Amsterdam, 1627), bk. 8, tab. 6. Art: Odoardo Fialetti. Copperplate engraving: Francesco Valesio. 41 × 26 cm. Hagströmer Medico-Historical Library.*

and bloodletting. He is the man who championed the use of anesthesia (he coined the word), and championed Semmelweiss's revolutionary research on "the contagiousness of puerperal [childbed] fever." And then campaigned to get doctors and surgeons to take precautions—handwashing—to avoid fatally contaminating patients with infectious matter.[2] But still relishes the lore of bygone medical follies, errant beliefs, and anatomical play. And is delighted to hand on that legacy.

And so Holmes relates how Firmin, in the course of dissecting "some poor wretch who had swung upon the gallows," may have "turned to his book, as he laid bare the mysteries of the hidden organs." Perhaps, he speculates, it might have been a well-used copy of Firmin's "precious Vesalius":

> ... or [Vesalius's] figures repeated in the multifarious volume of Ambroise Paré; [or] ... the Aldine octavo in which Fallopius recorded his fresh observations; or that giant folio of Spigelius just issued from the press of Amsterdam, in which lovely ladies display their viscera with a coquettish grace implying that it is rather a pleasure than otherwise to show the lace-like omentum, and hold up their appendices epiploicae as if they were saying "these are our jewels." (279)

It's a curious anecdote, at once celebratory and mocking. As a descendant of first-wave settlers (Holmes also coined the term "Brahmin" as a label for the "caste" of elite Bostonians he belonged to), Holmes surely knows that Firmin, who accompanied his father Giles Firmin Sr. on the voyage from England to Massachusetts Bay Colony in 1632, was not just an anatomist but also a pious Puritan minister who preached the Word in tracts and sermons.[3] Firmin urged Christian devotion upon his congregants and warned against sinful thoughts and theological error. Yet, in Holmes's reverie, Firmin breaks from his dissection to take pleasure in an anatomical peep-show, replete with "lovely ladies" (prostitutes?) displaying their anatomical wares in one of the great illustrated atlases of early modern Europe (Figs. 1.1–3). And here Holmes lets the mask slip a bit. Even as he marks the utter absurdity of early anatomical engravings compared to the sober pictorial conventions of modern times, his pleasure in the fanciful plates of yore, and their eccentric, mildly titillating showmanship, shines through.

What's odder still about Holmes's recital is that the most coquettish of Spigelius's figures, the ones that demonstratively hold up their jewels and show off their lacy *omenta*, are *not* "lovely ladies." On a few pages, Spigelius does feature female subjects in coquettish poses, but mostly he shows scenes of ladies posed in modestly welcoming postures to demonstrate the anatomy of the female reproductive system and various stages of pregnancy (Figs. 1.4–5). Some of the ladies in Spigelius's *De foetu formato* (Padua, 1626) are dissected in such a way as to resemble a blossoming flower. Not terribly modest that, but the showmanship resides in the hands of the anatomist and artist, and not in any (imagined) acts of cadaveric coquetterie.

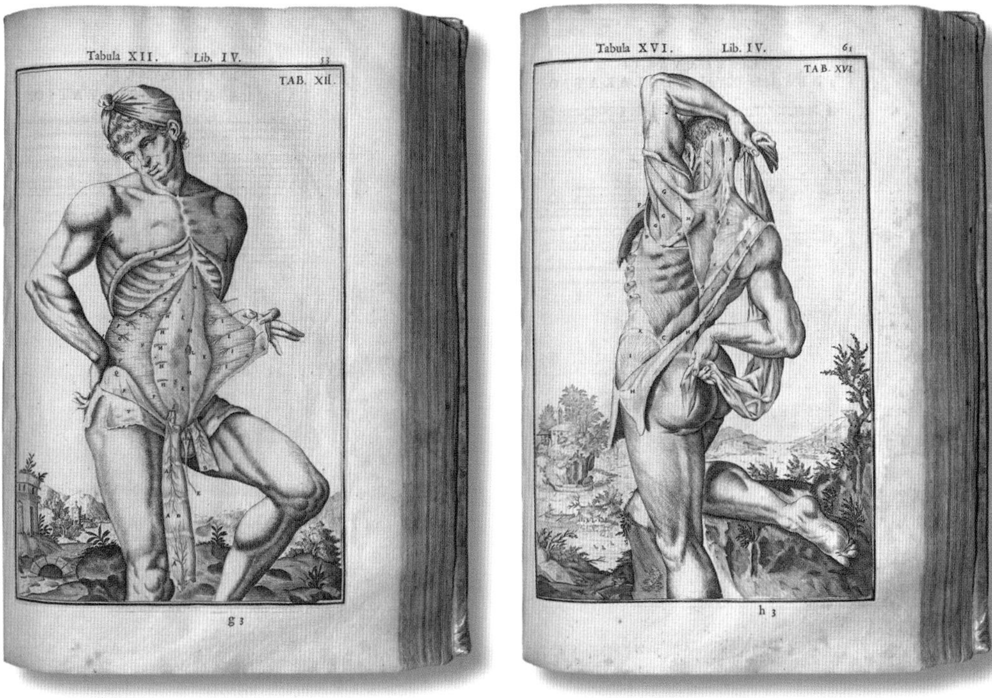

1.2–5 TOP ROW: *Anatomical cockettes. Adrianus Spigelius,* De humani corporis fabrica libri… *bk. 4, tabs. 12, 16.* BOTTOM ROW: *Some less immodest female performers.* BOTTOM LEFT: De humani corporis fabrica libri… *bk.8, tab. 19.* BOTTOM RIGHT: De foetu formato *(Padua, 1626), tab. 4. Art: Odoardo Fialetti. Copperplate engraving: Francesco Valesio. 41 × 26 cm. Hagströmer Medico-Historical Library.*

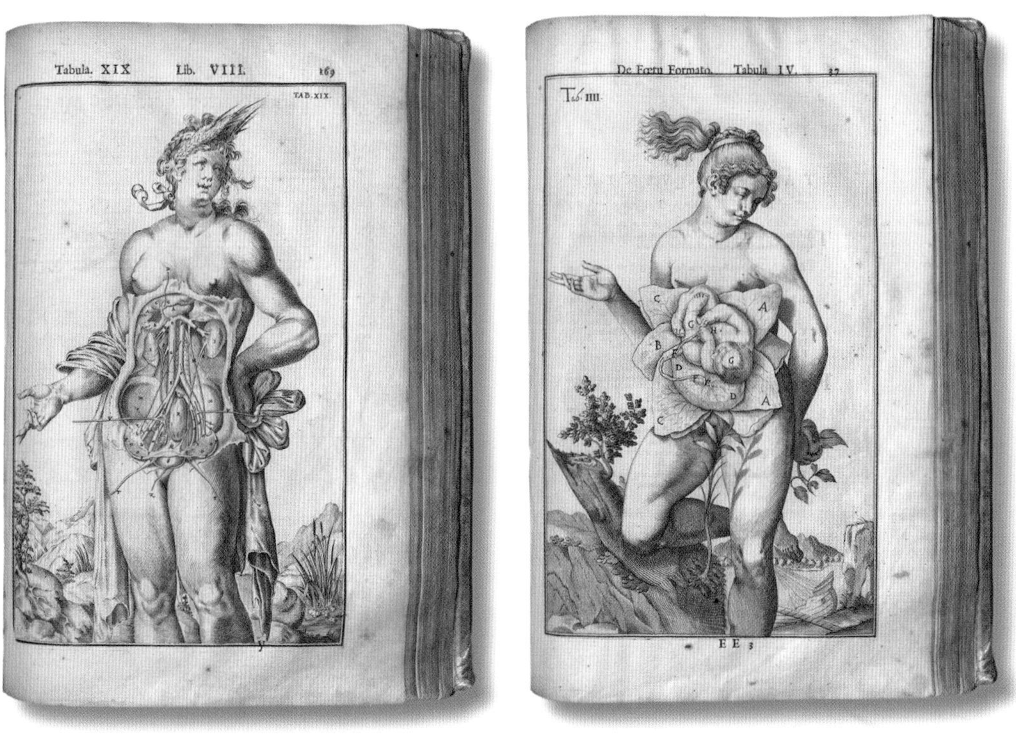

The anatomized ladies may flirt a bit with the reader, but do not display their *omentum*, and no jewel-like *appendices epiploicae* are displayed (as far as I can see). No, in Spigelius's Amsterdam folio of 1627, the figures who most theatrically "display their viscera with a coquettish grace" are *male* (Figs. 1.1–3).

To our twenty-first-century eyes, then, Spigelius's flirty men may be accounted not only as odd, but *queer*, a *prima facie* case of seventeenth-century anatomical voguing. (Padua is burning.) But not the way Holmes tells it. That salient fact of campy showmanship is overlooked. Or suppressed.

It's hard to say why. Holmes could have consulted his own copy of the rare 1627 first edition of the Spigelius folio.[4] But maybe only gave the figures a cursory glance before writing up his lecture, and mistakenly took the flirtatious *coques* for coquettes. Or relied on faulty memory, and neglected to check his copy. Or was so blinkered by immersion in hetero norms as to not even see it.

Or ... maybe he was in on the carnivalesque jokery staged by artist Odoardo Fialetti at the behest of Giulio Casseri (*aka* "Casserius"), professor of anatomy at the University of Padua, in the folio that was completed and posthumously published under the name of his successor Adriaan van den Spiegel (*aka* "Spigelius").[5] Maybe Holmes kept his anatomical "cockettes" as a private pleasure, and was disinclined to publicly acknowledge the homoerotic flavor of the performance, reluctant to let his audience of young medical students in on the joke. Or maybe Holmes was (intentionally or not) translating Fialetti's polymorphously perverse display into an idiom of impropriety that he and the lecture hall attendees could more easily tolerate and comprehend: frat-boy gazing on female subjects. Maybe maybe maybe maybe.

Holmes, of course, was not just a celebrated champion of scientific medicine, but also a distinguished man of letters, a novelist, poet, journalist and the author of *The Autocrat of the Breakfast Table* (1858), which was regarded for a century or more as a classic of American comic literary prose. In that vein, the opening gambit of his 1867 lecture is a jesting act of historical ventriloquism. Double ventriloquism: Holmes inhabiting the figure of Firmin inhabiting Spigelius. An act that enables the Harvard professor to flaunt his love and knowledge of rare illustrated medical books—Holmes was an avid bibliophile (Fig. 1.6) and book-collector.[6] And bear in mind again the venue: Holmes concocted his anatomical puppet show for a convocation of male students and professors, an audience very likely including bibliophilic colleagues (and later expanded to a wider readership of medical men via publication in his collected *Medical Essays*).[7] To put a fine point on it: Holmes's rare Spigelius was an object of bibliophilic desire that enfolded objects of representational desire—images of flirtatious anatomized men miming female objects of desire. So: double, triple desire, at men, among men, between men. A travesty in gender and history and anatomy and bibliophilia. How very queer.

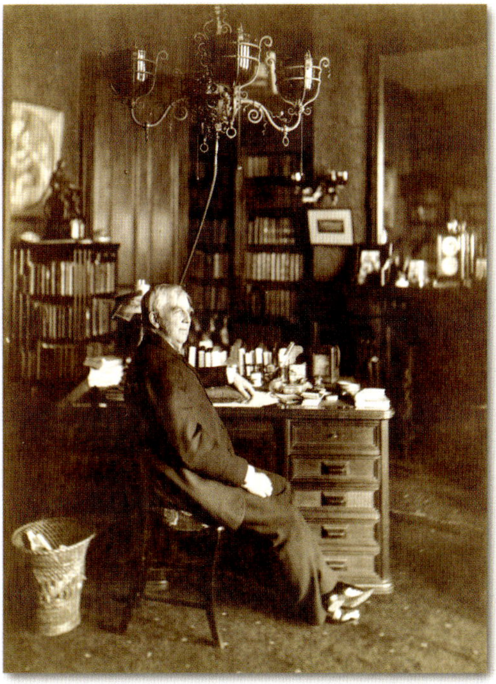

1.6 *Oliver Wendell Holmes Sr. in his office with some of his books (c.1890). Countway Library of Medicine, Harvard University, from an original in the Boston Medical Library.*

1.2 An advisory, an acknowledgment

And so to begin: a coy daydream about a seventeenth-century Puritan taking pleasure in an anatomical striptease, narrated in a prologue to a mid-nineteenth-century for-gentlemen-only lecture (later a printed essay) on scholastic and bedside teaching. And now, here in the twenty-first century, repurposed to introduce the work you are presently reading. Which is a book on perverse desire in the center and margins of the eighteenth- and nineteenth-century anatomical figure—and on the queerness of certain anatomical illustrations and the men who made them, gazed upon them, studied them, collected them. In the foreground: works by William Cheselden and Joseph Maclise. Behind and ahead of them: Casserius and Spigelius, Gautier Dagoty, Paolo Mascagni, Jones and Richard Quain, John and Charles Bell, J.-B.-M. Bourgery and N.-H. Jacob, M.-P.-C. Sappey, Baron Dupuytren, Henry Gray, William Hunter, and many others. (Familiar names to those who know the history of medicine ...)

In the pages that follow, we will read images from the past, up close and at a distance: medical and artistic renderings of dead and dissected bodies (mostly naked, mostly male), erect and flaccid penises, open and closed vaginas, buttocks and rectums. And we'll think about perverse desire and same-sex erotics, and how once upon a time such things were mixed up with sober professional conduct, scientific investigation, art pedagogy and connoisseurship. And with politics, ideology, social standing, friendship, and sexual identity.

Corporeal estrangement stood at the center of the anatomical enterprise. The dead body, full of horrific smells, atrocious sights and infectious perils, was made to perform provocations which tested, informed and entertained anatomists, medical students, onlookers. And also—via specimens, models and pictures—a more distant and more public viewership. Medical students were notoriously prankish, high-spirited, even riotous, in dissecting rooms, graveyards and anatomical lectures. Those outrages were met with efforts to impose limits, at a bare minimum decorum. And, in some respects, so it is today. In keeping, then, with present-day ethical protocols, here's an advisory: if you don't wish to see, you may at any time depart these pages (as if anyone needs my permission).

I hope you decide to stay the course. But before we get properly started, in the interests of full disclosure I need to make a confession: I take pleasure in all of this. I delight in the beauty, sensuality, eroticism, burlesquerie, high artistry and low, the sheer peculiarity—as did the men who are the protagonists of this book. If I get carried away with my appreciation, and indulge in something approaching an "erotics" (as Susan Sontag once urged her readers to do, without ever really explaining what that might mean), please bear with me.[8] Our historical actors had to disavow or conceal or encode their pleasure. I don't. You don't. But, even so, the sources and nature of that pleasure cannot be plain and simple. It has a differential history, objects, effects. Which are worthy of consideration.

If the images here discomfort you, that's also worth considering. You may feel disturbed by the sight of so much exposed skin and so many opened bodies. And so many penises and rectums (a few vaginas too). Or resent the anatomists and surgeons and artists who made provocative or demanding or seductive images from cadavers and dissections (without ever thinking to ask anyone's consent) (Fig. 1.7). Or become irritated with me for foisting those things upon you. Whatever the case: please suspend judgment ... Breathe deep, and follow me into the lost world of anatomists, artists, readers, collectors, cadavers, and queer anatomies ....

If you do follow, I think it will pull on you like it pulls on me. We're TV-watchers, phone-users, museum-goers, novel-readers, video-gamers, podcast-listeners. We watch read hear and play. We like to set our bodies aside and distract ourselves, temporarily relieve ourselves of the pressure of history and necessity, the incalculable weight density mass. Instead, we float away on media clouds. Phantasmic forms play-act before us. Sometimes violent sometimes rosy sometimes sexy sometimes monstrous ... And, in the moment, we're colonized, re-made, hooked. We take the pipe, inhale, dream on.

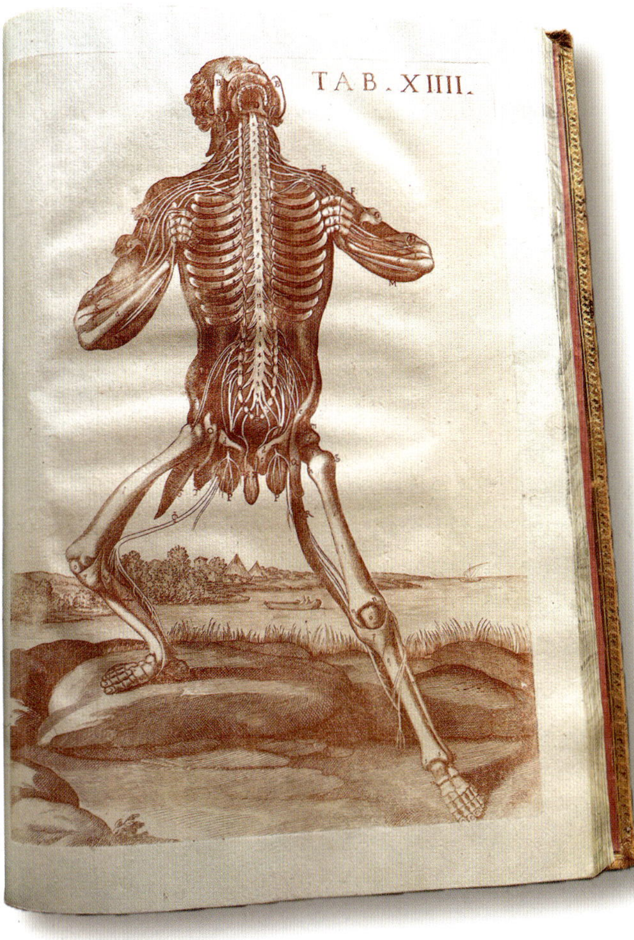

1.7 *A dissected man confronts the reader. High spirits within the anatomical image. Pietro da Cortona Berrettini,* Tabulae Anatomicae… *(1618; Rome, 1788), pl. 14. Copperplate engraving. 44 × 31 cm. Hagströmer Medico-Historical Library.*

That's heady. Heads spin. But even high-flying escapism relies on toil, politics, traffic management, chores. And all of that heady fantasy happens in our fleshy bodies, in the gravity that crushes us, in the humidity and temperature and the past that molds us and shapes our world. Your head is attached to a neck which tapers off into collarbones lungs guts and so on … You turn pages, scroll down, follow the figures, in and out of rhythm, with fingers and breath and blinking eyes. "What else do you read a book with, but your body and your history?" poet/novelist Patricia Lockwood practically shouts from the middle paragraphs of a review essay. "What do you read a book with? Your wrong clothes, wrong shoes, wrong words, wrong mind?"[9] Wrong body. Wrong is the only option. Wrong is the only way to read, and write, and make pictures. Especially in anatomy, a restless field that, over hundreds of years, continually figured and disfigured and refigured dead bodies in dissecting rooms, lecture halls, museums and illustrated books (later in photographs, motion pictures and digital interactives). Changing sensibilities, technologies, politics, research agendas, ethical codes. Bodies with no heads. Heads with no bodies. Mouths, feet, skin, muscles, veins, nerves, innards, hands, genitalia. Methodical. Estranging. Discrepant. Wrong. Queer.

THEORY

2.1 Queer explains everyone

And that's how to read this book. Which is inspired by Eve Kosofsky Sedgwick's *The Epistemology of the Closet,* one of the foundational texts of queer studies and theory, published way back in 1990.[10] Queer theorists theorize the power relations, politics and lived experience of "mismatches between sex, gender and desire." They finger everything that "troubles" gender, identity, and the male/female binary. Variations and deviations of all kinds.[11] Which is important because, as Kosofsky Sedgwick argues, normative and abnormative performances of gender—masculine/feminine, hetero/homo, dominant/submissive, pure/impure, generic/anomalous—always fluctuate in push/pull dialogues with one another. Always make sense or nonsense in relation to each other.[12] One side always conjures the other (the Other, in critic-speak). If so, the *queer* of queer theory doesn't *only* belong to, or explain, self-identified *queers*. Queer explains *everybody*, including the very straightest, self-identified (even homophobic) (especially homophobic) *straights*. (Whether they know it or not.) And queerness stands at the very center of the anatomical illustration—and the very center of "Western culture as a whole." Not just a marginal effect.[13] Not just for marginal people. Oliver Wendell Holmes Sr. was a medical and literary celebrity and lion of Boston society (and the father of three children, one of whom became a Justice of the US Supreme Court). Adriaan van den Spiegel (*Spigelius*) was the professor of anatomy at Padua, one of the great universities of Europe, and at the forefront of anatomical research.

So marginal and dead center. But difficult to pin down. Cultural critics and activists originally offered *queer* as a critique of *gay*, *lesbian*, *homosexual*—categories which seemed to be evolving into stable—in their own way normative—identities.[14] At its inception, *queer* was oppositional and wayward. "Queer," Rosemary Hennessy insists, "is a mark of the instability of identity." Queerness "highlights the arbitrariness of the neat distinctions ... between masculine and feminine," and between hetero- and homosexual desire and performance.[15] And the impossibility of any way to absolutely define and enforce those lines. Queer can include male effeminacy or hyper-masculinity. Female masculinity or hyper-femininity. Desire between men or between women. Or between humans and animals, or humans and things. Really all sorts of erotic attachments to persons, body parts and objects, obsessions, positions. But not necessarily.[16] It all depends. *Queer* resists definition.

Even so, *queer* especially belongs to those who feel and avow their queerness, and who are especially attuned to the dynamics of queer subject formation and feeling. Queer theory is queer. José Esteban Muñoz, for example, understands queerness as a sensitizing mode of desire that enables one to "see and feel beyond the quagmire of the present" (*Cruising Utopia*). And, for Peggy Phelan, this exquisite sensitization is simultaneously emplacing and displacing, embodying and disembodying. So that "something substantial can be made from the outline left after the body has disappeared" (*Mourning Sex*). Phelan goes on to talk of an "affective outline of what we've lost" in the wake of AIDS, which "might bring us closer to the bodies we want still to touch," and which we might somehow redeem via "art with real bodies."[17]

If Phelan and Muñoz evoke contemporary experience (and in the case of Muñoz, even "queer futurity"), other twentieth- and twenty-first-century writers conjure an idiosyncratic blizzard of feelings and acts. Personal and collective, past and present, imaginary and real, comic and tragic, affectively potent. Shame and shaming. Prideful defiance. Confusion. Willful transgression. Travesty. Grief. Ecstasy. Numbness. Heightened sensation. Casual fornication. Romance. Fixation, obsession, fetishism. Queer sensitivity.

2.2 Queer history

Maybe that's specific to our time and we're led astray if we transport our *queer* back into the distant past. Queerness, of necessity, is historical, situational, relational (Fig. 1.8). What was normative in Periclean Greece and Augustan Rome appears to be very unlike what was normative in Georgian Britain, even if Georgians looked to antiquity for moral, cultural, political and aesthetic exemplars. Art historian Whitney Davis, setting the table for his study of eighteenth- and nineteenth-century "queer beauty" and aesthetics, urges us to "notice the erotic entanglements of art in its social milieu … [and] corporeal and communal contexts."[18]

His historical actors were entangled in their world. We're entangled in ours. Outside this book, you can hear warnings: Beware of entanglement. The historian George Kubler long ago cautioned readers that "Our signals from the past are very weak and our means for recovering their meaning … are most imperfect."[19] It's an epistemological error to export our analytic categories and descriptive vocabulary back into the past: we naïvely think we're following a thread, but the past is frayed, or spun from entirely different fibers. The historian Arnold Davidson, following Michel Foucault, argues that "an analysis of late antiquity and early Christianity would reveal … an experience of the flesh quite distinct from, and not to be confused with, our experience of sexuality." The "conflation of these experiences," via our own "coarse epistemology," leads us into "a disfiguring, disabling anachronism":

> It is this automatic and immediate application of concepts, as though concepts have no temporality, that allows, and often requires, us to draw misleading analogies and inferences that derive from a historically inappropriate and conceptually untenable perspective.[20]

Concepts have temporality. Yes. Our perspectives are time-bound. Yes. But it is the very difference between then and now that enables us to place our

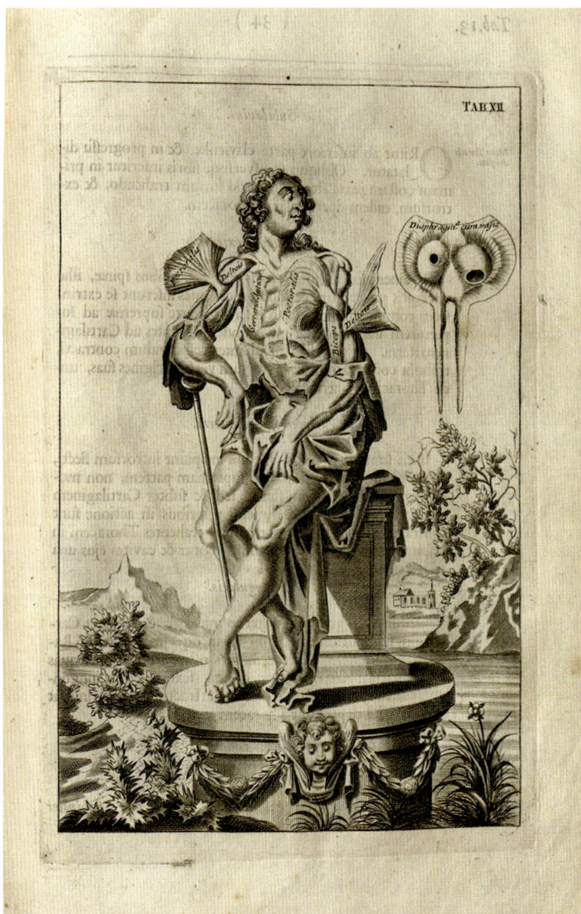

1.8 *John Browne,* A Compleat Treatise of the Muscles, as they appear in the Humane Body, and Arise in Dissection *(London, 1681), pl. 12. Copperplate engraving. 32 × 29 cm. Hagströmer Medico-Historical Library. A foppish courtier postures atop a pedestal, legs crossed as if dancing a dainty step: one of a series of anatomical travesties. (In reality the nobility and gentry were protected from dissection—anatomists used the bodies of prisoners, outcasts and the poor.)*

concepts and systems as products of our distinctive times and locations, and not of some essential unchanging human nature. Even so, there must still be commonalities in human experience that our current vocabulary and analysis can partially capture and translate. Because we're not entirely worlds apart—otherwise societies, cultures and persons, past or present, linguistically or geographically distant, would be utterly undecipherable, inaccessible to historians, anthropologists, translators and go-betweens.[21] As we heed Davidson's caution, then, let's posit that our personal and recent historical experiences of queerness can sensitize us to comparable dynamics in eighteenth- and nineteenth-century life, at least what we can make of it. With our queer eyes, maybe we can make out the expressively queer "affective outlines" of anatomical figures and their anatomical creators in bygone times—who also made "art with real bodies." (Literally. The medium of human flesh.)

Gary Ferguson, writing on same-sex identity and relations (and same-sex marriage!) among certain groups of men in early modern Rome, gets it just about right: while we shouldn't look to the past for "mirror images of ourselves," we also shouldn't presume a total "breach between 'us' and the rest of history."[22] If "the past is a foreign country" and "they do things differently there" (L.P. Hartley's still useable if shop-worn maxim), it's not *utterly* foreign.[23] Rather than "stress the alterity [otherness] and unintelligibility of disappeared or now-supposed-alien understandings of same-sex relations," Kosofsky Sedgwick urges us to "invest attention in those unexpectedly plural, varied and contradictory historical understandings whose residual … forces seem most palpable [to us] today." Palpable because people in past or distant locations lived lives that resonate and dissonate with our lives. With skillful reconstruction, we can make approximate sense of them, even feel something of their experience. (This is a tricky line to dance on. Foucauldian warnings against anachronistic conflation may end up justifying a kind of epistemological nihilism, a refusal of imaginative reconstruction. And then, paradoxically, a reimposed embargo on the recognition of expressions of queer desire. In a casual aside that tacks against the drift of his larger argument, Davidson himself allows that "The lengths or depths to which some will go to deny what is visibly evident is rather remarkable.")[24]

2.3 The gaze and its objects

If anatomical dissection and representation can activate a certain kind of queerness (and vice versa), then queer theory should supply us with useful models and descriptive terms for tactics and settings. Such as: *the closet*, *queer space*, *drag*, *shadows*, *camp*, *flagging*, *passing*, *flaunting*, *cruising*, *clubbing*, *voguing*, *panic* … Another favored term is *the gaze*—meaning originally a kind of intensive, entranced looking (watching, surveying, studying)—which is also a keyword in visual culture and film studies, feminist theory, and the writings of Michel Foucault. In those settings, the gaze, especially "the medical gaze," has mostly been figured as oppressive.[25] The person, body part or thing gazed upon is "constituted" as an object by the gaze (and its technologies), and so fixed, and robbed of agency, objectified. Foucault, with early nineteenth-century anatomy top of mind, says "cadaverized."[26] But not so fast. The gaze is dynamic, complex, multidirectional, generative. Even if it seems unmediated, it always depends on mediation: technologies, procedures and staging devices, such as the drawn or printed illustration, the microscope, the dissection, the display vitrine, the peep-hole, the spotlight, and even, on the periphery, the proscenium, picture frame and gallery wall. The gaze turns back on itself, has recursive effects. The object being gazed upon, even a cadaver or a picture of a cadaver, stages a return of sorts (Fig. 1.9). "The object stares back" (proclaims art historian James Elkins, echoing Lacan, from whom a lot of *gaze* talk ultimately derives): sometimes it even waves hello and bats its eyelashes. The initiator of the gaze is divided by the gazing act, invests the object of the gaze with agency, or

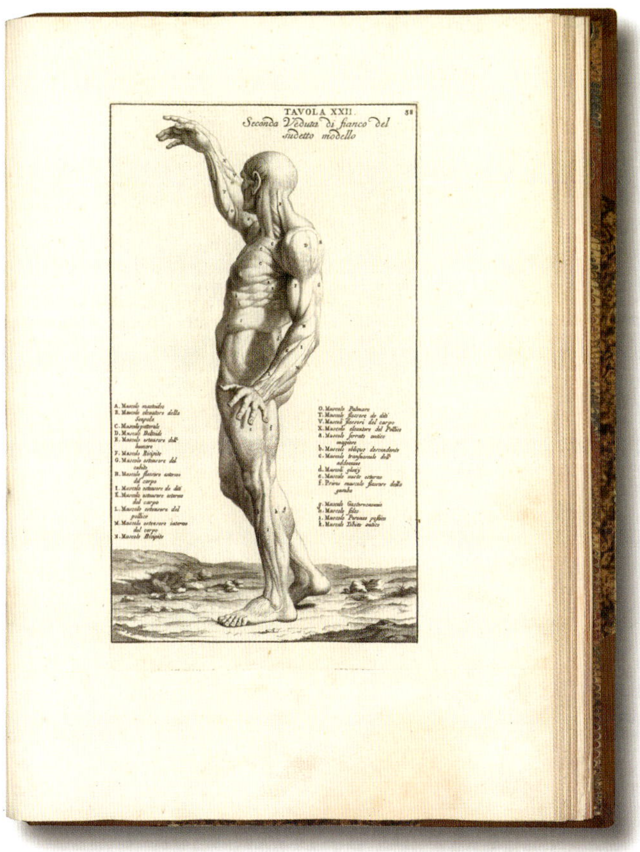

1.9 *Bernardino Genga,* Anatomia per uso et intelligenza del disegno ricercata non solo su gl'ossi, e muscoli del corpo humano *(Rome, 1691), pl. 22. Art: Charles Errard. Copperplate engraving. 47 × 32 cm. Waller Collection, Uppsala University Libraries.*

a simulation thereof, and in so doing makes a divided self, a splintered displaced subjectivity.[27] Foucault: "the observer and … observed take part in a ceaseless exchange. No gaze is stable: … subject and object, spectator and model, reverse their roles into infinity."[28]

Objects exercise an odd kind of agency, especially on the people who make them. Who can never entirely control their creations. Material things have qualities we don't account for (or don't want to account for). We never entirely control them or ourselves—there's always some partly or entirely unconscious expression in the form, content, staging, or framing. Resistance, defiance, transference, projection. And always some measure of contingency and materiality. Happy and unhappy accidents. Side effects. Non-effects. Because: we can't entirely control what goes on outside of us. We can't dictate the distribution, reading and reception of what we create. And we're constrained by time, opportunity, resources, materials, skill, knowledge, and co-workers. The anatomist has to cope with patrons, body provisioners, prosecutors, colleagues, students, artists, engravers, publishers, printers, legal authorities, the lay public. And bodies.

The point is this: anatomical images and objects perform. Spigelius and his cadavers directly refer to theater and dance in their poses, gestures, and settings. And that was conventional practice in early modern anatomical illustration. But anatomical figures aren't limited to light entertainment and burlesquerie. They're more varied and powerful than that. They can refer to all sorts of performances—social, religious, historical, athletic, military, funerary, pedagogical, etc. And to embodied experience—life and death, beauty and ugliness, desire and disgust, sickness and health. Some images signify strongly, others are tempered or dull. Levels of coherence and incoherence vary. But with all of that, there's also a cumulative impact. Anatomical images come in bunches, and in categories and genres and styles, which collectively have ramifying cognitive effects. Anatomical specimens and charts and illustrations have authority. And generate self-referentiality. When you refer to them, you refer to yourself, make yourself over. You're looking at yourself and something else.[29]

In the eighteenth and nineteenth centuries, the character of anatomical performance changed, but the anatomical illustration still put on a show for its viewers. Take, for example, these four plates (Figs. 1.10–13) from M.-P.-C. Sappey's 1874 study of the lymphatic vessels, which uses delicate filigreed lines of mercury injections to create patterns on the surface of the body. In Figure 1.10, hypnotic eyes unrelentingly stare back at the anatomist and the reader. Detached from the face, the mouths below appear to be on the verge of addressing (or kissing) the reader. In Figures 1.11 and 1.13, the torso shows

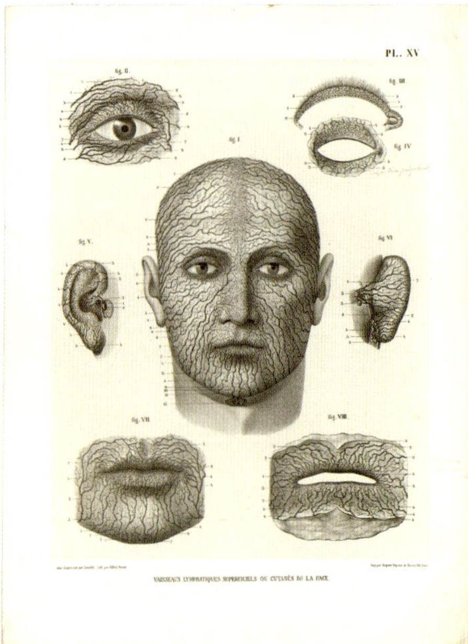

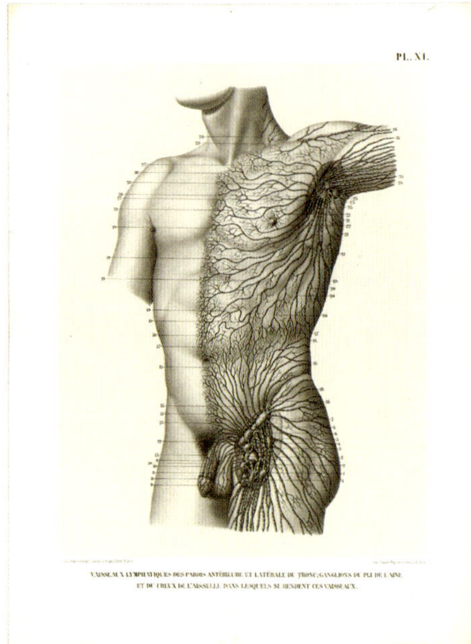

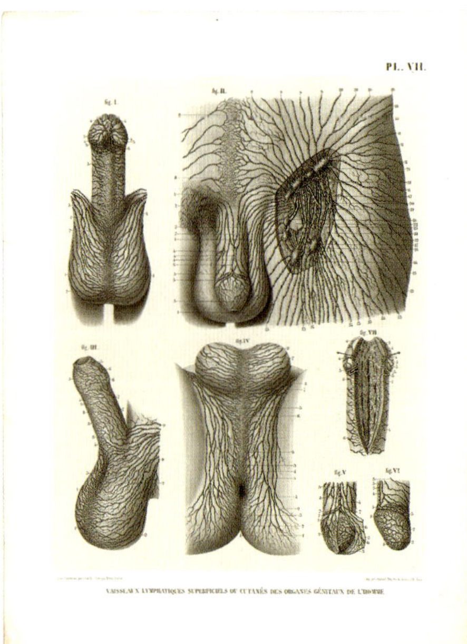

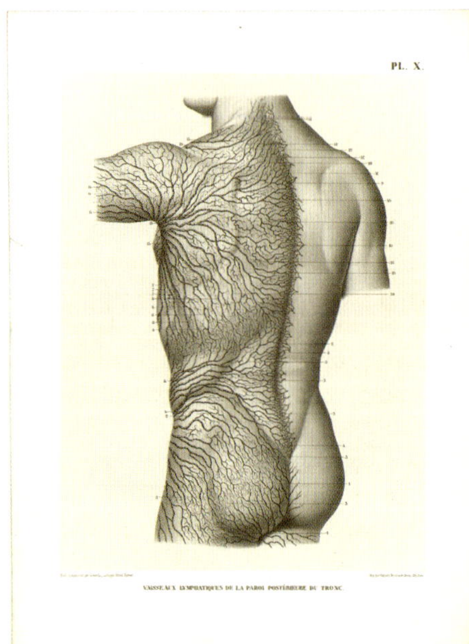

1.10–13 *M.-P.-C. Sappey,* Anatomie, Physiologie, Pathologie des Vaisseaux Lymphatiques… *(Paris, 1874). Art: Jean-Baptiste Léveillé. Lithography: Alfred Poirier. 54 cm. Hagströmer Medico-Historical Library.* TOP LEFT: *An almost extraterrestrial universal human emerges from lymphatic vessels on the surface of the face (pl. 15).* TOP RIGHT: *Lymphatic vessels make sensual tracings on the front surface of a masculine body (pl. 11).* BOTTOM LEFT: *Lymphatic vessels trace the surface of the male genital (pl. 7).* BOTTOM RIGHT: *Lymphatic vessels trace the posterior contours of a masculine body (pl. 10).*

off (the standard term is "demonstrates") Sappey's astonishing injection technique, artist Jean-Baptiste Léveillé's bravura draughtsmanship and Alfred Poirier's bravura lithography. And (together with nearby Figure 1.12) also flaunts genitals, flesh, and a fine masculine figure. That confrontational face ... Those oddly patterned defamiliarizing surfaces and demonstrative torso ... The lingering, meditative tracings on the skin ... The otherworldly classicism ... Even the little lines with numbers (call-outs to the captions and text) that make an odd radiant glow as they tether the body and its parts to the world of language and discourse ... Is that "queer"? Is this the sort of thing that queer theory provokes us to think about and *feel*? And can "importing queer notions into the world of critical theory," as Caroline Evans and Lorraine Gamman advocate, help us to comprehend, reconstruct, and take pleasure in, "perverse but enjoyable relations of looking" in seventeenth-, eighteenth- and nineteenth-century anatomy?

Much of the critical discourse on the gaze emanates from feminist theory, and deals with the emotional and moral wounds the objectifying male gaze inflicts on living breathing women at work, in the home and in every other situation.[30] There is a very long history of efforts to empower male gazers and to induce/coerce women to perform for the gaze, submit to it, internalize it. And a long history of efforts (of varying effectiveness) to suppress the emergence of a "female gaze."[31]

But also a long history of efforts, in proscriptive law and through prescriptive norms, to *constrain* the male gaze on the unclothed female subject. Even if gazing is a privileged activity, the gazer himself also comes under regimes of governance, becomes an object of the gaze. Critical communities of onlookers will direct their gaze upon the gazer and generate commentary and analysis. The gazer is subjected to policing, discipline, often mockery, and often enough an odd mixture of mockery and incitement. In different historical moments, that policing performs different functions: patriarchal territory-marking, protecting the market value of female virginity, coping with sex panic over the erotic power of women, etc. And these efforts co-exist with the emplacement of well-defined zones where men are licensed, even encouraged, to gaze intensively on unclothed *male* subjects—especially in medicine and in fine art. The training and policing of the male gaze, then, had the paradoxical effect of intensifying the erotic frisson that female subjects were taken to generate in every zone.[32] And, by marking a boundary between men and women, also had the effect of creating dedicated spaces (physical and discursive) in which homoerotic desire could blossom and flourish. Paradoxes that only a (feminist) theory of queer can account for.[33]

2.4 Proliferating views, intensified viewing

But *the gaze* is not a single thing. Its exponents may aspire to create an "absolute eye" (Foucault again), yet there are many kinds of looking—intensive looking—medical, aesthetic, pornographic, economic, religious, and so on.[34] Many "ways of seeing" (as John Berger famously demonstrated in his landmark BBC series and paperback) and many roles, sciences, institutions, connected to those ways. And so, an expansive vocabulary of looking-words: staring, glancing, peeking, peering, scrutinizing, picturing, surveying, inventorying, spotlighting, examining, targeting, scanning, searching, peeping, reading, tracking, sizing up. And many specialized domains—each with its own gendered rules and history and modes, some brightly performative, others circumspect or entirely screened off. And each with its own technologies and genres and protocols of representation.[35] Art historian Anthea Callen contrasts the casual "disembodied" sightseeing of the nineteenth-century "urban *flaneur*, the self-conscious Baudelairean stroller of the Parisian streets" with the "embodied physicality of the plurisensorial," "loquacious" medical gaze. Which was attached to, and generated, an apparatus of formal and informal discussions, lectures, demonstrations, "pathological cabinets," "grand rounds," wall charts, journal articles, atlases, textbooks, photographs, wax casts and models, etc.[36] And proliferating viewing devices, a prosthetics of viewing: magnifying glasses, binoculars, microscopes, telescopes, projectors, spectroscopes, eventually X-rays.[37] All formalized and institutionalized and technologized in their historical moment — particular locations and audiences, particular scopes, particular methods. (Oliver Wendell Holmes, the anatomy professor whose lecture starts off this book, invented the hand-held stereoscope, a device that facilitated the sharing in parlors and classrooms of immersive three-dimensional views of exotic scenes and objects. Scaled down to the size of rectangular "stereo-cards" and stored in a box with hundreds of such cards, in series, those views were transformed into indexed, archived equivalents.)

In clinics, dissecting rooms, laboratories, lecture halls, morgues, museums, and printed publications, anatomists gazed intently and expansively. And orchestrated those gazes for students, colleagues and a wider public. As did artists. Who made anatomical figures and scenes, with details and flourishes, on paper, canvas and blackboards, in ink, paint, chalk, marble, bronze, and wax. Which drew on well-established spectatorial tactics, customs, genres, even as medical researchers and artists (sometimes the same person) developed new techniques and strategies and instruments ... All designed for the proliferation and circulation of intensive viewing—the visual rhetoric and practice of the new science of the sixteenth and seventeenth centuries carried forward and expanded in the eighteenth and nineteenth centuries. What historians Simon Shaffer and Steven Shapin term "the multiplication of witnesses" went hand in hand with the multiplication of staged easily transportable sights for witnesses to see.[38]

Whether viewed directly or remotely via prints and illustrated books, or even "virtually" (that is, re-staged in the imagination stocked with a palette of visual experiences and descriptive narratives), the procedures of looking and view-making were themselves gender-coded. And laden with affordances for queering. Frank Nicholls, an eighteenth-century English anatomist, regarded the ability to look with calm discernment upon anatomically mutilated corpses as a sign of manly virtue and warned his students to arm themselves against the critics of anatomical butchery and their "effeminate lies."[39] Women wouldn't have been allowed to attend Nicholls's lectures. But even in Nicholls's time some women clamored to receive anatomical instruction and, a generation or two later, the right to dissect. Some of them eventually succeeded in doing so, at the risk (or for the benefit) of "de-sexing" themselves in the process.

As the eighteenth century transited into the nineteenth, the cultivation of the senses, especially the visual, became a nearly pervasive theme of literature, philosophy, and art pedagogy and criticism. And medical pedagogy and discourse. Fueled by Romanticism and Napoleonic "great-man-ism", there was a tendency toward gaze inflation, a kind of hyper gaze-ism. In the arts, essayist William Hazlitt in an 1824 article took "genius" to be the result of a heightened "power of original observation" (a gift which an anointed few were born with, but which others could perhaps cultivate through intensive training).[40] The philosopher Ralph Waldo Emerson, in an influential essay published in 1836, imagined that, in a transcendent state, emancipated from "all mean egotism," one would metamorphose into "a transparent eye-ball," purified, all-seeing, spirit, "part or particle of God."[41]

Tropes of the medical gaze couldn't top that, but had their own grandiose intensity. In a story published the very same year, Balzac figured the surgeon's gaze as a masculinist "godlike eye" through which the great surgeon could see "into the sufferer and his malady by an intuition, natural or acquired, [and] ... to grasp the diagnostics peculiar to the individual, to determine the very time, the hour, the minute when an operation should be performed, making due allowance for atmospheric conditions and peculiarities of individual temperament."[42] Sight and insight become indistinguishable. Seeing is seeing-into. Which generates images, words, thought pictures. Joseph Maclise, who we will meet later on in this book, a mid-nineteenth-century surgeon-anatomist who was also a gifted medical illustrator, connected his illustrations to the "mental vision" that a surgeon must use to "draw a distinct picture" of an anatomical region prior to surgery, a distinct picture in one's mind.[43] Drawings figured the gaze; the gaze figured drawings. On paper and in the imagination.

That level of intensity transforms the gazer. Foucault tells us that the gaze "constitutes" its object *and* its subject: the thing under scrutiny but also the scrutinizer and field of scrutiny. And goes on to explain that the apparatus of policing and shunning and studying and sorting, initially designed to survey, understand, condemn, cure or suppress desire, actually brings desire out of obscurity, propagates vocabulary words and practices and technologies and spaces. And objects and images. Which come to define and invest desire, produce and instantiate our categories of "sex," "sexuality," "homosexuality," "heterosexuality," "perversity," "deviance" and so on. Pathologize yes, but also naturalize. And incite. Leading, beyond that, to an ever-intensifying sense of interiority—and historicity—two kinds of depth—to go along with the proliferation of surfaces and objects.

And thus, Foucault argues, the gaze effects a redistribution of "the original distribution of the visible and invisible," and, by something more than association, the object of the gaze comes to seduce, and remake, even the sexologist and the policier. The gaze instigates queer displacements of desire.[44] And another queer effect: It's hard to keep modes of gazing apart. Curiosity and desire in scientific gazing and erotic gazing spill over into each other. Both are characterized by a passionate yearning to know and possess. And even employ the same technologies: A telescope designed to search the night sky can be used to peer through a window into a neighbor's apartment.

2.5 An odd term

Queer itself is an odd term, ill-defined and arguable. Its current usage grew out of the worry that the fight for homosexual rights was leading to a domestication of erotic expression and identities, a dulling of critical edges ("homonormativity"). *Queer* became a brand for a critique, a way out of territory disputes among LGBTs, and an alternative or complementary identity. Also a way in to new territory disputes: queer theorists are a disputatious bunch. Who sometimes tie themselves up in knots trying to keep queerness separate from same-sex desire and identity. Let's not worry too much about that. Queerness can take the form of a refusal to identify and perform as well as the perverse determination to identify in opposition to norms, queer theorist Jenny Sundén argues.[45] There are lots of different ways to identify or refuse identification, lots of different ways to queer (verb) and be queer (noun). Queerness resides in actions and objects as well as persons.

Let's also grant that the objects discussed in this book are queer in the old-fashioned sense: peculiar, eccentric, contrary, out of joint. And the queer of queer theory isn't entirely applicable to eighteenth- and nineteenth-century medical illustrations and objects. But any quick dismissal would be unwise. Queer theory gives us new eyes to see old objects, new words to describe and analyze, new thoughts to think. Queer theory has brought forth brilliant scholarship on medieval poetry, Renaissance painting, Nietzsche and Melville, comic books, electoral politics, video-gaming, fashion photography, all sorts of artifacts. In which queer desire and queer sexual expression—not always same-sex—take stage center or strategically occupy and overflow the margins.

Art historian Abigail Solomon-Godeau abstains from using "queer" as a category of analysis in *Male Trouble*, her groundbreaking 1997 book on the "crisis in male representation" in Revolutionary and post-Revolutionary

France. *Male Trouble* investigates the cultural meaning and political valences of the numerous paintings and sculptures of supine naked "ephebes" (young men, androgynous, effeminate, peri-adolescent). Queer theory was well underway, but Solomon-Godeau hedges on whether those works of art were motivated by homoerotic desire (and whether we should even care) (although she obviously does care).[46] The very question is taken to be anachronistic, irrelevant, a trap.

But, even if eighteenth- and nineteenth-century artists and anatomists didn't have access to our conceptual vocabulary of "queer" and "homosexuality," scholars can't entirely do without it: the very act of writing history involves translation and interpretation. "Being bound to the vocabulary of their own time," historian Blair Worden reminds us, "historians ... translate the thought of the past every time they recount it."[47] As we strive to understand and even resurrect the vocabularies, grammars and scenographies that structured the life-experiences and decisions of our historical actors, our own time-bound experiences provide us with new terms and concepts that sensitize us and help us to imaginatively reconstruct, and rethink, the past. And then rethink the present. The coming of online networks and interactive digital media is one such set of experiences (which have transformed our understanding of earlier successive media revolutions). Queer is another.

2.6 Default genders of anatomy

So here is an anatomical object designed as an instructional aid for the classroom and lecture hall: *Dr. Franke's Phantom* (Figs. 1.14–15), a life-size flap anatomy, manufactured in New York in 1891 and marketed in Germany. With over 100 flaps, like a Swiss army knife with too many blades. To be stood up before an audience and opened flap by flap, as a lecturer demonstrates. Containing: A whole course of lectures on medical topics—the systems of the body, the five senses, the dangers of corsetry, first aid and minor surgery, human reproduction. All packed into a masculine "heteronormative" figure (the top layer). Who is equipped with penis and testicles ... And who is also 5-ways pregnant.[48]

Which is certainly odd, even though the sellers and users of *Dr. Franke's Phantom* somehow never troubled themselves to comment on this queer bit of gender trouble. That failure (or refusal) to notice was perhaps due to the fact that, for centuries, the adult male body served as the default object in anatomical study (and every other domain of study).

Before the last third of the nineteenth century, art academies mostly used unclothed male models and cadavers to teach anatomy and to practice figure drawing. Anatomical atlases featured male bodies to illustrate *human* anatomy. In medical texts, the female body was mostly taken to be a special

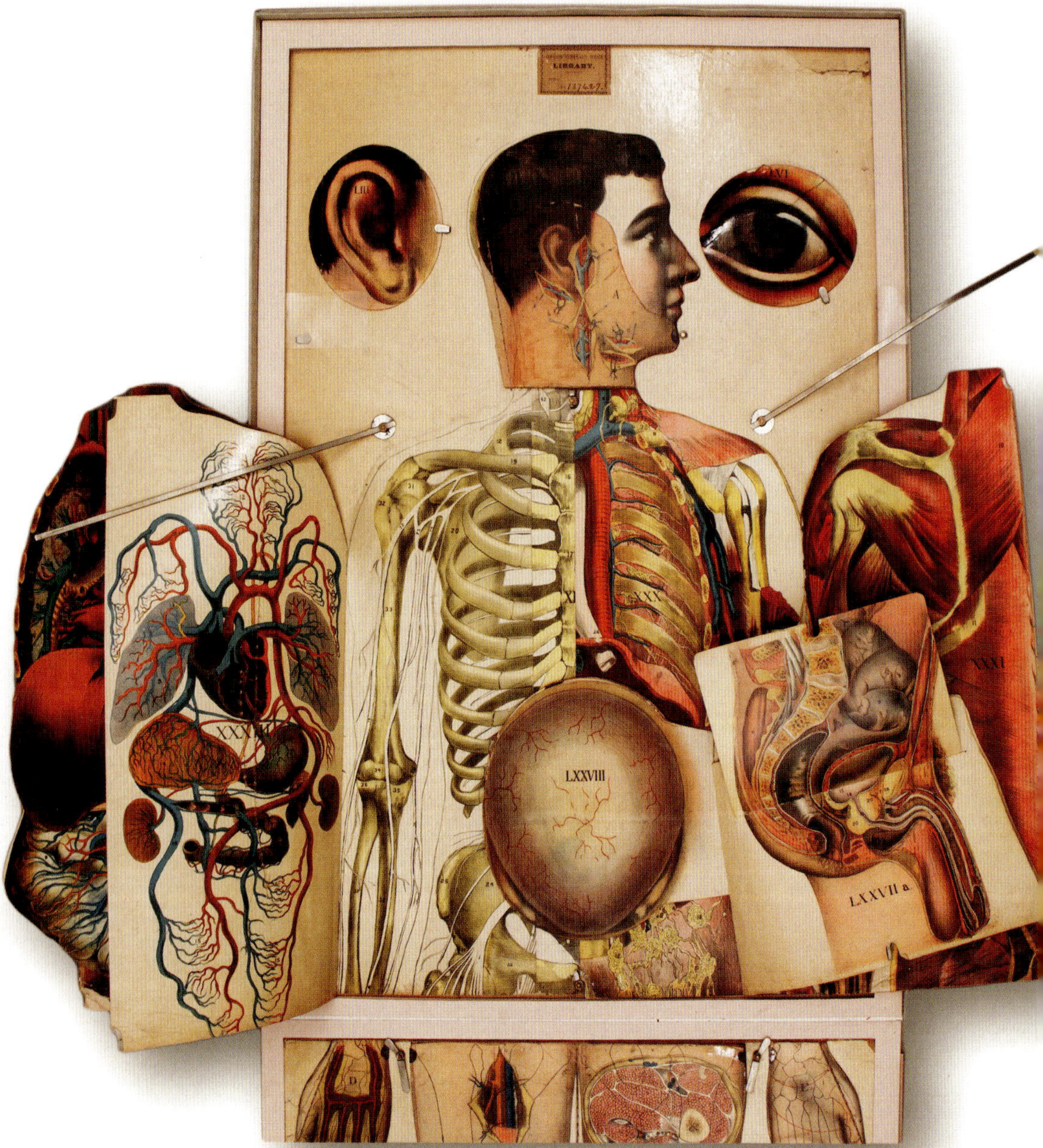

1.14–15 ABOVE: *Man with child, pregnant.* FACING PAGE: *Man with child, pregnant, with child in position to be delivered, one of five ways.* Dr. Franke's Phantom *(Berlin, 1891). Flap anatomy. Chromolithography. 91 × 175 cm (unopened). National Library of Medicine.*

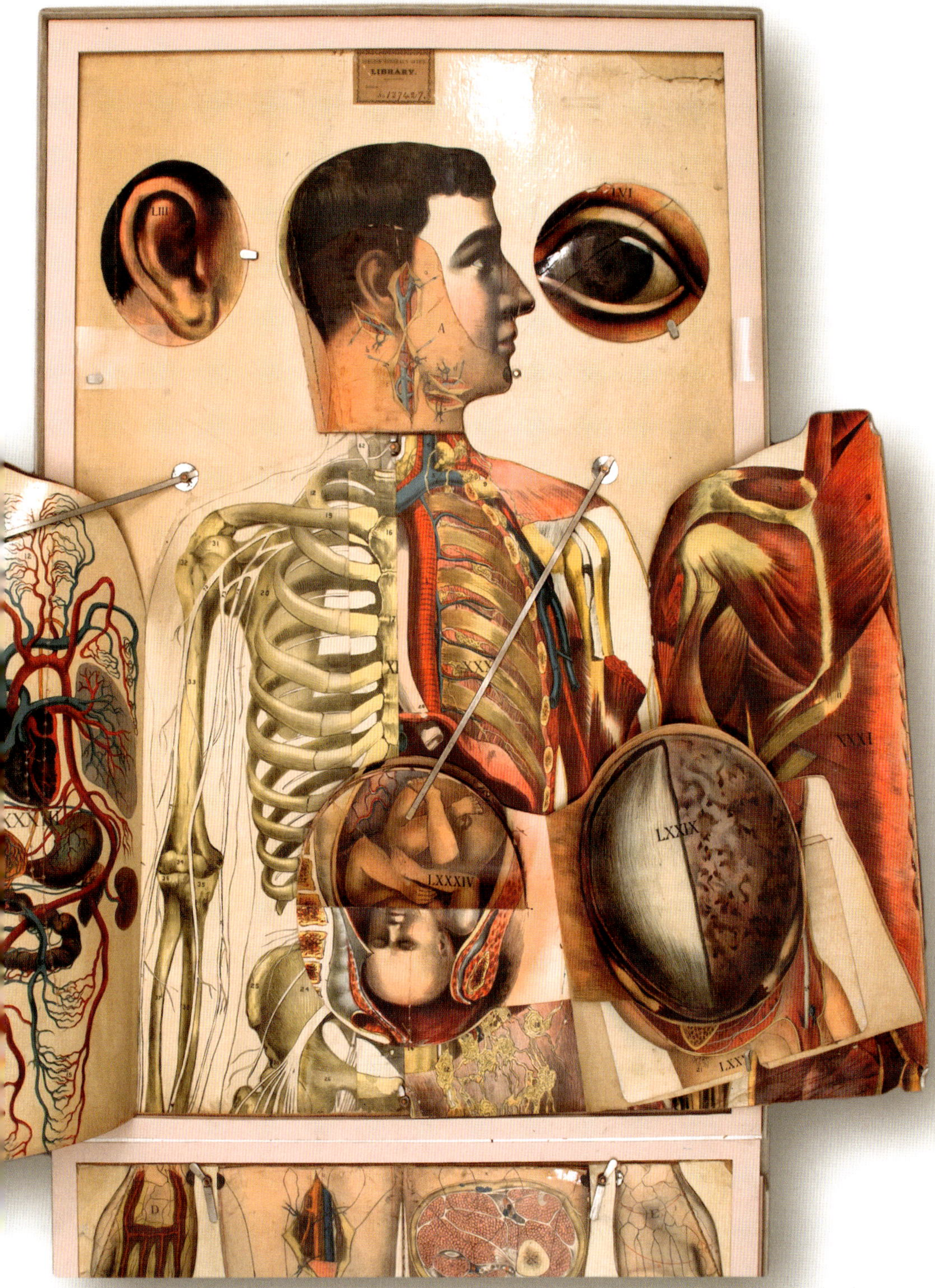
LIBRARY
LIII
LVI
A
LXXXIV
LXXIX
XXXI
D
E

case, displayed primarily to illustrate the female reproductive system and the anatomy of childbirth. That convention of display—which flowed freely from presumptions of male dominance—was bolstered by the belief that—whether the subject is a living model or dissected cadaver—masculine musculature is more legible than female musculature (in women the muscles tend to be less well developed and obscured by "adipose membrane," a layer of fat). And therefore male bodies are more suitable for anatomical demonstration.[49] This anatomical preference for the male body was likely also braced by a species of heterosexual panic over the power of the naked female body, especially the genitals (and pubic hair), to incite desire and immoral sexual behavior.[50] Perhaps safer, then, to focus on men. As if male bodies couldn't also incite.

So not entirely safe, especially when it came to genitalia. *Dr. Franke's Phantom* had genitals of both sexes in the underlayers, however, many atlases concealed or omitted the genitals entirely, especially ones for schoolchildren and the special sections included in "home health" encyclopedias. But the male uro-genitary system was of course treated in specialized studies on venereal disease, the preparation of anatomical specimens, and surgical works on operations for the "cutting for stone" and other problems.[51]

And there were also specialized studies of female subjects. In his harshly realistic *Anatomy of the Human Gravid Uterus* (1774), William Hunter signaled a strong commitment to showing what the eye sees ("the mark of nature"), using the body of a woman who died in late-stage pregnancy—genitalia centrally visible (as it must be in such studies), with legs chopped off above the knee, like ham-hocks (Fig. 1.16).[52]

Hunter was celebrated for his contributions to obstetrical science. And also for his unsparing, even shocking, choice of subject and style of presentation. Asserting professional, class and gender privilege, Hunter went right to the edge of representational probity.[53] (A probity which wouldn't have been nearly so accommodating to a life-size atlas featuring the male reproductive system, an *Anatomy of the Human Engorged and Ejaculating Penis, exhibited in figures*.)[54]

So the division: The female figure was the main event in books and lectures on the female reproductive system, pregnancy, childbirth, lactation. And the main event in fairground exhibits and "anatomical museums" which catered to the lay public, and its growing desire to know the science of the human body—as part of the curriculum of Enlightenment and post-Enlightenment science. While also appealing to prurient interest. The exhibition of instructive wax and papier-mâché models—"Anatomical Venus"—showing stages of pregnancy, and childbirth provided the medical justification for displays of recumbent female flesh, including genitalia (Fig. 1.17).[55] As did displays of the horrifying effects of venereal disease, in wax, papier-mâché—and sometimes actual specimens in glass jars. All at the edge of representational probity.

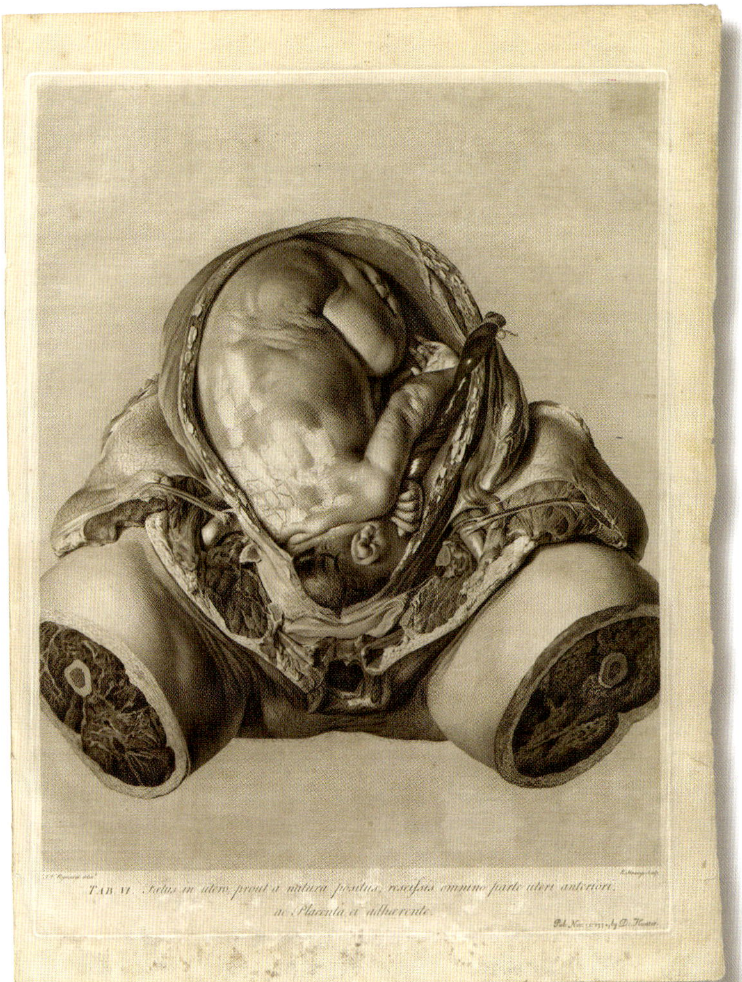

1.16 *William Hunter, "[T]he child in the womb, in its natural position,"* Anatomy of the Human Gravid Uterus *(London, 1774), pl. 6. Art: Jan Van Rymsdyk. Copperplate engraving. 62 × 45 cm. Hagströmer Medico-Historical Library. "Every part is represented just as it was found; not so much as one joint of a finger having been moved to shew any part more distinctly, or give a more picturesque effect."*

The female nude, without any display of genitalia, was of course featured in paintings and sculptures exhibited in galleries of art, churches and on the walls of townhouses and country manors—and in art academies, studios and drawing classes, where students drew from nude classical sculptures (usually casts or copies, but in the right location, originals), and increasingly, as the nineteenth century wore on, lightly clothed or naked female models.[56] The subject of female anatomy was vital to the enterprise of European art,

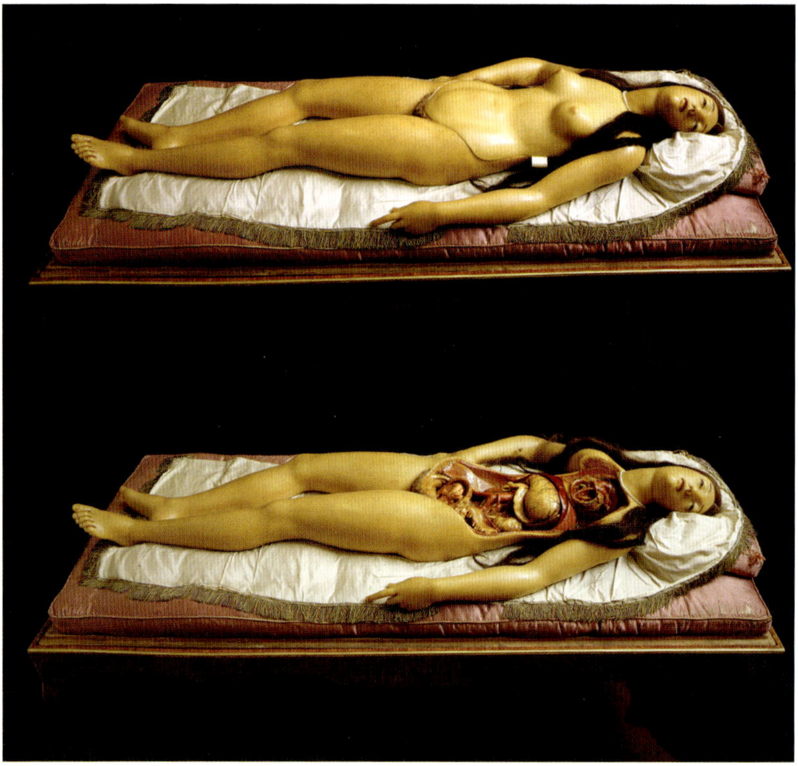

1.17 *Workshop of Clemente Susini, "Anatomical Venus" (Florence, 1780–2). Wax, "dismantable model," life-size. La Specola, Florence. Photo © Raffaello Bencini / Bridgeman Images.*

and the male gaze on the female body therefore a vital topic for artists and collectors. Yet the male body was the main event in most illustrated anatomies (Figs. 1.8–9, 11–13, 18), whether aimed at professional medical men, artists or students.[57] And that, as we shall see, had some very queer consequences.

2.7 Homoerotics queered

Now to clarify: queerness is often taken to be an identity. But here we will treat it as a condition that comes unbidden out of sheer inexplicable contingency. Often from the disciplining of gender performances and sexual expression from early childhood onward, the unintended consequence of rewards and punishments, ranging from mild discouragement to shunning, shaming and acts of violence. Queerness appears in objects and subjects, persons, images, artworks and scenes that contain irresolvable contradictions, and that become vehicles for the nurturance and expression of—sometimes panicked aversion to—queer desire. Some of that queerness may "rub off" on, or "stain," producers or users of those objects, and contribute to the making of dissident identities or dissonant personalities. Queer eccentricity may also be something claimed as a special privileged identity by people who have a privileged standing, sometimes the very people who enforce gender codes, such as doctors and teachers and the clergy. Those privileged characters may even flaunt certain forms of queerness—often read as mere eccentricity—as a perk of academic achievement or social standing. No matter, queer performances are always open-ended, incomplete, difficult to sustain or subject to censure. On the outside, there are many sets of eyes, searching, peeping, assessing, sharing comments and judgments. Queerness is hard to navigate. Failure is always possible.

Especially when it comes to erotic expression. Sex between men, often men and boys, was universally condemned as "shameful," "unnatural." Notwithstanding the tacit acceptance of everyday same-sex relations aboard ships and in prisons, frontier mining towns, and boarding schools—and notwithstanding the emphatic representation of male beauty in the fine arts and sporadic flaunting of moral propriety by privileged aristocrats—in eighteenth- and nineteenth-century Europe, homosexual acts and male effeminacy could

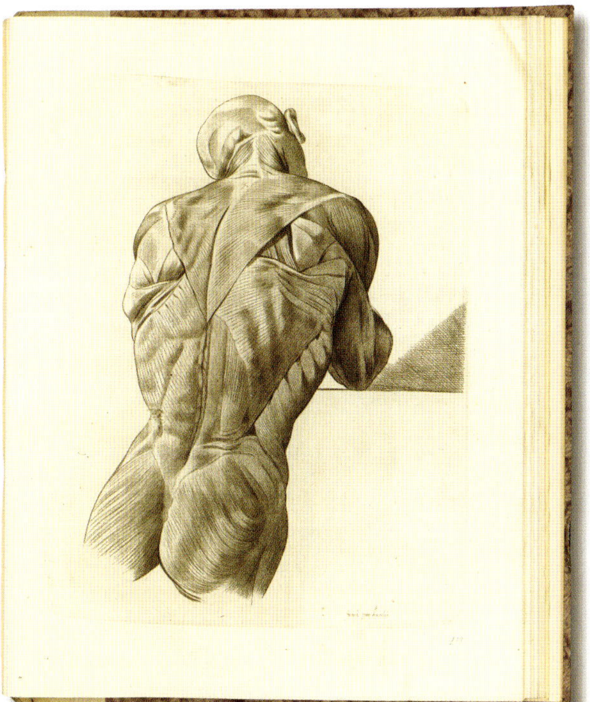

1.18 *The male body in art anatomy. Jacques Gamelin,* Nouveau recueil d'ostéologie et de myologie, dessiné, d'après nature... *(Toulouse, 1779), 110. Copperplate soft-ground etching: Jacques Lavalée. 54 × 40 cm. Waller Collection, Uppsala University Libraries.*

be punished with social exclusion, public humiliation, blackmail, beatings, or worse.[58] And there might be dire legal consequences. In England, sodomy was outlawed as "an unnatural crime." Yet, as urban, industrial, commercial and institutional spaces proliferated, very often sorted into male- and female-only zones, so did opportunities for contact between men, between boys, between men and boys. And recurrent panic over those contacts. Which (like relations between men and women) were not always consensual.

Men who took the "female" role in "sodomitical" relations, and male effeminacy and cross-dressing, were especially condemnable. An anonymously-authored 1855 London pamphlet alleged that:

> The increase of these monsters in the shape of men, commonly designated *Margeries*, *Pooffs*, etc., of late years, in the great metropolis, renders it necessary for the safety of the public, that they should be made known. The punishment generally awarded to such miscreants is not half severe enough, and till the law is more frequently carried to the fullest extent against them, there can be no hopes of crushing the bestiality. The wretches are too well paid—they being principally, it is well known, supported by their rich companions—to care a jot about a few months' imprisonment.[59]

The misdemeanor of dressing "in woman's clothes for immoral purposes," and the felony of sodomy—not yet packaged together under the rubric of "homosexuality"—were only sporadically and inconsistently policed.[60] Sodomy was a graver offense. Before 1861, the maximum penalty was death by hanging, at the judge's discretion. But given the limits of state and civilian surveillance, and the undoubtedly large numbers of sodomitical acts, prosecution was erratic and the maximum sentence rarely imposed. Men who were convicted were mostly "remitted" to incarceration with hard labor or transportation to the colonies, or flogging (a common punishment for all sort of offenses in the Royal Navy and army). In 1861 the maximum sentence was reduced to 10-years-to-life-in-prison. Flogging in the Navy was entirely discontinued in 1879, but remained on the books in civilian jurisprudence until 1940 (though seldom inflicted outside of occasional waves of moral panic).[61] Lesser offenses like public cross-dressing, "indecent assault," and "attempted sodomy" remained subject to lesser terms of imprisonment, fines, dismissal from employment, or discharge from service.[62]

With all of that risk, tactical retreat became all the more appealing and expedient. Which could take the form of a withdrawal into complete invisibility, or some perilous balance of situational discretion and expression. "A normality," novelist Tom Crewe reckons, "perhaps compromised and limited, shadowed by guilt or suspicion or fear ..." Because, while legal penalties and social excommunication were dire, they could only reach so far:

> The vast majority of gay men in the past lived their whole lives in contravention of the law without being caught in its clutches. They don't show up when we flash our torch across the legal records, or over the archives of the famous.[63]

Don't show up. Didn't want to show up.

2.8 The epistemology of the anatomical closet

So consider *the closet*. A metaphor that comes into common usage in the middle decades of the twentieth century to denote a condition of smothered homosexuality, suppressed desire, hiding, shame, longing. *The closet* is claustrophobic, a space of isolation where unwelcome feelings are contained or denied. A lonely place, where expression is secret or entirely thwarted; identity is negated, or never allowed to emerge and flourish.

But that's not the whole story: *the closet* can also be a hothouse, a place where desire can grow, intensify, come to know itself. Until a breaking point. When it comes out into the open: a coming out, a crisis of self-emancipation. (The standard account.) Or maybe there is no coming out, just a murmuring inner dialogue conducted among constituent parts of a divided self. Or a coded partial disclosure that closeted persons of similar interests can detect and decrypt, and use as a point of contact.

In eighteenth- and nineteenth-century Europe that coded disclosure could take place through the production, collection, sharing of anatomical experiences, images, objects, figures. It's anachronistic to invoke *the closet* when it comes to the eighteenth and nineteenth century. But useful, as a way to think about how libidinal investments might be buried in the anatomical image—how anatomy might be a domain where "the love that dare not speak its name" could show, even flaunt, itself, in the pages of a book or folio of prints or the shelves of a collection, while remaining under cover. A closet of sorts.

In this construction, repression creates, proliferates, intensifies, the very categories it aims to forbid and extinguish.[64] *The closet* is not necessarily a grave where desire comes to die, but can be a private and provisionally safe queer space—shielded from public spectatorship and policing—where desire comes to the doorstep of self-awareness, is imaginatively free to take shape, self-nurtured and articulated, in reverie and in linguistic and visual and gestural code. And in meaning-laden silence, undeclared arousal, and "the telling secret."[65] Jenny Sundén theorizes closeted silence as a dark but positive "obscurity," a kind of deliberate, defensive "opacity" (borrowing a term from Édouard Glissant and Nicholas de Villiers).[66] Which might be for sharing: a *closet* may also be a *club* (members only). Whose mysteries can be kept safe from prying eyes and wagging tongues, in a society increasingly policed in networks of conversation, letter-writing, press reportage, and yes by actual policemen and informants. Or it might be a place for eavesdropping and gazing outward, spying, through a keyhole or peephole or slat, that familiar contrivance of the Victorian novel and pornography.

Can we then say that the closet and the gaze are a pair—and that both are a necessary precondition for the "invention of homosexuality" (Foucault again) and new kinds of queerness? Along with an important material precondition: the proliferation of new private spaces in the architecture of the nineteenth-century home and city, an actual proliferation of private rooms equipped with closets.[67] Closeted representation, representational closets. Private spaces. Queer spaces ... Opaque, but full of meaning. The closet occludes, negates the gaze, but creates sequestered and imaginary spaces for self-reflection, gazing and sharing. Privacy. Private society. And not just a special space: a special interval of time and heightened feeling. Literary historian Matthew Bevis tells us that "to watch" (let's say *gaze*) and "not merely to see," is "to elongate and think through"—feel through—"the act of looking."[68]

Still, you've got to wonder ... Wittgenstein concludes the *Tractatus* with a curtain-closing aphorism: "whereof one cannot speak, thereof one must be silent." But when same-sex desire and its objects are unavowed, and evidence is limited, what can we really say? What can we know, how do we know it, how should we put it into words, when "closeted-ness itself is a performance initiated ... by the speech act of a silence"?[69]

This is the problem Kosofsky Sedgwick so cogently addresses in *The Epistemology of the Closet*. "Epistemology" is a fancy word (a buzzword in recent scholarship) with a rhythm that rolls off the tongue. But it's much more than that. In philosophy and the history of science, epistemology is the problem of knowledge. How do we know what we know? How do we come to take sources and judgments as trustworthy? In given historical sites and moments, what are knowledge production's political social conceptual conditions and protocols, and how do those change over time? How is knowledge registered, circulated and archived? Which methods, media, genres, idioms, principles, ethos, performances are requisite and which debarred? What roles do institutions and designated spaces play? What qualifies a person to undertake study? What personal and social attributes are helpful or mandatory? How should scientists and scholars comport themselves, among colleagues and in public? And, since anatomy is a field in which art and science converge, and art also makes truth claims: how have truth claims in art developed historically in cohabitation with, or opposition to, the truth claims of science? Questions.

Kosofsky Sedgwick allows there can be no epistemological certainty when it comes to a system of meaning that is systematically cloaked, covered over in plausible and implausible deniability. But, she argues, if we only credit what is epistemologically secure, we miss the whole show. In such circumstances, an insistence on certainty is obtuse (and no fun). Wittgenstein's translator, Frank Ramsey, goofing on his heavily closeted friend, reworks the aphorism: "What we can't say we can't say, and ... can't whistle it either."[70] A quip which winks at melodic undertows of signifying gestures, a kind of queer, partly decipherable, music. But, from a distance, how can we "grasp ... the motors of concealment" and hear "the specific language of a person hiding himself"? (The quest that Rowan Williams, writing on Dostoyevsky, urges upon us.)[71] Kosofsky Sedgwick doesn't prescribe any particular method, but she does demonstrate one: an eclectic mixture of narration, contextualization, genre analysis, biography, theoretical musings, close and distant reading: an open-ended back-and-forth of provisional questions, provisional answers. Then more questions.

OBJECTS

3.1 Mystery men, mute images

And that's how we'll play it. Our actors are mystery men, don't declare themselves. Maybe don't have anything to declare. Or maybe they do. Or don't know that they do. But they do leave hints, marks, "tells"—historian Carlo Ginzburg calls them "slender clues"—sometimes in print, marginalia, scribbles, often in images.[72] Which point emphatically, or coyly wink, or subtly redirect us ... or lead us astray. Or don't point at all, just leave trails of unresolvable incoherent feeling. Historians are more comfortable with strong evidence of intent, most of all in writing. But even seemingly clear declarations can contain double, triple meanings, contradictions, halting approximations of meaning, or lies. Which is why close reading is so often revelatory. And if that's true for text, then what of mute illustrations, where the hand of the artist may betray carefully protected feelings, and meanings might lurk in the margins or lie buried dead center? Genre and custom give us all sorts of formulas and instructions on how to read, but images (more than texts?) often exceed their remit.

For example, this gaily hand-colored engraving (Fig. 1.19) from Paolo Mascagni's life-sized spectacular (posthumously published) *Anatomia universa* (1823–30) performs something that goes beyond the instrumental purpose of illustrating the surface anatomy of the back of the arm, lower back, buttocks and rectum.[73] Maybe it was meant to be a cruising figure, a flirt. As if the figure has a hanky stuck in his anatomical back pocket, or the tracings on the body are sexy tattoos or a form-fitting body suit ... If so, was the expressive power of that perverse flirtation intensified by the fact that anatomists had, over the previous century, mostly rejected the flirty poses and winking gestures of early modern anatomy as untrue to nature, and unbefitting serious scientific study? Was its gaudy coloration a flaunting display of anatomical dandyism, a deliberate affront to new norms of anatomical sobriety and scholarly comportment? (The stripteasing cadavers of Spigelius and Fialetti that appear in the opening pages of this book are just a sampling of the inebriated performances staged in early modern anatomical atlases.)

Mascagni stood on the cusp of a change in the conventions of medical representation. The anatomical figure had long been a vehicle for idiosyncratic clowning, horror shows, allegorical play-acting, Biblical allusions, Hermetic correspondences, memento mori, and peep-show eroticism. And often enough—given the centrality of the anatomical figure of Man as an emblem of the universal human—homoeroticism. Illustrated anatomy was an unpoliced borderland. But in the last third of the eighteenth century, medical and surgical anatomists started to place limits on poses and settings.[74] There was no longer room for cadaveric dance, play, flirtation or clowning ... except in the anatomy of fine art and art pedagogy. Anatomical illustration

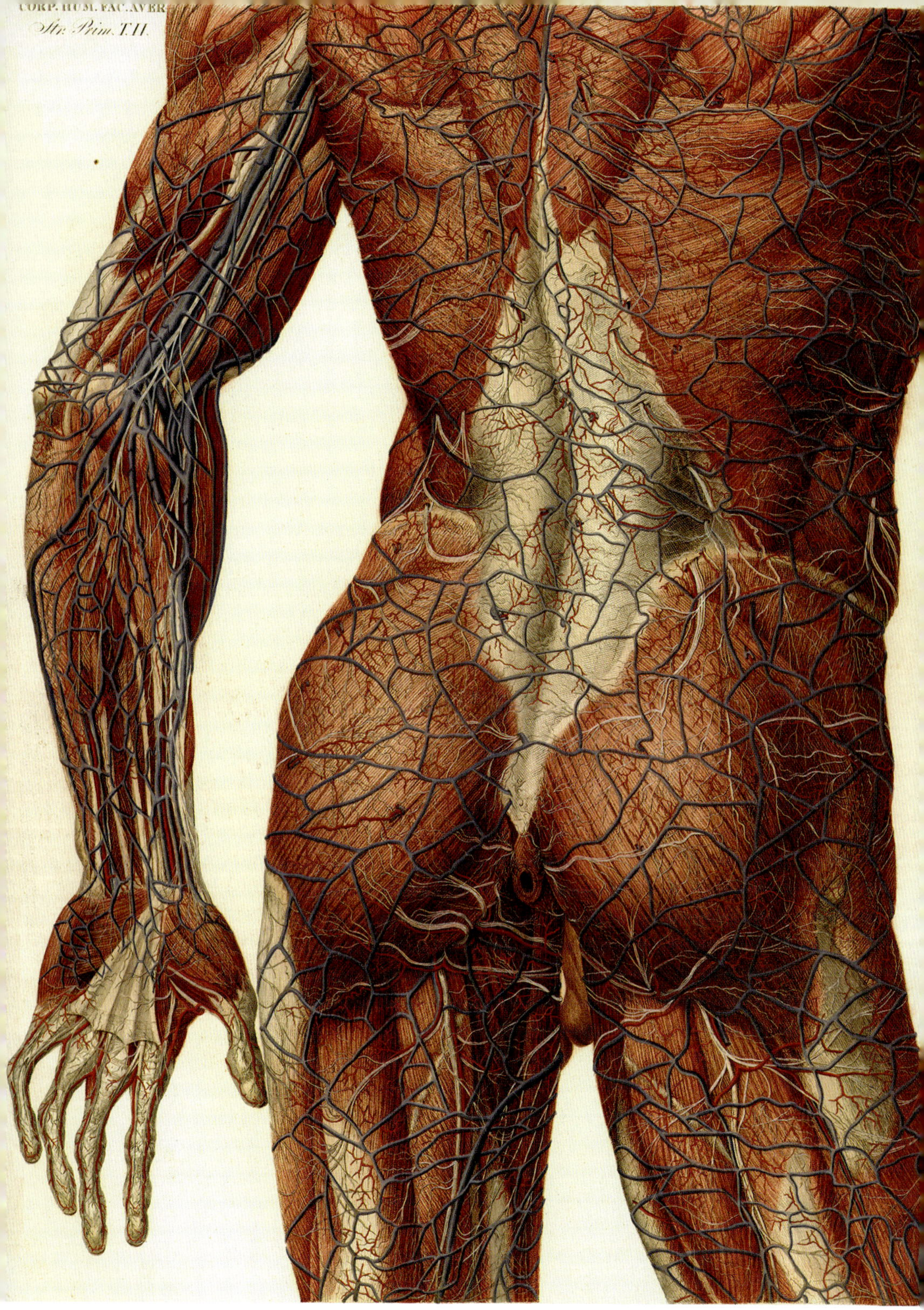

1.19 *Flaunting? Flirting? "Back, Stratum Primum,"* Paolo Mascagni, Anatomia Universa *or* Grande Anatomia del Corpo Umano, *pl. 2 (Pisa, 1823–30). Art: Antonio Serrantoni. Hand-colored copperplate engraving. 99 × 72 cm. Hagströmer Medico-Historical Library.*

was divided into separate spheres. Art got to keep metaphor, affect, drama, allegory, scenography, danse macabre. And sexy bodies in dramatic movement and repose, female and male, with an emphasis on skin surfaces and skeleto-muscular structure.[75] Medicine got the remainder: spectacular pathological specimens and conditions, as seen on the skin of the living or extracted from the innards of cadavers; unsparing pictures of dissected bodies and parts; peacefully sleeping corpses; earnest neoclassicism; moody Romantic poses; skeletons; fetuses; gruesome surgical operations.

The body, naked and in various states of dissection, still continued to take center stage. The erotics of medical and surgical anatomical illustration, however, went untheorized and unmentioned. Scottish anatomists John Bell and William Hunter, who forthrightly set out criteria for how anatomical subjects should be illustrated, never explicitly discussed flirtation or sensuality or provocation in the essays that prefaced their illustrated publications, but affected to disdain all forms of representational play.[76] And again, that's the problem for historians: should we bracket the question of erotic valences as a kind of unknowable dark matter—disqualify ourselves on the grounds that we will be tempted to fill up the epistemological void with our own *aisthesis* and erotics? Or take interpretive liberties and read the silence, caution, reticence, discretion?

Here we'll take liberties. Because efforts to police and punish expressions of same-sex desire nearly always produce queer results: representations disguised, encoded, contorted (even unconscious, given that human beings aren't transparent to themselves). If so, scholars can and should undertake open-ended investigation and translation, reasonably speculate—play with it—as long as evidentiary limits are respected, and, *pace* Davidson, changes in conceptual categories are critically registered and accounted for. It has been argued that simple epistemological modesty demands that we abstain from interpretation: interpretive nihilism.[77] The inevitable erosion and loss of evidence confronts us with insuperable obstacles: "the past rewilds itself, oblivion springs up out of it like a forest" (says poet-essayist Maria Stepanova), helped along by the deliberate suppression and destruction of materials.[78] Sometimes amounting to clear-cutting. But the interpretations offered here—even ardent conjectures—are in no way confining. Other interpretations can be productively compounded with or set in opposition to them. Yet, notwithstanding open-endedness, we can all agree: interpretations are good to argue over. And some are better than others, according to whether they are supported or contradicted by logic and/or a "preponderance" of evidence (as in American civil law). This book won't make an open-and-shut case. Our remit, again, will be to ask questions and to imaginatively reconstruct our historical actors and their image-work, through close and contextual reading and looking. And, counteracting a long history of denial, to credit the possibility, the likelihood, of coded expressions and erotic valences.

The stakes in all this, Kosofsky Sedgwick tells us, go beyond just the chronicling of a marginalized, stigmatized group's history. Because "the structuring of same-sex bonds," and even the coded expression of same-sex desire, "in any historical situation marked by inequality and contest *between* genders, [will] be a site of intensive regulation that intersects virtually *every* issue of power and gender ..." (emphasis added).[79] And, really, are any historical situations not so marked?

Some of those situations seem, well, conspicuously *marked*. Jones Quain's top-end anatomical atlas, *The Muscles of the Human Body* (London, 1836) features images of skinned, dissected men, and parts thereof—a subject for medical practitioners *and* practitioners of figure drawing, painting and sculpture—really anyone with a cultivated appreciation of classical art and learned discourse. The figures demurely abstain from homoerotic winking. No flirtation or theatrics. Some do speak softly in the dialect of British homoerotic classicism (which wasn't exactly homegrown: most of the plates are copied from an 1822 atlas published in Paris and authored by Jules Cloquet).[80] But the demeanor of the figures is sober, demure, all business (Fig. 1.20).

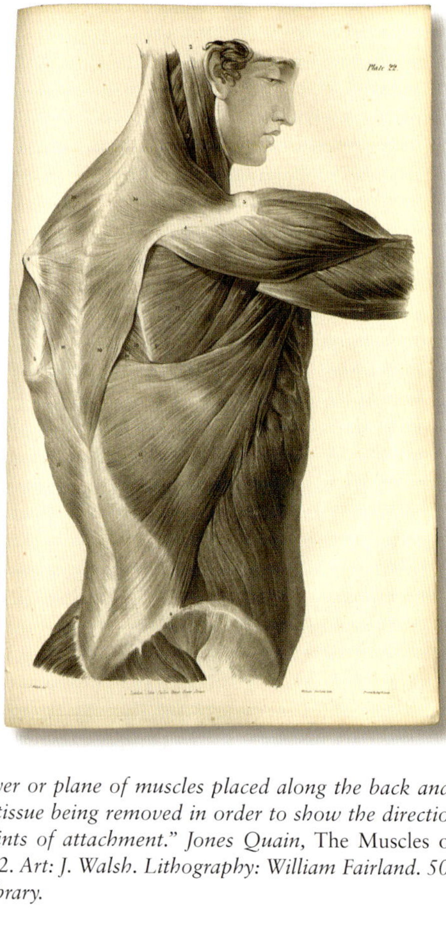

1.20 *"[T]he first layer or plane of muscles placed along the back and side of the body: the skin and the cellular tissue being removed in order to show the direction of the fibres in each muscle, and their points of attachment." Jones Quain,* The Muscles of the Human Body... *(London, 1836), pl. 22. Art: J. Walsh. Lithography: William Fairland. 50 × 32 cm. Hagströmer Medico-Historical Library.*

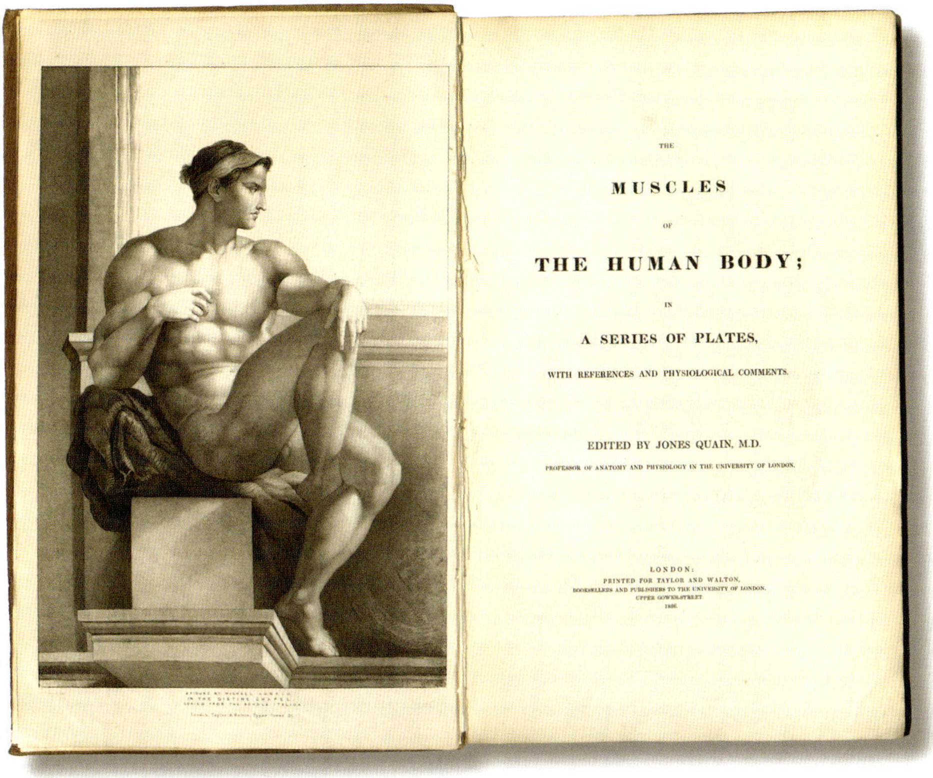

1.21 *"A figure by Michel Angelo in the Sistine Chapel copied from the Schola Italica...", in Jones Quain,* The Muscles of the Human Body... *(London, 1836). Lithography: William Fairland. 50 × 32 cm. Hagströmer Medico-Historical Library. The lithograph follows Michelangelo's original fresco, but exaggerates the young man's musculature. Both versions show his legs coyly crossed to reveal the peek-a-boo tip of the penis. But in the fresco his right elbow rests on a stack of oversized acorns that visually rhyme with the tip of the penis. The lithograph replaces the improbable acorn with a bolt of folded cloth.*

Except for the frontispiece. A lithograph, based on a Michelangelo painting which, rather than showing off a dissected body or skeleton (as one might expect), features a buff and very naked young man, coyly presenting himself in a richly sensual display of hyper-muscular masculinity—along with a peek-a-boo glimpse of the tip of his penis (Fig. 1.21).[81] The kind of exaggerated beardless, body-hair-less youthful masculinity that flips over into coyly eroticized androgyny that Solomon-Godeau writes about: the ephebic young man as object of desire, a very Greco-Roman inflected desire. Quain's frontispiece gestures toward the large cultural domain—fine art—in which ideals of masculine beauty, the male nude, and especially Michelangelo's nudes, occupied a place of privilege, the privilege held by possessors of cultural capital (and plain old capital). Quain comments in the text that the figure "has been selected for its fine and muscular proportions."

But the presentation of a Michelangelo meant more than that. In the 1830s, Michelangelo's place in the pantheon of great artists, great men of culture, was unassailable—his association with anatomy, anatomical dissections, and masculine musculature was totemic. His homosexual inclinations were not. (Or not yet: the outing of Michelangelo took place later in the century.) Even so, the visual reference to Michelangelo afforded Quain with an opportunity to display homoerotic male nudity. Which was not an arcane taste. Not difficult to find: Quain was an eminent professor at the University of London, at the center and not the margins of British anatomy and medical society. And the frontispiece nude—the first figure to greet the reader, just opposite the titlepage—was not an add-on or throwaway but almost a mascot, an emblem of the stratospheric moral and aesthetic ideals, standards, purposes, *and* pleasures, that licensed and animated anatomical study. (Later on in *Queer Anatomies*, we'll meet up with his brother, Richard Quain, who was the author of a grander and more sensual anatomical atlas, and also professor of anatomy at the University of London. Not a coincidence, family connections mattered in British medicine.)

Oh yes, Jones Quain leaves us one more thing to account for: figure 1 of plate 48 (Fig. 1.22), which shows a penis, pinned through the foreskin, and erected to a standing position. This, in an atlas mostly devoted to "the muscles of the human body" where it wouldn't be expected. The penis, if it receives any consideration at all, is usually placed in a section on the arteries or uro-genital system, where it may or may not be shown in the erect position. Anatomical atlases devoted solely to the musculo-skeletal system are often practical, designed for beginning medical students and artists. No need for an erect penis there. And even atlases that aim to be comprehensive often overlook the erect penis. Quain, following Jules Cloquet, doesn't.[82] (But also doesn't survey the female body in his study of "the human body," make of that what you will.)

Plate 48's two "preparations," male (top) and female (bottom), demonstrate, without comment, some muscular differences between the sexes.[83] And also demonstrate uro-genitary differences. The number 15 at the base of the penis identifies "the tube of the urethra"; and number 16 the "corpus cavernosum penis at the right side." The corpus cavernosum being not a muscle but a sponge-like region of erectile tissue, which contains most of the blood in the penis during an erection. The caption declines to note that Quain is here taking the opportunity to show off a beautifully dissected penis made erect via the injection of wax or some other substance, rendered beautifully by artist and lithographer J. Walsh. (Make of that what you will.)

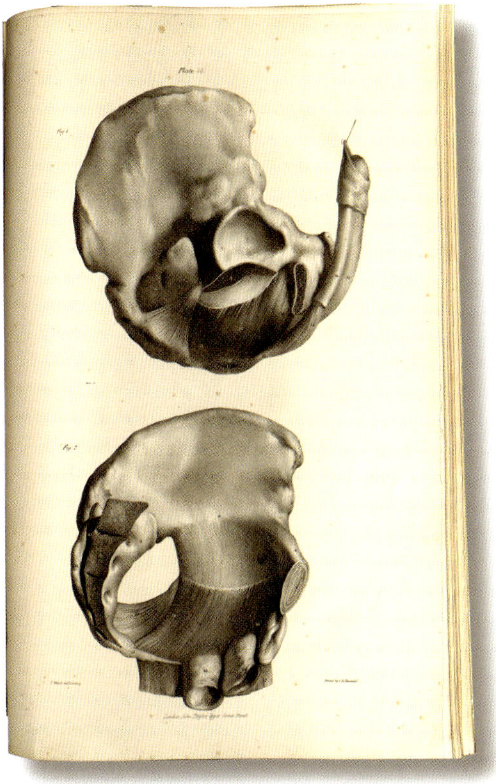

1.22 *Jones Quain,* The Muscles of the Human Body… *(London, 1836), pl. 48. Art: J. Walsh. Lithography: William Fairland. 50 × 32 cm. Hagströmer Medico-Historical Library. "Fig. 1. A lateral view of the perineal muscles is given here in order to show the levator ani muscle. The greater part of the ischium, with part of the os pubis, is cut away at the right side, so as to expose the extent of the levator ani muscle and its points of connection… 15. The tube of the urethra. 16. The corpus cavernosum penis at the right side…" Fig. 2 of the plate (at bottom) shows "a lateral section of the pelvis" dissected from a female cadaver.*

3.2 The mystery penis

Quain's plate is our jumping off point, so now let's parachute into more epistemologically insecure territory. About 20 years ago, doing research for an exhibition on the history of anatomical illustrations, I troll through the catalogue of the National Library of Medicine (NLM). I'm searching for illustrations in the works of François-Joseph-Victor Broussais, an influential medical authority of 1820s and 1830s France. Broussais's publications, it turns out, are surprisingly devoid of images, but the NLM catalogue does list an "atlas" of the history of medicine by his son Casimir (Fig. 1.23). It has one illustration. Which, I hope, might be one of those allegorical or historical scenes which show great men of medicine performing dissections amidst emblems of anatomy. (I'm collecting things like that to go in the exhibition.)

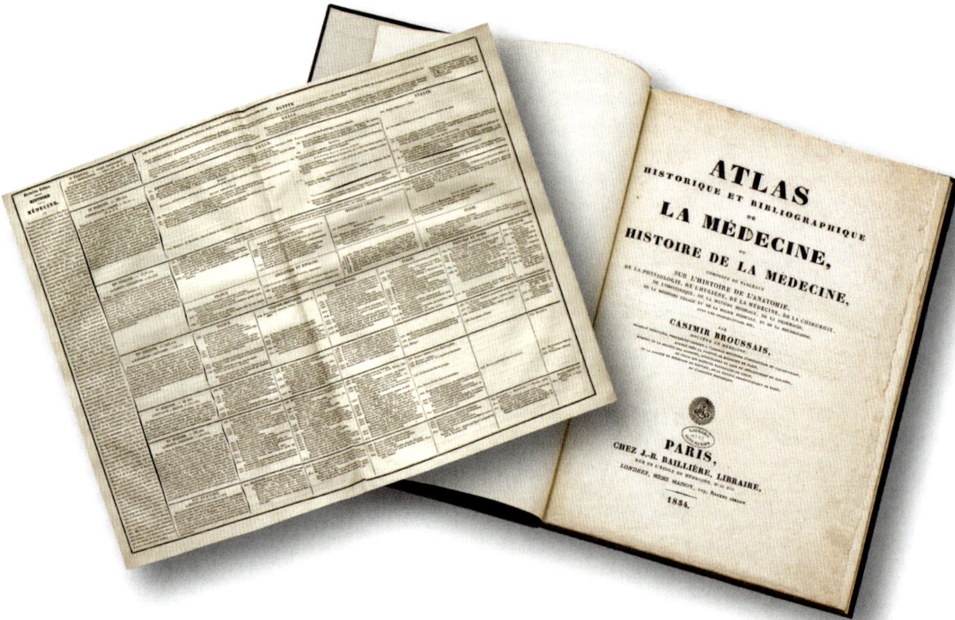

1.23 *Casimir Broussais,* Atlas historique et bibliographique de la médecine*... (Paris, 1834). New York Academy of Medicine.*

But instead, amidst pages of columns of tiny type, I find this, in the middle of the book, a centerfold (Fig. 1.24). A fine uncaptioned lithographic print.[84] Which shows the anatomy of the bladder. Like the penis in Quain's plate, the erection of the penis here is an incidental effect, here achieved by the insertion of a catheter.

Illustrations of an erect penis were sometimes included in nineteenth-century books on "generation" (human reproduction), and the penis injected via catheter to a state of erection might also appear in works on urology and urologic surgery, and very rarely in a work of general anatomy like Quain's. In this particular image, a catheter is inserted into a penis in order to inflate the bladder with water, via an undepicted syringe, with the likely aim of demonstrating the preparation of the bladder for "the cutting for stone," and to demonstrate the anatomy of the bladder (which would be difficult to see were it not inflated). The illustration is a useful picture for a surgeon.[85] An unusually artful useful picture.

But Casimir Broussais's *Atlas historique et bibliographique de la médecine,* with its long lists of great achievements and important publications in the history of medicine, has nothing to do with that. The illustration of an erected penis and inflated bladder cannot belong to this book.

So why is it there? My guess is that it was taken from some near contemporary work on uro-genital surgical anatomy, yet to be identified, perhaps a folio of unbound lithographs. And placed, folded-up, inside the Broussais *Atlas*, for safekeeping. By a doctor or surgeon who admired the precision and clarity of the dissection, the fine technique of the artist and lithographer, and above all the erectness and beauty of the penis. And who wanted to have it easily accessible, close to hand, but not in plain sight. In other words, the *Atlas* might have served as a plain brown wrapper, a device to mask a guilty (or shameful) pleasure, a hiding place ...[86]

Admittedly a conjecture. But bolstered by the fact that, from the 1600s onward, anatomical specimens of male genitalia, along with the syringes and catheters used to inflate them to erection, acquired erotic associations among men of medicine and the lay public (who had a growing familiarity with those instruments as both medics and laity increasingly deployed them

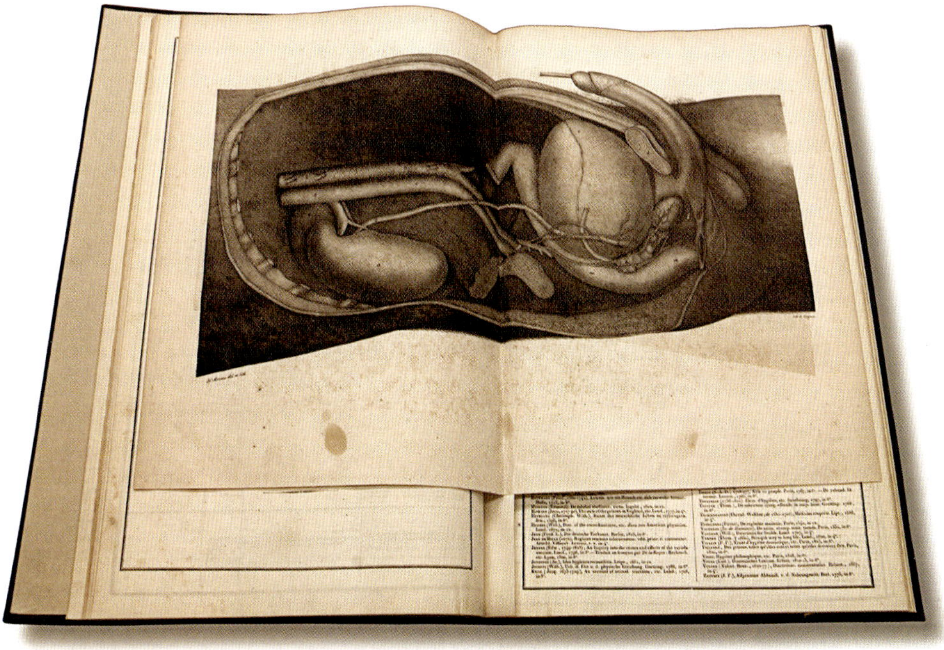

1.24 *An orphan lithograph, c.1820s. Printer: "Martin". Lithography: [Pierre] "Langlumé". Bound into Casimir Broussais,* Atlas historique et bibliographique de la médecine *(Paris, 1834). National Library of Medicine.*

to treat medical conditions, including those afflicting the sexual organs). And so, according to historian Darren Wagner, the syringe, along with or in place of the erect penis, began to frequently appear in pornographic illustrations and descriptive prose, even as Johannes Ladmiral, John Hunter, Alexander Monro *primus*, and other anatomists took great pride in preparing specimens of "a spectacularly injected penis," along with illustrations of them. (Monro bragged of "making the Prettyest preparation.") Wagner reports that "this low association of syringes" with the organs of generation became:

> even more evident in the literary record, where syringe became a bawdy metaphor for penis ... The use of syringes in anatomical preparations emphasized [the]

> mechanical properties of penile function … During the long eighteenth century, syringes retained dirty connotations regardless of who wielded them. Conversely, imagining how penises and ejaculation worked would have often conjured up notions of syringe mechanisms. More than just figurative speech, the analogy between penises and syringes was realized in various ways, such as the invention of dildos …[87]

OK, that's something. But before saying farewell to our fine and mysterious urogenitary lithograph, consider this: Before the twentieth century, it's hard to find beautifully rendered illustrations of an erect penis. In fact, as a subject of representation, there was no polite way to make, show, or collect an image of an erect penis, EXCEPT in an anatomical illustration directed to medical eyes (Fig. 1.25).[88]

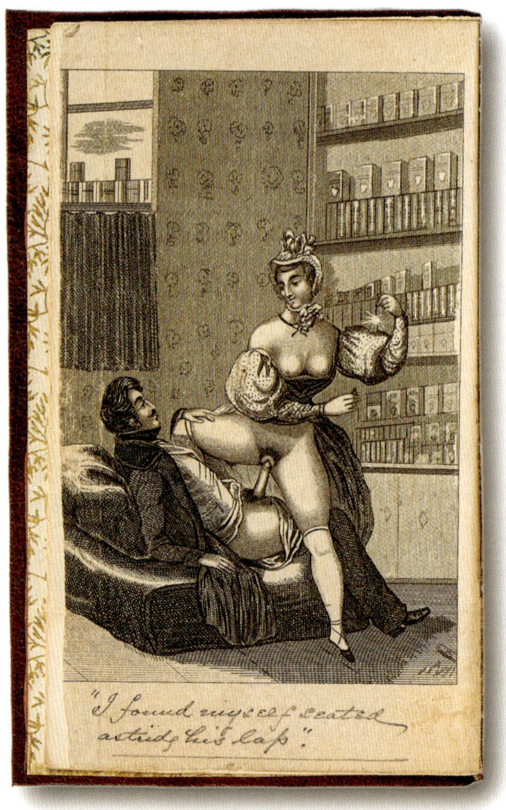

1.25 *The erect penis: an impolite representation. "I found myself seated astride his lap,"* The Life and Adventures of Cicily Martin *(New York, 1846), pl. (after 184). Art/lithography uncredited; 16 cm. American Antiquarian Society. Bawdy images typically featured the erect penis in acts of heterosexual vaginal coitus, and not acts of masturbation, oral or anal sex. The quality of artwork varied from crude to competent, and couldn't be considered "fine."*

3.3 The penis and medical eyes

But doctors weren't the only ones equipped with medical eyes. The general reading public, men and women of the middling and working classes, while lacking in access to elite publications, also acquired a modicum of familiarity with medical concepts and images via attendance at popular lectures on "physiology" (which typically featured wallcharts, lantern slide projections, and wax and papier-mâché models), and the reading of popular illustrated books and pamphlets on health (authored by doctors and pseudo-doctors). And also of course consultation with doctors and surgeons. Anatomical terms and the medical nomenclature of disease entities, symptoms, character and constitution circulated in serial fiction, weekly and monthly newspapers, theatrical performances, classroom instruction and everyday conversation.

Ordinary people also had access to illustrated books, articles and pamphlets on "anatomy," "physiology," "marriage," "organs of generation," and "venereal maladies"—a mixture of popular health and science that later came to be called sexology. A few of those works (Figs. 1.26–28) featured workaday diagrams of a penis, mostly shown as a body part and unconnected to an entire body. Presented in a putatively anatomical medical context, framed with medical justification. "Adapted for every man's private use." "For men only." Private. (But in a print publication nonetheless, and therefore of course public.) Women, with their "fragile" constitutions, and children, so innocent and impressionable, were to be protected from pictures of male genitalia.[89]

Such books occupied a low position in the hierarchy of cultural goods, were subjected to a good deal of sneering and sniffing by the medical profession and social elites. And were beset by controversy—condemned as immoral, an incitement to sexual desire. They were at the racy end of the market for works on "popular" medicine and health, and considered to be vulgar (by many people) in both subject matter and style adjacent to explicit pornography. And therefore subject to censorship.

Publishers and authors risked fines, confiscation, and even imprisonment. But did so because the books made enormous profits. There were, however, limits: the illustration of male and female genitalia was a bright line to cross. Some books had them; many didn't. The depiction of penile erection was an even brighter line, and for most publishers a step too far. While many books discussed or alluded to penile erection, very few dared to show it. (Fig. 1.27, from *The Male Generative Organs in Health and Disease,* only ventures to suggest it.) (And no popular medical book depicted the act of coitus: that space was left unfilled.)

Authors and publishers (often the same person) who did sally forth into that contested borderland did so without much regard for aesthetics. Unlike Jones Quain's plate 48 and our catheterized mystery phallus, their

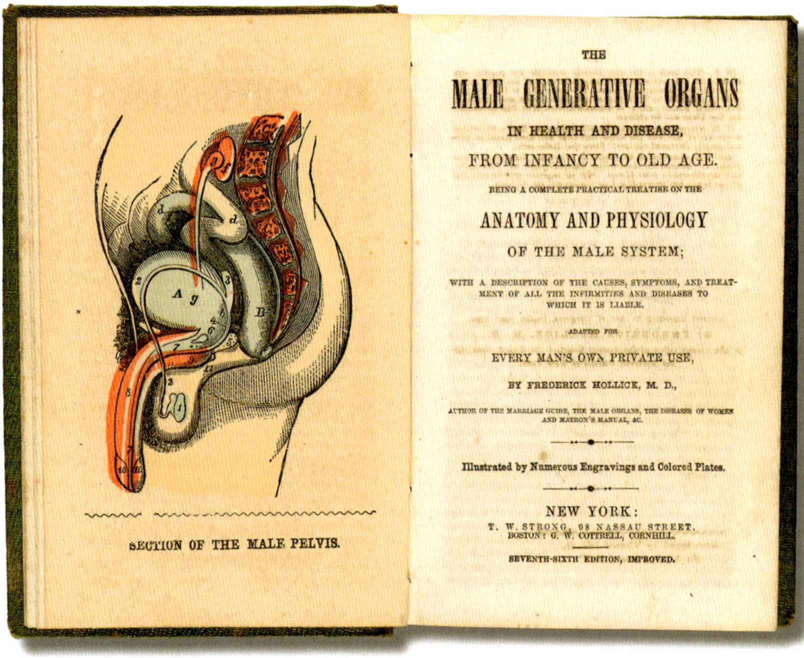
SECTION OF THE MALE PELVIS.

THE

MALE GENERATIVE ORGANS

IN HEALTH AND DISEASE,

FROM INFANCY TO OLD AGE.

BEING A COMPLETE PRACTICAL TREATISE ON THE

ANATOMY AND PHYSIOLOGY

OF THE MALE SYSTEM;

WITH A DESCRIPTION OF THE CAUSES, SYMPTOMS, AND TREATMENT OF ALL THE INFIRMITIES AND DISEASES TO WHICH IT IS LIABLE.

ADAPTED FOR

EVERY MAN'S OWN PRIVATE USE,

BY FREDERICK HOLLICK, M. D.,

AUTHOR OF THE MARRIAGE GUIDE, THE MALE ORGANS, THE DISEASES OF WOMEN AND MATRON'S MANUAL, &C.

Illustrated by Numerous Engravings and Colored Plates.

NEW YORK:
T. W. STRONG, 98 NASSAU STREET.
BOSTON: G. W. COTTRELL, CORNHILL.

SEVENTH-SIXTH EDITION, IMPROVED.

1.26–27 *The penis in popular anatomy and sexology.* TOP: *Frederick Hollick,* The Male Generative Organs in Health and Disease... *(1850; New York, 1851) ["seventh-sixth (sic) edition, improved"; a few months later the book was up to the "120th edition, enlarged and improved"], frontispiece. Art uncredited. 21 × 35 cm. Archives & Special Collections, Columbia University Health Sciences Library.* BOTTOM: *"Penis Cut Through Vertically,"* The Male Generative Organs in Health and Disease *(New York, 1853), 130. New York Academy of Medicine.*

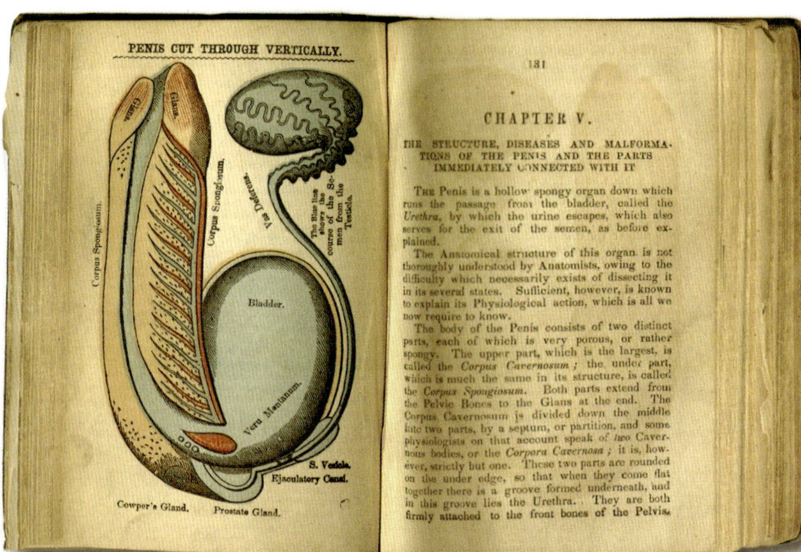
PENIS CUT THROUGH VERTICALLY.

131

CHAPTER V.

THE STRUCTURE, DISEASES AND MALFORMATIONS OF THE PENIS AND THE PARTS IMMEDIATELY CONNECTED WITH IT

The Penis is a hollow spongy organ down which runs the passage from the bladder, called the *Urethra*, by which the urine escapes, which also serves for the exit of the semen, as before explained.

The Anatomical structure of this organ is not thoroughly understood by Anatomists, owing to the difficulty which necessarily exists of dissecting it in its several states. Sufficient, however, is known to explain its Physiological action, which is all we now require to know.

The body of the Penis consists of two distinct parts, each of which is very porous, or rather spongy. The upper part, which is the largest, is called the *Corpus Cavernosum*; the under part, which is much the same in its structure, is called the *Corpus Spongiosum*. Both parts extend from the Pelvic Bones to the Glans at the end. The Corpus Cavernosum is divided down the middle into two parts, by a septum, or partition, and some physiologists on that account speak of *two* Cavernous bodies, or the *Corpora Cavernosa*; it is, however, strictly but one. These two parts are rounded on the under edge, so that when they come flat together there is a groove formed underneath, and in this groove lies the Urethra. They are both firmly attached to the front bones of the Pelvis.

illustrations were not finely made works of art that could be said to have aesthetic as well as scientific merit, were very far from fine. The vaginas and penises of popular sexology were crudely drawn, devoid of sensuality. Even so, the mere representation in print of male or female genitalia, in any form, even a sober anatomical diagram, generated a red-colored buzz, an erotic frisson. Which was represented in the images themselves by their red coloration.[90] The popular anatomies of the 1840s and 1850s weren't subtle.

Take, for example, the erect penis on exhibit in *The Silent Friend* (Fig. 1.28) of 1847—a "Medical Work treating on the Anatomy and Physiology of the Organs of Generation and their Diseases," an open domain that included "onanism," "mental and sexual incapacity and impotence," "venereal and syphilitic maladies," and "observations of marriage and its impediments." That small volume—probably sold in an "anatomical museum" that was attached to the office of "consulting surgeons" who treated venereal disease—had at least one foot in the red-light district of print culture, a line that only the most daring publications danced upon.[91] The authors and publishers of such works (often one and the same) well knew that, to defuse the charge of naked obscenity, a penis had to be cloaked in a covering text written by a doctor of medicine (or a claimant to that credential) and had to take the form of an anatomical diagram that was decorated with medical/moral nomenclature, fancy words. And framed with explanations, mostly on two themes: (1) knowledge of the anatomy and physiology of human reproduction would demystify sexuality and domesticate or tamp down desire; and (2) knowledge of the medical and moral dangers posed by promiscuity, over-excitement, "onanism," syphilis, etc. would deter readers from engaging in masturbation and sex outside of marriage. Authorities were thereby signaled (though rarely persuaded) that the publication was on the safe side of the border separating medical sexology from pornography, even as buyers were signaled that there was sexual content to be had ...

The double signal was not necessarily disingenuous. Most medical men and many members of the public took the pernicious effects of masturbation on the nervous system and physical vitality as an article of faith. Syphilis and other sexually transmitted diseases did run rampant (sexological authors claimed to offer effective treatment, but there were no effective cures). And some writers were sincerely committed to bringing anatomy and physiology—the science of the human body—to the lay public, including working people, women, and children, for ideological and moral purposes, including the tamping down of intemperate desire (sometimes linked to the temperance movement). Many of them sincerely wanted to democratize medical knowledge and society, while at the same time offering their services as medical advisors and provisioners of (onsite and mail-order) cures. In the US, Frederick Hollick, Edward Bliss Foote, Charles Knowlton, best-selling authors all, were self-identified radicals, reformers, democratizers, *and* vendors of publications, products and services.

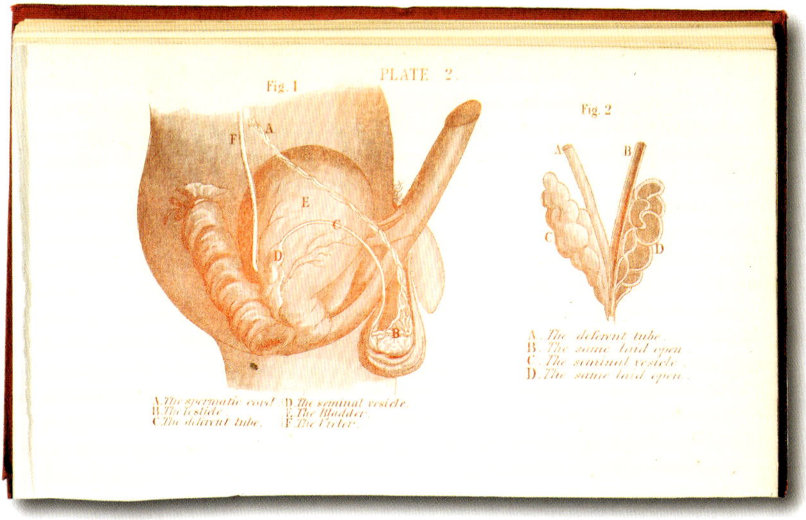

1.28 *R. & L. Perry & Co. ["consulting surgeons"],* The Silent Friend... *(London, 1847), pl. 2. Art/lithography uncredited. 17 cm. The Bodleian Libraries, University of Oxford. One of the very few medical publications that dared to show the penis erect.*

But the risks were real. Hollick was twice brought to trial in the 1840s in Philadelphia (but never convicted): he was accused of circulating "lewd pictures: colorful anatomical plates that boosted book sales" and showing audiences life-size "anatomical models" of naked dissected women (papier-mâché manikins imported from France). In the mid-1870s Foote ran afoul of Anthony Comstock and the Society for the Suppression of Vice for selling "obscene" material through the mail (a rubber "womb veil" and accompanying pamphlet explaining female reproduction and how the device should be used to prevent conception). He was convicted, and fined what was then the considerable sum of $3,500. (His son, Edward Bond Foote, coined the word "contraception.")[92] Yet profusely illustrated works by Hollick and Foote on health, medicine and the anatomy and physiology of sexuality continued to be published and read, into the early decades of the twentieth century. (Hollick's sexological *Origin of Life*, first published in 1845, achieved its "500th edition" in 1883.)

3.4 The closet's edge

"Anatomical" and "physiological" health publications were hugely popular, selling hundreds of thousands of copies. And sexual acts and relationships were everywhere, between men and women, but also same-sex and intergenerational couplings, and of course masturbation. Sex workers catered to common and special preferences. All of that tacitly known, and in some ways far less regulated than in our own times. Philip Van Buskirk's voluminous diaries of life aboard US Navy ships, kept over many years from the 1850s until late in the century, uniquely detail working-class illiterate and semi-literate sailors routinely engaging in sexual acts with each other, often in long-term relationships, often between adult men and teenagers or even boys (ships employed boys and teenagers until checked by child labor laws). According to Van Buskirk, "Certainly ninety percent of the white boys in the Navy of this day ... are, to an extent that would make you shudder, blasphemers and sodomites."[93]

Van Buskirk's private diaries never spell out what "sodomites" actually do. Zoned out of polite conversation and discourse—only referred to in mixtures of euphemism, allusion, gesture or condemnation—sex of all sorts was the glue which held the social and cultural universe together. And pulled it apart. Sex marked a boundary between speech and desire; between mannered literate middle and upper classes and the impolite illiterate poor; men and women; day and night.

Sexology did business on the borderline, provisioned the public with a medical and scientific vocabulary of bodies and parts, in diagrams and illustrations and charts, of things that otherwise could not appear in polite publication and mixed company.[94] The sexologist offered physiological justification for sex talk and sex itself. Sexual gratification was vital to adult health, Hollick and Foote argued, where desire was "awakened by a worthy and attractive object" of the opposite sex.[95] That was a radical idea.

Yet, until Kinsey, even sexology had hard limits. No medical or moral justification could ever be mounted for promiscuity or masturbation or sex outside marriage. And no mention ever made of same-sex desire. That was outside the pale of even the most transgressive popular sexologist.[96] Unmentionable, unthinkable.

Until, nearly all at once, John Addington Symonds, Havelock Ellis, Richard von Krafft-Ebing, Sigmund Freud, and Magnus Hirschfeld came along to break the spell, amidst much controversy and tumult, with "the invention of *homosexuality*" and a descriptive technical vocabulary of sexual "psychopathology" (*aka* "perversion").

So here too we come to an edge. Over the course of the nineteenth century, as discourse and apparatuses of regulation grow, the edge of the closet becomes ever more evident and well defined, yet ever more porous. The closet is consolidated, even as intermediate zones and sequestered spaces for queer sexuality flourish.

That sets the table. We've addressed issues, talked things over, and looked at: the mystery lithograph ... the anatomical plates of Jones Quain and Mascagni and a few others ... Dr. Franke's Phantom ... Sappey's mercurial injections ... Spigelius's strip-teasing self-demonstrating cadavers (via Holmes's recital) ... popular anatomical illustrations of genitalia, published in books which hovered near or on the line ... and a pornographic illustration well over the line.

Those materials can now serve as a shaky foundation upon which to build an argument: A medical book (and a medical library) can be a closet or a queer space or a club. And an anatomical illustration can be an object of desire, a queer object of queer desire ... Going further: certain anatomical illustrations were (and are) peculiarly suited to offer up queer objects for solitary contemplation. And for shared viewing in formal and informal clubs—the "secret museums" of wealthy collectors and the wood-paneled libraries and fireplaced meeting rooms of Royal Academies and Colleges and other elite medical and scientific societies.[97] *(And also in these pages, amongst ourselves.)*

So, here's what's next: We go on an immersive tour of images, first concentrating on the eighteenth century (Part Two) and then the nineteenth (Part Three), and think about aesthetics, the gaze, connoisseurial sociability and judgment, scientific merit, locations, careers, clubs, closets and other matters. As we go, we'll take an all-of-the-above approach: Close reading, contextualizing, contrasting—a mélange of comparativist, iconographical, genre-analytical, sociological, historical methods. And the objects of our study? Scientific representations of male (and some female) genitalia, muscled bodies, postures of bondage and submission, grazing fingers, and skin—all emanating from a cultivated and perverse aestheticism or maybe just an aisthesis, *the cultivation of the senses that was antecedent to and a corollary of scientific knowledge production.*

The images appear in works that aspire to the highest ideals and standards of scientific method and objectivity and publication. Which is also part of the queerness of it all. Our hypothesis: The anatomical image—idiosyncratic, full of meanings, sometimes contradictory, sometimes incoherent—did many kinds of work for the people who made and looked upon them. And gave rise to social, intellectual, scientific, and affective situations that afforded queer, erotically charged, experiences of making and viewing.

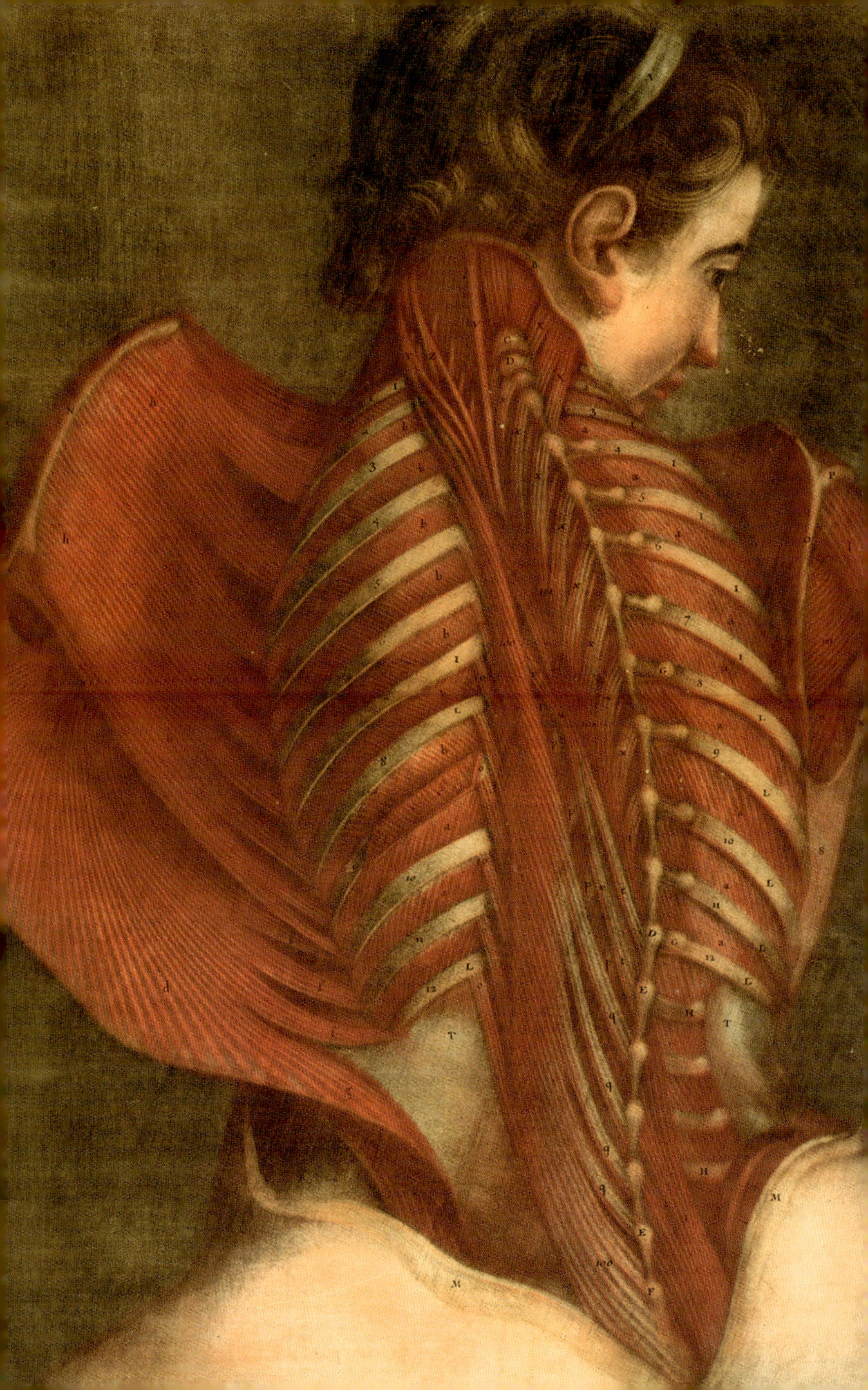

PART TWO

Connoisseurship, taste and "the beauty of the plate"

GAUTIER

1.1 Hungry eyes, science and the anatomical mezzotint

Popular anatomies disavowed pleasure and desire. If images of genitalia were presented, they had to be innocent, licensed with medical and moral purpose. Nothing to please the eye or spark the imagination. No grace notes. But for a very different group of readers, an elite of well-placed doctors, surgeons, scientific-minded intellectuals, and collectors, whose "judgments of taste constitute[d] a will to distinction," the anatomical object could do double duty as a more fulsome erotic object.[1] And exclusive and expensive anatomical publications—whether focused on art (the nude) or medicine—had plenty of grace notes—and were collectable just like paintings or sculptures. A gentleman's collection, historian Sarah Bull tells us, might "include pornographic novels," but also "medical and scientific works, writings on ancient artefacts, translations of foreign literature, court reports, legal texts, religious tracts, Greek and Roman classics, and 'gallant' novels ..."[2]

2.1 *Jacques-Fabien Gautier [Dagoty] & [J.-F.-M.] Duverney,* Myologie complette en couleur et grandeur naturelle... *(Paris, 1746[–48]), pl. 14. Color mezzotint. 61 × 46 cm. Archives & Special Collections, Columbia University Health Sciences Library.*

That was a market attended to in eighteenth-century France by artist-anatomist-printmaker Jacques-Fabien Gautier Dagoty (1716?–85), one of the first great exponents of the color mezzotint (though not its inventor: Gautier learned the technique, some say stole it, after a six-week stint in the workshop of Jacob Christoph Le Blon).[3]

In an age when printed illustrations were nearly always monochrome (unless laboriously colored by hand), mezzotint was a brilliant new multi-color printing process. The trade in illustrated books was booming when Gautier, an artisan from Marseille, came to Paris to seek his fortune. Setting up shop, he sought to capitalize on his unique color printing skills to court elite patronage and acceptance as a scientific gentleman.[4] (In mid-career he added "Dagoty," his mother's maiden name, as if ennobled, but without an apostrophe. His son, Arnauld-Eloi, assumed the name of "D'Agoty.")[5] These aspirations converged in his illustrated publications (Fig. 2.1). Which were vivid, weird, impressive, and pricey. Gautier's color printing process was labor-intensive, time consuming, requiring three or more copper plates per print, and specially prepared inks.[6] Some of his richly tinted mezzotints were 1:1 scale, life-size, designed to be bound into folio-size books or assembled together and hung on a wall like a painting. For an extra fee, purchasers could even have a print varnished to make it resemble an oil painting.[7]

Gautier's accomplishments as a printer were undeniable (despite the ongoing dispute about priority) and the king recognized him with a 30-year *privilege du Roi*, a royal license. But Gautier also craved recognition as a contributor to the new science. His membership in the *Académie des Sciences* of Dijon (1750), a more-than-respectable provincial society, attested to his scientific commitments. As did his self-published, and mostly self-written and self-drawn, *Observations sur l'Histoire Naturelle, sur la Physique et sur la Peinture* (1752–5), an illustrated journal devoted to matters of anatomy, medicine, zoology, botany, microscopy, art and physics.[8] But his attack on Newton, in a pamphlet on the generation of colors, elicited a rebuke from Goethe who dismissed Gautier as "an active, quick, rather impulsive man, certainly gifted but more than befittingly aggressive and sensational."[9] Later attempts to present his scientific work to the *Académie des Sciences* in Paris and the Royal Society in London, historian Sarah Lowengard tells us, were met with stone-cold rejection.[10]

If Gautier had any scientific bona fides—apart from the technology of color printing—it was in anatomy. In the 1730s and 1740s anatomy was fashionable. Anatomical lectures at the Jardin du Roi, the premier center for scientific research in France, were open to the public, and audiences flocked there to watch the dissection of cadavers. In those years, Paris became famous for its private courses in anatomy and abundance of "anatomical material." Students from all over Britain and Europe came to get instruction and hands-on experience. (Cadavers were hard to get in their native lands.)

Gautier took his private lessons, "for several years," from Jacques-François-Marie Duverney (1661–1748), anatomical lecturer at the Jardin du Roi (for the purpose of learning to make anatomical illustrations).[11] And he advertised his first major publications in anatomy, *Myology Complete in Color and Life-size* (1746) and *The Anatomy of the Head* (1748), as based on "pieces dissected and prepared by M. Duverney."[12] Duverney was credited as the author. His name and the Jardin du Roi association lent an aura of authority to Gautier's atlases.

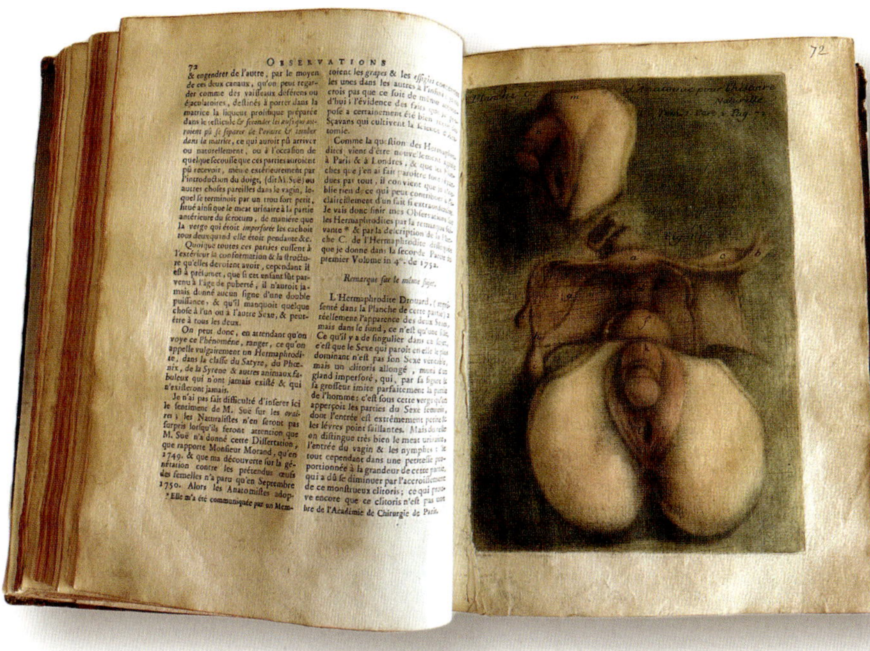

2.2 *The genitalia of Michel-Anne Drouart, in J.-F. Gautier [Dagoty],* Observations sur l'histoire naturelle, sur la physique et sur la peinture... *(Paris, 1752), 72. Color mezzotint. 27 × 20 cm. Hagströmer Medico-Historical Library.*

After Duverney's death, in 1748, and a brief collaboration with surgeon-anatomist Antoine Mertrud (d. 1767) on a study of Michel-Anne Drouart, the famous hermaphrodite, Gautier was on his own (Fig. 2.2).[13] His new anatomical publications, he claimed, continued the plan devised by Duverney, but Gautier now took the lead as dissector, and claimed the title of anatomist, as well as artist and printer.[14]

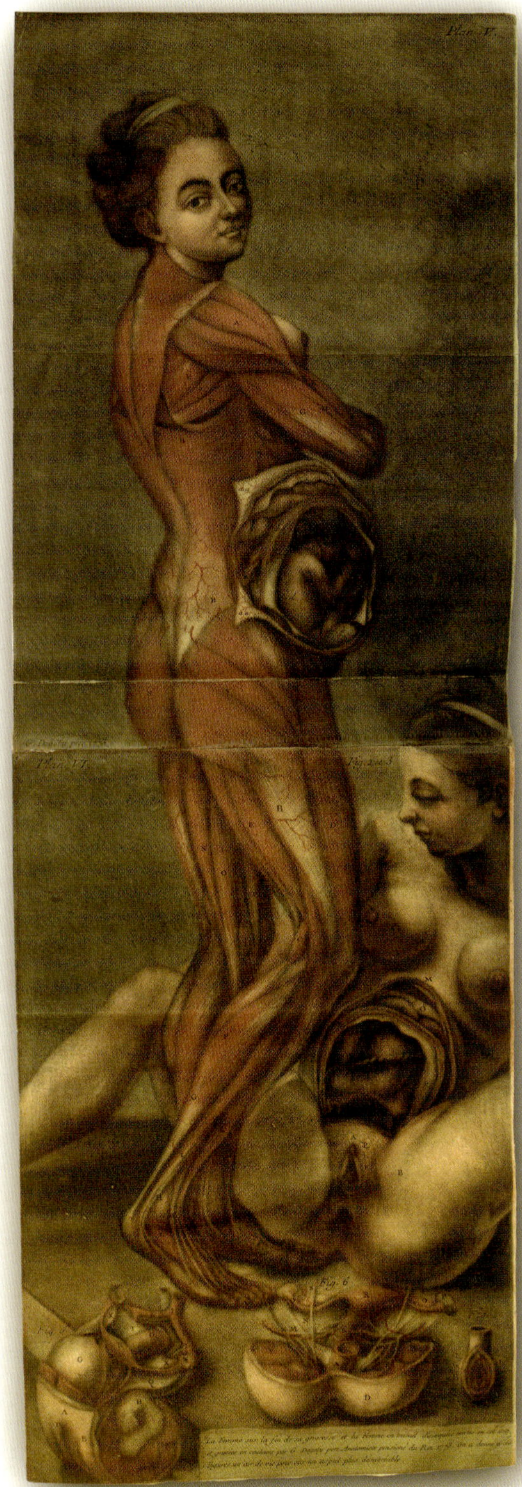

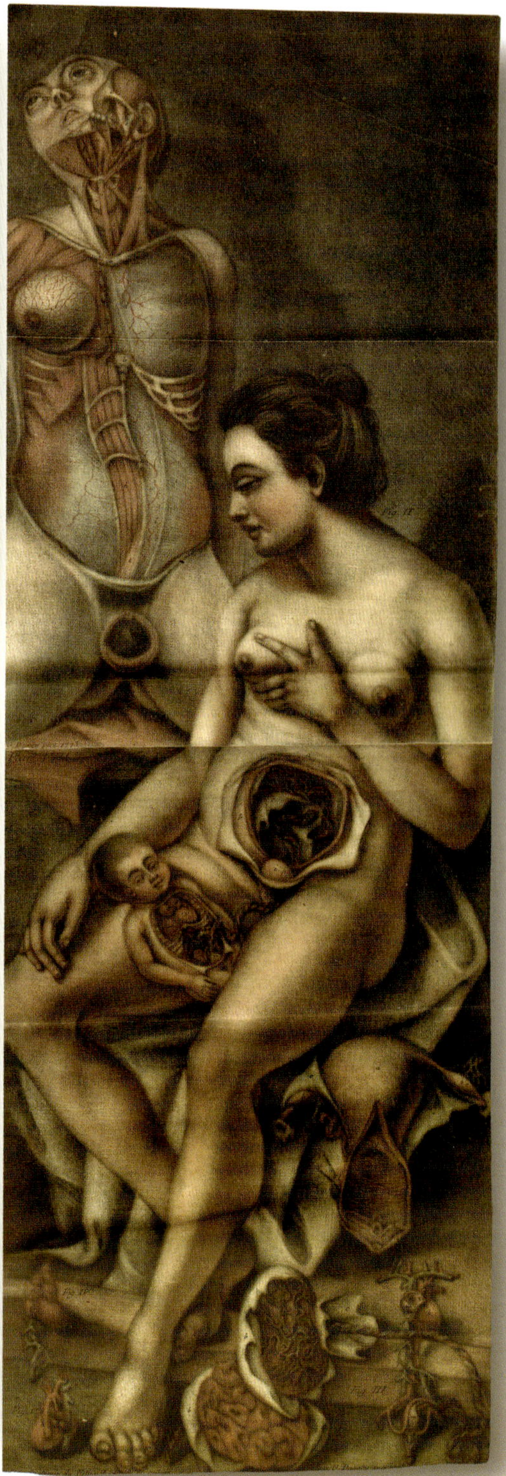

Anatomy was a subject well-suited to show off his mastery of color printing and a different kind of mastery, a mastery of the cadaver and the dissected body. And, of course, the dissected female body. This wasn't anatomy in a homoerotic closet, but in an exclusive social circle, a heteroerotic men's club. Gautier's mezzotints are provocative, often playful, sometimes sexy. The naked female body and body parts—female beauty—are extravagantly displayed. In the plate on the right (Fig. 2.4), that hand squeezing the breast (to illustrate how milk is expressed), the open hole in the genital region, the head looking skyward, a pose associated with the passion of Christ and the saints. (The imitation of Christ.) And, for good measure, a dissected infant wedged between her thighs. In the plate on the left (Fig. 2.3), a young naked dissected woman sitting on the floor with genitals and rectum open at the foot of another woman—who is both écorchéed and pregnant. Figures anatomized, yet vibrantly alive (but not the baby which looks like a dissected doll). The very composition of the scene: a live woman in the foreground, the dead dissected woman behind her. So much is going on ...

1.2 Anatomical provocations and the senses

And outside the frame: The scientific gaze and a male erotic sensibility focused on an odd assemblage of female objects. Gautier never pledges allegiance to any movement, but are his atlases pandering to the cult of *libertinage* and its provocations? Libertinism combined critiques of Christian morality and theology with all sorts of philosophical interests, including *histoire naturelle* and *philosophie naturelle*—the new science. An overweening interest in the human body was part of the package.[15] Eighteenth-century learned discourse was full of anatomical and physiological metaphors—the body as economy and polity, and vice versa—and arguments based on the mechanics of sensation.[16]

Libertinage, of course, was not just a set of talking points, but a philosophy of living, a justification for pleasure-taking, emancipated from traditional moral strictures. Eventually it would receive extravagant articulation in the works of the Marquis de Sade (1740–1814). In *The 120 Days of Sodom*, Sade refers to "the most convincing wax representations of dead bodies" (props for a scene of staged debauchery). He knew wax anatomies. Did he also know Gautier's mezzotints?[17] (It would be a shame if he didn't.)

Sade, the libertine, revels in sodomy, cruelty, pleasure and transgression, Gautier in death and viscera. Both men provoke readers with strange scenes and difficult objects, the human body in extremis, morbid perversity. Ugly beauty. Beautiful ugliness. And both men, in their chosen medium, mount

2.3–4 *Jacques-Fabien Gautier Dagoty,* Anatomie des parties de la génération de l'homme et de la femme *(Paris, 1773). Color mezzotints. 41 cm.* LEFT: *pl. 5.* RIGHT: *pl. 6. New York Academy of Medicine.*

challenges to the senses (Fig. 2.5). This at the high point of philosophical sensationism: the idea—famously expounded by Condillac in his 1754 *Traité des Sensations*—that knowledge fundamentally derives from the senses. Which was adjacent to the idea that sensual pleasure is good in its own right and not to be deplored (hedonism). And which motivated lively philosophical and scientific debates on the cultivation and physiological mechanics of the senses. Which Nicolas Le Cat, author of *Traité des Sens* (*Treatise on the Senses,* 1742) and other anatomists contributed to (Fig. 2.6).[18] As did Gautier Dagoty (Fig. 2.7).[19]

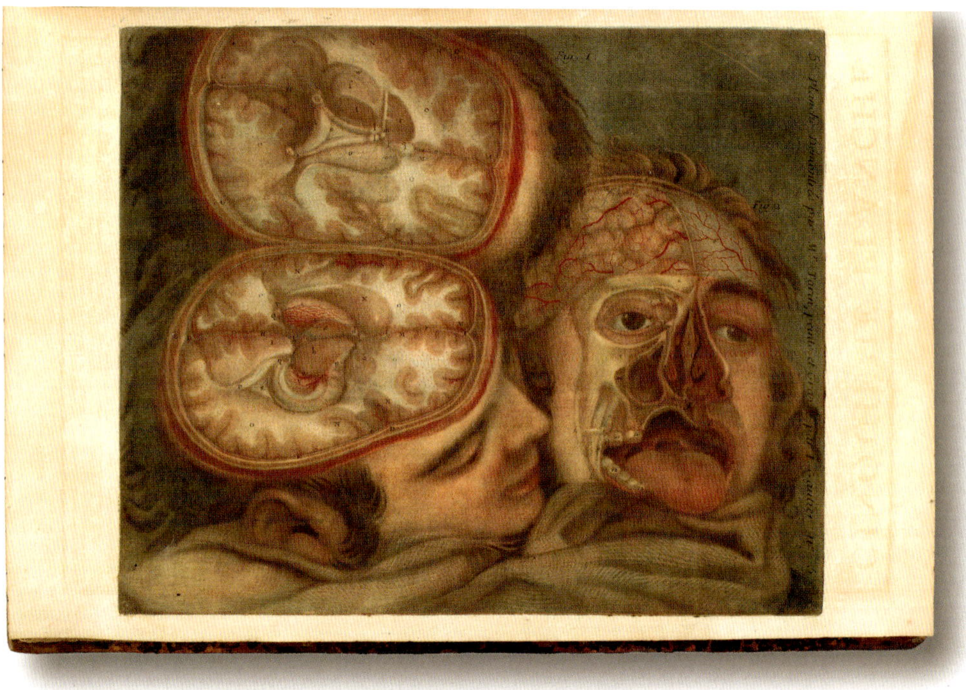

2.5 *Organs of sense, sensing, desire, in an oddly intimate scene of horror. Jacques-Fabien Gautier [Dagoty] & [J.-F.-M.] Duverney,* Anatomie de la tête, en tableaux imprimés qui représentent au naturel le cerveau sous différentes coupes, la distribution des vaisseaux dans toutes les parties de la tête, les organes des sens et une partie de la névrologie, d'après les pièces disséquées et préparées par M. Duverney... *(Paris, 1748), pl. 5. Color mezzotint. 55 × 39 cm. Archives & Special Collections, Columbia University Health Sciences Library.*

And that justified Gautier's penchant for showing off dissected ladies and lady parts (Figs. 2.1–3, 2.8), and also sometimes male organs, as in the still life with erect penises on the right (Fig. 2.9). His concentration on organs of sensory pleasure was oddly transgressive, an eccentric presentation of objects that even the most licentious eighteenth-century painting wasn't permitted to show. While the prefaces and captions assert a scientific justification, and situate Gautier as an anatomist in the grand line of contributors to medical science—the big names who claimed priority in the discovery of parts and functions—he himself never made any discoveries, major or minor, had no students or theoretical innovations. No one could take him for a great authority.

He offered readers a system of visual pedagogy, a full *cours d'anatomie*, not just reproductive anatomy. But the excised genitals, brilliantly colored, arranged as a bizarre juxtaposition of dissected objects, can't be strictly

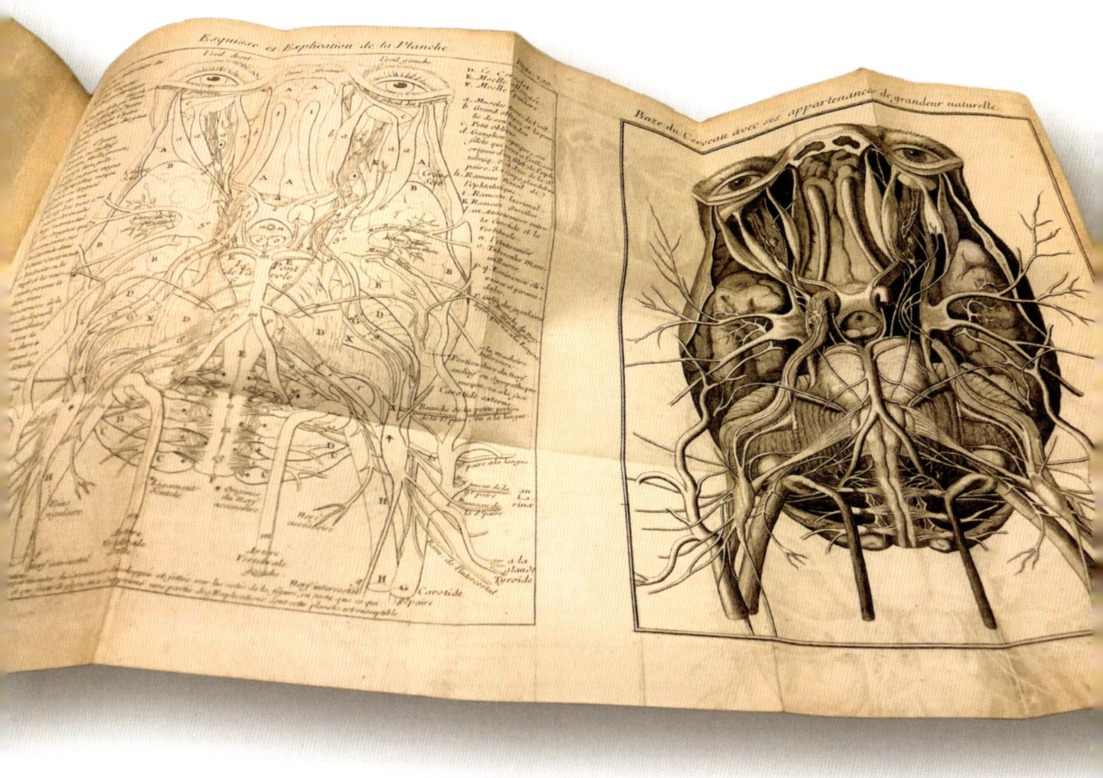

2.6 *The anatomy of the gaze. Claude-Nicolas Le Cat,* Traité des sens *(1742; Amsterdam, 1744), pl. 1. Copperplate engraving, fold-out. Book: 13 × 20 cm; foldout: 44 × 30 cm. Hagströmer Medico-Historical Library.*

for pedagogical purposes or scientific study or demonstrations of printing technique.[20] While some of Gautier's illustrations were life-size, suited for wall-hanging as visual aids for anatomical instruction, we don't know they were ever used in classrooms, lectures or dissecting rooms or to decorate the walls of learned societies. His mezzotints, full of vibrant reds, use the objects of anatomy—the dissected body, especially dissections of women and female body parts — to inflame the senses of the (male) viewer. Gautier's son, Arnaud-Éloi Gautier d'Agoty (1741–80, or 1783), who worked in the

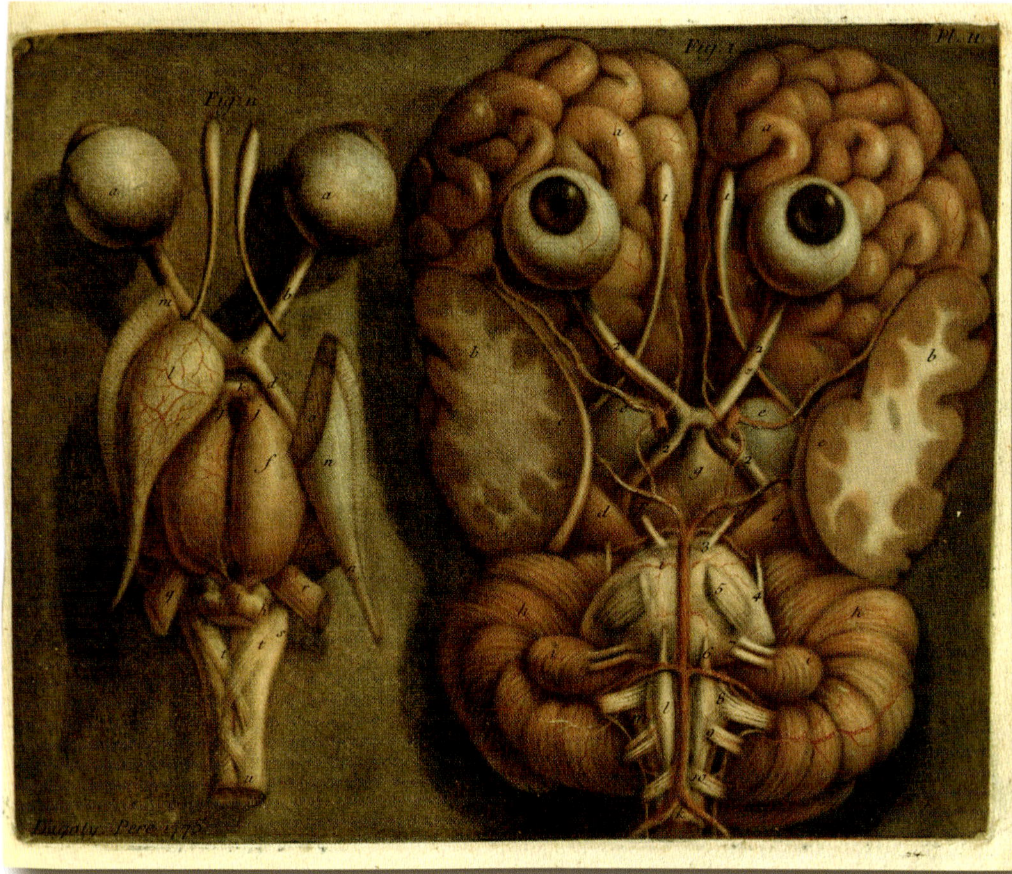

2.7 *The anatomy of the gaze three decades later. Jacques-Fabien Gautier Dagoty,* Exposition anatomique des organes des sens, jointe la névrologie entière du corps humain… *(Paris, 1775), pl. 2. Color mezzotint. 42 × 27 cm. New York Academy of Medicine.*

family business, offered a half-hearted justification for that: "For men to be instructed, they must be seduced. But how can anyone render the image of Death agreeable?"[21] Yet, as any reader of Sade can attest, in the anti-ethos of libertinage, the image of Death and anatomical horror, within or alongside female bodies, could be very agreeable, perversely agreeable.

Gautier was a provocateur. As an artisan on the periphery of the medical and art establishment, his main chance was to carve out a unique high-end niche in the print marketplace: freaky color-saturated large-size anatomical illustration was his and his alone. While some of his mezzotints gestured toward female beauty and feminine graces, others affected a flaunting grotesque ugliness. He printed only in small runs, and left behind no school or style of medical publication. The rarity, novelty, artisanal skill, scientific subject matter, and queer provocation—the dissected human body, genitalia, images of taxidermied and dissected animals (also a bit of botany, microscopy and hermaphroditic freakery)—made his works worthy of a kind of arguable connoisseurship.[22]

Arguable because the level of artistry fluctuates: his drawings are often crude, sometimes terribly crude. Gautier had some difficulty with the rendering of figures. It's hard to know how potential purchasers responded to that. Likely the novelty, grotesquery and scientificity of the subject matter, and brightness of his colors, outweighed the clumsiness of his pencil. Gautier claimed that he alone could provide readers with images whose colors accurately corresponded to what the anatomist sees when he cuts into a fresh cadaver: a weighty claim. And consider that the printed colored image was novel and charming enough to be a collectable category. (Other printers who specialized in color did a good business with flowers and other traditional subjects of fine art: images of beauty.)[23] Consider also that the artwork of contemporary French anatomical atlases was not particularly wonderful.[24] So perhaps Gautier's most artful and painterly plates came near to meeting connoisseurial and scientific standards—even if they never remotely approached the high-water marks in anatomical image-making set by Govard Bidloo (1649–1713), William Cowper (1664–1723), Bernhard Sigfried Albinus (1697–1770), Albrecht von Haller (1708–77) and William Hunter (1718–83). Those acclaimed anatomists also featured provocative subjects and images—ugly, monstrous subjects, beautifully rendered—but they were mostly inoculated from criticism by medical and scientific credentials, social status, and the brilliance of their sharply delineated (monochrome) plates. Made by artists of distinction.[25]

Yet, even with small print runs, inept draughtsmanship, and lots of question marks, Gautier had reach. Pehr Floding (1731–91), "professor of anatomy and perspective" at the Academy of Art in Stockholm, wrote in his notebook (*c.*1780) what must have been a common assessment among medical men and teachers of art in France and beyond. (Floding studied and worked in Paris in the 1750s and 1760s.) The mezzotints "are quite splendid but also confused. In Gauthier's hand, the art of combining all the colors of the parts ... has not reached the perfection it requires ... also, the plates are incredibly expensive ..."[26] Still, Johan Gustaf Hallman (1726–97), a pupil of Linnaeus, deemed them valuable enough to purchase for his library in Sweden.[27] And Gautier had customers enough, inside and outside of France, to support his business and growing family for a period of more than forty years.

We might label him an outlier, and his mezzotints a kind of "outsider art." But that assessment is complicated by his scientific commitments and insider customers: men of the nobility, the haut-bourgeoisie. Who could afford the costly sumptuous images, with their red-saturated views of sexual anatomy, flayed cadavers, diseased and deformed genitalia, which were deemed unsuitable for impressionable youths and women. Given anatomy's prominence in the curriculum of Enlightenment science, ladies with philosophical interests might have also sought out his mezzotints, but Gautier's customers were gentlemen collectors of learning and "taste," men with medical and scientific interests, and at the head of the pack, wealthy physicians and surgeons.[28] Medical gentlemen.

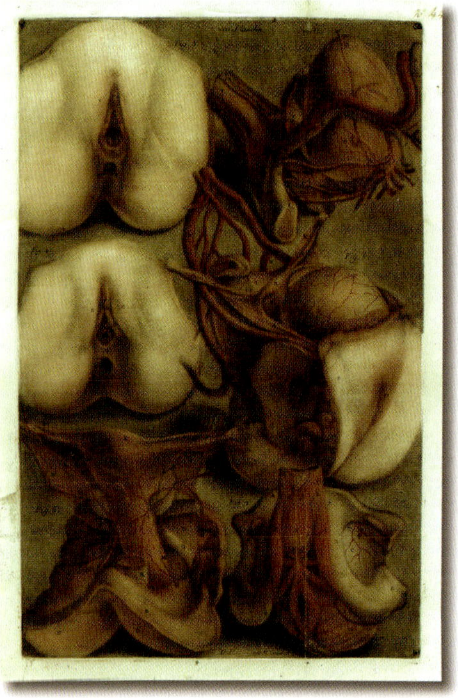

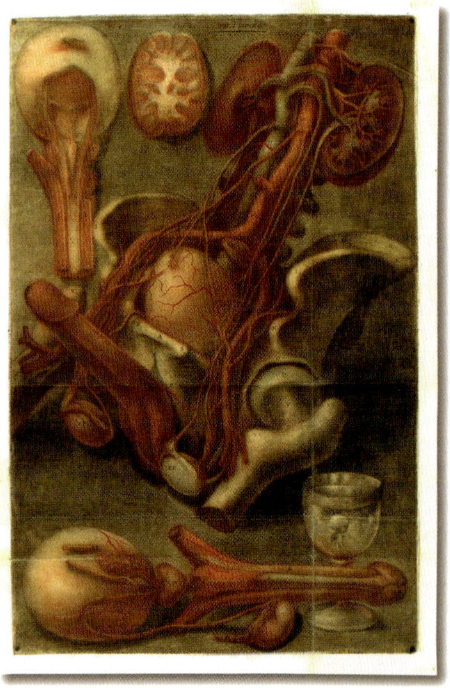

2.8–9 *Jacques-Fabien Gautier [Dagoty] & [Jacques-François-Marie] Duverney,* Myologie complette en couleur et grandeur naturelle.... *(Paris, 1746[–48]), pls. 7–8. Color mezzotint. 61 × 46 cm.* LEFT: *Dissected rectums, vaginas, and other parts of the female genitourinary tract.* RIGHT: *Still life with erect penises and parts of the genitourinary tract—and a homuncular fetus in a wineglass. (The fetus in a wineglass also appears elsewhere in Gautier.) Hagströmer Medico-Historical Library.*

"Taste" (in French *goût* or *goust*), was a keyword, connected to sense, sensation and the sensory apparatus, discernment, refined sensibility, superior breeding and temperament, maybe an inborn sixth sense. It was an expansive and ill-defined category among privileged men, who considered themselves free to gaze upon, savor and collect images and objects otherwise regarded as base, contaminated.[29] They were beyond reproach. But Gautier's questionable social status—an artisan who got his hands dirty—and the dubious moral and aesthetic status of his mezzotints—their wayward ugliness, corporeality, erotics—must have placed a mark, a stain, upon the artist-artisan turned anatomist. *Philosophes*, medical professors, aristocrats, the wealthy, collected his publications, but was he welcome in their libraries and salons? Probably not. And that cold or indifferent reception would have rankled Gautier, an arriviste who never quite arrived. According to historians Corinne Le Bitouzé and Morwena Joly-Parvex, over the decades Gautier's scientific texts, "often abstruse and based on pseudo-experiments turn more and more to self-justification" and grievance. He craved validation. And maybe the lack of it destroyed him. He died in 1785, shortly after suffering the humiliation of learning (from notices in the press and not any direct communication) that the Dijon *Academie des Sciences* had expelled him from its ranks.[30]

The problem of the gaze, for Foucault and for feminist theory, is the problem of desire. Intense looking is objectifying, the foundational procedure upon which methods of division and analysis can be deployed. According to its seventeenth- and eighteenth-century exponents, scientific practice and discourse should be disinterested, disembodied, objective. (Along the same lines, Jonathan Richardson, an eighteenth-century exponent of the new "science" of connoisseurship, who we will shortly encounter, called for a parallel ethos of connoisseurial detachment.)[31] *The scientific eye is a scope, should have no bias, no stake in outcomes.*

And yet the gaze, so thirsty for understanding and control, is an act of possession that captures both object and viewer. The view inflames the viewer. The viewer hungers for the view. And that initiates a collapse, a merging of subject and object—almost a lovers' gaze, an alternating current of reciprocal identification, a humming oscillation of object-subject transference. Which in turn, may seed the growth of an identity formation, a fellowship of gazers, social or professional.

And the medical illustration is a locus of those gazes and gaze effects, a space where they can converge and intensify.

CHESELDEN

2.1 "The beauty of the plate"

And that in turn leads us to reflect upon the privileged men who directed and shared the medical gaze, who cultivated the sciences of gazing, the gazes of science, and who avidly produced and collected scientific images of beauty, desire, spectacular monstrosity, and curious anomaly. Such as Gautier's near contemporary, William Cheselden (1688–1752), an eminent surgeon and medical author who was regarded as one of the most distinguished British anatomists of his generation. Consider this copperplate engraving (Fig. 2.10), which first appears in his 1740 edition of *Anatomy of the Human Body*, the book which, over many decades, had the widest circulation and readership of any anatomical text in eighteenth-century Britain and North America. The plate shows "the famous statue of Hercules and Antaeus," ostensibly to demonstrate the structure and musculature of

T.AB.XX.

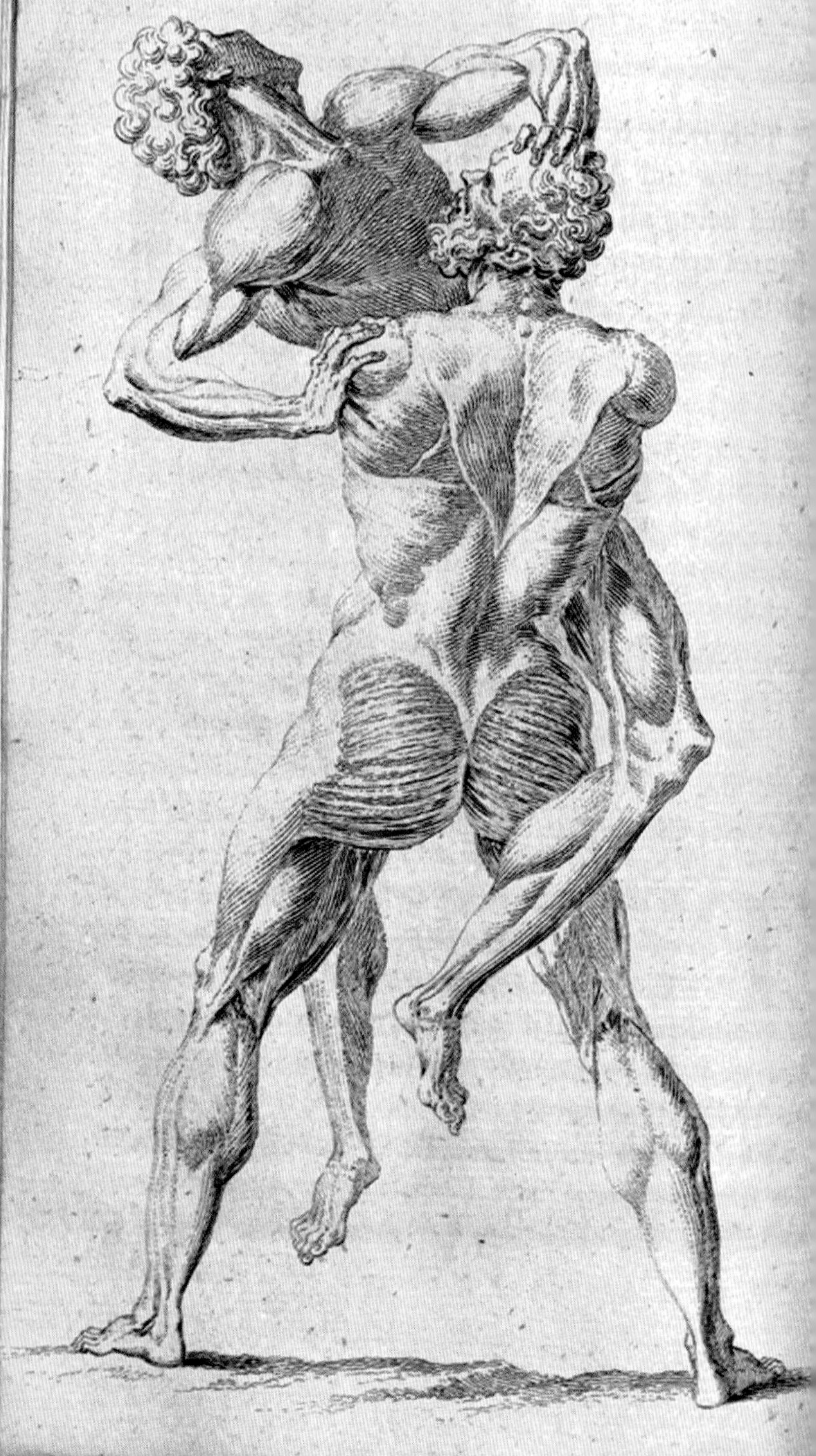

TAB. XX.

This table is done after the famous ſtatue of Hercules and Antæus. The muſcles here exhibited being all explained in the other plates, the figures are omitted to preſerve the beauty of the plate.

the buttocks, shoulders and back.[32] One naked muscleman (Hercules) grips the other (Antaeus) in a peculiar embrace that looks as much like a rape scene as a wrestling match. On the facing page, Cheselden comments: "The muscles here exhibited being explained in all other plates, the figures," the little numbers that key the illustrated parts to an accompanying caption, "are omitted to preserve the beauty of the plate." To Cheselden, the plate's "beauty" is self-evident, needs no explanation or qualification. The inclusion of "figures" would be disfiguring. (That wasn't uncommon: other eighteenth- and nineteenth-century medical authors singled out favored images for similar treatment.)[33] But you might wonder: What makes this particular plate beautiful? Why does it merit privileged treatment?

Like Gautier, Cheselden was a striver, but as a country gentleman's son come to London, a bit more secure in his social status and prospects. Given his evident talent as a bright young surgeon and anatomist, he could realistically entertain the ambition to participate in Enlightenment discourse and social circles.[34] In that discursive world, aesthetics was the philosophy of beauty and the senses. The beautiful. Which, by centuries-long association, had an ambivalent connection to erotic desire and pleasure in both male and female beauty.[35]

But Beauty has to transcend desire, rise above mere sensual pleasure and desire. To get its capital B, embodied beauty has to be attached in some way to the theory of beauty (aesthetics), and receive representation and commentary in cultivated text and conversation, and in painting, drawing and sculpture. A man or woman may be beautiful, may be a very great beauty, but when he or she embodies Beauty, his or her body materializes an abstraction, a platonic ideal, and so corresponds to the beauty of the great art of antiquity and the Renaissance, and present-day "masters."[36]

In this cultural logic, Beauty becomes discernible as an object when it is perceived and appreciated by cultivated minds in dialogue with other cultivated minds. The philosopher-politician Edmund Burke, for example, engages in precisely this kind of dialogue when he remarks to his readers, in a "short review of opinions," that "beauty, and the passion caused by beauty ... is different from [mere] desire."[37] Beauty is a kind of juried desire, "a social quality" (Burke again) rarefied or raised above bodily desire, only made apparent through a series of artful mediations and group endorsements, and in this way absolved, made innocent, inoculated against sordid pleasure-seeking. Which then gives the cognoscenti a moral license to do just that. Seek pleasure.[38]

What is beauty? How is it discerned? How is discernment acquired? What prerequisite qualities mark a man of discernment? These were

(PREVIOUS PAGE) 2.10 *"...the figures are omitted to preserve the beauty of the plate." William Cheselden,* Anatomy of the Human Body *(10th ed.; London, 1773), 130–1, tab. 20. Copperplate engraving: Gerard Vandergucht. 21 × 13 cm. Hagströmer Medico-Historical Library. This plate first appears in the 5th edition (1740).*

vitally important questions for Jonathan Richardson the Elder, the Earl of Shaftesbury, Edmund Burke, Alexander Baumgarten, William Gilpin, David Hume, Immanuel Kant, Francis Hutcheson, William Hogarth, and Richard Payne Knight, all widely-read exponents of the then new and fashionable field of aesthetics. In Cheselden's time, the philosophy of beauty and the procedures of discernment had an avid readership. Hume, writing "Of the Standards of Taste" (*c.*1745), argues that beauty is a matter of "delicacy of the imagination," "sensibility of ... finer emotions," "sentiment." Qualities that only certain people, a certain class of people, may possess. Hume shies away from any consideration of how a social consensus forms around the standards of taste. He wants everything to happen in the Mind. Yet in the interstices of his argument even Hume has to acknowledge that assessments of beauty are arrived at through a process of discussion, debate and negotiation: "Every one talks of it." "[T]he general rules of beauty are of use: ... being drawn from the observation of what pleases or displeases, when presented singly or in a high degree ..."

But Hume wants to base the standards on something more secure than mere personal opinion or group discussion. His language is disembodying: he declines to specify any forum of presentation, or person or persons who might make use of the rules of beauty in speech or transactions. Dramatis personae, scene, plot, all of that, are left to lurk in the discursive shadows. Hume again: "And if the same qualities ... affect not the organs, with a sensible delight or uneasiness we exclude the person from pretensions to this delicacy." In other words, without an accrediting constitutional appreciation of beauty, no (hypothetical) person can play the role of legitimate tastemaker in the community of tastemakers. Hume, like most of his philosophical contemporaries, is keen to naturalize and essentialize the workings of Mind and "organs" of sensibility: the apprehension of beauty happens in the senses. And he therefore brackets the social settings, conversations and transactions in which questions of beauty and taste are decided. By the mid-eighteenth century, there were hundreds of formal all-male clubs, by century's end thousands, and many more informal cliques.[39] But the connoisseur, the collector, the dealer, the spectator, and their formal societies and wider circles of association, stand outside the text, go unmentioned and untheorized in Hume's treatise. Yet those are the very people to whom his treatise is addressed. Hume writes to provide them—his readers—with a model and a vocabulary for the making of aesthetic judgments that will ultimately contribute to the shaping of collective aesthetic wisdom.[40]

Which is a big gap. Historians have shown that the connoisseurial circle served as a kind of "knowledge community," functionally equivalent to the "scientific communities" that sociologist of science Thomas Kuhn famously showed to be central institutions in the production of scientific knowledge. Which the British elite developed under the influence of Italian, French and latinate discourse (and therefore labeled themselves with terms adapted from that discourse). *Connoisseurs* clustered in groups of *virtuosi* and *dilettanti*, elite groups of men who dined and drank together (alcohol, coffee, tea), and who traveled and collected and partied together, occasions that were full of serious and erudite conversation and witty or supercilious banter. *Virtuosi* focused on a broad curriculum of natural and man-made "sciences"—physics, chemistry, philosophy, anatomy, etc.—which included art and architecture. *Dilettanti* focused on a broad curriculum of art and architecture and semi-competitive collecting, but also took interest in, and often collected, natural knowledge. The men, societies and cliques that claimed those labels overlapped—many men sought to embody connoisseurship, virtuosity and dilettantism. And in those places, art opinion, criticism, study, consensus and dissensus, rested on a "social epistemology" of group deliberation, in text and conversation, reinforced by formal instruction in art (drawing and history) and the market pricing of artworks. Always subject to the vagaries of fashion.[41]

And "influencers." All aesthetic judgments were not equal. Writing decades earlier, when the term *connoisseur* was very new to the English language,[42] Jonathan Richardson also wanted to individualize and disembody beauty, but his more practically minded *Two Discourses* of 1719 focuses on the role of tastemaker, the "connoisseur" (who is a person and a type): "None sees as a Connoisseur does ... He ... sees Beauties in Pictures and Drawings which to Common Eyes are Invisible ..."[43] Abstract "Beauties," appearing in all kinds of unexpected locations, are here contrasted to the easily visible beauties that are accessible to "common eyes," belonging to those who, for example, might seek gratification in views of naked, erotically desirable women, and men. Common eyes, yes. The distinction of Taste was, of course, also a distinction of class. ("Meaner sorts" of people in late seventeenth- and eighteenth-century England, art historian Carol Gibson-Wood has shown, also looked upon paintings and sculptures, of whatever quality they had access to, and also bought them in bunches, of whatever quality they could afford, to decorate their meaner homes. And claimed some distinction of Taste in relation to their peers and people of adjacent rank.)[44]

But if Beauty was useful in making social distinctions, it was also troublesome: Polarities could always be reversed. Erotic desire was directly expressed or indirectly encoded in the beautiful figure, in the making of it, the viewing of it, the acquisition and display of it. The moral legitimacy of the naked or partly naked figure as a subject for the appreciation of viewers—its Beauty—its status as an object embodying Beauty—depended on transcendence and a disavowal of erotic interest. Otherwise the figure was pornographic, base, corporeal, vulgar. And, by extension, so was the person attending to it. Lord Shaftesbury, writing in 1713, warned against "this *false Relish*, which is govern'd by what immediately strikes the Sense" (Body!), rather than Reason and Spirit (Mind!).[45]

Yet, even transcended in a kind of disavowal, the figure was still there in plain view for those who might take an erotic interest ("false Relish"). And that tension was the crux of a vital question in connoisseurial deliberations: Is this particular work of art (and the figures contained within it) merely beautiful (or not even that) or is it a figure of Beauty? And to what degree—in recondite allusion? jesting banter? open admiration?—may connoisseurs, singly or in a group, share, hint at, openly take pleasure in, the desirous view?[46] Richardson wants to dissociate the connoisseur—who approaches works of art with expert knowledge, judicious assessment, reason, and a discerning eye, but also maybe, some kind of communion with or purified passion for the art object and the figure(s) represented in it—from those who merely seek to acquire beautiful works of art for the prestige of acquisition or the base enjoyment of desirous looking and erotic gratification.[47] But once you've passed the test, and qualified for connoisseurship, what then? What sort of sociability occurs among connoisseurs in the group of cognoscenti? What happens when it's time to let your hair down, and speak and act freely?

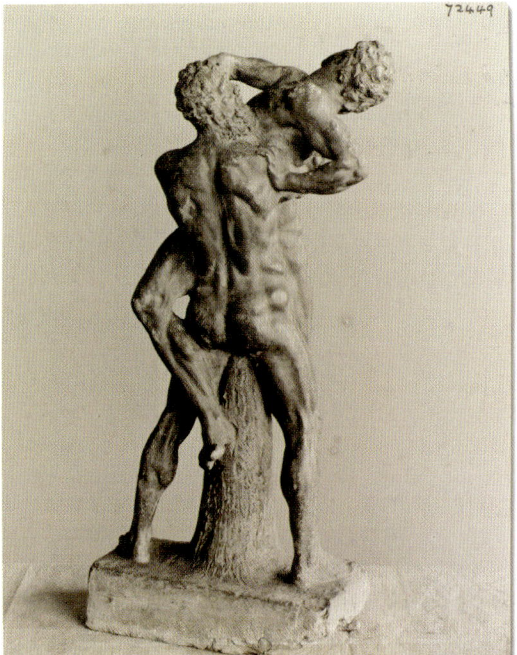

2.11 *Stefano Maderno,* Hercules and Antaeus. *Sketch model, unfired clay. (Florence, c.1622). 59 cm. © Victoria & Albert Museum, London.*

2.2 What is beautiful?

But before we get into all that: a complication. Let's stipulate that, even though Cheselden pauses to remark on the beauty of his Antaeus and Hercules pair, a beauty that could be said to reside in the artistry of the composition and execution of the image, the copperplate engraving actually falls a bit short, more than a bit. Printed in an ungrand middling-sized book format, the rendering of the contest between the two strongmen is slightly klutzy, earthbound, fails to transcend.

However, that merely competent illustration references the hand of a prior and more gifted artist, and a more aesthetically satisfying work: Stefano Maderno's sensuous and graceful bronze sculpture of Hercules and Antaeus. We don't know if Cheselden's plate was based on a direct view of the shiny bronze (Maderno made several copies), a clay sketch model, a tabletop figurine, or on some now lost pencil-drawn study (Fig. 2.11). No matter: Maderno's statue was well regarded (although just one of several well-regarded versions of the Hercules-Antaeus encounter)—and tabletop plaster and bronze models circulated widely.[48] And we don't know who drew the artwork for the plate: Cheselden himself or someone else working under Cheselden's direction. Cheselden's plate translates most of Maderno's design, only removing some buttock and shoulder skin (a partial écorché to make it more anatomical) and removing the (to our Freudianized eyes, phallic) pillar that serves as a structural support for Maderno's sculpture.[49] But the fluidity of line, the sensuous bodily surfaces, are lost in the translation from statue to the engraving. The anatomical illustration is a credible reference to a classical ideal but only that, it doesn't do justice to Maderno's sensually playful original. Even so, Cheselden's plate could have generated sparks for readers who fancied an oddly intimate scene of rough embrace and struggle for dominance between two very naked muscle-men of classical antiquity.[50]

Intimate but not so beautiful. Except by association, as a reference to Maderno's original and, in back of that, to the enchanted world of classical and neoclassical mythology (where Hercules had long been a canonical figure in poetry and art, becoming even more prominent after the 1546 recovery of the the Farnese Hercules). And to ideals of masculine power. And to the cultivated appreciation of disembodied abstracted Beauty that, via a chain of mediations, paradoxically, is ultimately derived from actual sweaty entangled bodies—and which licenses enjoyment of same.[51]

2.3 Connoisseurial judgment and anatomy

Art and anatomical science came together first in Renaissance neoclassical drawing, painting and sculpture, a marriage consummated in the illustrated works of Vesalius and his successors. And in the art academy, a school for the formal study of art, where the subject of anatomy was a foundational part of the curriculum. The anatomy taught there was exclusively skeleto-muscular, the structures of the body, the mechanics of bodily motion, and the anatomy of gesture, facial structure and expression—subjects useful to artists in portraiture and the staging of religious, mythological and historical scenes, scenes of everyday life and the picturesque. Art anatomy focused on the anatomy of strong, muscular, naked men. Muscles were larger and more manifest in male bodies, so thought to be better suited for figure study. But the male figure was also the template of the human, Man. According to art historian Nicholas Penny, at the art academy founded by the Carracci family in sixteenth-century Bologna (an influential model for subsequent schools), "The male body was held to be the divine form: the proper object of study and veneration."[52]

Anatomical correctness was one of the criteria by which art was adjudged. And therefore a concern for connoisseurs and collectors. And a matter which William Gilpin (1724–1804) repeatedly turned to in his little book of 1768, *An Essay Upon Prints: Remarks Upon the Principles of Picturesque Beauty, the Different Kinds of Prints, and the Characters of the Most Noted Masters; illustrated by Criticisms Upon Particular Pieces* ...[53] Gilpin, an artist as well as a writer, and one of the foremost exponents and explainers of "the picturesque" and "picturesque beauty," also attended to beauty in the representation of figures. In paintings, he tells us, "drawing has more of nature in it, and more of effect: but the student in anatomy finds more precision in the print; and can more easily trace the line, and follow it in all its windings through light and shade" (38). Engravings, then, have this particular virtue.

Gilpin goes on to discuss various artists and engravers, assessing their anatomical competence, and weighing that against their other virtues and faults ("Some Cautions that may be useful in collecting Prints"). Let's eavesdrop a bit, take in some of his connoisseurial shop-talk:

> [Karel] Du Jardin understood the anatomy of domestic animals perhaps better than any other master. His drawing is admirably correct and yet the freedom of the matter is preserved. He copied nature strictly, tho' not servilely; and hath given us not only the form, but the characteristic peculiarities of each animal.[54] (140)

Yet a knowledge of anatomy, while necessary, is not the sole criterion of artistic value: "The great excellency of" Raymond La Fage's sketches, he opines, "lay in drawing; in which he was perfectly skilled. However unfinished his pieces are, they discover him to be admirably acquainted with anatomy and proportion." But "[t]here is very little in him besides, that is valuable..." (99).[55]

As for Hogarth's anatomy, Gilpin judges it to be entirely lacking, but the deficiency is overcome with the artist's sheer wit and liveliness:

> Of the muscles and anatomy of the head and hands he had perfect knowledge; but his trunks are often badly moulded, and his limbs ill set on. I tax him with plain bad drawing, I speak not of the niceties of anatomy, and elegance of out-line: of these indeed he knew nothing; ... yet his figures upon the whole are inspired with so much life, and meaning that the eye is kept in good humour. (171–2)

Given all of this emphasis on anatomy in art training and connoisseurship, medical authority was potentially also aesthetic authority. Thus, upon

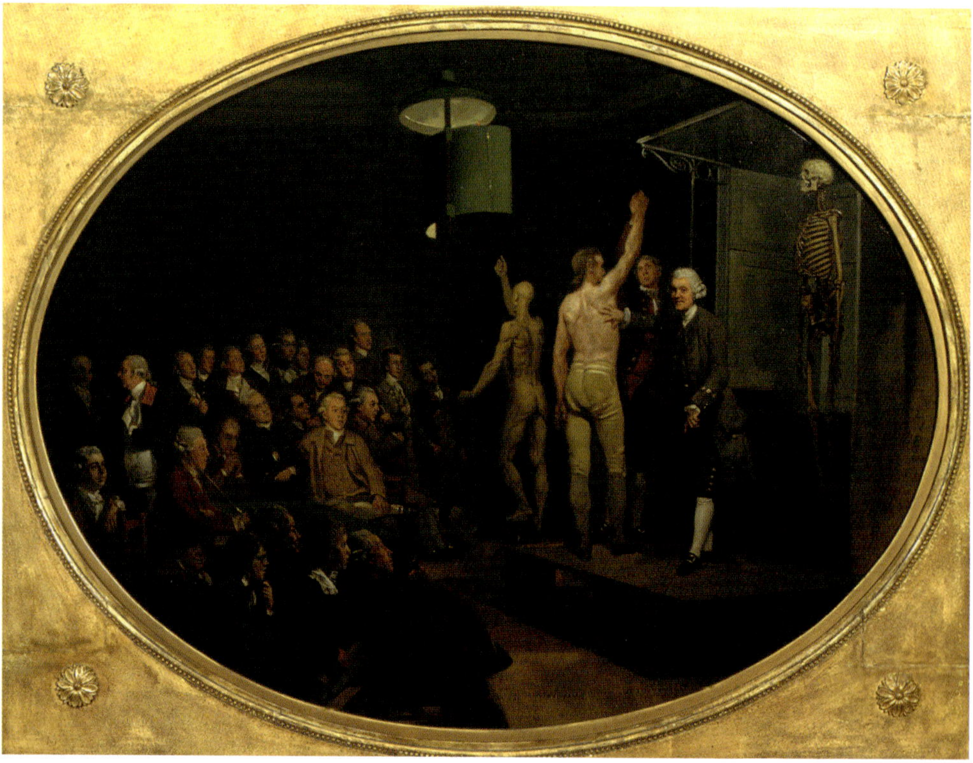

2.12 *Johan Zoffany, "William Hunter Lecturing to an audience of artists and students at the Royal Academy" (1770–2). Oil on canvas. 77 × 104 cm. © Royal College of Physicians, London.*

its founding in 1768, the Royal Academy of Art recruited the eminent anatomist William Hunter, to teach anatomy (Fig. 2.12).[56] It was common practice for art academies to hire anatomists to teach anatomy, sometimes including dissection. Instructors in other subjects, such as the sculptor John Flaxman (1755–1826), also placed great importance on anatomy. In his lectures at the Royal Academy, Flaxman narrated the history of sculpture as a history of the progress of anatomical knowledge.[57] The Egyptians knew less than the classical-age Greeks, who knew less than the Hellenistic Greeks and the Romans, who knew less than the Renaissance masters, who knew less than modern Europeans. The painter Benjamin Robert Haydon (1786–1846) credited the advance of the visual arts to the advance of medical knowledge: "our artists now ... know a good deal, because our surgeons know so much!"[58] Art and anatomy shared the methodology of close observation and fine distinction, as drawn by pencil, pen, brush and scalpel. (And so did physic and surgery with their increasing methodological stress on observation and description of patients, body-parts, and pathologies.)[59]

In Cheselden's time, anatomical lectures and illustrated books often addressed multiple audiences: doctors, artists, book collectors, the natural-philosophically-minded intelligentsia. The preface to the 1713 first edition of *Anatomy of the Humane Body* proclaims that the book is "design'd for the use of Those who study Anatomy for their Entertainment," as well as students of "Physick and Surgery."[60] Anatomy, Cheselden expects, is a subject that naturally piques the curiosity of the public. Interest in it will be universal, a key part of a curriculum of improvement and refinement that appeals to a range of social types, crossing some lines of social distinction and occupation: the same range of types who would have attended Cheselden's public course of lectures, and dissections. Which, according to an advertisement in the *London Daily Courant* of 1721, were "chiefly intended for Gentlemen" (and therefore "such Things only will be omitted as are neither Instructive nor Entertaining, and Care will be taken to have nothing Offensive"). *The Anatomy of the Humane Body* was initially sold as an adjunct to the course. The lecture series promoted the book; the book promoted the lectures.[61]

The "politeness" was partly rhetorical. The appeal of public lectures lay very much in anatomy's transgressiveness: dissection of dead bodies (and "objectionable," "offensive" odors emitted), skeletons displayed, the viscera revealed, sexual anatomy. The opportunity to look behind the curtain at secret knowledge and freaky cases (hermaphrodites, diseased genitals, deformities). Translation from bodies and specimens to printed images and wax models obviously mitigated some of that, made anatomy politer. But not entirely polite. And anatomy, in the flesh or in print, was therefore something the fairer sex and children were to be protected from. Women were not easily received into anatomical circles, even if those circles intersected the literary and philosophical circles of the salon, where women could display sparkling wit and erudition in mixed company. *The Anatomy of the Human Body* spoke to men, a broad spectrum of middling and upper-class men, in the idiom of plainspoken manly gentility. It was not a fancy, large-format production for patrons and collectors: Cheselden attended to the high-end market with his *Osteographia* of 1733. His *Anatomy of the Human Body* didn't put on airs. It bundled together anatomical expertise, unornamented speech, and aesthetic gestures as signifiers of culture and attainment. Genteel, enlightened, manly. Or at least aspiring to that.[62]

2.4 Cheselden's figures

Cheselden's chatty aside about the beauty of his Hercules-Antaeus plate, then, tells us that, even in an ostensibly scientific work, the illustration (and text) can serve as prompts for shared conversations, and shared opinions, about Beauty and Art and works of art. And it tells us that the art-referencing anatomical illustration, and by extension the entire field of anatomy, was a cultural good attached to a certain group and class of men, and a class ideal, a contribution to the multifarious pile of cultural goods that defines the cultivated gentleman and the gentleman doctor. The "beautiful" illustration (and beautiful book) may be a conveyor of knowledge, but it's also a prop. The appreciation of Beauty, of beautiful objects (and illustrations of beautiful objects), becomes a way to pleasurably (sometimes competitively) demonstrate a shared filiation with classical art, fine books, anatomical medicine: emblems of civilization. And also an opportunity to enjoy the rarefied appreciation of beautiful bodies in suggestive poses.

And with that comes the possibility that disavowals or the pretense of supposedly disinterested judgment may serve as camouflage, an affordance for disavowal. Consider then another beautiful figure from Cheselden (this one disfigured by call-out numbers), a muscle man in a compromising position, this time in bondage, tied to a tree, possibly referencing the Greek mythological figure Marsyas, who was tied to a tree and flayed by Apollo, or possibly St Bartholomew, St Sebastian, or Prometheus, male figures who were also tied to trees and subjected to rough treatment (Fig. 2.13).

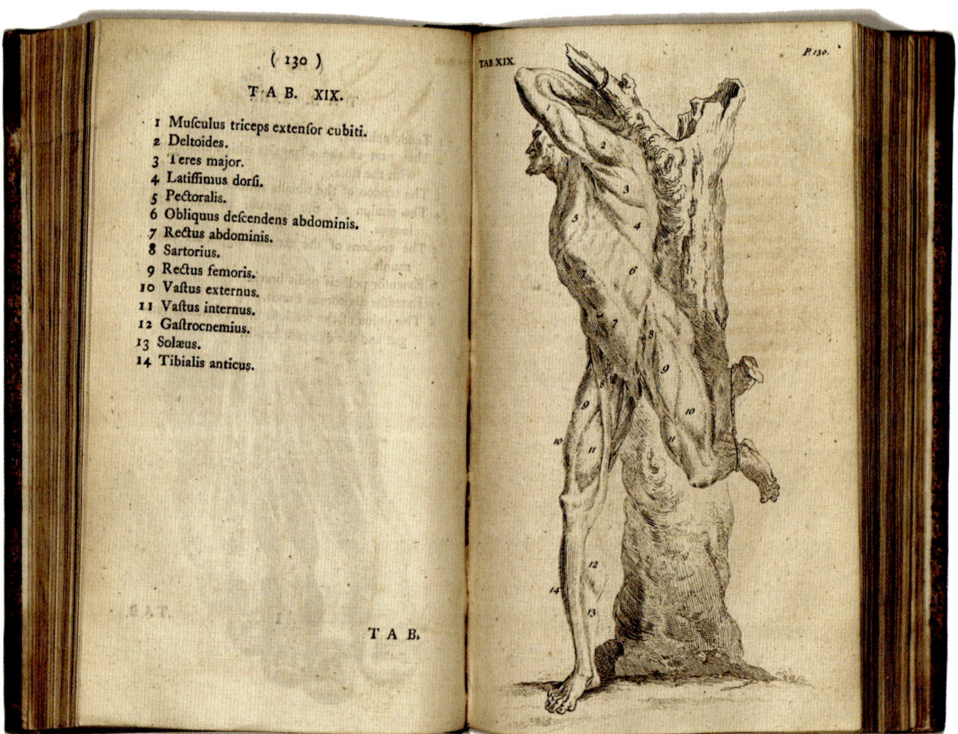

2.13 *William Cheselden,* Anatomy of the Human Body *(1740; 10th ed.; London, 1773), tab. 19. Copperplate engraving: Gerard Vandergucht. 21 × 13 cm. Hagströmer Medico-Historical Library. The pose has an anatomical justification: The raised arm and leg demonstrate sets of muscles that would otherwise be obscured.*

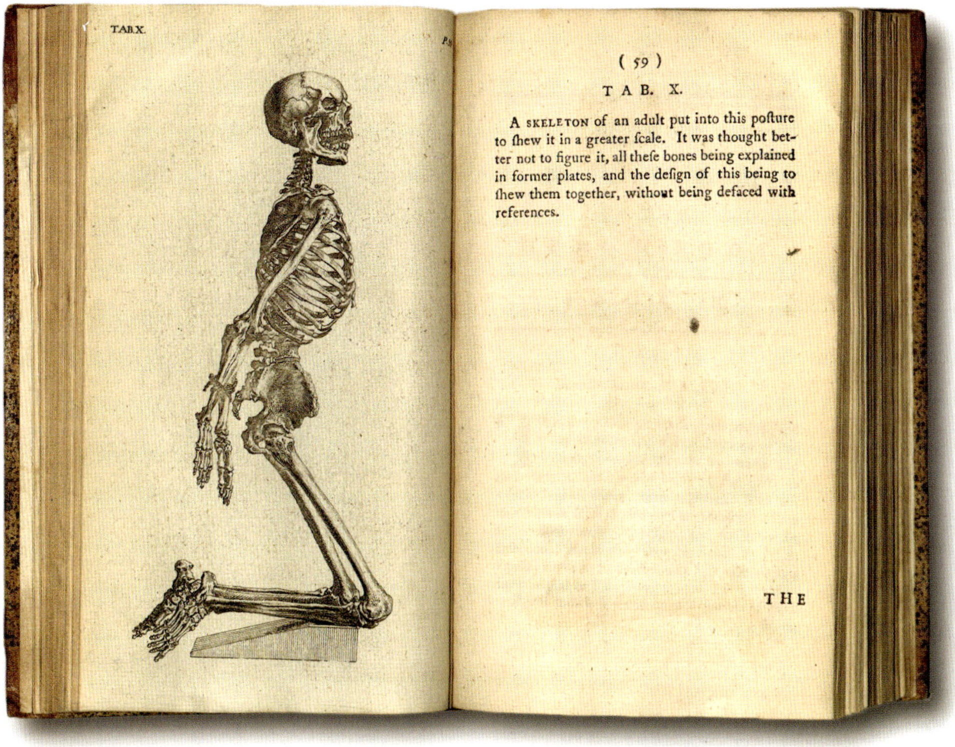

2.14 *If Death is a captive, who is his captor? William Cheselden,* Anatomy of the Human Body *(1740; 10th ed.; London, 1773), tab. 10. Copperplate engraving: Gerard Vandergucht. 23 × 16 cm. Hagströmer Medico-Historical Library.*

(The tree and male nude in Cheselden's plate bear some resemblance to Christophe Veyrier's mid-seventeenth-century sculpture of Marsyas bound, but Cheselden's nude is thicker and more mature, Michelangelesque.)

The study of the male form—again, a subject for both medical anatomy and art pedagogy—was for over a thousand years a central preoccupation of European figurative art. No wonder then that anatomical atlases referred, directly or indirectly, to the favorite subject matter of painting and sculpture, the figures of classical gods and heroes and the tortured, flayed saints of Christian iconography, even Christ himself. Their nakedness and contorted poses justified by its reference to a religious, mythological or historical scene, and by the pedagogical need to instruct students on the proportions of beauty, and the musculature of the torso, especially muscles that were otherwise hard to show. If anatomy begins in the willful violence the anatomist does to the dead, a kind of domination by dissection, anatomical representation extends that by giving expressive force to scenes of sadism and bondage, dominance and submission, a masculine figure conquered.

That could receive representation even in the (by default, masculine) figure of the human skeleton. Death the conqueror, figured as a teasing, mocking master of humanity, was a favorite trope of memento mori, endlessly elaborated in the *danse macabre*. Cheselden's kneeling skeleton (Fig. 2.14), with his hands tied behind, might be read as a reversal of the trope: Death the conqueror is conquered. (But then who is his captor?) Or maybe visualizing this moral proposition: in death we are all conquered, forced to submit. (But is there pleasure in submission? The kneeling figure seems to be smiling in mockery, as skeletons are so often wont to do, pleasurably entertained and simultaneously a pleasurable entertainment.) While Cheselden, as usual, doesn't address these non-anatomical matters, he accords his allegory a measure of aesthetic privilege by again declining to include call-out numbers that would "deface" it (as with his Hercules/Antaeus plate).[63] But mind that the allegorical particulars are attendant upon a practical consideration: in a small book format, the binding of hands behind the back makes the most economical use of the limited territory of the page. This pose allows Cheselden to show his figure "in a greater scale." In his folio-sized *Osteographia*, the very same skeleton is shown, hands unencumbered, placed in front and extended in freely offered prayer.[64] The memento mori figure there plays the role of a proper Christian supplicant (or makes a travesty of it).

2.5 The figure of Cheselden

Now, as far as we know, there is nothing written by or about Cheselden that suggests he had a secret life, or took inordinate pleasure in looking at or doing anything "untoward" with other men or male bodies, whether in the dissecting room, the hospital, the art gallery, the pub, the salon, or bed. Cheselden was married with a daughter. But it only takes a glance at Cope's biography of Cheselden to get the gendered flavor of the great surgeon's sociability: Cheselden inhabited a man's world. The son of a moderately prosperous gentleman-farmer and landowner, he came to London from a village north of Leicester at age 15 to undertake a surgeon's apprenticeship, devoted himself to his studies, started his medical practice and very popular lecture series at age 23, married well, and cultivated a large assemblage of male friends and associates, mentors and protégés. His social world was a thicket of man-talk and man-action. As an ambitious young anatomist and surgeon with interests in natural philosophy, the search for patronage, patients, friends and allies was key.[65] Cheselden's anatomical publications (and lectures) played an important role in that search. He first contributed to the *Philosophical Transactions* of the Royal Society, and was made a Fellow, in 1712 at age 24. Over time, his circle came to include medical and surgical colleagues, poets, painters, politicians, gentlemen and aristocrats (Figs. 2.15–16). He was friends with the poet Alexander Pope, the painter William Hogarth, the eminent naturalist, collector and physician Sir Hans Sloane, and a bevy of other physicians and surgeons, including the wealthy and distinguished Dr Richard Mead (to whom

The Anatomy of the Human Body is dedicated).[66] As a surgeon, he attended Alexander Pope and Sir Isaac Newton (in his last illness), and in 1727 was appointed surgeon to Queen Caroline (to whom *Osteographia* is dedicated).[67] In his social world, women were patrons, wives, mothers, daughters, sisters, friends, hostesses, lovers, "muses," servants, whores, and in his professional work, patients and nurses. Men and women socialized in mixed groups at all sorts of occasions, and conversed on matters aesthetic, philosophical and political in salons and over dinner.[68] But the intellectual worlds of anatomy and art, and the illustrated publications where those worlds converged, were male-dominated spaces, full of deep friendship, and also rivalry (sometimes

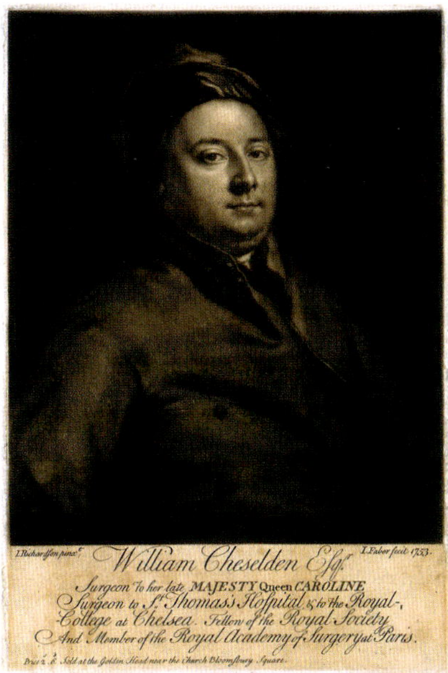

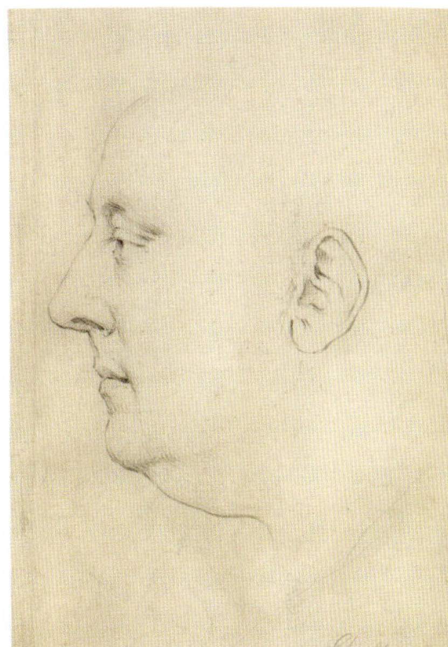

2.15–16 *Two likenesses of William Cheselden.* LEFT: *An official portrait; the printed caption lists positions that Cheselden held. Mezzotint: J. Faber, 1753, after an oil painting by Jonathan Richardson the Elder, c.1730. 32 × 22 cm. Wellcome Collection.* RIGHT: *An intimate portrait, by engraver Gerard Vandergucht (1733). Pencil on laid paper. 36 × 28 cm. © Royal Academy of Arts, London.*

good-natured, sometimes venomous).[69] And within those spaces there was a consensus on the appreciation of, and deference to classical antiquity and post-classical invocations of classicism, with all of their (unacknowledged) homoerotic valences. Amongst men, whose commitment and competence and preferences varied.

Cheselden was not in the forefront. According to Joseph Frank Payne's chatty, condescending entry in the old *Dictionary of National Biography*, Cheselden

> is said to have had a taste for literature and pretensions to critical judgment, which on one occasion misled him (in the presence of Pope himself) into denying

that the fourth book of the 'Dunciad' could be by the author of the first three. His true bent was evidently mechanical, and it is stated, on the authority of Faulkner's "History of Fulham," that Cheselden drew the plans for the old Putney bridge. He was also a keen patron of athletic sports, especially boxing. His disposition was gay and genial. He was fond of society and evidently popular. To his patients he was kind and tender-hearted.[70]

2.6 The learning curve

If artist-philosopher Jonathan Richardson the Elder was Cheselden's closest cultural/intellectual companion, the character of their social circles and sociability may perhaps be discerned by a reading of Richardson's 1719 double treatise, *An Essay on the whole Art of Criticism as it Relates to*

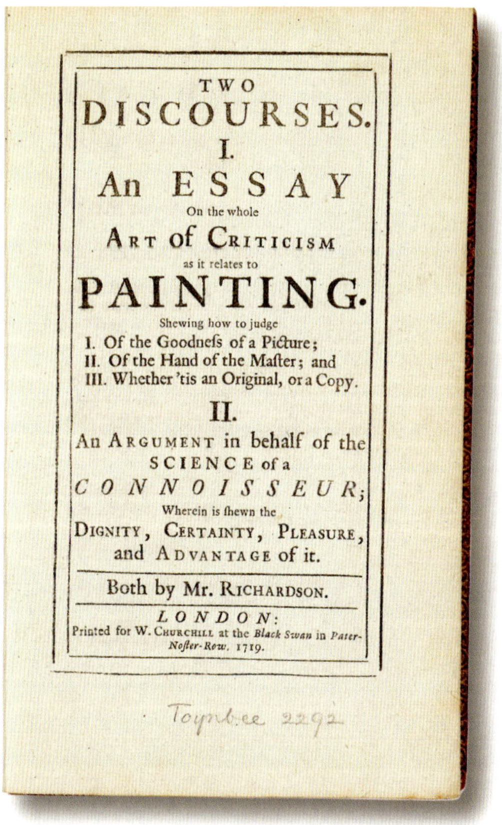

TWO
DISCOURSES.
I.
An ESSAY
On the whole
ART of CRITICISM
as it relates to
PAINTING.
Shewing how to judge
I. Of the Goodneſs of a Picture;
II. Of the Hand of the Maſter; and
III. Whether 'tis an Original, or a Copy.
II.
An ARGUMENT in behalf of the
SCIENCE of a
CONNOISSEUR;
Wherein is ſhewn the
DIGNITY, CERTAINTY, PLEASURE,
and ADVANTAGE of it.

Both by Mr. RICHARDSON.

LONDON:
Printed for W. CHURCHILL at the *Black Swan* in *Pater-Noſter-Row*. 1719.

2.17 *Jonathan Richardson the Elder,* Two Discourses: I. An Essay on the whole Art of Criticism as it Relates to Painting; II. An Argument in Behalf of the Science of a Connoisseur, Wherein is shewn the Dignity, Certainty, Pleasure, and Advantage of it *(London, 1719). Richardson was both a collector and a painter, and Cheselden's good friend. 20 cm. The Bodleian Libraries, University of Oxford.*

Painting and *An Argument in Behalf of the Science of a Connoisseur, Wherein is shewn the Dignity, Certainty, Pleasure, and Advantage of it* (Fig. 2.17).[71] Richardson was one of the most influential and respected British painters of his day. He was also an avid and influential collector of books, prints, paintings and (especially) old master drawings.[72] He was also an important theorist. Richardson's two discourses provide an aesthetic

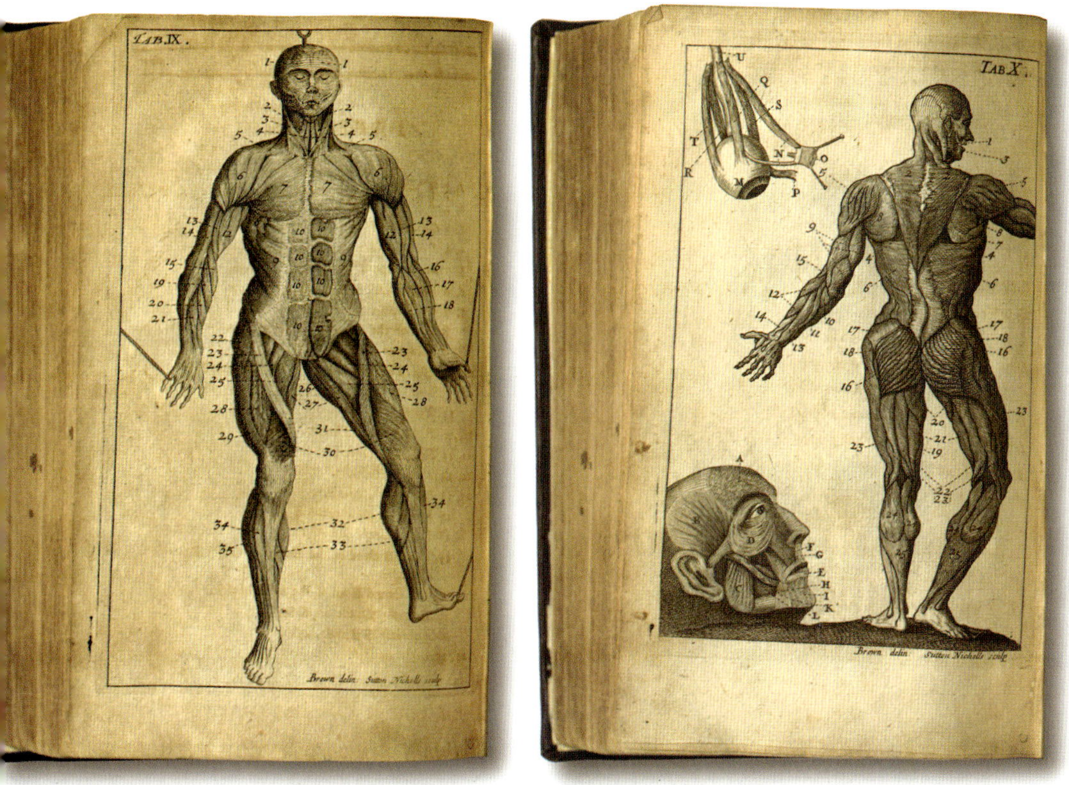

2.18–19 *The anatomy of the human body before Cheselden comes to Beauty and classicism. William Cheselden,* Anatomy of the Humane Body *(1st ed.; London, 1713), tabs. 7–8. Artist: "Brown." Engraver: Sutton Nicholls. 23 × 16 cm. New York Academy of Medicine.*

and moral introduction and guide to a collective high connoisseurship of shared venues, views, opinions, and pleasures. A social space: "I open to Gentlemen a New Scene of Pleasure, a New Innocent Amusement, and an Accomplishment which they have yet scarce heard of, but no less worthy of their Attention … My present business is … to persuade our Nobility, and Gentry to become Lovers of Painting and Connoisseurs."[73]

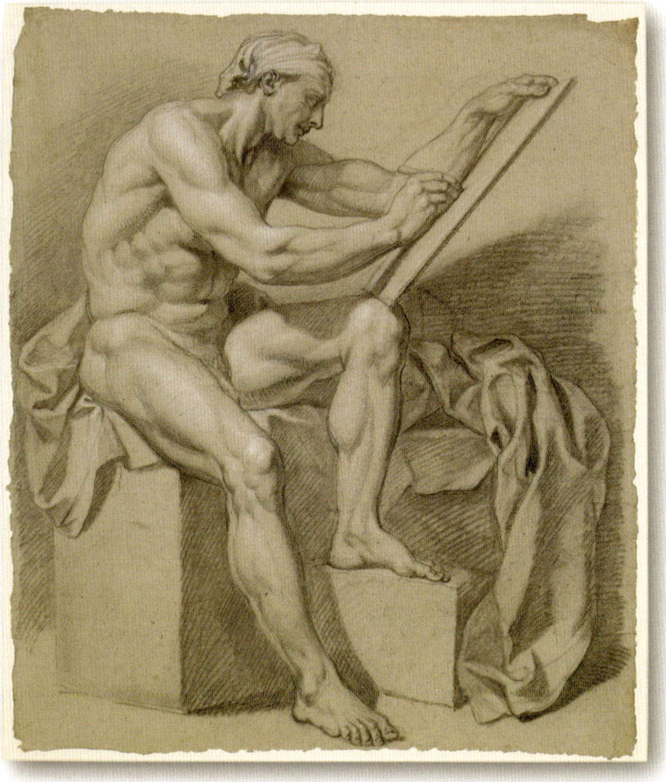

2.20 *Louis Chéron, drawing of a male nude. Black chalk, touched with white, on grey paper. c.1720. 65 × 56 cm. © The Trustees of the British Museum.*

His essay goes on to offer practical guidance: advice on how to determine "the goodness of a picture," the attribution of the artist (or authorship), "whether 'tis an original, or a copy"—key questions, procedures and topics that glued together the disparate network of elite collectors, public discoursers, middleman culture brokers, and aspiring beginners. Group standards and judgments, forged in friendly and not so friendly disputation, and a group relish in appraisal, reception and ownership, mattered a lot.[74]

But there was a learning curve. Cheselden's own connoisseurship was a work in progress, something he worked hard to cultivate over many years, perhaps spurred on by Richardson's friendly encouragement. The first edition of his *Anatomy of the Humane Body* (1713), which came out when Cheselden was only twenty-five, was marketed as an adjunct handbook to his course of public anatomical lectures. It featured crude illustrations (Figs. 2.18–19) by a journeyman artist and journeyman engraver.[75] In 1720 Cheselden started taking classes in drawing at "The Academy for the Improvement of Painters and Sculptors by drawing from the Naked," conducted by drawing masters Louis Chéron (1660–1725) (Fig. 2.20) and John Vanderbank (1694–1739), who earlier had been Jonathan Richardson's student. The two men offered the best instruction available in England at the time—William Hogarth, Joseph Highmore, William Kent, who went on to be leading lights of British painting, all studied at the academy.[76] Cheselden surely had practical reasons for seeking instruction, to help improve the quality of his preparatory anatomical and surgical drawings, and to ground his collaboration with artists and engravers. But drawing classes were also part of the curriculum of genteel education, an aid to refinement. The training would have contributed to Cheselden's growing appreciation of classical and post-classical figurative art, with its strong emphasis on anatomical representation, as well as helping him to develop a more able hand and discerning eye. An aesthetic upgrade.

The first tangible fruits of his studies came with the publication of his quarto atlas *Osteographia, or the Anatomy of the Bones* (1733), a big jump in artistic quality from previous publications, a leap into a sophisticated Netherlandish naturalism (blended with a bit of baroque post-Vesalian theatrics). The titlepage depicts Cheselden using a camera obscura to draw a skeleton, aided by his assistants. In the preface he takes full credit for the illustrations, citing the control he exercised over the artwork to ensure accuracy and quality: "I always directed; sometimes in the drawings with the pencil and often with the needle upon the copper plate."[77]

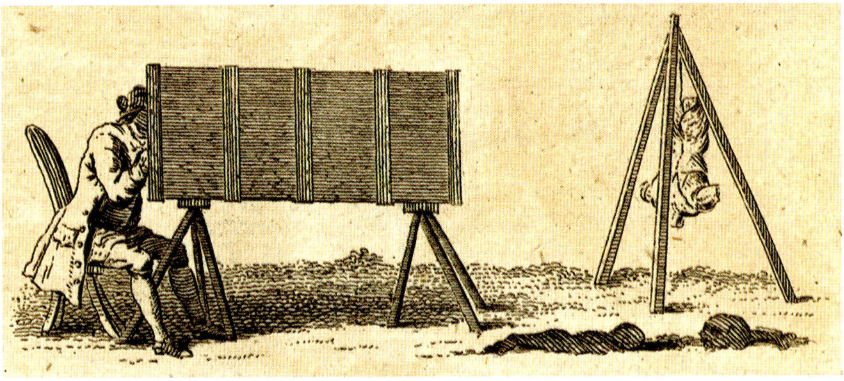

2.21 *Detail from titlepage: Cheselden looking through the camera obscura at an anatomical specimen (the same torso featured in tabs. 12–13 [*Queer Anatomies*, figs. 2.23–24]); the ground is casually littered with other specimens. William Cheselden,* Anatomy of the Human Body *(1740; 10th ed.; London, 1773). Copperplate engraving: Gerard Vandergucht. Hagströmer Medico-Historical Library.*

A few years later, in 1740, Cheselden issued the fifth edition of *The Anatomy of the Human Body*, which added the man tied to the tree, Hercules and Antaeus, and other plates—and deleted the clumsy plates which disfigured earlier editions. And with that, Cheselden took a few giant steps into the world of the classicist Beauty. Which, among cognoscenti, was a kind of gold standard, the centerpiece of an enduring connoisseurial consensus, exempt from the vagaries of fashion—even if the merits of particular artworks were always open to debate.[78] Of course the merits of particular anatomical works were also debatable, so the fifth edition also carried an epistemological claim: the artwork accurately represents the anatomy of the body and what the anatomist sees. And to symbolically attest to the accuracy of the depictions, the image of the camera obscura image from *Osteographia* shows up for the first time on the titlepage of *The Anatomy of the Human Body,* and was retained in subsequent editions (Fig. 2.21).

Naturally, those improvements weren't cost-free: Cheselden's publisher substantially increased the price of the book, making it less accessible to the common class of readers.[79] But Cheselden didn't entirely abandon those readers—or entirely remake himself into a refined connoisseur. His sensibility mixed refinement with the down-to-earth practicalities of the surgical profession, and he continued to feature crowd- and profession-pleasing odd cases, such as the genitalia of two hermaphrodites, a woman with her guts hanging out, and the case of Samuel Wood, a miller whose right arm was torn off in an accident (Fig. 2.22) (cases which also had the virtue of raising philosophical questions on the senses and the nature of gender). The accompanying plate shows the torn arm in the foreground, almost grasping for life, as Wood in profile demonstrates his armless shoulder. In the background: the windmill where the accident happened, set in the picturesque English countryside.[80] One is tempted to say: No classicism or gentility here! But there's the drapery (bandage? ripped shirt?) wrapping the left uninjured shoulder (the suggestion of a toga?), the miller's Roman nose, the peaceful vista, even the way Wood's torso is planted in the landscape like a monumental sculpture. So perhaps a bit of eccentric classicism. Awkward grace notes.

Gentility defined itself in opposition to vulgarity but didn't attempt to extinguish it. Rather it lorded over, condescended to it. If the gentleman wasn't disgusted, he might be amused. Or take high-minded pity on the vulgarity of it. Or ignore it. Or, best of all, collect it. Cheselden seems to have had a mixed sensibility, suitable to a man of his mixed social and professional trajectory, mixed roles and locations (the parlor, the waiting room, the learned society, the dissecting room, the tavern, the coffee house, and of course the wounded or diseased body). Anatomy and surgery were, by their very nature, at the center of things yet also in the borderlands, and some very rough borderlands.

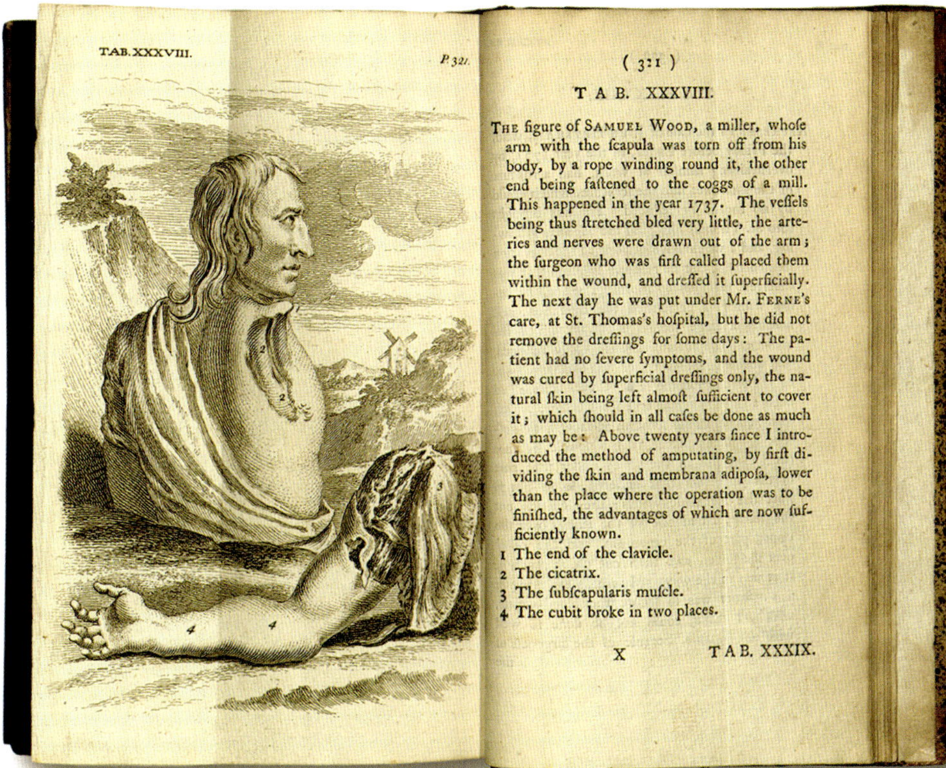

TAB. XXXVIII. P. 321.

(321)

TAB. XXXVIII.

The figure of Samuel Wood, a miller, whoſe arm with the ſcapula was torn off from his body, by a rope winding round it, the other end being faſtened to the coggs of a mill. This happened in the year 1737. The veſſels being thus ſtretched bled very little, the arteries and nerves were drawn out of the arm; the ſurgeon who was firſt called placed them within the wound, and dreſſed it ſuperficially. The next day he was put under Mr. Ferne's care, at St. Thomas's hoſpital, but he did not remove the dreſſings for ſome days: The patient had no ſevere ſymptoms, and the wound was cured by ſuperficial dreſſings only, the natural ſkin being left almoſt ſufficient to cover it; which ſhould in all caſes be done as much as may be: Above twenty years ſince I introduced the method of amputating, by firſt dividing the ſkin and membrana adipoſa, lower than the place where the operation was to be finiſhed, the advantages of which are now ſufficiently known.

1 The end of the clavicle.
2 The cicatrix.
3 The ſubſcapularis muſcle.
4 The cubit broke in two places.

X TAB. XXXIX.

2.22 *William Cheselden,* Anatomy of the Human Body *(1740; 10th ed., London, 1773), 320, tab. 38. Copperplate engraving: Gerard Vandergucht. 23 × 16 cm. Hagströmer Medico-Historical Library.*

2.7 Headbutting disputation

"Taste," the critical discernment of beauty and quality, while perhaps not universally practiced, would have been a precious concept in many of Cheselden's circles. It was the work of such circles to make assessments about what was "agreeable" and what was "distasteful," what was masculine and what was "effeminate", what was worthy and what was unworthy, and police those assessments through formal and informal rewards and punishments. Gatekeeping. But within such groups members could take privileges, enjoy banter, even take in street entertainments, and other vices. Cheselden and friends were parties to a pact between consenting gentlemen, but pacts varied among and within different groupings. What was deemed valuable or permissible in one circle, might be condemned in others.[81]

And that could be the occasion for opinion-makers to put their opinions into print as a way of vying for a place in the hierarchy of connoisseurship and the various clubs, formal and informal, which constituted it. And so in his little treatise of 1753, *The Analysis of Beauty: Written with a View of Fixing the Fluctuating Ideas of Taste*, the artist William Hogarth dismisses the "middling connoisseur" who naively assumes that "no profile has beauty without a very straight nose, and if the forehead be continued straight with it, he thinks it is still more sublime." The beauty of figures, Hogarth insists, is curved and sensuous, and not to be forced to conform to straight-lined geometry and geometrical diagrams. To prove the point, Hogarth cites that paragon of classical androgynous beauty, the "easy and gracefully-turned attitude of the [statue of] Antinous," the young man who was the favorite of the emperor Hadrian.[82]

Taste was made for disputation. And Cheselden's images, and character (Figs. 2.23–24), were not exempt. John Douglas, a prominent fellow surgeon, publicly and aggressively contested the merit of Cheselden's premium

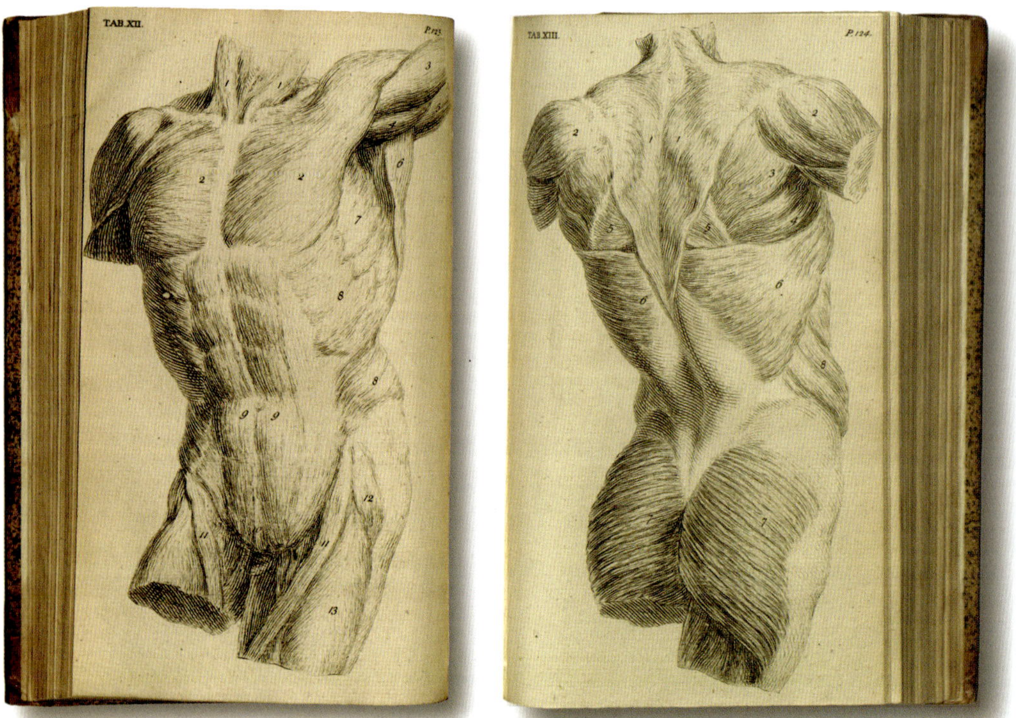

2.23–24 *Anatomical beauty, for artists, doctors and cultivated readers. William Cheselden,* Anatomy of the Human Body *(10th ed., London, 1773), tabs. 12–13. Engraver: Gerard Vandergucht. 23 × 16 cm. Hagströmer Medico-Historical Library. The torsos with their sensuous curves replace the clumsy musclemen of the first edition (*Anatomy of the Humane Body*, 1713, tabs. 7–8 [*Queer Anatomies*, figs. 2.18–19]).*

publication, *Osteographia*. Douglas's 1735 pamphlet, *Animadversions on a Late Pompous Book, Intituled, Osteographia: or, The Anatomy of the Bones* mocked Cheselden's "florid" language, typographical errors, intellectual emptiness, anatomical blunders, lack of originality, and failure to achieve real beauty in his illustrations.[83] (Douglas's brother James, a physician and anatomist, sided with his old friend Cheselden in the dispute.) Cheselden somehow weathered the storm.

Headbutting disputation. Yet there was a consensus on certain standards and ideals. Given the importance assigned to anatomy in aesthetics, natural history and philosophy, Cheselden the eminent anatomist was well-positioned to gain the respect of "Gentlemen of good Taste," cultivated men who could "tell us of a great many Senses, Tastes, and Relishes for Beauty, Harmony ... in Painting and Poetry and ... a Relish for a Beauty in Characters, in Manners" (Scottish Enlightenment philosopher Francis Hutcheson's sensationist formulation).[84] And so, aided by his surgical talent, illustrated publications, strong alliances, and sociable interactions, Cheselden became an iconic figure of British medicine and culture. And was joined to the large cohort of tastemakers who bequeathed the concept of "taste" to later generations (and ultimately to us). William Wadd, writing some seventy-five years after Cheselden's death, described the surgeon alongside his cohort, not quite at the highest rank, but as a high-level fellow traveler: "the companion and friend of the great master-spirits of the age, the men of genius and taste."[85]

BETWEEN MEN

3.1 Between men: Connoisseurs, collectors and anatomy

All of this connoisseurship and friendship took place "between men." Which happens to be the title of yet another seminal work by Eve Kosofsky Sedgwick, an extended riff on masculine sociality and its troubled ramifications, as manifest in some canonical works of literature.[86] In the eighteenth and nineteenth century, unequal, sex-segregated social arrangements, Sedgwick argues, provided ample opportunities for the growth of intense "homosocial" attachments between men. Who defined themselves and their cohort groups in opposition to feminine sociability and aesthetics, with queer consequences: affordances for both male hypermasculinity and effeminacy.

Homosocial associations were forged and renewed by the sharing, exchange of and competition over women, but also books, opinions, paintings, meals, drinks, witty banter, gambling, adventures. Shared connoisseurship and viewing of beautiful or exotic or ingeniously-crafted things—and shared pleasure in study, acquisition, collection, ownership—formed the basis of shared, often intensely felt, companionships. All of which occasioned intensive gazing and incessant discussion on the merits of things, in conversation and written discourse. Including the objects of anatomy—beautifully wrought sculptures, drawings, prints and paintings of beautiful nude and partly-clothed, or partly-dissected, men and women—and authoritative, expensive, artfully illustrated, handsomely printed, books and engravings, often over-sized, dealing with the *subject* of anatomy. Which stood atop the hierarchy of medical publication.[87]

The role played by book collecting and personal libraries was not trivial. Here's literary historian Fiona Stafford describing the world of Jane Austen's *Pride and Prejudice* (1813), and the library of her heroine's suitor, Mr. Darcy:

> [T]he gentleman's library was as much a status symbol as well-managed parkland. A fine book collection was an essential part of the estate and a clear sign of good taste, breeding, and, above all, wealth. Libraries filled with valuable books had been a prominent feature of country houses since the seventeenth century, while many new Georgian mansions boasted splendid rooms lined with magnificent oak shelving to accommodate rows of leather-bound treasures. Books, like dinner services, cutlery, carriages, and servants, wore their owner's distinctive livery and were arrayed in neatly matching polished rows.
>
> During the 1790s ... book buying ... became a matter of high fashion ... Prominent ... figures such as Earl Spencer and the Duke of Devonshire attracted international attention by lavishing their largesse on books a phenomenon that inspired the Earl's private librarian, Thomas Frognall Dibdin, to [write] ... a "bibliographical romance" entitled *Bibliomania; or Book Madness*. Diagnosis of "this fatal disease" was not very difficult: symptoms included a thirst for "black letter" printing, uncut pages, hand-coloured illustrations, and fine bindings.
>
> The obsession with book buying continued to grip Britain in the early nineteenth century, partly fuelled by the sudden availability of treasures from the deposed French aristocracy, partly in imitation of British royal tastes. Anxieties about safe investments made books an attractive, long-term commodity, while the fashion for luxury volumes grew ever more extravagant.[88]

Status, competition, yes. But book collecting and the space of the library did all sorts of social and intellectual work, work that performed philosophical, political and aesthetic attachments. Art historian Viccy Coltman focuses on classicism, but let's add "anatomy" (so intimately connected to classicism) to the mix. The library, according to Coltman, was where "the culture of education, imitation, competition, and conversation"—with "the material culture of the ancients" at its privileged center—was "packaged for possession by an elite British audience ... The library embodied antiquity in its textual *and* material incarnations," in its architecture and decorations, and "deluxe library volumes."[89] And, among those volumes, were deluxe works of anatomy which featured renderings of classical and neoclassical nudes for anatomical study, and/or dissections of bodies designed for use in the study of classical and neoclassical art. (For a prime example, see Bernardino Genga's *Anatomia* of 1691; Figs. 1.9 and 4.5.)[90]

It took capital to collect books and build a library—and a lot of capital to buy obscenely expensive anatomical atlases like Mascagni's massive and brilliantly-colored *Anatomia universa* and Hunter's *Gravid Uterus*, and rare books like a first or second edition of Vesalius. But for those with smaller purses, maybe a bit lower down in the social hierarchy, there were books, new and used, to be had at more affordable prices. Men desirous of pursuing the encyclopedic knowledge associated with the curriculum of Enlightenment philosophy and "improvement"—many of them physicians (who made up a considerable percentage of the membership of the Royal Society and other learned institutions)—spent time and resources acquiring and building up their personal and family collections.[91] Which testified, by means of bindings, arrangement on the shelves, and sheer bulk, to one's social status and intellectual agendas. But books could also perform, Stafford tells us, "a surprising range of social functions":

> A book might be a means to attract attention or a screen to hide behind, a refuge from social hubbub or a cue for conversation, a way to fend off unwelcome encounters or to further a flirtation. Social anxiety could be masked or exposed through the careful deployment of a polished volume ...[92]

To take one small example of how anatomy figured in homosocial collecting culture (and the diffusion and extension of that culture), consider Thomas Jefferson (1743–1826), on the outer periphery of the culture of connoisseurship in faraway Virginia, but a man of wide-ranging "philosophical" interests and friendships, and some resources. And therefore an avid book collector. According to Library of Congress librarian Michael North, Jefferson was "a bibliomaniac," who "wanted books on any subject," though "not a connoisseur in the sense of wanting the first or finest edition of a book," and not someone who spent a lot of money on fancy bindings (as aristocratic book collectors often did).[93] Aesthetics wasn't his central concern—he was most of all a connoisseur of law, political discourse, and rhetoric. But he bought and decorated his home with paintings, prints and sculptures, socialized with aesthetes, and was a dedicated enthusiast of Enlightenment encyclopedism. Which contained within its capacious ambit those two entangled fields of knowledge, aesthetics and anatomy.[94]

His book collection amounted to 6,487 volumes (in 1815, the largest personal library in the United States, when Congress purchased it to replace the library burned by British troops during the War of 1812). And alongside volumes on political and moral philosophy, history, architecture, rhetoric, religion, painting, gardening, mathematics, agriculture and many other topics, his library included works on medicine, surgery and anatomy by William Hunter, Descartes, Cuvier, Winslow, Blumenbach, John Bell, *and* "Cheselden's Anatomy, 8°," a 1763 eighth edition of *The Anatomy of the*

Human Body (which contains one annotation in Jefferson's own hand, written in Greek).[95] And also a small shelf of books on aesthetics, including Jonathan Richardson's 1719 *Argument in Behalf of the Science of a Connoisseur* and William Gilpin's 1768 *Essay Upon Prints*.[96] (What Jefferson thought about them, or whether he actually read them, we know not.)

There was nothing straightforward in all of this. Complicated conditions marked the connoisseur's performance and identity: contradictions. Men gathered in various places, private and public, to exchange and display opinionated discernment, sometimes contentious, sometimes agreeable. The objects of collection and study could occasion serious discussion (sometimes in correspondence, as Jefferson's many letters show). But gatherings were also full of opportunities to take and share pleasure—conviviality, jesting pranks, cutting wit, drinking, smoking, and what historian Kate Davison calls "intimate bawdiness."

All under the eyes of group members and sometimes outside observers.[97] Which then became a topic for fictional narrative, visual depiction, and social commentary, and often (in all of those modes) the subject of satire.[98] In Richard Cosway's 1775 group portrait (Fig. 2.25), one of the connoisseurs stands close, gazing upon the sculptures of female nudes with rapt attention. But just behind him, two men appear to be sharing snuff or exchanging money. A third glances sidelong at the exchange, while at the same time conversing with a fourth man who reaches behind a drape. A little further off, a seated connoisseur looks at the nudes through a small magnifying glass, his gaze narrowed, as if trained on some telling aesthetic or anatomical detail. But his interests surely lie elsewhere: pants open, his left hand is in his pocket, masturbating unobserved (except by us).[99] One wonders: is it only a shared interest in female beauty that brings these five men together? or shared interest in the cultural cachet and monetary value of classical sculpture? Or savory male sociability compounded of all those things? Cosway the painter (himself an art collector and periwigged fop) stands outside the scene, sharing the joke with his viewers, rendering a good-natured judgment: pretentions to manly connoisseurship and elevated appreciation can also be a worldly spectacle of sophomoric fraternalism, money-grubbing corruption, and prurient interest in the female body.[100] A bit sordid. A bit of a travesty. Even self-mockery. But all in good fun. No one is offended.

Charles Townley (1735–1805), the wealthy collector who stands second from the left showing off some sculptures recently acquired on travels in Italy, was one of Cosway's friends. And liked Cosway's painting enough to pay £100 for it, maybe commissioned it.[101] The "conversation piece," a popular genre in Townley's day, was designed to prompt friendly banter and comment, and, in this case, provide a reassuring bit of double-consciousness,

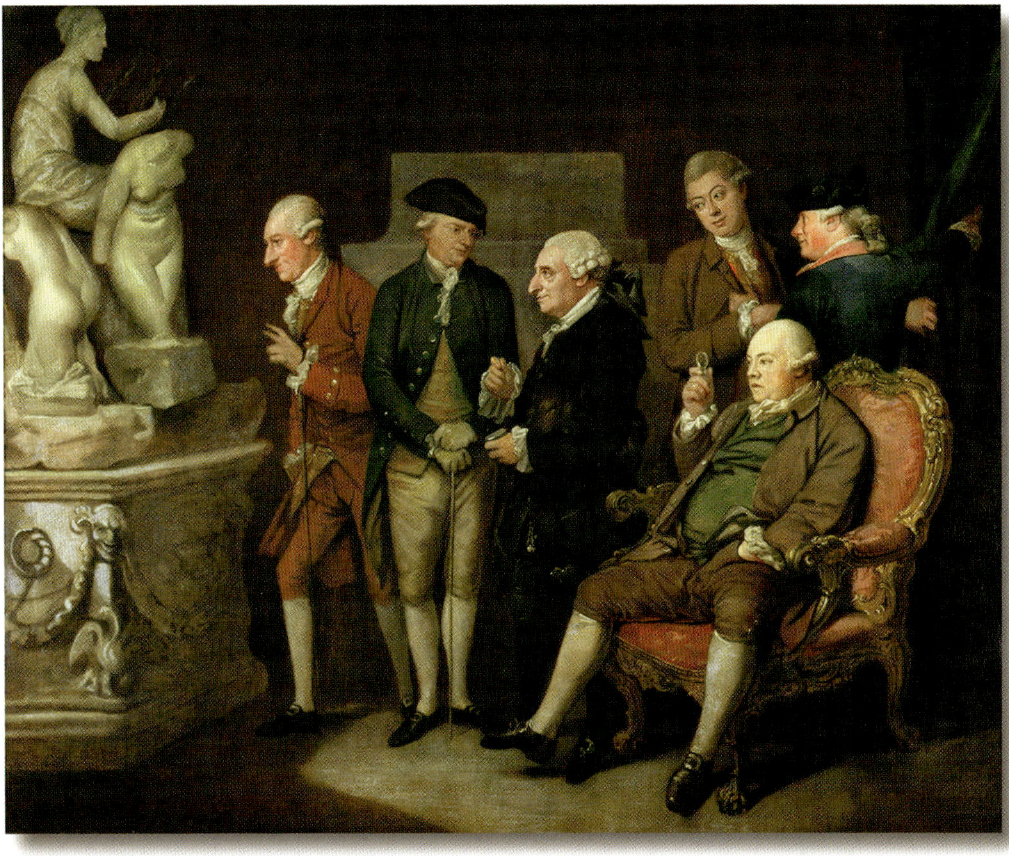

2.25 *Between men... A travesty of masculine disinterestedness. Richard Cosway, "Group of Connoisseurs" (1775). Oil on canvas. 84 × 105 cm. Burnley Borough Council, Towneley Hall Art Gallery & Museums, UK.*

amongst the men depicted and their larger circles, who got to see it hung on the wall during social occasions hosted by the collector.

The scene marks a moment in Townley's upward trajectory. During a spell on the Continent he has acquired valuable antiquities. Returning to England, he moves from his country seat in Lancashire (Towneley Hall) to London. His collection becomes the centerpiece of a new and improved reputation, new friends, and eventually membership in the Society of Dilettanti (1786), the very exclusive club (all-male, as all such clubs were) that stood at the very pinnacle of British collecting culture. And then, five years later, election to the Royal Society (1791), the very exclusive (and all-male) club that stood at the very pinnacle of British learning and erudition.[102]

3.2 Conversations and "conversation pieces"

Membership in such societies occasioned something more than just an attachment to learning and an appreciation of art. The Society of Dilettanti had a membership consisting of the highest intellectual and political strata of British society. "Behind the Dilettanti's façade of intellectual decorum," historian Jason Kelly reports, "was a realm of homosocial convivium."[103] The Society had a reputation for blow-out drunkenness, foppery, and rakish debauchery, at home and in Italy, where *dilettante* Sir William Hamilton, British ambassador to the Kingdom of Naples, merrily harvested antique erotica—dildoes, dildo-like votive objects, and ancient representations of the Roman god Priapus, leering and flaunting enormous erections. Hamilton's priapic objects were a much-admired coup of antiquarian collectorship. Which the Society celebrated by commissioning the printing of an expensive privately published, lavishly illustrated volume (a work that itself quickly became a collectable rarity), *An Account of the Remains of the Worship of Priapus* [*Priapeia*] (1786), only for members and worthy friends in high places.[104] Hamilton wasn't the only *dilettante* collecting priapic erotica: so did Richard Payne Knight, the *Priapeia*'s author. And so did Townley. Who was well acquainted with both men and who, of course, wouldn't have been one to deplore the excesses of connoisseurial comportment and interests, and any attendant moral and social consequences.

Others did. The connoisseur's hyper-masculine libertinism could cause offense. Yet fawning appreciation and preoccupations with finicky questions of attribution, authenticity, classical ideals of beauty, and relative merit might register as unmanly and unvirtuous, even farcical. In a treatise originally published in 1713, Anthony Ashley Cooper, the Earl of Shaftesbury (1671–1713), mocked the effeminating effects of connoisseurship—"I like! I fancy! I admire!"—and worried that some part of high cultivation wasn't very high or smart or sincere. The superficial enjoyment of a painting's decorative features, its bright colors, and flashy details—that was the kind of viewing that women were said to do. The sharing of collecting and viewing interests and experiences should mark a gender distinction. And a class distinction: Shaftesbury sprinkles the words "common," "vulgar" and "vulgarity" throughout his letters and essays.

Gentility, then, was a tightrope: one shouldn't be too full of oneself or too disparaging of inferiors. "Men of Sense and Breeding," Shaftesbury argues, should embody deeply held moral and aesthetic concerns, and perform them with "Discernment" and "Grace."[105] Which even men of breeding and rank need to cultivate by practice and study. While also taking pleasure in witty banter and the "Amusements of Gentlemen." Because too much pedantry is unsociable, tiresome, pretentious:

> ... [E]ven rude Nature itself, in its primitive Simplicity, is a better Guide to Judgment, than ... pedantick Learning ... Tis no wonder, if after so wrong a ground of Education, there appears to be such need of Redress, and Amendment,

> from that excellent School which we call the World. The mere Amusements of Gentlemen are found more improving than the profound Researches of Pedants.[106]

And don't be preachy or overly moralistic, Shaftesbury cautions. Be tastefully free in your performance of "Taste":

> Some by mere Nature, others by Art and Practice, are Masters of an Ear in Musick, an Eye in Painting, a Fancy in the ordinary things of Ornament and Grace, a Judgment in Proportions of all kinds, and a general good Taste in most of those Subjects which make the Amusement and Delight of the ingenious People of the World. Let such Gentlemen as these be as extravagant as they please, or as irregular in their Morals ...[107]

But not too free, other writers countered. How you do tastefulness either bolsters or undermines your manliness and moral condition, and therefore your reputation. In *Things as They are: or, The Adventures of Caleb Williams*, William Godwin's enormously popular novel of 1794, the hero Caleb lauds the character of the country squire Mr. Falkland with these Shaftesburian accolades: "Learned without ostentation, refined without foppery, elegant without effeminacy!"[108] Unlike his enemies, Falkland gets it just right, retains his masculinity and virtue against the pull. Godwin, a radical egalitarian and not of the upper crust, likes protagonists who embody an expansive, morally founded ideal of "taste", "refined sense" and "discernment," which virtuous and intelligent men *and* women, of any rank, are capable of achieving (through the acquisition of literary, artistic, musical erudition and accomplishments and moral virtue rather than appreciation and possession of collected objects).[109]

But maybe connoisseurship, by its very nature, tends to debase its practitioners.[110] Vicesimus Knox (1752–1821), a headmaster, Anglican priest, and essayist, in a chapter denouncing the ostentatious deployment of the French language and French airs in British society (written at a time when Britain and France were at war), opined that:

> Taste unsupported by good sense becomes *fastidiousness*; a quality of weak and vain minds. It is derived from affectation, effeminacy, and insolence, and it commonly renders its possessor unhappy and ridiculous. It is the parent of false *connoisseurship*, and of every species of foppery and unmanly refinement.[111] (emphasis in original)

For Knox, the very sound of *connoisseur*, a French import, connotes a louche pretension, an insufficiency of masculine virtue and power. Left unsaid was the unsayable but not unthinkable possibility that the "unmanly" connoisseur might take as much pleasure in male nakedness as Cosway's connoisseurs take in the female.[112]

Also left unsaid, was anything about the moral *virtues* of manly connoisseurship. Which could direct masculine attention to a *masculine* aesthetic object, as in Joseph Wright of Derby's "Three men viewing the Gladiator by candlelight" (1765) (Fig. 2.26). The rapt contemplation of an art object here is earnest, morally elevating. In an intimate gathering around a tabletop copy of the Borghese Gladiator, Wright's connoisseurs train their collective gaze on the gladiator's buttocks, groin and torso, a picture of male beauty rendered by Wright with no obvious salacious intent—and no imputation of salacious intent to the men portrayed.[113] The statuette of the gladiator, a canonical sculpture and a paragon of supple nude masculine athleticism, provides ample affordances for appreciative viewing and study.[114] Which the observers in Wright's painting gracefully supply. Without in any way undermining their own masculinity. Quite the opposite. Wright's chiaroscuro piles on opportunities for connoisseurial appreciation and sharing among the gladiator's three manly viewers. (No effeminating or pretentious periwigs! No distractions!) Also illuminated, in the background, to the right (partly obscured), a skillfully rendered drawing

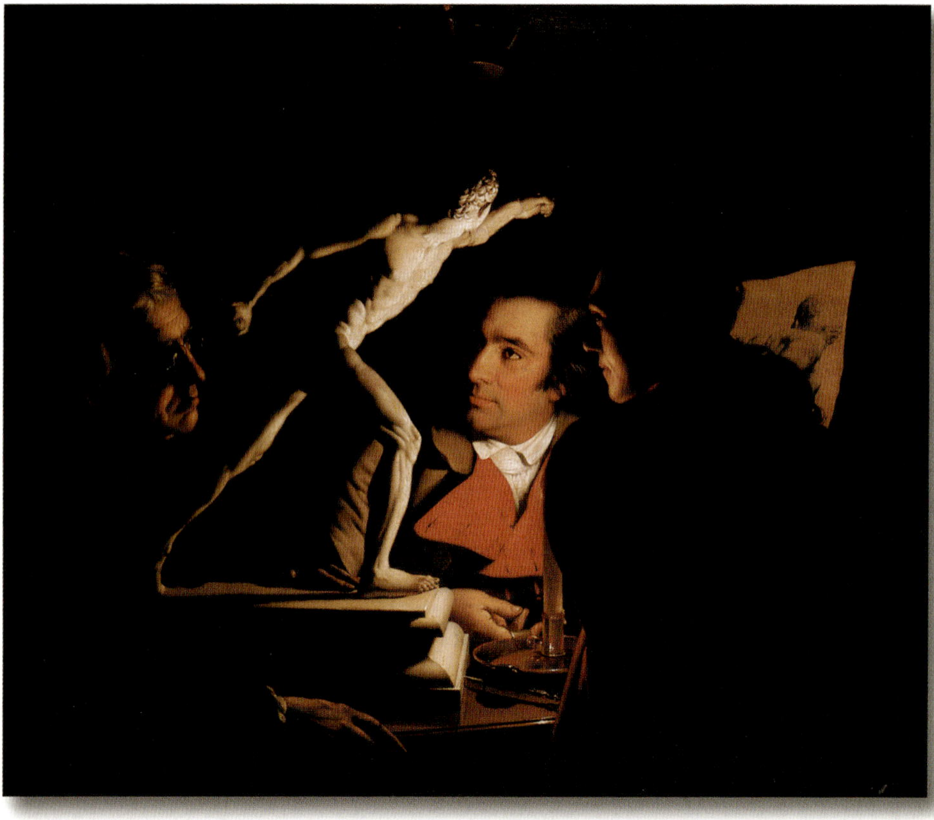

2.26 *Joseph Wright of Derby, "Three men viewing the Gladiator by candlelight" (1765). Oil on canvas. 103 × 122 cm. Private collection, on loan to National Museums Liverpool, Walker Art Gallery.*

of the gladiator, stood up on an easel for additional study and comment. And maybe freshly drawn for that purpose, the drawing of classical art objects being a key part of drawing pedagogy but also art appreciation and study of the human form.

Standing outside the frame of Wright's painting, we (echoing the men in the picture) are recruited to bathe in the glow of that shared connoisseurial study—this is also a "conversation piece"—and to share that intensely appreciative gaze with appreciative fellow viewers in the art gallery or collector's home. A ramifying friendly circle of virtuous connoisseurship which converses on matters like the distinction between "taste" and "genius."[115] Candle-lit intimacy. Candle-lit enlightenment. (A smaller monochrome engraving of the painting, published a few years after Wright first exhibited his painting, welcomed a larger viewership into the connoisseurial circle.)[116]

The burgeoning culture of connoisseurship—the depiction of men taking pleasure in works of art—was a congenial subject for eighteenth-century painting, drawing, engraving, private letters, printed fiction and non-fiction (especially in the domain of pleasurable periodical journalism), and in structured and unstructured conversation. It is the subject of good-natured satire in Cosway's painting, but outright celebration in this 1782 oil painting by Johan Zoffany (Fig. 2.27). In which the wealthy collector Charles Townley (him again!) and a different set of periwigged friends, with books at the ready, take their leisurely pleasure in Townley's gallery of antiquities, with its many nude and partly clothed figures.[117] On the floor, the satyr Silenus sits with legs apart, genitals exposed, and nearby, a book lays opened to an illustration of that very sculpture.[118] The books work to authorize the art, and vice versa. And both work to bolster the status of the collector. The transit between art object and printed engraving was a cultural amplifier, a mutually affirming certificate of aesthetic and historical significance and value.

So was the painting, commissioned by Townley—shown sitting apart, far right, with an open book on his lap and dog at his feet—which served as a visual synopsis of his brilliant collection, wealth and discernment—and the erudite fraternal sociability it occasioned. A very public (ostentatious) summa. Not a realistic representation of how the collection was actually arranged, but the collection re-staged to promiscuously gather all the works together, in one place for the delectation of Townley and friends. A scene invented, as if a prompt for viewers to imagine what one might hear if you could only eavesdrop upon the cultivated remarks that passed among the four chums. (Townley acquired the Discus Thrower, his prize collection piece, after the painting was completed. In 1791 he had Zoffany paint the sculpture into the scene.)[119]

Elite connoisseurship was a small world. Circles of sociability overlapped and intersected. Cosway and Townley were friends. Zoffany and Cosway were both fellows of the Royal Academy. Cosway, himself a collector and

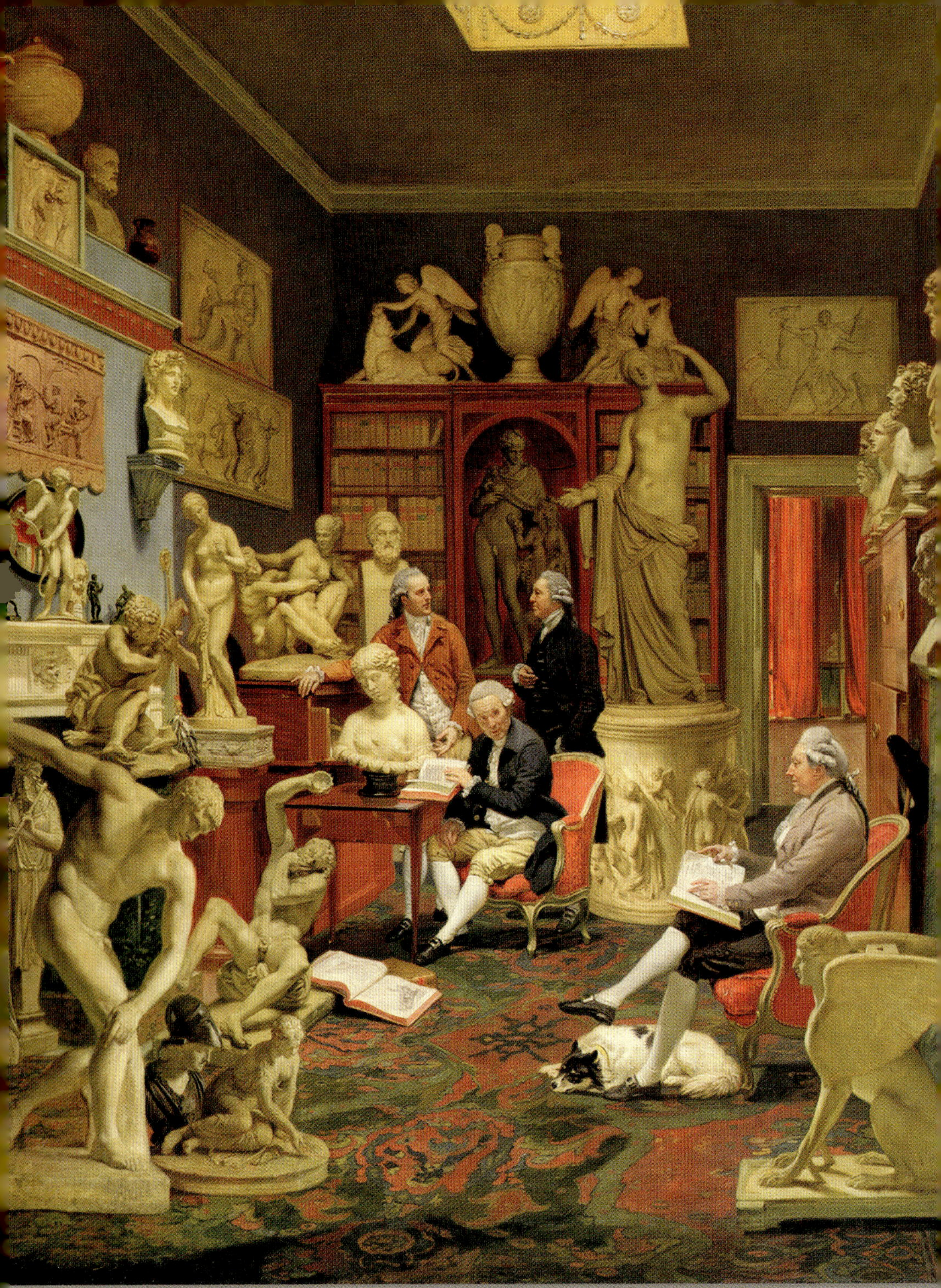

2.27 *Johan Zoffany, "Charles Townley in his Sculpture Gallery" (1782). Oil on canvas. 127 × 102 cm. Burnley Borough Council, Towneley Hall Art Gallery & Museums, UK.*

art dealer as well as an artist, also advised wealthy collectors like Townley. In Paris in 1786, Cosway socialized with the Prince of Wales, the Duc d'Orléans, and the self-proclaimed Baron d'Hancarville (aka Pierre-François Hughes, an art dealer and rake who Townley hired to catalog his antiquities, and who was pictured sitting almost dead center in Zoffany's painting of Townley's collection). (According to Jason M. Kelly's definitive history of the *Dilettanti,* the *Worship of Priapus* "owed its greatest intellectual debt" to d'Hancarville.)[120] Also among the revelers in Paris: Thomas Jefferson (then the American Minister to France), who had a friendship, likely an affair, with Cosway's wife Maria.[121]

Elite medical men, like other professionals, also took part in connoisseurship: two of the men depicted in Cosway's painting were doctors.[122] Physician-collectors could occupy very high places in the hierarchy of collectors. Dr Richard Mead, cited earlier as a good friend of Cheselden, owned a large and much-admired collection that included works by Rembrandt, Titian, Holbein, Watteau, Dürer, Carracci, Poussin, Rubens and Van Dyck, along with a personal library of over 10,000 books.[123]

3.3 Eyes on the gaze

The performance of gentlemen collectors and connoisseurs was an easy target for satirists, as in Thomas Rowlandson's depiction of a clutch of "Connoisseurs of Art" (Fig. 2.28). Eyes on the connoisseurial eye ... Which Rowlandson skewers as entirely masculine and absurdly, myopically, desirous, hungry for framed art objects and even more for the naked female bodies that appear within the frame.

Acts of intensive looking can gather a crowd—eyeballs recruit eyeballs. Gaze, if you will, but know that you yourself may be exposed, caught in the act, and then gazed upon. Rowlandson's dramatization of the connoisseurial scene, one of many that he did over the course of his career, is a kind of acting out, a bit of shaming that sets the satirist and his viewers in ambivalent judgment over connoisseurial homosociability. Some mixture of bemusement and critique, but also a dollop of shared self-mockery. Many of the people who bought and collected Rowlandson's prints undoubtedly saw a bit of themselves and their friends in the satire. Likely, so did Rowlandson. The cartoonist lived in the hubbub of late eighteenth-century British life, and offered his farcical scenes as clear-eyed though slightly tipsy pictures of everything that was going on around him. One could render judgment lightly and still enjoy the fun. Over-refinement, or the pretentious mimicking of refinement, resulted in very unrefined behavior: bug-eyed clubbiness, degenerating voyeurism, moral laxness, unmanliness. Which might even conduce to effeminacy and same-sex attachments among viewers, who might go from avidly drooling over objects featuring feminine beauty to objects featuring masculine beauty ...[124]

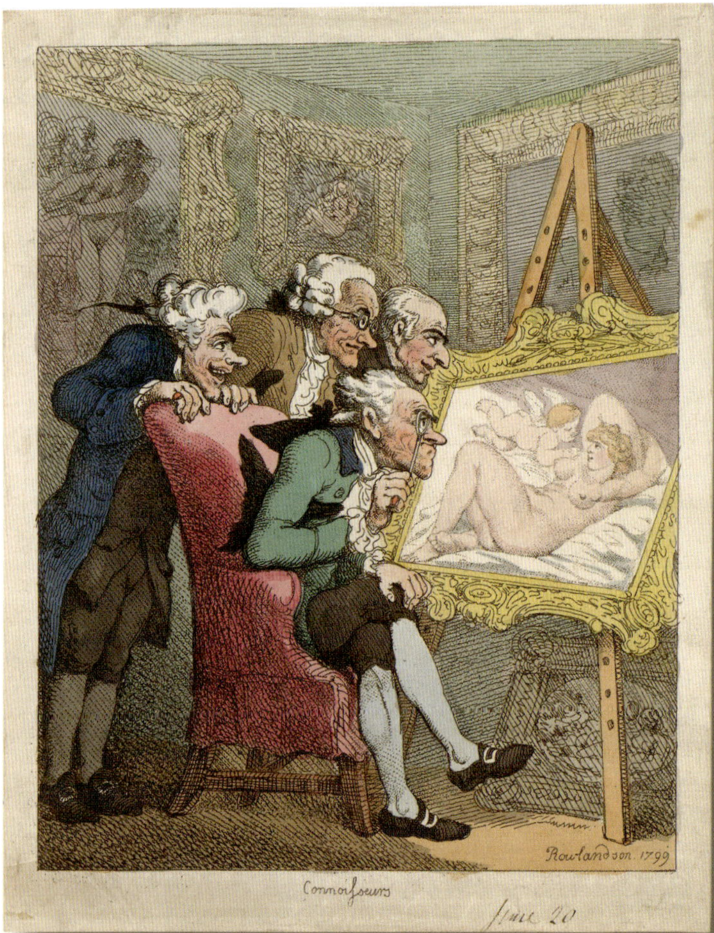

2.28 *Thomas Rowlandson (1757–1827), "Connoisseurs of Art" (London, 1799). Hand-colored etching. 27 × 21 cm. Metropolitan Museum of Art.*

To protect themselves from such feelings and appearances, members of such clubs might indulge in conspicuous displays of insult and physical violence against effeminate men, sexual objectification of women, misogyny, whoring, debauching, or just jesting banter and mockery (the idiom of Rowlandson's satire). Which would go some way toward affirming the manliness of group members. Or not. For most of the eighteenth century, men of the upper elite had privileges. Men at the bottom had a different kind of free pass, no one expected them to do anything but show deference to superiors. But throughout the social spectrum, homoeroticism and homophobia were paired ends of a gradient, part of a larger cultural logic, a regime governing homosocial behavior "between men." If, as Jeffrey Weeks argues, "men are socialized … by being taught they are not women," homosocial groups of men often socialize themselves by acting in opposition to male effeminacy. Or, if they had leave to queer that, by giving themselves permission to play the feminine, sometimes in the company of women, sometimes only among likeminded men.[125]

3.4 Between men: A continuum of attachments

The complicated dynamics of men interacting with each other and performing their political, social and aesthetic commitments and judgments in galleries, coffeehouses, clubs, and other public spaces, provided the basis for the emergence of idiosyncratic homosocial expressions of fellow feeling.[126] As we have seen, in the male networks and clubs of eighteenth-, nineteenth- and early twentieth-century Europe and America, sex-exclusive groupings within sex-exclusive institutions, there were many artful representations of naked women to share and savor. And many artful representations of naked men. And, as Kosofsky Sedgwick demonstrates in readings of literary sources, there was always a potential—danger, opportunity—that bonds among "secret sharers" could intensify into shared homoerotic feelings. Often matched by outbursts of homophobic rage. Abigail Solomon-Godeau, looking at the late-eighteenth-, early-nineteenth-century art world (mainly French), describes a "homosocial continuum" of attachments, ranging from group gathering and fellow feeling, to intense but chaste "romantic" friendship, maybe ripening into something more than that.[127] Same-sex desires could perhaps be privately indulged—and tolerated at certain times and in certain protected spaces—more latitude for foreigners abroad, more latitude in the upper reaches of the aristocracy and the church, and mostly tacit acceptance for sailors and other working-class men—but open expression was risky. Disclosure might trigger panic and chastisement from authorities and peers, but was mostly discouraged by informal policing: gossip, shaming, shunning, queer-bashing, blackmail, etc.

Why? Because sexual contact between men, by longstanding custom and rule of law, was decreed to be a crime against nature. Shameful. According to historian Harry Cocks, between 1780 and 1830, there was a new intensifying "consciousness" in Britain that moral and legal sanctions against "indecent behavior," "buggery," "unnatural acts"—especially displays of male effeminacy—should apply to the ruling elite, as well as to other classes.[128] The spaces for expression of same-sex desire were increasingly monitored and constrained, even as more spaces opened up to avoid monitoring. And so a culture of concealment developed: the closet, many peculiar closets.

The settings? Homosociality, and homoerotic sequelae, occurred up and down the social scale, among and between men of different social and hierarchical standing. Some at the center of power, others at the far edges, still others somewhere in the great in-between. Particular groups of men, and exchanges between groups—particular institutions—had their own particular homoerotic potentials, protocols and expressions. There was a boarding school effect: sex-segregated homosocial institutions—the art academy, the medical college, the association, the university college, the club—nurtured homoerotic feelings within peer groups. All within a matrix of power differentials: teachers taking liberties with students, upper-level boys with lower levels, etc. …[129]

Class always mattered.[130] Same-sex attachments were often enough connected to an absolute lack of privilege, something for the wilds of working-class life, or conversely an elite sense of privilege—the upper-class man forging links to likeminded members of his rank or perversely degrading himself with social inferiors, protégés or dependents. Or, more positively, finding emotional fulfillment and connection to a peer, or someone a rank or two below, or often enough someone in, or beneath, the class of men who served him every day, and who took intimate care of his body and his needs in childhood, adulthood and old age. Or there might be no attachment at all, just monetary transactions or non-consensual contact. In another book, we might consider same-sex encounters and attachments from the affective point of view of working-class men (and the homoerotic interactions that occurred within their own class and circles). But here we are concerned with "respectable" professional men, elite men—arrayed in medical societies, clubs, universities, hospitals, etc.—and a certain class of shared objects: illustrated anatomical books and prints. And the "source material" for many of the illustrations: working-class cadavers. Class mattered.

3.5 Between men: Surgical masculinity and objects

The conversation-piece paintings of Cosway *et al.* put on view a masculine subculture of dealers, collectors, voyeurs and aesthetes. A man's world. Surgery was also a man's world. Scottish surgeon John Bell, describing the "character and manners" of the profession in the year 1810, uses these terms: "address" (directness), "intrepidity," "courage," "presence of mind," and "dexterous" manual power. Discerning diagnostic gazes, manly resolve. Such qualities "enable[d] a surgeon to bear up undismayed against alarms and accidents when his own reputation is at stake."[131] In contrast to the genteel physician, the surgeon was figured as a man of strength and action. He dealt with blood and bones and pus and lesions, had to move decisively and quickly, hold down patients, cauterize wounds, remove stones, cut away growths, saw off parts. And spent much time with cadavers, dissecting to gain surety of hand-and-eye and familiarity with the interior of the body, especially the arteries. This was before anesthesia (introduced in the mid-1840s), antisepsis (first demonstrated in 1867), blood transfusion (early twentieth century), and rigorous protocols of surgical hygiene (which began to take hold only in the 1880s). The surgeon got dirty and bloody. He had to have a strong stomach, manfully ignore cries of pain and other displays of atrocious suffering, "amid the cruelty of a needful and dangerous operation" (John Bell again).[132] The surgeon wielded the same sharp instruments used by barbers, carpenters and butchers. And sometimes had a military or naval association: the battlefield and sailing ship were male-only places where surgery was frequently required and performed. If the surgeon also taught or studied anatomy—as was often the case—he would have to obtain, handle, dispose of, or collect specimens from, a succession of dead bodies and body parts. Bell uses the adjectives "fearless," "relentless," sometimes "hardened," although never "cruel." And emphasizes that the surgeon's "good name"—as assessed by peers and benefactors—depended on comportment under trying conditions.

Dirty, difficult work. Surgery was a liminal occupation, a profession certainly and not a trade, but without any guarantee of social acceptability, or a big income. Even so, Bell argued for a democratic and compassionate surgical gentility, and there were "surgical gentlemen."[133] While traditionally the surgeon was ranked below the physician, the social standing of surgeons in general rose over the course of the eighteenth and nineteenth centuries (especially after the division of barbers and surgeons into separate guilds in the mid-eighteenth century and the passage of the Apothecary Act of 1815, which attempted to set higher educational standards and separated the surgeons from the apothecaries). And genteel or not, master surgeons were often credited with fine discernment, tactile sensitivity and delicacy (and a fine command of needle and thread). The learned surgeon consulted medical books with detailed, often artful, illustrations and greco-latinate technical discussions—and often enough collected such books, and maybe took an antiquarian interest in rarities.

And, as with everything else in eighteenth- and nineteenth-century Britain, surgery was organized hierarchically. At the highest rank, surgeons treated high-born patients and socialized with them. Some were themselves members of the gentry, by birth or through rising. Some were even honored with knighthood (e.g., Charles Bell and Astley Cooper). Below them were strivers who (sometimes ambivalently) aspired to rise. Such men would be expected to display a modicum of manners, have a decent library, framed paintings, decent clothes and other visible forms of "refinement"—and were appraised on the quality of their possessions and attainments. Yet there was also a hierarchy where surgeons were ranked by the caliber of their resolute manliness, surgical strength, speed, craftsmanship and cool determination, and the values of the two hierarchies often clashed.[134] Surgical identity was complicated. Performed before disputatious circles of onlookers who were as eager to pass judgment as they were to close ranks around friends, social peers and protegés, surgical reputations were difficult to establish and sustain.

We have seen that art pedagogy, connoisseurship and anatomy were closely linked. Surgery and anatomy were closer still, the links forged precisely in the teaching and taking of courses of gross anatomy in medical school, as well as extracurricular anatomical instruction and activities. Art historian Alan C. Braddock, writing on the painter Thomas Eakins and his circle of mid- and late-nineteenth-century Philadelphia art students, artists and medical men, observes that "anatomical bodies facilitated a fraternal discourse broadly shared by artists and physicians." And surgeons too.[135] Who all took in a common set of experiences: the appropriation of bodies (bodysnatching!), dissection in class and private studies, collective commentary and storytelling, along with all sorts of verbal and practical jokes regarding matters anatomical.[136] And, with all of that, opportunities for socializing within and across class lines—friendship—and the corollary nurturing of shared medical, scientific, and aesthetic interests.

As the eighteenth century transited into the nineteenth, connoisseurship burst its bounds. The culture, social circles and erotics of art appreciation and collecting metastasized. Literacy became more widespread. The production of books, prints, art objects, antiquities, naturalia and exotica proliferated and diversified, as did the passionate collecting of used and rare objects, especially books. Which was accompanied by a kind of celebratory virtual collection of canons of great works and pantheons of great artists, writers, scientists, doctors, etc. At the same time, connoisseurship underwent a partial democratization. The unusual collection, the valuable collection, could serve as a vehicle for upward cultural mobility or aspirations thereto. Though still mainly coded as masculine and elite, increasingly women and people of middling income levels took part. There were bargains to be had, obscure treasures to be discovered; the hunt itself was a source of pleasure.

And so was the figure of the collector. Who could be portrayed in novels and short stories as an eccentric, foolish, maybe loveable character, or maybe snooty, degenerate or demented—a man (always a man) who lingered within his personal museum or library, and lusted after first editions and rarities. (Often the plot turned on someone driven by collecting obsessions to steal from an antiquities dealer, museum, library, church or fellow collector ...)[137]

Over the succeeding generations, connoisseurship intensified, a feedback loop nurtured by the genre of art criticism (especially the writings of Joshua Reynolds, William Hazlitt and John Ruskin) and the growth of print media, literacy, journalism, art academies, university education, public museums, galleries and art markets. As more people joined in (and connoisseurship was increasingly redefined as expertise in art history and appreciation), social, intellectual, and aesthetic bars were raised.[138] *Art was valorized as an ever more transcendent realm; the genius an ever more transcendent figure; the masterpiece an ever more transcendent object. People started crafting new art styles, movements, projects, and personae that took account of those new investments; masterpieces were concocted, lines were crossed (transgression! transcendence!), insiders were initiated, outsiders condemned or shunned.*

Jumping ahead to the last decades of the nineteenth century, the culture of sophisticated gazing and connoisseurial discernment even gave rise to Oscar Wilde's odd synthesis, "the critic as artist," which raised the critic above artists and the objects of criticism. And gave rise to new performances of quivering sensitivity, hyper-discernment, and erotic perversity—ambivalently masculine and feminine and other—the Aesthete, the Decadent, the Avant-Gardist.[139] *In the fictions of Henry James and other* fin de siècle *writers, the same heightened discernment had social implications. If you could read works of art and discern the marks of the artist, you could read the marks of a person. A person's tones, gestures, stylistic choices and preferences in dress, décor and taste in art also suggested one's erotic attachments, maybe amounting to an unmasking, if the signaling wasn't overt and deliberate. (But, as always, there were counter-narratives: Maybe connoisseurial discernment co-existed with or fostered an utter lack of social, moral or economic discernment ... Or people made fools of themselves via incompetent displays of good taste and erudition ... The stuff of comedy or pathos ...)*

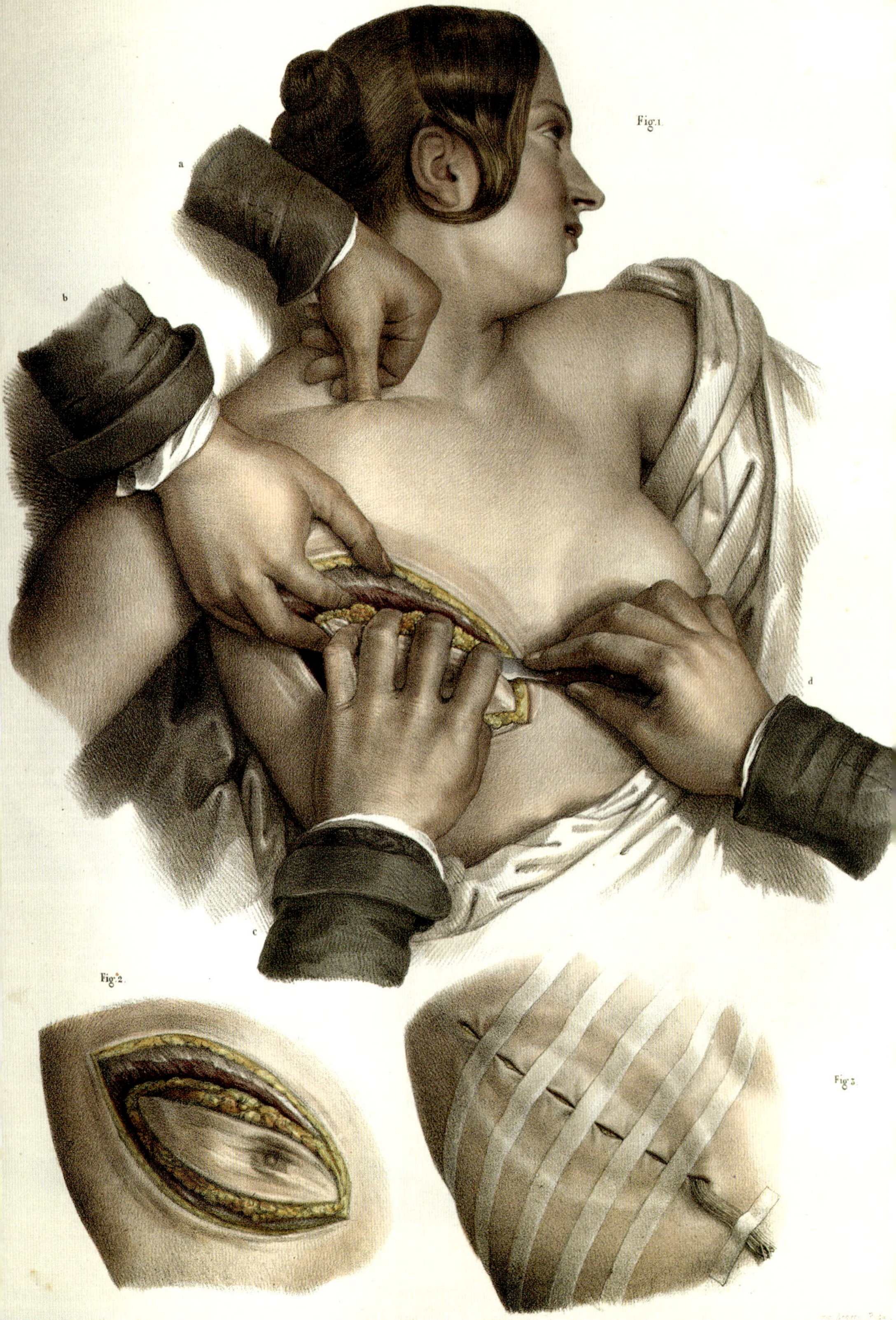

… nature par N. H. Jacob.

PART THREE

"Overshadowed by the artist": Mr Joseph Maclise's queer anatomy

PROLOGUE: NICOLAS-HENRI JACOB

1.1 Medical eyes, surgical hands

As the number of trained surgeons multiplied in the latter half of the eighteenth century and first half of the nineteenth, so did the middle and upper social and intellectual registers of British surgery. And so did the production of objects and experiences for sharing among surgical men and their cultured friends, who consulted and collected anatomical publications from all over Europe. Such as the multivolume image-laden *Traité complet de l'anatomie de l'homme* (1831–54; 2d ed., 1866–71) of surgeon-anatomist Jean-Baptiste-Marc Bourgery (1797–1849). And his collaborator, Nicolas-Henri Jacob (1781–1871), who unusually for a medical illustrator, received full credit on the titlepage as "professeur-dessinateur-anatomist" and co-author.[1] (As well he deserved: the first edition had 3,750 illustrations in total, more than 2,000 by Jacob himself and the rest made under his direction.)[2]

The images are extraordinary. Take, for example, this illustration from volume 7 (Fig. 3.1). Two sets of masculine hands operate on the body of

3.1 *J.-B.-M. Bourgery & N.-H. Jacob, "Removal of the breast,"* Traité complet de l'anatomie de l'homme... *(Paris, 1831–54), v. 7 (1839–40; 2d ed., 1866–70), pl. 27. Chromolithograph. Art: N.-H. Jacob. 33 × 44 cm. Hagströmer Medico-Historical Library.*

a beautiful and supine woman. The scene—demonstrating the surgical removal of a cancerous tumor of the breast—is a brilliant composition brilliantly executed. Jacob was a gifted practitioner of Jacques-Louis David's "corporal aestheticism" (as a young man, he trained in David's workshop)—but was just as much under the influence of Jean-Auguste-Dominique Ingres, who expertly used color and shading to show body volume, texture, and silky, creamy perfect skin.[3] So: a polished work of high artistry, worthy of the Salon des Beaux-Arts, presenting a desirable young woman with fashionable hairdo and rouged cheeks, undergoing the torment of a distressing operation, eyes open, awake (anesthesia hadn't been invented yet), but absent any expression of torment. Like many other illustrations in the *Traité complet*, it is offered both as a how-to guide to a difficult operation, and a visual delight. A provocation and an incitement. Almost a fever dream. And a celebration of surgical mastery and the recently perfected technology of color lithography (at least in the second edition, the first edition has beautiful hand- and stencil-coloring). An unusual scene, for medical eyes, cultivated eyes.

Nearly identical hands share the surgical work, evoking both the haptic experience of surgery and the touch of masculine hands on naked female flesh.[4] A set of touchings, which in turn are offered for sharing among those who will have access to the plate in a fine medical library or who can afford to subscribe to the folio in installments (expensive) or purchase individual volumes (very expensive) or (from 1854 on) the full set of eight volumes and later supplements (obscenely expensive).[5] The *Traité complet* outdid all competitors: its illustrations were more comprehensive, colorful, precise, demonstrative, pedagogical, horrific, aggressive, numerous.[6] And more beautiful, in the idiom of illusionistic beaux-arts perspective. In every respect, extravagant. And, in the aggregate, oddly playful, theatrical, voyeuristic. Full of sensual mimetic representations of surgical hands on and in bodies. The reader gazes upon the patient, who doesn't, can't, return the gaze. The surgeon appears only in the form of disembodied hands, and multiples thereof. Otherwise, he exists by inference, present in the text but outside the printed image. Relations between undepicted gazer and gazed-upon figure are asymmetrical. Spirit (epitomized by the sight-unseen surgeon, and reader/viewer) operates upon matter (the pictured patient and cadaver). Subject tops object.[7]

The illustration records a transgression, a crossing of boundaries. Elizabeth Stephens, in her essay "Touching Bodies: Tact/ility in Nineteenth-Century Medical Photographs and Models," argues that the "erotics of touch" is "a relation of mutuality and reciprocity between two bodies ... a point of contact in which to touch is always also simultaneously to be touched": "[T]ouch is foundational to the relationship between subjects ... the point of intersection between ethics and erotics."[8] If so, the touching depicted here violates that mutuality and reciprocity. The mastectomy scene pairs the opportunity to see (what modesty shouldn't consent to) with an opportunity to touch (what virtue shouldn't consent to). All imaginary: this is just representation of touch, not touch itself. But from those double transgressions, committed upon an object of desire, and licensed and compelled by surgical necessity, an erotic frisson is constituted. Stephens speaks of "the sexualization inherent in the construction of medical knowledge itself."[9] But, as we've already seen, and will see again, some constructions are more sexualized than others.

The Parisian medical establishment never rewarded Bourgery with any high position, but the *Traité complet* hit a sweet spot in the market for medical publications. It became a standard reference work—notwithstanding the high cost—every good medical library had to have it. And it helped to inspire a new style of lithographic illustration that used high artistry, precise rendering, and brilliant color to convey the sensual experience, the feel, of surgery (and pathology, obstetrics, dermatology, histology, and anatomical dissection).

The plates burn with a kind of erotic intensity. But what objects of desire? Bourgery and Jacob mostly focus on dissected bodies and body parts, and complex, to us bizarre, surgical operations. One set of showstoppers: the surgical cuts, down to the bone, right through bone. Another set: the atlas's nude and semi-nude figures. Female nude and semi-nude figures certainly (famously, a spectacular depiction of a caesarian), but a preponderance of male figures (Fig. 3.2). Beautiful faces, beautiful bodies, subjected to horrific or just peculiar scenes of surgical-anatomical intervention. Readers got to see a nearly endless succession of creamy textures, jagged ruptures, deep wounds, bold incisions and perfect stitches—images that nearly pop off the page, drawn and printed with consummate artistry. In books that were themselves objects of desire, arrayed in libraries alongside other works of bibliophilic desire. (And not far away: prized collections of specimens, models, instruments, *objets d'art* and *naturalia*.)

Jacob and Bourgery were especially acclaimed for their comprehensive drawings of hands on and in bodies, step-by-step detailed depictions of surgical operations—a genre of illustration that went way beyond anything nonmedical artists might attempt in gory scenes of the martyrdom of the saints and historical atrocities, or sexy scenes of nude heroes and woodland nymphs from Greco-Roman antiquity. Medical men, of course, were trained and licensed to look upon difficult subjects. And, by virtue of class and gender, licensed to exercise a privileged gaze upon potentially erotic subjects.[10]

And so were collectors and connoisseurs, who were famously fraternal (though socially exclusive). The wealthy bibliophilic physicians and surgeons who built up large libraries of expensive and rare books also socialized with nonmedical collectors. You can easily imagine those nonmedical men, eager to peek behind the professional curtain, browsing the libraries of medical friends (or libraries of clubby scientific societies) or even themselves acquiring the atlas.[11] In order to take in the arcane and intense sensations that medical illustrations induced. Because medical publication was in so many tantalizing ways exempt from the strictures that governed the representation of bodies in other domains.[12] (The same class of nonmedical gentlemen used their pull to observe surgeries and dissections, and to go on private and group tours of the Parisian morgue.)[13] Added to that, *Traité complet*, like other renowned medical publications, participated in the visual rhetoric of modernity and emancipatory science. Mid-nineteenth-century collectors who identified with Enlightenment encyclopedism performed that attachment in the acquisition of scientific books—such as *Traité complet*, a grand encyclopedia of anatomy and surgery.

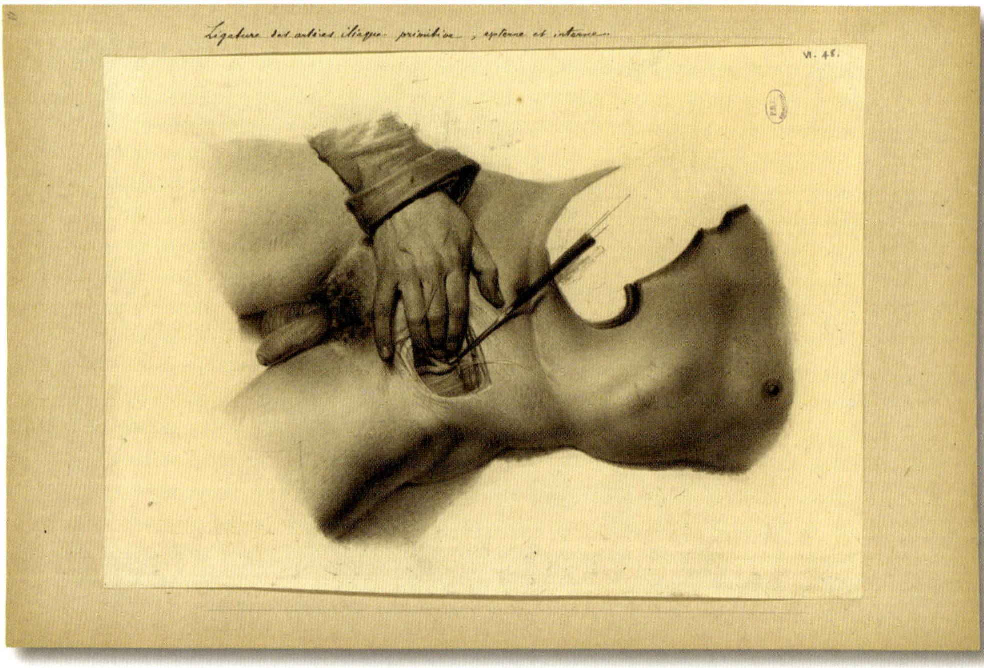

3.2 *Nicolas-Henri Jacob, "Ligature des artères iliaque primitive, externe et interne" (c.1840) [ms. 81, t. 6]. (Preparatory drawing for* Traité complet de l'anatomie de l'homme, *v. 6 (1830–40), pl. 48.) 39 × 28 cm. Bibliothèque Interuniversitaire de Santé Médecine – Université Paris Cité.*

It all sounds a bit boundless. Yet even Jacob had to negotiate boundaries. Compare his preparatory drawing of "The ligature of the iliac arteries" (Fig. 3.2) with the finished lithograph (Fig. 3.3). The drawing shows a hand inside a surgical cut in the body of a well-proportioned, almost classical, masculine torso. The image fades out above the right nipple (leaving space for an undrawn left hand that will hold the surgeon's probe). Below the cut, Jacob artfully renders the penis. An almost independently sensate pinky lingers, not far away (slightly apart from the other fingers), right at the border where pubic hair leaves off.

In contrast, the printed lithograph covers up: it wraps both ends of the anatomical subject in fabric, a framing device that protects the modesty of the reader (and the anonymous patient/cadaver?) and hides the penis. And yet, upon closer inspection, the penis remains discernible under the finely rendered folds of cloth. Is Jacob dancing on the line, enjoying himself, teasing his audience? (Jacob, of course, didn't invent the tactic of draped disclosure. Leo Steinberg, in his controversial article on early modern depictions of Christ's penis, drily notes that "it had long been the special pride of Renaissance painters to make drapery report subjacent anatomic events.")[14]

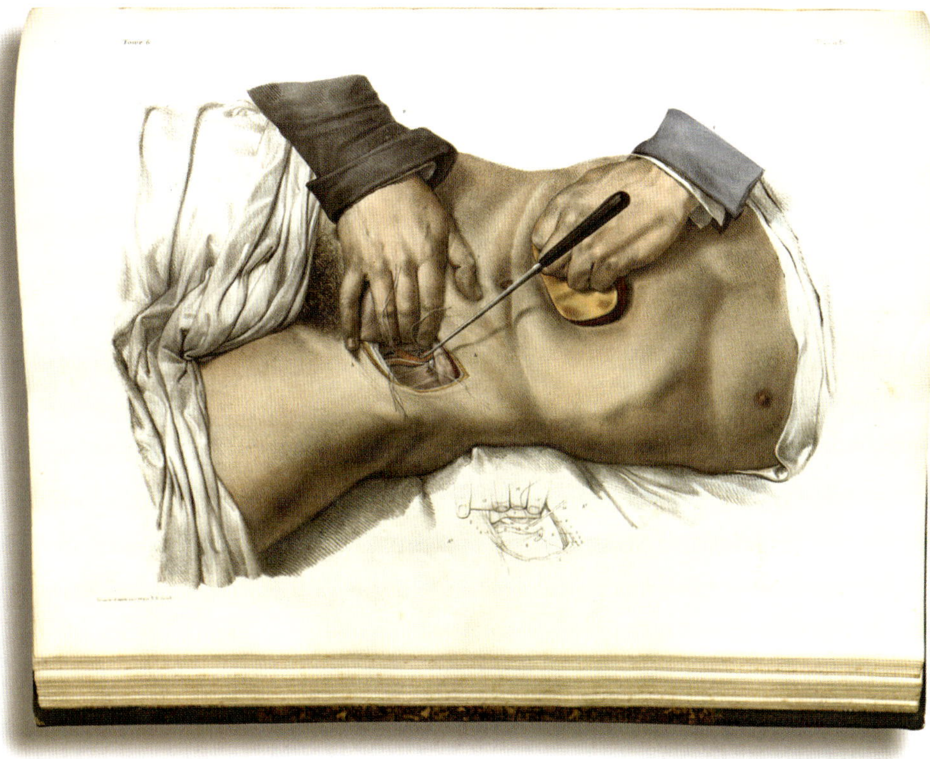

3.3 *J.-B.-M. Bourgery & N.-H. Jacob, "Ligature des artères iliaque primitive, externe et interne,"* Traité complet de l'anatomie de l'homme *(Paris, 1832–56), v. 6 (1839–40) (2d ed., 1866–71), pl. 48. Art: N.-H. Jacob. Chromolithograph. 33 × 43 cm. Hagströmer Medico-Historical Library.*

Maybe Bourgery or publisher C.A. Delaunay asked Jacob to make the cover-up, but Jacob probably didn't need any prompting. The standard editorial practice in mid-nineteenth-century medical illustration was to omit or minimize things that were irrelevant or distracting, especially if that thing was a penis. For a formally-trained artist like Jacob, the preparatory drawing was a stage in a process, a place to show figures in the nude, fully undressed, to get a better sense of the underlying form of the bodies, and then overlay clothes or drapery in the finished version.[15] Embedded in this method, was a hierarchy of structure—skeleton > écorché > nude > dressed—that was a foundational part of the curriculum of drawing pedagogy.[16] And the nude stage of that hierarchy (often connected to the study of live nude models) provided the opportunity for private sensual enjoyment—often (though not always) followed by a seemingly more modest covered public presentation.[17]

More broadly, one wonders, how did the representational guard-rails around the penis in Jacob's medical illustrations compare with those prevailing in the academies and ateliers, where an artist like Jacob would have been trained and acculturated? Happily, we have a fine depiction of such an establishment, a scene in which the male body and genitalia are in the process of receiving representation: Martin Ferdinand Quadal's monumental 1787 painting, "The Life Class of the Vienna Academy" (Fig. 3.4).[18] Quadal gives viewers an almost synoptic view: a classical statue

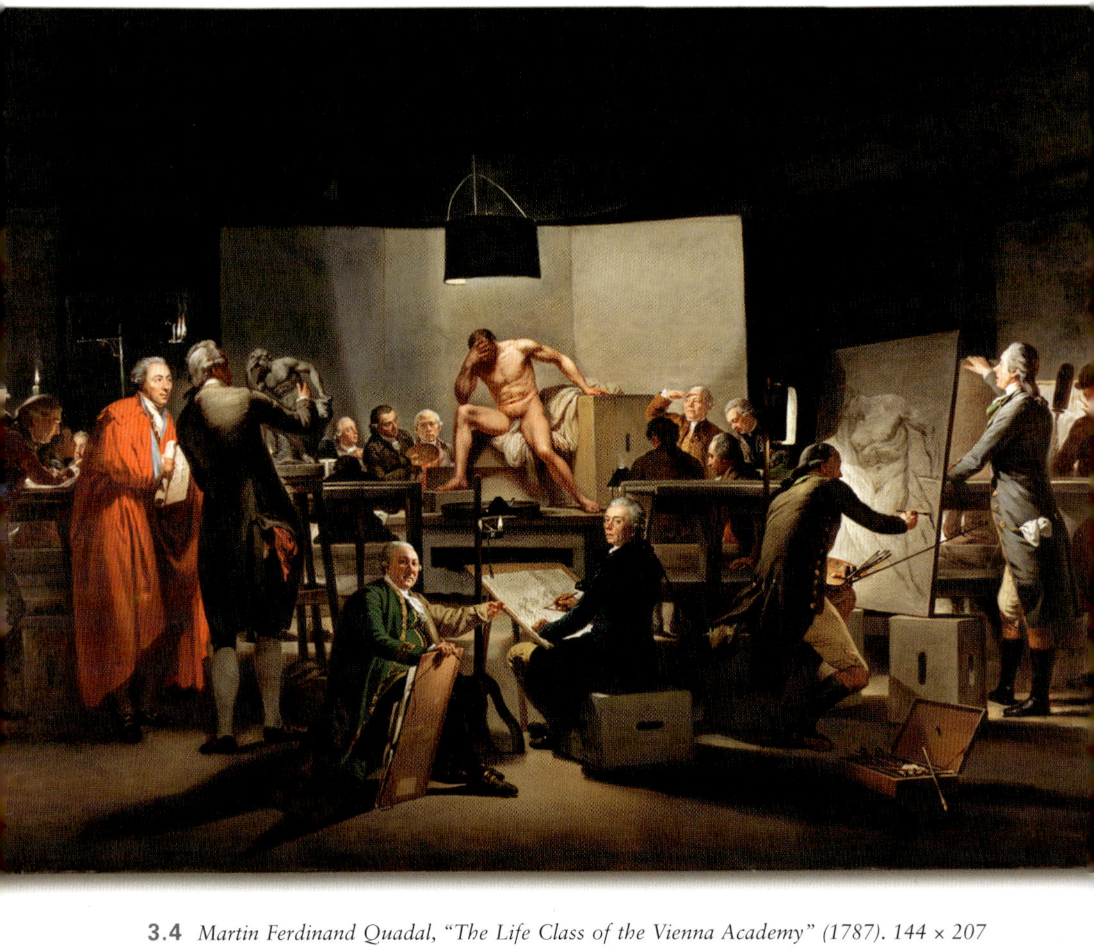

3.4 *Martin Ferdinand Quadal, "The Life Class of the Vienna Academy" (1787). 144 × 207 cm. Gemäldegalerie der Akademie der bildenden Künste Wien / Academy of Fine Arts Vienna, Paintings Gallery.*

of a male figure in the nude; a live model positioned in the same pose as the statue, and artists (all men), making paintings and drawings, *ad vivum* (from life) with the model in the place of privilege.

Notice the treatment of the penis. The model's penis, at the very center of the painting, is exposed—almost highlighted—but still concealed by an almost vanishingly minimal bit of wrapping (another "report of a subjacent anatomic event"). Other anatomical details—pubic hair, the ball sac—are similarly suggested and obscured. Toward the rear, at left, we can see the statue on which the model's pose is based, but here too no view of a penis (or a fig-leaf) is presented, the groin being conveniently blocked by a figure in the foreground (which saves Quadal the bother of having to cope with that problem). To the right we see a painter's monochrome rendering of the model, which represents the figure with a signal difference: a much larger piece of cloth has been added to obscure the penis and surrounding area. Stepping back, arrayed in a ring around the center, there are more artists—all busied with the work of drawing, painting, studying, discussing.

If the focal point of Quadal's painting is the center of interest, then the thing in the center, the penis, is precisely what cannot be represented. Which raises more questions: is Quadal being true to life here? Or concealing the fact that the model actually exposed his genital region, without any concern for his own modesty or corrosive moral effects on the assembled artist-viewers? We have no way of knowing—Quadal protects us (and himself) from the worry of any confrontation. Either way we have the final result: a polished demonstration of Quadal's painterly and compositional mastery, showing a scene of art pedagogy in the salon of one of its most prestigious institutions, where he himself was painting-and-drawing master, organized around ... what? Hmmm ...

JOSEPH MACLISE

2.1 The mystery of Mr. Joseph Maclise

Traité complet was widely influential in France and Germany. Its comprehensive coverage, anatomical-surgical erudition, sensual aesthetics, provocative staging, precise rendering, and perfect printing set a high bar for the generations of studio-trained medical illustrators that followed. Across the Channel, the only atlases that came anywhere close were those featuring the drawings of Joseph Maclise (1815–91), a striver who studied anatomy and surgery in London and Paris in the late 1830s and 1840s, where he would surely have encountered the work of Jacob and Bourgery, and maybe the men themselves.[19] Maclise, a brilliant dissector and gifted draughtsman, though never a gallery artist, situated himself in the grand Renaissance tradition of perfectionist, volumetric figure drawing and its artful synthesis of *disegno* (composition and line), naturalistic rendering, ideals of beauty and anatomical proportion, and male nudity. Art. He also situated himself in the grand post-Vesalian tradition of top-shelf medical and surgical anatomy. Science. Yet he idiosyncratically departed from the conventions of both domains. Such as the convention of genital discretion: Maclise didn't cover up or minimize his irrelevant penises.

We don't have his thoughts on that. Maclise was a loquacious and opinionated writer on medical and scientific topics, but entirely reticent about his stylistic decisions, aesthetic influences, social life, feelings and erotic attachments. He left behind no diaries, no letters, no self-portraits, almost no puzzle pieces: only a thin trail of circumstantial evidence (mostly crumbs from the leavings of his older brother, the celebrated painter and illustrator, Daniel Maclise). He did, however, leave us many extraordinary anatomical illustrations. Which, he assured readers (in the preface to his *Surgical Anatomy*), would enter "the understanding straight-forward in a direct passage"—as any true representation must. And as words cannot.[20] That assurance was linked to a strong but circular claim: that his renderings offered a kind of reliable witness to his dissections, where the precepts of "transcendental anatomy" were plainly revealed. Forms of Nature were self-evident in his representations. Almost a revelation. "A picture of form," he declared, "is a proposition which solves itself."[21]

Yet his pictures don't really solve themselves, or anything else. The man and his pictures are a mystery. Even so, following Kosofsky Sedgwick's lead, let's entertain the possibility, that in some queer and occluded fashion—perhaps not fully apparent even to Maclise—he unveiled himself in his image-work, sent out flares of homoerotic desire.[22] Not only that, of course: his "pictures of form" offer many open-ended propositions, from which many possible interpretations might be derived. Yet, if they don't enter "understanding" straightforwardly in any direct passage, they do have tendencies. A deeply felt mimetic sensuality. An overabundant pleasure in male bodies, line, texture, and the showmanship of anatomical representation. An argumentative assertion of principles and positions. And, as I will demonstrate, a queer erotic intensity.

His first major publication featured drawings, "from nature and on stone," for Richard Quain's *Anatomy of the Arteries of the Human Body*.[23] Issued in two formats—an oversize volume (1844) published in installments (and then as a bound volume), and, in 1846 an even larger "Imperial" folio of unbound lithographic plates ("the figures the size of life")—it is a *tour de force* in its dimensions, erudition and beauty. (*From nature*, a formulaic phrase, signaled a commitment to faithful representation of an actual subject on view by the artist, without embellishment or invented detail. Similarly, *the size of life* was a guarantor of fulsome representation and avoidance of the distortion and loss of detail that inevitably comes with the reduction of scale.)[24]

Reviewers loved Maclise's "delineations." A reviewer of the first two installments singled him out as an "artistical talent of the very highest order," and added this connoisseurial comment: his plates "will bear comparison with any of those splendid specimens of anatomical drawing, so abundant on the continent, but heretofore so very rare in our own country ..."[25] There was, it seems, something *continental* about Maclise's approach. This perhaps wasn't merely a euphemism for *sexy*, but points to a hard-to-define quality which a cultivated eye would discern as aesthetically distinct from, and superior to, the fine British illustrated anatomies of the period, respected, in some cases venerated, works by Charles Bell, Astley Cooper, John Lizars, etc. The reviewer didn't go beyond his suggestive remark (book reviews in medical journals tended toward brevity), but it's likely he was gesturing toward the plates of Bourgery and Jacob, with all of their polish and sensuality.

Consider then plate 51 (Fig. 3.5) from *Anatomy of the Arteries*. Upright, as if alive, a dissected body demonstrates the anatomy of the superior mesenteric artery. A cord keeps the right hand suspended at the breast—there's a bit of puppetry. The fingers appear to be pointing to, touching, the heart. The gesture is "heartfelt." Perhaps a signal, to Maclise, and to us. As if that dissected body has a will of its own (but without the menace that attends a horror-movie ventriloquist's dummy).

The wealth of extraneous detail—Roland Barthes's famous "reality effect"—attests to the verisimilitude of the scene, demonstrates Maclise's commitment to truth-telling and command of illusionistic perspective. We're seeing with his anatomical eyes.[26] Reality. But a curated reality. Maclise choreographs his scene to highlight selected features and textures, his scalpel and pencil lead the viewer on a tour of the body and a lesson in thoracic anatomy. And in that way produces what Lorraine Daston and Peter Galison call "a reasoned image."[27]

Yet the artist is also leading his readers and himself astray, into something beyond reason. There is the neatly arranged rupture of the cut ... Those subtle shadows and contours ... The undissected skin surfaces contrasting with, or fencing off, the rococo intestines as they nearly spill over onto the clean-shaven pubic area and testicles. Maclise could have covered the genital with a sheet, as Jacob and Quadal did, or left it out of the picture. Like the dangling hand, the penis is entirely unrelated to the subject under demonstration. But Maclise still contrives to show it hanging front and center: a provocation, when you consider that the conventional thing was to cover it or crop it out (unless the image is demonstrating a uro-genital topic).[28] And even more provocative if you consider that in classically-influenced academic art, even where there is a commitment to realistic depiction (Maclise's tradition), penises were usually sized discreetly, disproportionately small, if not entirely obscured by a fig-leaf or some other device.

Maclise's aphorism speaks of "the picture of form," but what of the form of this picture?[29] The mesenteric artery is framed by the intestines, which are

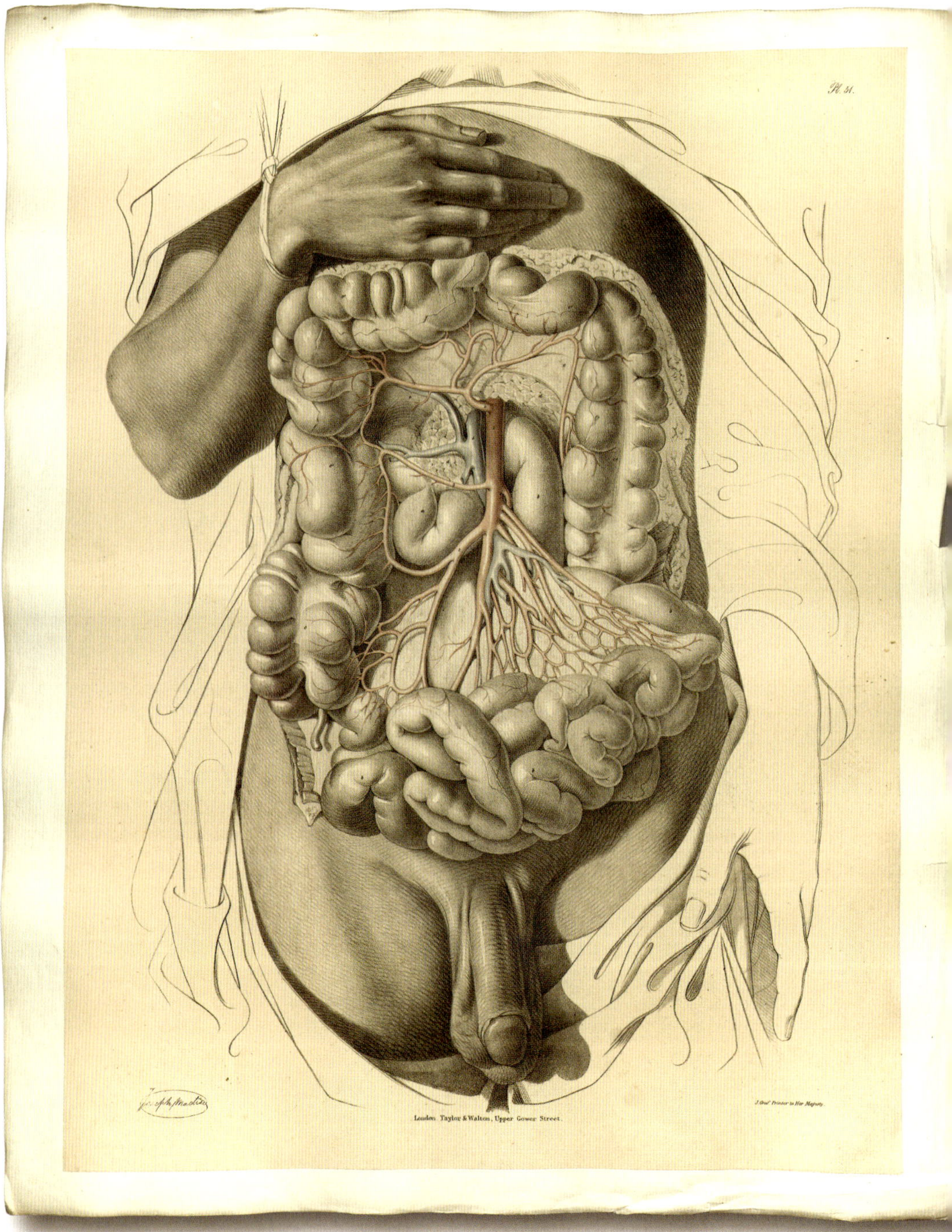

3.5 *"Superior Mesenteric Artery," Richard Quain,* The Anatomy of the Arteries of the Human Body *(London, 1844), pl. 51. Art: Joseph Maclise. Lithograph. 68 × 55 cm. Hagströmer Medico-Historical Library.*

framed by the anatomist's cut, which is framed by the skin of the cadaver, which is framed by the *non-finito* outline drawing of the swirling sheet, with the left hand completing the circle (and then framed by the negative space around the whole). Frames around frames. Almost a rosette. The plate demonstrates a bravura dissection no doubt, flaunts the anatomist's erudition and skill with the scalpel.[30] But also flaunts the artist's bravura draughtsmanship, command of line and shadow and space, compositional gifts—and command of lithography. (Maclise is "drawing on stone.") Flaunting in multiples.

And what else? That exceptional male genital calls on the viewer to take notice ... So do the luscious skin surfaces ... that hand touching the breast ... the invisible line that connects the hanging hand at top to the dangling penis at bottom ... The wallow in aestheticism ... The too-much-ness ... Is Maclise "queering" the picture, flaunting himself? (His signature is bold, expressive. Anatomical illustrations aren't usually signed by the artist.) That cadaver's hand gesturing to the reader ... that's Maclise showing *his* hand, orchestrating a hothouse scene of erotic interiority. (For some readers, nothing is signified, it all flies under the radar. Others feel the heat, but say nothing aloud ...)

2.2 Misters Quain and Maclise

Maclise was the artist; Richard Quain (1800–87) the author. A wealthy "professor of descriptive anatomy" at the University of London, and a Fellow of the Royal Society, Quain was born into a lower echelon of County Cork's upper crust (his father was said to be a "retired gentleman living upon a small estate"). Upon his arrival in London, he quickly got a leg up from his elder brother Jones Quain, who was already established as a medical professor at the university (Fig. 3.6). Over the course of his career, the younger Quain ascended to the top tier of British medicine, a status confirmed by his eventual assumption of the office of President of the Royal College of Surgeons (1868) and appointment to the position of "Surgeon Extraordinary" to Queen Victoria.

Said to be "strictly conservative" in politics and quarrelsome in temperament, Quain held that surgeons should be men of culture and discrimination, and not just crude mechanics of the body. And, as a gentleman of some means, he had the resources to subsidize the costly production of a super-sized beautifully printed atlas that would stand as an exemplary work of both high science *and* high artistry. Something extraordinary, a masterpiece, a monument. And designed to be so. Quain wasn't highly regarded as a surgeon or lecturer, and had published little of consequence.[31] So he aimed very high with the *Anatomy of the Arteries*. And maybe staked more on it than he could comfortably afford. Sales weren't good, perhaps because, unbound, the folio cost £12 10s (advertised as "an unusually low price," but still pricey).[32]

Like most of his contemporaries, Quain had a strong historicist sense of himself and his times, and saw the medical professions, with their commitment to scientific medicine, as vital contributors to the progress of civilization. In the preface, he situated *Anatomy of the Arteries* right beside the canon of eminent atlases, works by Haller, Scarpa and Tiedemann that stood high atop the hierarchy of medical publication.[33] Quain was bidding for entry into the pantheon of great medical publications and great medical men, a place in medical history, the kind of thing that historian Chris Haffenden calls a

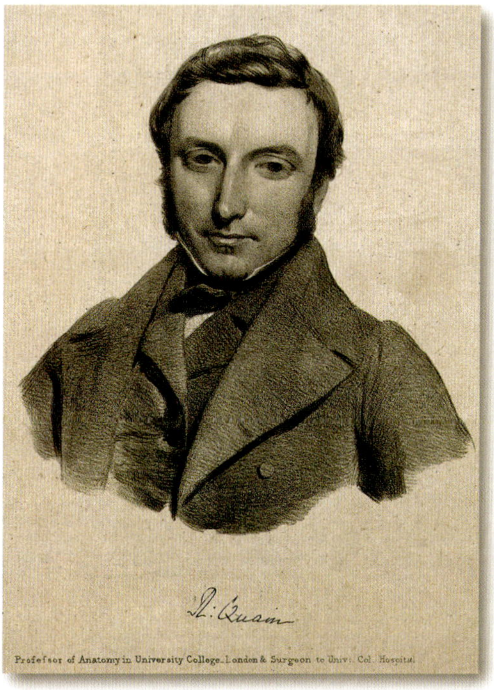

3.6 *Portrait of Richard Quain as a young man (London, c.1832). Lithography: T. Bridgford. 20 × 25 cm. Wellcome Collection.*

"self-monumentalizing," "self-historicizing" performance—a "strategy for posthumous recognition" but also for recognition in the here-and-now of the ongoing historical stream.[34] Quain perhaps also had a personal agenda, to outshine his brother Jones, who had not so long ago published his own elephant-folio *Series of Anatomical Plates in Lithography* (1836–42) (see Figs. 1.20–22). (According to historian W.F. Bynum, after 1831 "relations between the brothers were not cordial.")[35]

Joseph Maclise (1815–91), Quain's "friend and former pupil," was also born in County Cork.[36] Fifteen years younger, Maclise was the son of a Presbyterian Scottish regimental soldier turned tanner and shoemaker: humbler stock.[37]

But ambitious: his first course of study was with artist John Woodroffe's Anatomy School in Cork, where he studied both medical anatomy and "the Anatomy of Painting" (like his brother Daniel before him). Maclise then left home to study anatomy and surgery at the University of London, with Quain, Robert Liston, and Samuel Cooper, and then Paris.

Initially, he attracted notice as a radical in the testy debates over "transformism" (in the decades before Darwin entered the fray).[38] At the same time he established himself as a working surgeon and medical illustrator of uncommon ability.[39] In that early period, Quain acted as mentor and protector, a bond likely forged from their Cork connection. With the accolades garnered for the plates of the *Anatomy of the Arteries*, Maclise was raised up from Member to Fellow at the Royal College of Surgeons. From there he went on to produce his own atlases, most notably *Surgical Anatomy* (1st ed. 1851; 2d ed. 1856), which was also large format, though smaller than the Quain folio. *Surgical Anatomy* was a critical and even financial success—"surpassed the expectations of its author and publisher" by selling out the thousand copies of its first printing in only a few months—and earned Joseph some income (though not enough to live on). But after failing to get an appointment as "Assistant-surgeon" at University Hospital in London, Maclise failed to win any other hospital or university position.[40] His career ambitions, maybe his social aspirations, were thwarted.[41] Maclise never equaled the high professional standing of Quain or the high cultural standing of his brother Daniel.

Perhaps he consoled himself with the prospect of a place in medical history. "Surgeons, like great singers ... are ... the heroes of a moment," performers who flash only briefly in the spotlight, declares Balzac in an 1836 short story: "The glory of a surgeon is like that of an actor: ... their talent leaves no trace when they are gone." But an anatomical atlas does leave a trace. And an oversize, spectacularly beautiful atlas, a spectacularly memorable trace.[42]

2.3 Queer bedroom scenes

To get a fuller sense of Maclise's aesthetic maximalism and ambition, consider plate 62 of *The Anatomy of the Arteries*, depicting the operation for lithotomy (Fig. 3.7). It's all a bit much. Ostentatious virtuosity. Confrontational, fulsome representation of skin surfaces. An approach which Maclise justifies in later writings with a surgical rationale: "The surface of the living body is ... a map explanatory of the relative position of the organs beneath ..." The picturing of skin surfaces—even those not adjacent to, or systemically connected to, dissected areas—is "an aid," which furnishes "the memory with as clear an account of the structures" as if they were "perfectly translucent."[43]

That principle furnishes Maclise with something else: an opportunity to stage a queer anatomical bedroom scene. Plate 62 features a supine handsome young man, legs spread apart with exposed genitalia amidst rumpled sheets. The masculine body is placed in a female subject position—a pose typically used in obstetrical situations and often depicted in obstetrical illustration.[44]

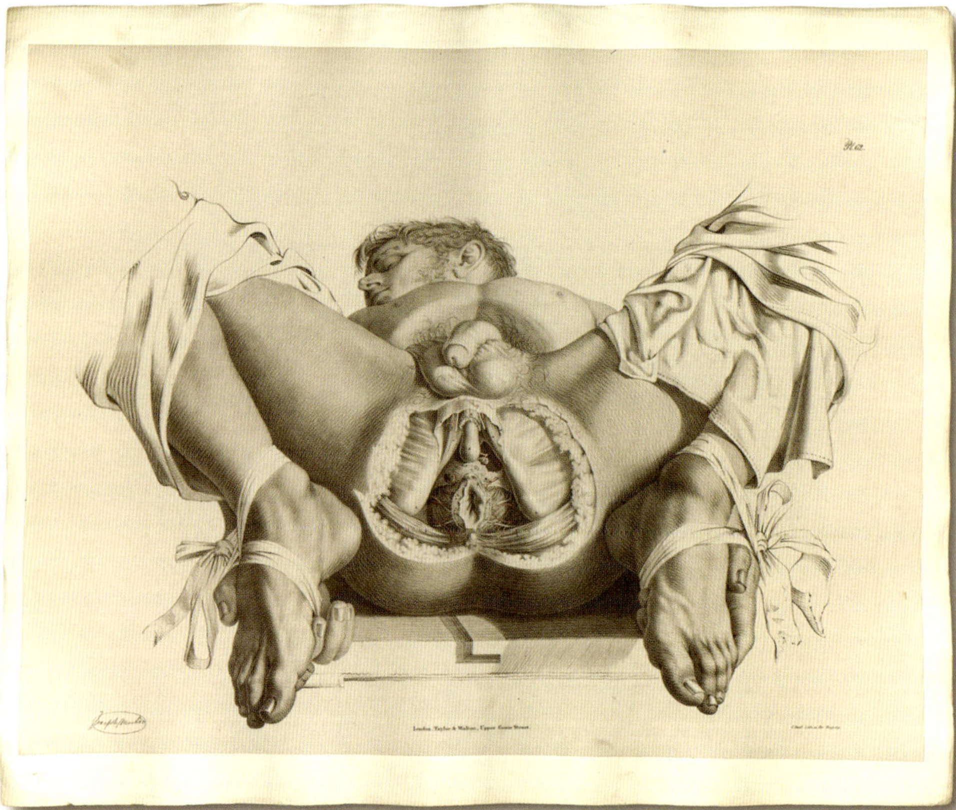

3.7 *"A deeper dissection of the Perineum. The Pudic artery and the artery of the Bulb are shown," Richard Quain,* The Anatomy of the Arteries of the Human Body *(London, 1844), pl. 62. Art: Joseph Maclise. Lithograph. 68 × 55 cm. Hagströmer Medico-Historical Library.*

The folds of fabric and naked body frame a dissection revealing at its center the open rectum. It is an arresting image (the second plate of a pair), an arresting arrangement, simultaneously intimate and theatrical. (The imperial folio format encourages Maclise to make horizontal compositions.)

A corpse obviously cannot resist, but the body in death becomes noncompliant ("dead weight," *rigor mortis*). And so to arrange the corpse in a position favorable to both dissection and the artist's view, the cadaver's arms are tied to his ankles. To our eyes the tying-up suggests coercion, but other details signal consent, as in consensual sexual bondage: the hands that hold the ankles are compliant. At the same time, the figure itself appears to be asleep or lying still in anticipation, an "animated" cadaver at rest. If the man is dead, why tie his hands? Is that really necessary?

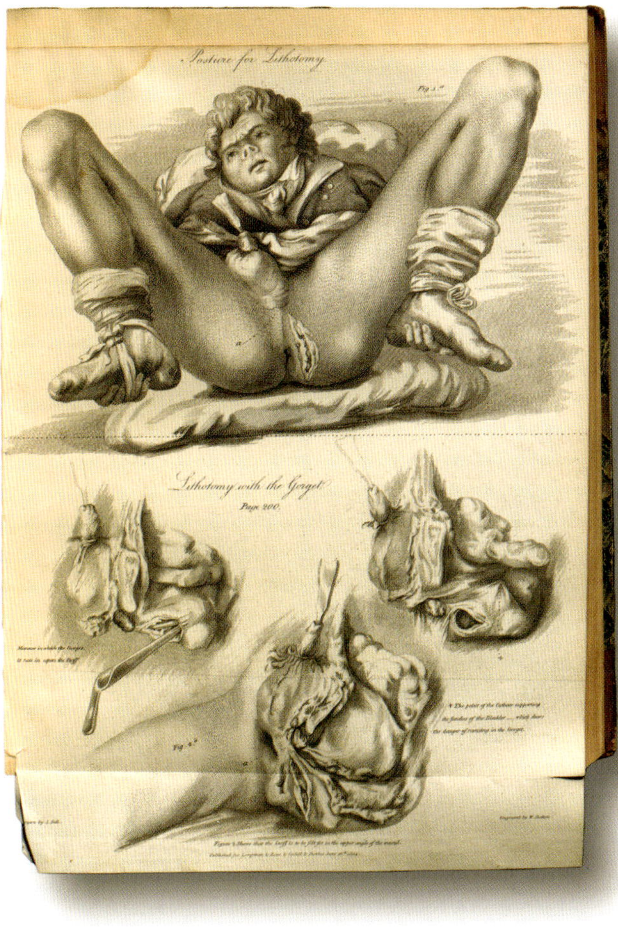

3.8 *"Posture for Lithotomy," John Bell,* Principles of Surgery *(3 vols.; Edinburgh, 1801–8; 2d ed., London, 1815), v. 2, fig. 1 (fold-out facing p. 200). Art: John Bell. 24 × 29 cm. Osler Library, McGill University.*

But the logic of the pose becomes apparent once you account for the illustration's iconographical origins and purpose—to show the anatomical structures and positioning a surgeon would need to know when "cutting for stone." Maclise's plate is likely inspired by or in dialogue with an illustration that appears in John Bell's *Principles of Surgery* (3 vols.; Edinburgh, 1801–8), an awkward engraving of a living patient waiting to undergo, and just having undergone, the cutting for stone (Fig. 3.8).[45]

Lithotomy was a difficult procedure: only the unremitting agony of a blockage could make someone so desperate as to submit to the risky and painful operation. The surgeon had to keep the patient's legs parted and fixed to suppress flinching, shuddering, and other involuntary movements. Hence the tying of hands and feet. Maclise's plate rehearses the operation on a cadaver; Bell's on a (reluctant, unhappy) patient whose penis is tied off and bagged, as it would have to be during surgery. The aesthetic differences between the Maclise and Bell images are telling. Bell makes no attempt at graceful rendering. The visual argument is straightforward, if a bit cartoonish. Undignified, slightly off in proportions and perspective, the image is not one of his best. Certainly not beautiful—a useful image.

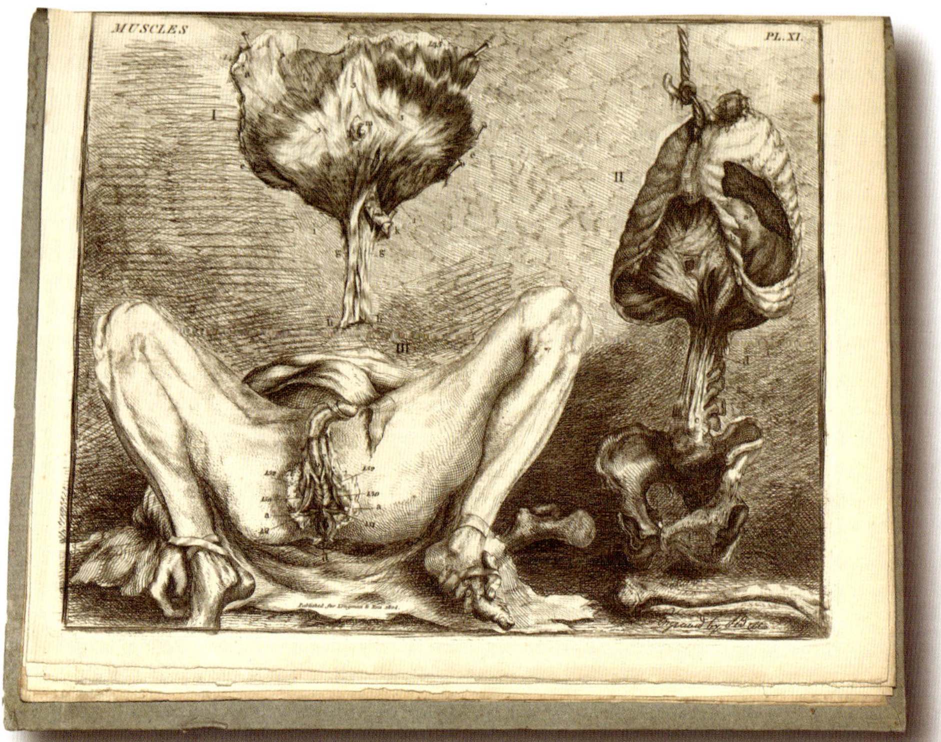

3.9 *"...the Diaphragm, and Parts of Generation, the hips and thighs being presented as in the operation of Lithotomy," John Bell,* Engravings of the Bones, Muscles and Joints... *(2d ed.; London, 1804), pl. 11. Art: John Bell. 26 × 21 cm. Hagströmer Medico-Historical Library.*

That fits with John Bell's persona as a gruff enemy of medical gentility and prettification. Roughly a decade earlier, Bell published *Engravings of the Bones, Muscles and Joints* (1794), which features flamboyantly ugly etchings of severed heads and mangled bodies abjectly plopped onto the dissecting table.[46] (The etching method encourages quick, sketchy lines, a kind of visual dynamism.) In the preface to that work, he deplores the fact that anatomists so often rely on professional artists whose "striving for elegance of form" introduces inaccuracies, falsifies the image. Like Maclise, John Bell was an anatomist, surgeon and artist—a brilliant artist, I think—but, unlike Maclise, an artist who never pretends to make works of Art. Bell's etchings are powerful, disturbing, deadly serious (yet morbidly playful). And among them is another illustration of the same subject, a harsh depiction of a very dead and entirely unanimated cadaver, trussed up and in the posture for lithotomy, without much ado, placed unceremoniously underneath an unpretty dissected-out diaphragm nailed to the wall, and next to a torso hanging from a rope (both torso and diaphragm are unrelated to the lithotomy operation) (Fig. 3.9).[47]

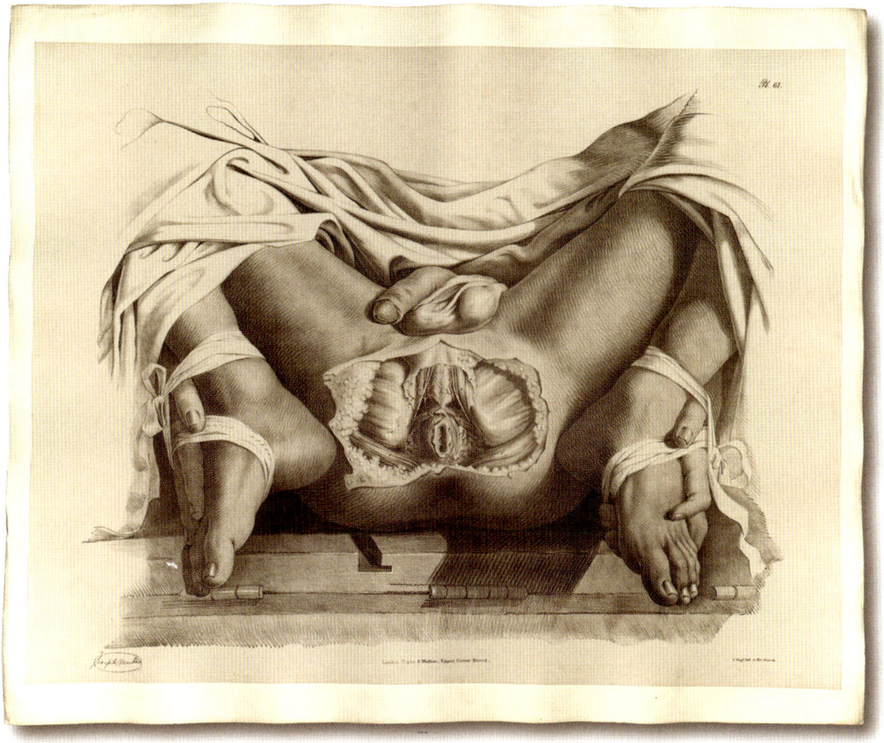

3.10 *"A view of the Arteries and other structures displayed in superficial dissection of the Perineum," Richard Quain,* The Anatomy of the Arteries of the Human Body *(London, 1844), pl. 61. Art: Joseph Maclise. Lithograph. 68 × 55 cm. Hagströmer Medico-Historical Library. "Male perineum, anus, pelvic floor, shown in situ. Penis and scrotum shown. Male cadaver, inferior view."*

The contrast between Bell's 1794 etching and Maclise is even more pronounced in Maclise's plate 61, the first of the pair on the anatomy of the perineum and rectum (Fig. 3.10). Which, contravening Bell, manages to combine great "elegance of form" with meticulous rendering, verisimilitude. Neither Bell nor Maclise show the cadaver's face, but Maclise decks out his subject with drapery around the genitals and dissected area. From the attention devoted to the carefully rendered folds of cloth that frame the anatomical object—echoed by the delicate folds of the testicular sac—it is abundantly evident that Maclise aspires to make Art in the grand tradition—even in the picturing of this unlikely subject.[48] Encouraged by the technical possibilities of lithography, which allow the artist to show subtle gradations of tone, Maclise orchestrates the contrast between surface textures, cloth, skin and the anatomical rupture—the flesh torn away to reveal the "superficial dissection." (Other plates show "deep structures.")[49] And somehow, without any theatrical contrivance, brings the dissected cadaver to life.

The feeling is grand, intimate, and immersive—the artist's private view projected onto a large sheet of paper, and thereby transformed into a printed monument. Maclise aims for a heedless transcendence, entirely sequestered from the growing debate over whether beauty was antagonistic to the goal of accuracy in science (an argument never entertained in Maclise's printed commentaries).[50] And utterly indifferent to the policing of representational boundaries that protect the category of Beauty from things like exposed rectums, testicles, viscera and anatomical destruction. The rendering of anatomical rupture, violation, and destruction with sensuality and grace makes a scene that looks real *and* beautiful, which is to say true.

A "technique of echoing bodily forms in drapery and upholstery," art historian Mechthild Fend notes, was "often used in eighteenth-century erotic art, in paintings by Fragonard" and in "Boucher's 1745 *Odalisque* where the forms of the reclining nude … are multiplied in the plush fabrics."[51] In both his dissection and his arrangement of reclining nudes (in plates 61 and 62) (Figs. 3.10, 3.7), Maclise plays with the difference between surface and underlying layers. Hardness, in the hardness of bone and muscle and the wooden table. Softness, in the smooth textures of skin and cloth. The approach is sculptural and tactile.[52] Maclise exquisitely renders skin contours and surfaces, especially around the area of the anatomical opening, which softens (feminizes?) the undressed masculine subject. His pencil is a caress, almost an invitation to touch (what cannot be touched). (And what of his scalpel?) It's as though "the alluring surface … 'solicits touch … as it prohibits it'."[53] Fend elsewhere suggests that anatomy is an unveiling and the skin a veil, "the symbolic removal of which results in the revelation of an 'inner truth' or essence." But Maclise reverses that. His anatomy dresses the body in sumptuous, silky hairless skin, stages a display of utter nakedness.[54] Would it be going too far to suggest that the deliberate stripping of skin is an echo of the stripping of clothing that precedes sexual intercourse? And that the revelation of "inner truth," anatomical unveiling, stands in for the revelation of hidden desire, an unmasking? … Desire held in an artful suspension of elements …

"Composition" was then a core subject of the art academy curriculum, and a key concern in the mid-Victorian art-critical, art-historical writings of Ruskin and Hazlitt. Maclise has a very compositional eye. The dissection of the perineum in plates 61 (Fig. 3.10) and 62 (Fig. 3.7) is a study in practical anatomy. But also a study in composition: that complexly arranged but partly symmetrical dissected subject draped in contingently random folds of cloth, decorated with fulsome detail up to the very edges of the drawing, against the surrounding air of the white page. The pulled-back sheet (in plate 61) and resting head and chest (in 62), the exposed thighs, penis, testicles, shadowy buttocks, and bound feet and hands: all

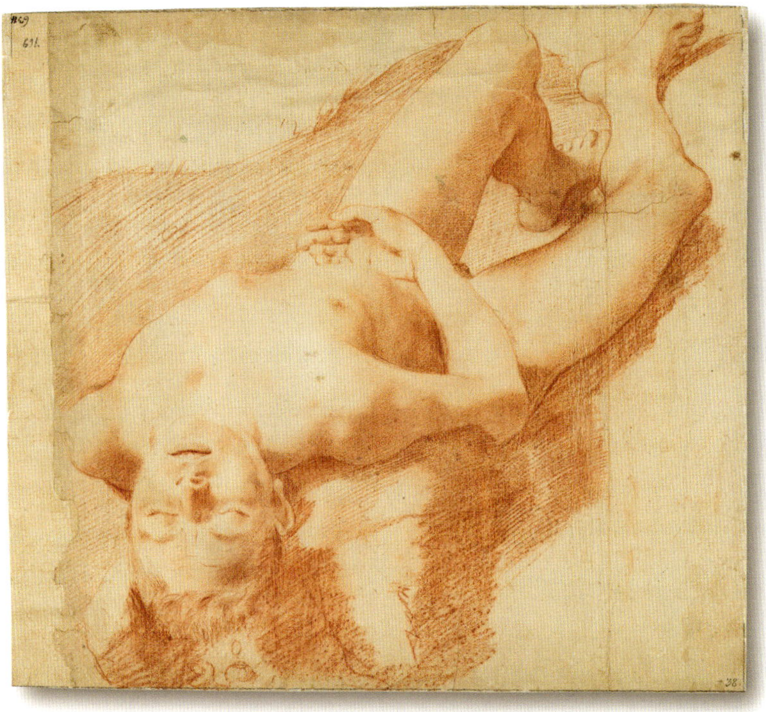

3.11 *Annibale Carracci, Figure study, nude (c.1584). Red chalk on cream paper. 36 × 40 cm. Photo: Cecilia Heisser. National Museum, Sweden. © Cecilia Heisser/Nationalmuseum 2015.*

combine to make a richly complex set of frames around the peeled rectum. At the same time, the folds of cloth partly covering the knees and thighs are nearly a landscape, almost geological. Stepping back to consider Maclise's lithotomies as a diptych, it's hard to say which part makes the strongest claim on the viewer, the rectum? Penis and testicles? The hands bandaged to the feet? the handsome face (in plate 62)? Or the mountainous horizon of rippled cloth (in 61)?

Maclise is pulling out all the stops, staging a performance in two iconographic domains: practical surgical illustration (as in Bell's "Cutting for stone") and the figure study for pleasure (as in any number of drawings by Annibale Carracci, such as the drawing above) (Fig. 3.11).[55]

2.4 Irrelevant penises (a gallery)

If the compositional talent and draughtmanship are extraordinary, so is Maclise's interest in the male nether regions. Is there another nineteenth-century artist who so lovingly and persuasively renders the scrotum, testicles, and penis? An uncovered penis appears 27 times in the *Anatomy of the Arteries*, often in scenes where it is irrelevant to the anatomical region demonstrated. In contrast, only one dissected female body appears among the folio's 87 plates: plate 59, which resembles plate 60 in every particular, with one signal difference: Maclise covers the undissected female genital region with cloth.[56] Was that because representational conventions concerning female genital modesty were more powerful than those that regulated the male? Or because Maclise took special pleasure in representing the male genitals?

We began our discussion of Maclise with his self-aware presentation of "The superior mesenteric artery" (Fig. 3.5) and its provocative male genital. But that plate is merely the most extraordinary of a series of plates demonstrating the anatomy of the viscera—a gallery of six sequential dissections, each featuring an upright headless figure facing the reader with penis hanging down. In each plate Maclise retains the irrelevant penis but excises other irrelevant parts of the body (the face, the head), except in two plates which also show irrelevant hands. A gallery of dissections, enfolding a gallery of dicks. Different shapes and sizes, some fully sheathed, some with the tip of the penis visible (Figs. 3.12–17).

That special interest didn't wane in Maclise's subsequent work. The 1856 edition of *Surgical Anatomy* shows the penis 43 times in 52 plates, sometimes at the margins, but often front and center (Fig. 3.18). Which undoubtedly reflects Maclise's interest as a practicing surgeon in regions where hernias, stones, and fistulas manifest, but also perhaps a special interest in young men, masculine bodies, and male genitalia. (Women, of course, also get hernias, stones, and fistulas. Yet Maclise only shows female genitals twice in *Surgical Anatomy* and only briefly discusses operations on women.) Other celebrated mid-century British anatomical atlases—the large-format lithographic atlases of George Viner Ellis (a former student of Quain) and Francis Sibson—demonstrate aesthetic virtues and showmanship.[57] But don't come close to achieving Maclise's intimacy, grace, perspectival depth, and erotic valences. More to the point: while confining themselves to mostly male cadavers, they avoid the groin. No penises appear, as the main topic or on the periphery. No contemporary British anatomist dares to gaze upon the groin as Maclise does. His penchant for drawing male genitalia is utterly unique.

3.12–17 *A gallery of dissections, a gallery of dicks (close-ups). Richard Quain,* The Anatomy of the Arteries of the Human Body *(London, 1844), pls. 49, 51, 52, 55, 53, 54. Lithographs. Art: Joseph Maclise. 68 × 55 cm. Hagströmer Medico-Historical Library.*

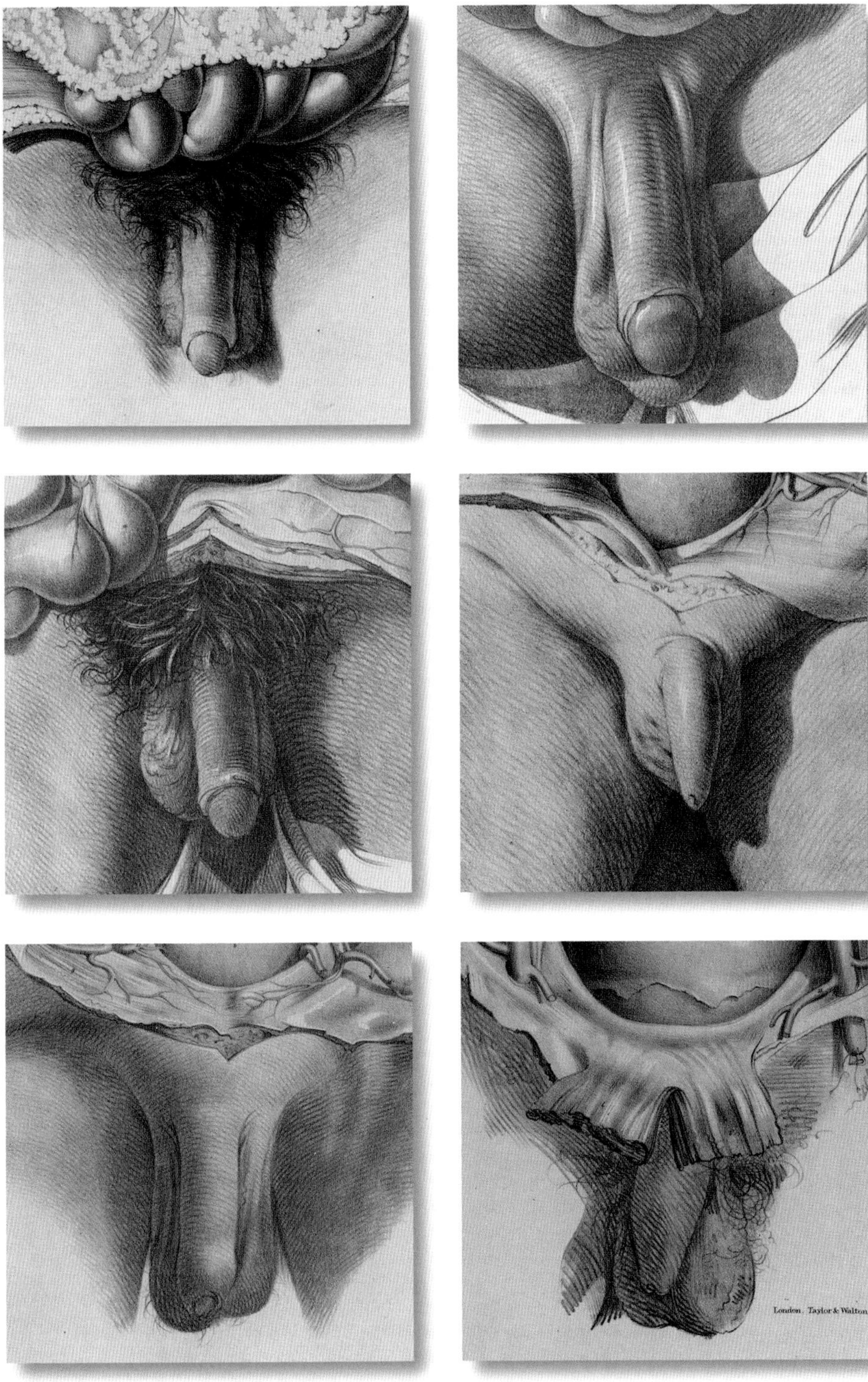
London. Taylor & Walton

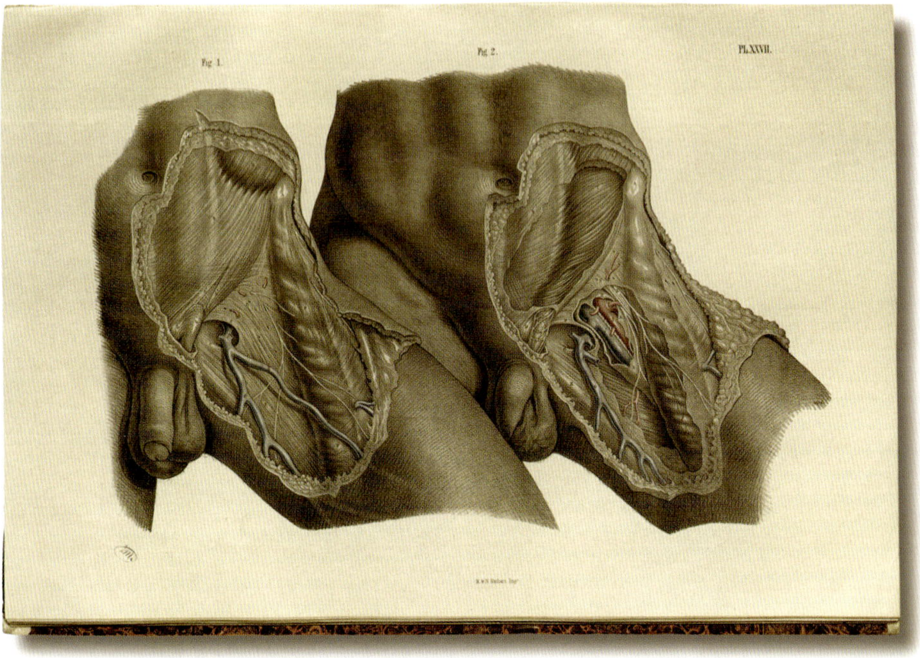

3.18 *"The surgical dissection of the superficial and deep structures of the inguino-femoral region," Joseph Maclise,* Surgical Anatomy *(London, 1856), pl. 27. Colored lithograph. 36 × 53 cm. Hagströmer Medico-Historical Library. "Hernial protrusions are very liable to occur at the groin."*

Let's stop here and take a breath. By now, dear reader, you may be wondering: So many dick-pics? Is that really necessary? *And I'm worrying:* My focus on penises, is it unseemly, infantile, impolitic, excessive or, a case of cherry-picking? *I blush to think of it (a blush generated out of an imagined dialog between me and my readers, so it's just me shaming myself). But hold on: let's take that discomfort to be a kind of "resistance" and analyze it. Which is what Leo Steinberg does in* The Sexuality of Christ in Renaissance Art and in Modern Oblivion, *an entire book on the representation of Christ's penis in early modern religious art. According to Steinberg, the poses and scenes depicted in Renaissance paintings, engravings and sculptures were deliberately and carefully chosen.*[58] *Everything represented there was purposeful and of theological significance. And therefore, art historians have been wrong to "tactfully" skip over Jesus's very visible penis (*"ostentatio genitalium"*), while comprehensively analyzing every other iconographic element.*

Steinberg argues that the reluctance of scholars, theologians and lay viewers to reflect upon the treatment of Christ's penis is the centuries-long legacy of the suppression of images and views of the male (and female) genital in public life. The numerous depictions of the infant Christ's penis—often shown being fondled or intently gazed upon—"remained unseen" (uncommented on) by art historians "because it was improper to notice and could not be conceptualized without shame."[59] *And, after Christ's penis lost its theological salience in the Reformation and Counter-Reformation, when a kind of panic took hold, the custodians of the art displayed in churches, museums and palaces ordered that penises be covered over with loincloths and other devices. So literally unseen. In our times, public views of the penis are also regulated, by statutory law, custom and written rules (don't do it on Facebook!), and by chiding, giggles, smirks, squirming avoidance, and tacit reprimand. If we deplore crude censorship, we still implicitly mark the borderlands of polite discourse with our reticence. Discretion. The refusal of discourse. Shame. Which in turn provokes resistance: coded or outright defiance, in the form of pornography, affront, queer expression. And, sometimes, insistent presentation in scholarship and cultural critique, such as may be found in Steinberg, and* Queer Anatomies. *So with that justification, let's hit play and get back to Maclise and his gaze upon the penis ...*

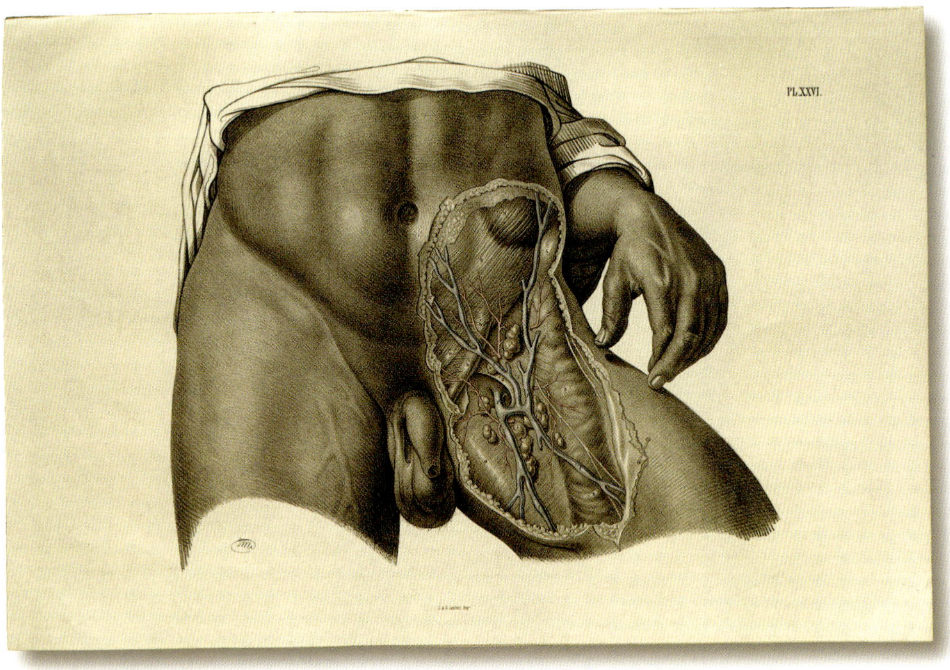

3.19 *"The surgical dissection of the superficial and deep structures of the inguino-femoral region," Joseph Maclise,* Surgical Anatomy *(London, 1856), pl. 26. Colored lithograph. 36 × 53 cm. Hagströmer Medico-Historical Library.*

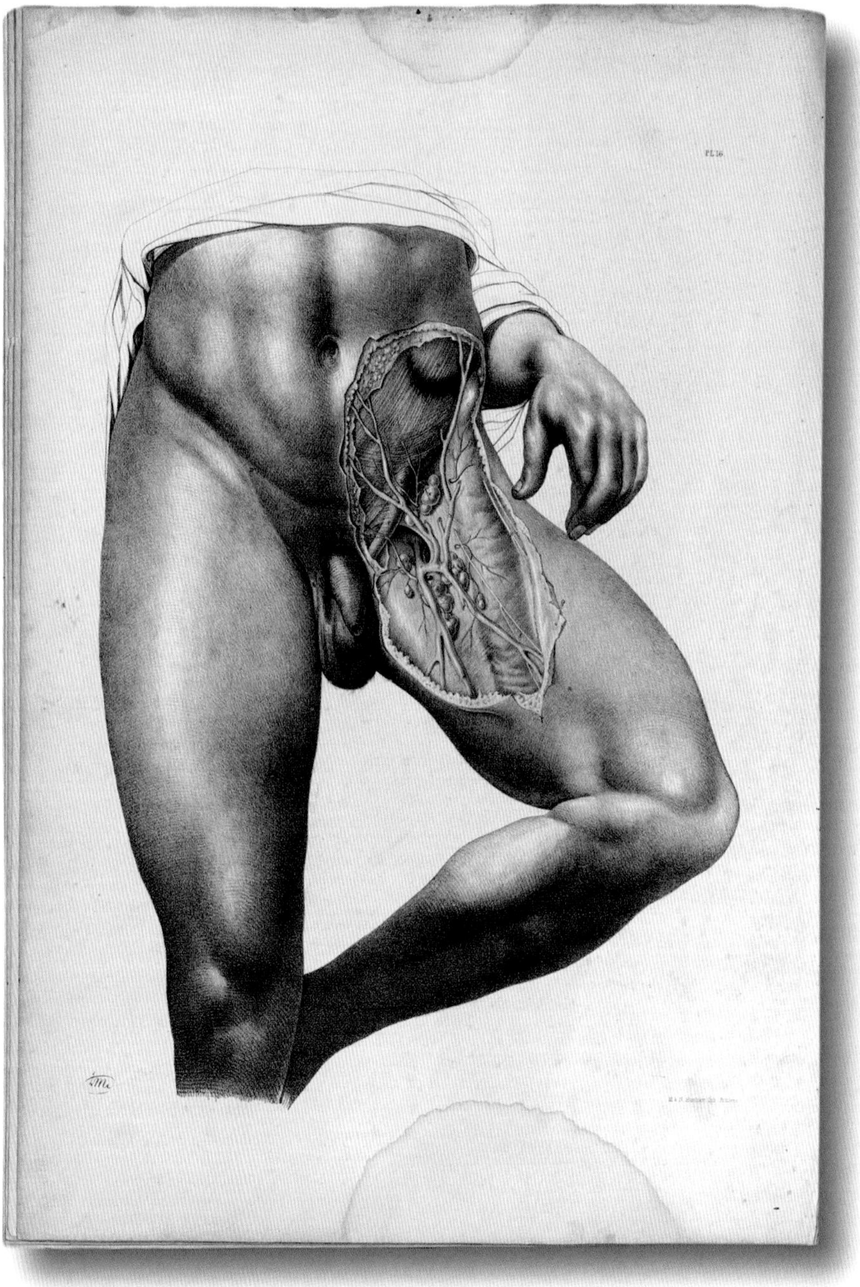

3.20 *"The surgical dissection of the superficial and deep structures of the inguino-femoral region," Joseph Maclise,* Surgical Anatomy *(1st ed., London, 1851), pl. 16. Colored lithograph. 54 × 38 cm. Wellcome Collection.*

2.5 Touching representation

But *gaze* doesn't capture the affective power of Maclise's visual presentation. For that, we need to return to touch, and the representation of hands touching skin and skin-to-skin contact. In plate 26 (Fig. 3.19), that sensual hand, gently grazing the outside of the thigh! Is that caress just another proxy for Maclise's desirous touch? Does it also double for the artist's *touche* with crayon, pencil, and brush?[60] In the 1851 first edition, Maclise shows a

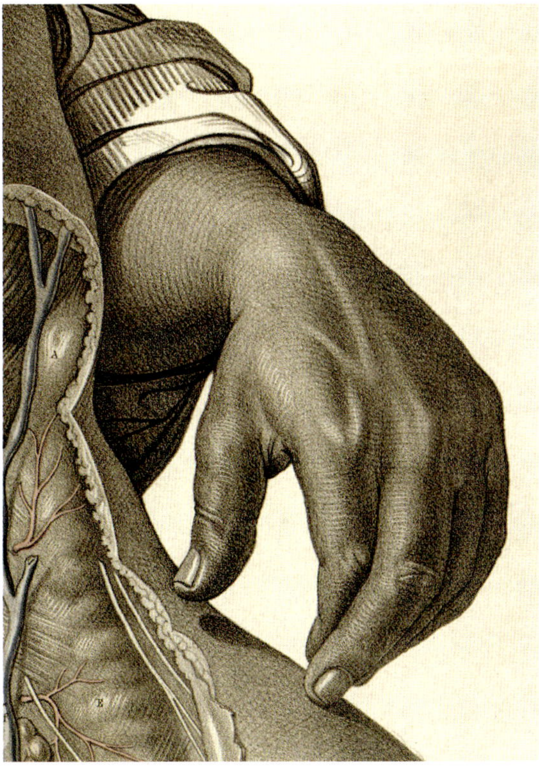

3.21 *Detail, "The surgical dissection of the superficial and deep structures of the inguino-femoral region." Joseph Maclise,* Surgical Anatomy *(London, 1856), pl. 26. Colored lithograph. Hagströmer Medico-Historical Library.*

bit more (Fig. 3.20). Below the shaved genital region, the subject's left leg appears to be touching the right leg, just in back of the knee, as if scratching an itch or performing a Scottish country dance or balletic *cou-de-pied*. Look again at plate 27, which initiates a small series of side-by-side dissections (Fig. 3.18). The penis on the right appears to brush the thigh of the figure on the left. It's rare to see two cadavers touch in anatomical illustration. This kind of touching is rarer still.

And once again, a bit much. Ostentatious virtuosity. But lest we (or Maclise's mid-Victorian readers) get carried away, Maclise offers a surgical rationale for his penchant for giving fulsome representation to skin: "The surface of the living body is ... a map explanatory of the relative position of the organs beneath ..." The depiction of skin surfaces—even skin far distant from the location of the surgical cut—is "an aid," furnishes the surgeon's "memory with as clear an account of the structures" as if they were "perfectly translucent."[61]

Yet the sumptuous display of skin does more than that. "Images of skin," Mechthild Fend reminds us, "can recall a double sensation of touching and being touched."[62] That happens in the positioning of the figures, but touching can also be discerned in the textures of the illusionistic rendering: light, shadow and surfaces created by line drawing. The fine cross-hatching itself records the caressing movement of Maclise's hand with pencil and pen on paper and then crayon on stone—and mimetically suggests the caressing movement of the hand of Maclise, the anatomist, the surgeon, the man, on the bodies of his subjects. Another echo: look closer at the hand in Maclise's plate 26 (Figs. 3.19, 3.21). The index finger seems to caress the middle finger. A caress within a caress. Exquisite sensation.

The trope of the visible brushstroke or drawn line as the record of a caress of the surface of the paper or canvas—and, by analogy, a caress of the body of the subject—was a part of the rhetoric of eighteenth- and nineteenth-century art discourse.[63] And by such means, Maclise's images manifest erotic valences as much in the representation of skin—and sensate touching fingers—as in the representation of the male genital. In his commentary on the anatomy of the hand, Maclise praises the hand's agency and powers, its "perfect ... prehensile and tactile functions": This "beautiful and valuable member" is "the material symbol of the immaterial spirit," "has a language of its own," is "the autograph of mind."[64] Maclise orchestrates a haptic imaginary in words, image, and line. (And if hand is an "autograph of mind", what is on Maclise's mind when he autographs the page and cadaver with *his* drawing and cutting and touching hand?)

Critics mostly loved Maclise's artwork. A reviewer in the *Edinburgh Medical & Surgical Journal*, commenting on the first three installments of *Surgical Anatomy*, singled out Maclise's "anatomical knowledge," "talents as a draughtsman," "great fidelity and accuracy," his "very correct and beautiful view" of dissected subjects in "the best and most effective positions ... before the eye of the beholder" so as to display them in an "impressive light."[65] But images like plate 27 (Fig. 3.18) push the limits. One reviewer deplored "the crowding of two anatomical figures on the same page." Was that criticism a displaced expression of discomfort with the erotic implications of such "crowding"? (And really, plate 27 doesn't look especially crowded. Given Maclise's compositional gifts, his plates rarely do.) With less space on the page, the smaller format 1851 Philadelphia edition separates the two figures, places them on separate pages.[66] (That edition, redrawn by an uncredited artist, closely follows the London edition, with some loss of detail and nuance, and, as we will later see, a few significant editorial changes.) In a larger format, it's economical to put more than one figure on the same page, and more pedagogically effective—the close pairing makes the comparison easier to see—but that tactical decision also becomes an opportunity to stage a teasing contact between bodies.

The convergence of artist's *touche* and anatomist's touch, those sensuous methods of studying bodies, was an oft-recited topos of art criticism and commentary. According to Fend, the eighteenth-century French portraitist Louis Tocqué, in an essay on painting, described how "the brush penetrates the body like an anatomist's knife":

> Rummaging through the inner parts while painting, the artist seems to feel his way with his brush, gaining insight into anatomical knowledge. This sensible brush leads the painter to "discover the muscles neatly," to organise the amorphous flesh, and enables him to represent the body with ease and precision simultaneously.[67]

But Maclise also works the analogy in reverse. Like a pen, the scalpel makes a composition out of the body, turns the body into a sketch, carves the body into a sculpture. Which are connected: the sketching of classical and Renaissance sculpture was a key practice in eighteenth- and nineteenth-century art pedagogy. Maclise is piling on, pleasuring himself with his double role as artist and anatomist. So, in *Anatomy of the Arteries*, in some plates,

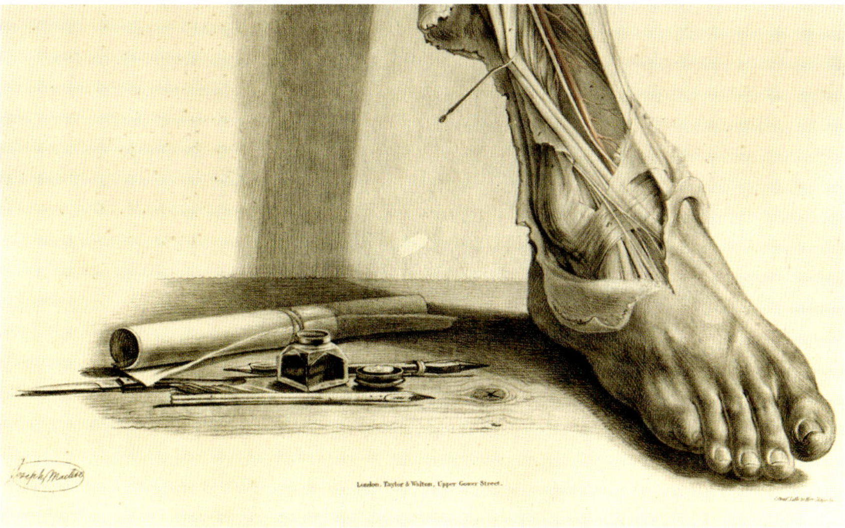

3.22 *Detail, "The anterior tibial artery," Richard Quain,* The Anatomy of the Arteries of the Human Body *(London, 1844), pl. 82. Art: Joseph Maclise. Lithograph. Hagströmer Medico-Historical Library.*

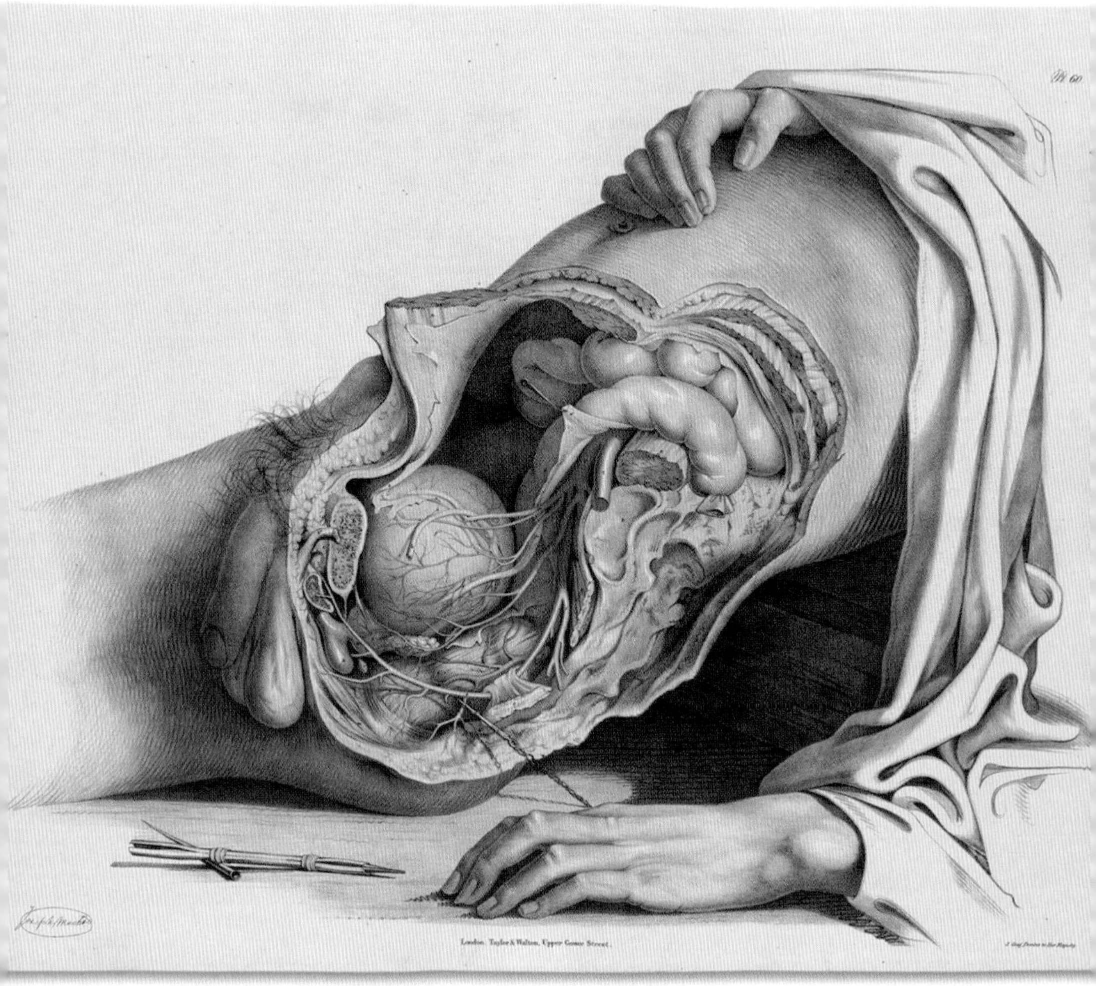

3.23 *"The arteries of the pelvis of the male," Richard Quain,* The Anatomy of the Arteries of the Human Body *(London, 1844), pl. 60. Art: Joseph Maclise. Lithograph. 68 × 55 cm. Wellcome Collection.*

Maclise depicts within the image the tools of the artist's trade: inkwell, paper, and pen (Figs. 3.22–23). And in still others, the tools of dissection and surgery: scalpels, knives, hooks, etc. And in a few images: both kinds of tools. Scalpel, pencil, chisel, burin, crayon, brush were, as Anthea Callen notes, "symbolically interchangeable" delineators, each instrument deployed by its practitioners with "manual skill, expertise, and dexterity," to instigate a "revelation" or visualization or scientific understanding.[68] And to instigate a revelation of feelings not quite defined, by drawing lines and making figures. Which are the feelings of Maclise the man as well as Maclise the artist. Because Maclise makes the kind of picture that art historian Victor Stoichita terms a "self-aware image."[69] Even as he lurks in the wings... always off-stage... in the closet?... Maclise can't help but point to himself and his work.

2.6 Cascading rhymes

Plate 60 is another *tour de force* in deep-focus, high-definition, illusionistic perspective (Fig. 3.23). The layered folds of fabric, pulled back like a curtain, rhyme with the deep and disruptive multi-layered dissection. The curvature of the anatomical cut and folded intestines rhyme with the curvature of the folded cloth. And with the penis (in the shadows) and testicles (curving the other way). Cascading rhymes. The cadaver's left hand seems to be crawling toward the pen (doubling as a scalpel) as the right hand emerges from the folds of the sheet, crawling toward the anatomical opening, feeling its own torso ... We're looking through Maclise's self-aware eyes, witnessing the anatomical scene he has choreographed, sharing his immersive gaze.

A deep, almost entranced, subjectivity corresponds to a panoptical penetrative objectivity. Maybe this dissected body "stares" back.[70] Not with eyes. (It has none.) But with hands, fingers ... There is, of course, no haptic equivalent for staring back, but Maclise's cadaver seems to grope ... touch ... feel itself ... reach out ... There's a residue of intentionality, the body willing itself to live, on the dissecting table and the page. Those riotous organs spilling out of the opened cavity, and those fingering hands ...

Contrast all that to the hands in N.-H. Jacob's illustrations (Figs. 3.1–3, 3.24). Which also evoke touch sensation, induce a kind of haptic empathy. But empathy with the hand of the surgeon and not the surgical object. Jacob brilliantly conveys the feeling of touching the body of the patient or cadaver. And models step-by-step surgical technique (solo and team). Shows where the surgeon's hand and fingers should go. How to hold the surgical instrument. How to cut through skin, bones, eyes, tongues, fingers, genitals. (Difficult to look at!) And how to open, hold, and close the wound, and sew it back together. Jacob's hands also do pedagogical work: they focus the reader's attention, direct the reader's eyes. Purposeful.

The hands in Maclise's plate 60 (and plate 51) do nothing of the sort. They are irrelevant, unpedagogical, unindexical. If anything, they distract the reader from surgical and anatomical business—and go unmentioned in captions and commentaries. Maclise presents many hands (a few purposefully depicting the anatomy of the hand) but never the surgeon's hand.

Distraction, of course, is a key technique of stage magic and mesmerism. Hypnotists rely on our habit of following the indexical hand to induce a trance that allows them to control the consciousness of a hypnotic subject. Are Maclise's cadaveric hands doing something similar? Is he entrancing us?

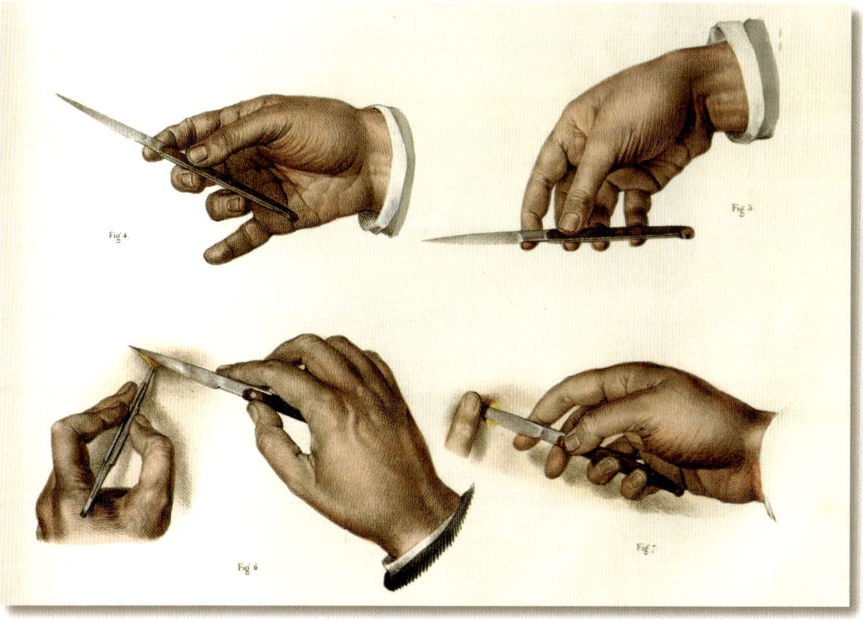

3.24 *Detail, N.-H. Jacob, J.-B.-M. Bourgery & Claude Bernard,* Traité complet de l'anatomie de l'homme, *v. 6, pl. 15 (Paris, 1866–71). Chromolithograph. 33 × 43 cm. Hagströmer Medico-Historical Library.*

Or entrancing himself, putting himself under with a bit of auto-suggestion? If the hands in plate 60 aren't a proxy for the surgical hand, then for what? The scene of plate 60 is oddly private, personal. Recruited to feel the feeling hands of an anatomical subject, the reader enters a space where Maclise's flashing desire momentarily becomes palpable. It's a perverse induction that transforms the reader into a more-than-eye witness. Those tracing fingers animate both reader and cadaver, and Maclise the artist.

This isn't gimmickry, but stylized realism, accomplished visual rhetoric, trained and redolent of the academy and the atelier. Three or four registers of beauty overlay each other: The beauty of the subject's hands (and genitals?). The beauty of the arrangement of the scene. The beauty of the dissection (which, any anatomist can tell you, has aesthetic dimensions). The beauty of the drawing and lithography. Taken together, they do more than merely persuade the viewer that the scene is true. The sharp focus and crisp details—the penis, testicles and scraggly pubic hair, the folds of cloth—the dynamism of the dissection—effect a merger, the melding of viewer, artist, and anatomical subject.

A queer convergence which demonstrates Maclise's anatomical *and* artistic powers. Which are not entirely separate matters. The shining beauty, precision, detail of the artist's rendering are distinguishing marks of *anatomical* excellence, as they had been for the grand productions of Maclise's eminent anatomical forebears: Bidloo, Haller, Scarpa, William Hunter, Tiedemann (all cited in Quain's preface to the folio), and the *Traité complet* of Bourgery and Jacob (uncited, but lurking in the background). Remember also the super-size format: the *Anatomy of the Arteries* is an "imperial" folio, life-size, 1:1 scale, printed on expensive paper—of a measure and quality that bespeaks the aspiration to create a masterpiece.[71]

Within such grand aspirations there was room for aesthetic variability. The conventions of anatomical illustration permitted a variety of approaches so long as the dissection and objects dissected were in some way true and legible. Maclise's approach depended upon impeccable draughtsmanship, compositional effects both subtle and heroic, fine imprinting of image on paper (also impeccable), and mastery of anatomical dissection. Overdetermined artfulness; artfulness in every possible register. Which attests to the authority of Quain and his protégé, their knowledge of anatomical principles, their privileged access to prodigious quantities of the best quality anatomical "material" (not always easily available), and slashing command of the dissecting knife. By those measures, Maclise and Quain together claimed a place in the grand anatomical tradition, the canon.

But Maclise had two canons in mind. The composition of the scene and its constituent parts and devices, the play of light and shadow, the big gestures and small flourishes (and even the flourish of the artist's signature), attest to the caressing brilliance and authority of Maclise's drawing hand and eye—and mark Maclise's filiation with the grand tradition of figure drawing so prized by connoisseurs: Art! A filiation that was his singular and private possession, not shared with Quain. And not shared with those eminent anatomical predecessors who had to negotiate the working process and results with an artist who was a collaborator: Bidloo with artist Gerard De Lairesse; William Hunter with artist Jan Van Rymsdyk; Bourgery with Jacob; etc. In those canonical atlases, there could be tensions between artist and anatomist, not just over terms of employment, but over terms of representation, delineation, lighting, texture, detail. If we credit historians Lorraine Daston, Peter Galison and Carin Berkowitz, there was a struggle for control between artist and anatomist—between Art and Nature.[72] A topic which William Hunter discoursed upon in his preface to the *Anatomy of the Gravid Uterus* (1774), and John Bell in his preface to his *Engravings Explaining the Anatomy of the Bones, Muscles, and Joints* (1794). Artists, they complain, were prone to introduce error and irrelevant material, and to beautify. (William Cheselden alludes to the problem in *Osteographia* [1733], when he depicts himself using a *camera obscura* as a guarantor of his atlas's faithfulness to nature, and points to his authority over his artists: "I always directed ..." And, as we have seen, he also took lessons in drawing.)[73]

The Bell brothers, John and Charles, circumvented that problem by making their own preliminary illustrations and etchings (a technique well-suited for quick impression), rendered with a plain-speaking provocative pictorial naturalism. In words and images, they mounted a contrarian critique of aestheticism and prettification, deplored the tendency of artists to strive "for elegance of form." And the images that they made affected a deliberate sketchiness, even inelegance, violated classical ideals of corporeal proportion, represented the ugliness and monstrosity of injurious wounds, decayed flesh, and anatomical mutilation.[74] The object, they argued, should be represented on the page as the anatomist's eye encounters it, without polishing or repair. The ugliness, the immediacy, performs their commitment to the real.

The Bells controlled image production and reproduction, with the ambition of being "true to nature." And so did Maclise, who performed and arranged his own dissections, depicted them in the idiom of realism, and made his own lithographic plates. But Maclise undertook a brilliant impossible synthesis: anatomy raised to aesthetic heights; drawing raised to anatomical heights. Beauty performed Maclise's commitment to the real. If there was plenty of mutilation, it was meticulously and beautifully rendered, with plenty of "elegance of form" and even some play. Maclise aimed to meet the highest standards of medical publication, but also the aesthetic standards of the "academicians" (formally trained fine artists) and collectors. Though he was aware of and admired Charles Bell—and paid homage to him in plate 65 of the *Anatomy of the Arteries*—he didn't imitate him (Fig. 3.25).[75]

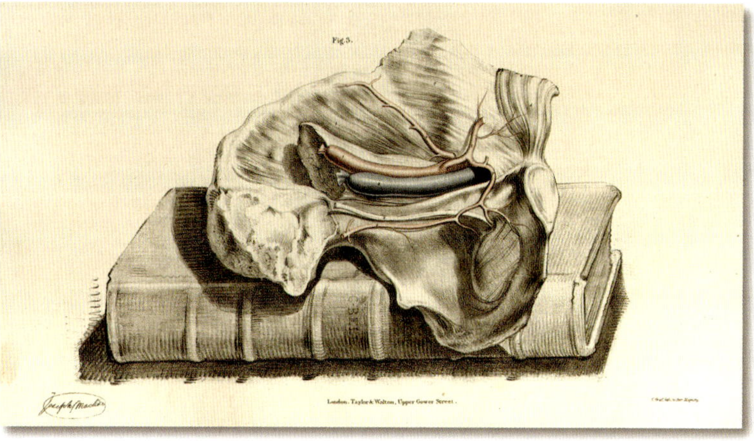

3.25 *A few of Maclise's plates feature sketches—though nothing as sketchy as the sketchiness of a Charles Bell etching. Here, placed underneath some sketches, Maclise pays homage by placing a specimen on a book with Bell's name on the spine. Richard Quain,* The Anatomy of the Arteries of the Human Body *(London, 1844), pl. 65. Colored lithograph. 67.5 × 55 cm. Hagströmer Medico-Historical Library.*

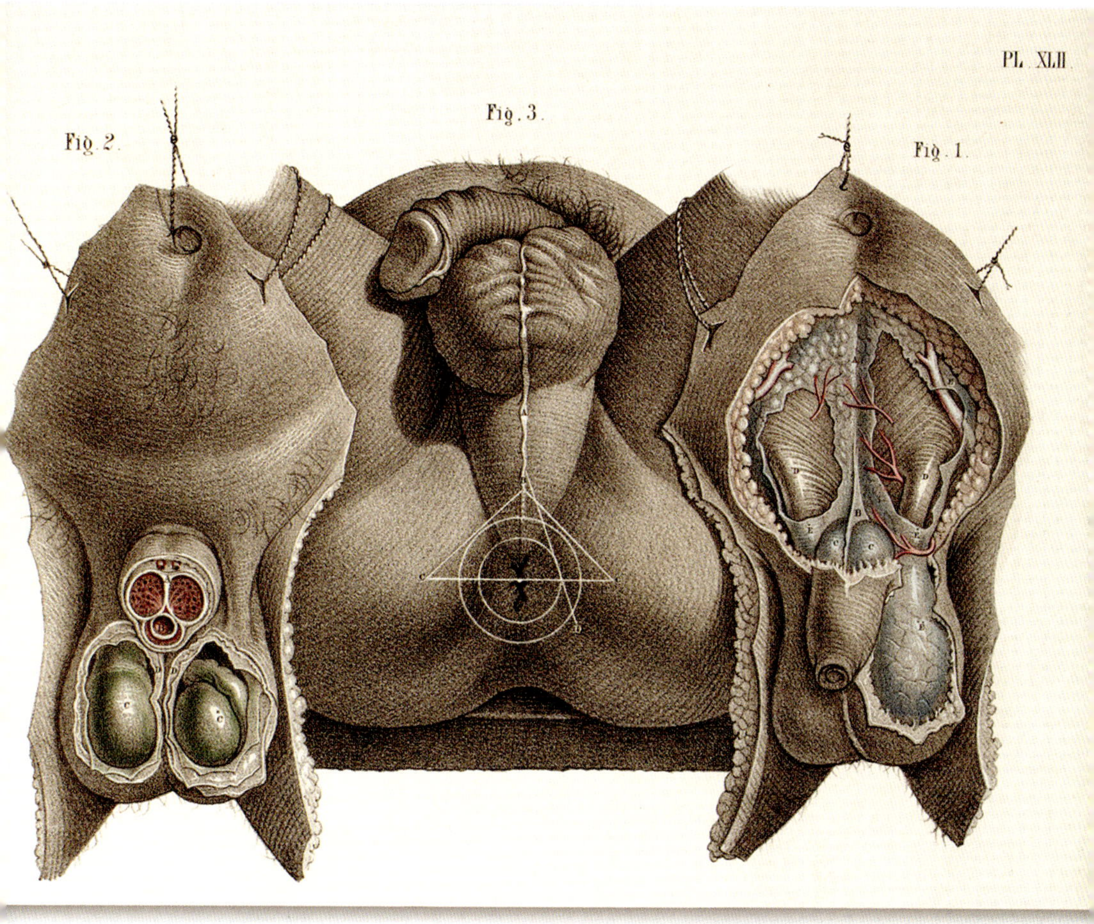

3.26 *Joseph Maclise, "The surgical dissection of the superficial and deep structures of the male perineum, lithotomy, etc.,"* Surgical Anatomy *(London, 1856), pl. 42 top, figs. 1–3. Colored lithograph. Hagströmer Medico-Historical Library. "The median line of the body is marked as the situation where the opposite halves unite and constitute a perfect symmetrical figure."*

2.7 The anus compared

In Maclise's concentration on the nether regions, he does not neglect the anus. Plate 42 of *Surgical Anatomy* has the whole package (Fig. 3.26), all of the variegated textures, rendered with fine draughtsmanship, in great detail. Or rather more than the whole package.

From Vesalius and Estienne through Ruysch, Bidloo, Albinus and Gautier Dagoty, there was a centuries-long tradition of eccentric anatomical showmanship on the page, echoing, and sometimes inspiring, the eccentric arrangements on display in anatomical classrooms, lecture halls, and museums.[76] Maclise mostly abstains from that tradition—his theatricality lies more in the play of textures, lighting, shading, and composition than in eye-popping juxtaposition and stagecraft—but here allows himself a moment. We're presented with an oddly symmetrical assemblage: two dissected specimens of male genitalia (detached from their bodies of origin) hung in front of (or from) the haunches of a dissected torso. The two sets of dissected genitals flank a complete (undissected) set composed of penis, testicles, perineum and anus: a queer triptych. A geometric diagram—a triangle superimposed over concentric circles—targets the anus, as a guide

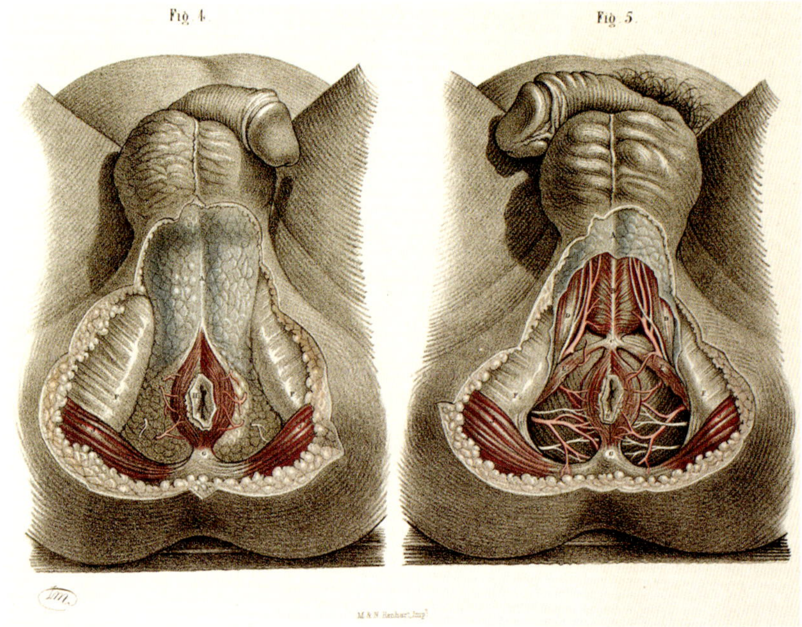

3.27 *Paired dissection sequence: penis right, penis left, off-kilter symmetry. Detail, "The surgical dissection of the superficial and deep structures of the male perineum, lithotomy, etc.," Joseph Maclise,* Surgical Anatomy *(London, 1856), pl. 42 bottom, figs. 4–5. Colored lithograph. Hagströmer Medico-Historical Library.*

for the surgeon to make his incision. It's yet another "transcendental anatomical" arrangement that scratches Maclise's platonist itch. The figure is an exercise in formalism: isosceles right triangles within triangles, cascading, echoing triplets. Maclise comments: "The median line of the body is marked as the situation where the opposite halves unite and constitute a perfect symmetrical figure." (Other drawings on the same page (Fig. 3.27) show a paired close-up sequence of the perineum dissected in two stages, with genitals atop, left-right, reflecting, and addressing, each other.)

The arrangement has a pedagogical purpose. A detailed knowledge of the anatomy of the rectum is necessary when cutting for stone and the repair of

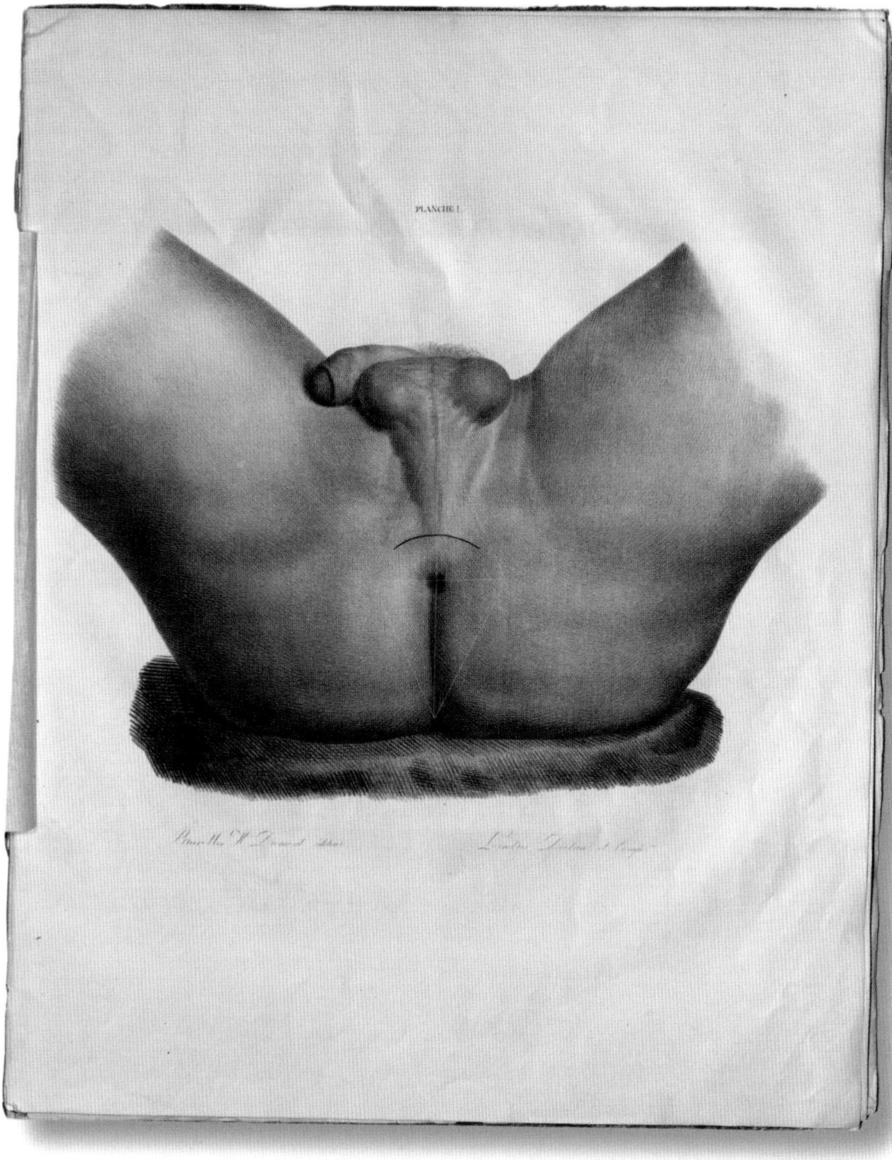

3.28 *Guillaume Dupuytren,* Abhandlung über die Steinoperation nach einer neuen Methode… *Trans. F. Reichmeister (Leipzig, 1837), pl. 1. [German trans.* Mémoire sur une Manière nouvelle de pratique l'Opération de la Pierre *(Paris, 1836).] Art: N.-H. Jacob. Lithography: [Pierre] Langlumé. 54 × 43 cm. Hagströmer Medico-Historical Library. Jacob also tackled the operation for stone in* Traité complet, *v. 7 pl. 64, showing the operation in steps, with hands emphatically on and in.*

fistulas and hernias. But one gets the sense that Maclise is piling on (literally and figuratively), enjoying himself.[77] And perhaps using the occasion of this plate to pay tribute to Nicolas-Henri Jacob. Maclise, who studied medicine in Paris in the 1830s and 1840s, would certainly have known that Jacob brilliantly essayed the same subject in a set of lithographic drawings for Dupuytren's celebrated 1836 grand folio treatise on a new method of cutting for stone.[78] The initial illustration (Fig. 3.28) of Jacob's sequence features a smoothly contoured groin, genitals and rectum (hairless save for a few pubic scraggles), which is also equipped with a triangular diagram (more subtle than Maclise's) and an arc (not a complete circle). Jacob's illustration is only the first of a set of spectacularly troubling images of surgical incisions and progressive dissections of the rectum (in the next plate Jacob takes the unusual step of depicting blood dripping from the semi-circular cut, as it would on a living patient and not a cadaver). The similarities between Jacob's illustration and Maclise's suggest a shared surgical interest and something more, a transmitted aesthetic, an influence.

And, via Jacob, this tenuously connects Maclise, through a few degrees of separation, to the mysterious unattributed orphan penis lithograph (Fig. 1.24) discussed earlier in this book. Pierre Langlumé, the lithographer for the Dupuytren-Jacob collaboration, was also the lithographer for that penis illustration (the attribution "lith de Langlumé" is discreetly tucked away in tiny letters on the lower right). And that raises the possibility that our finely rendered mystery lithograph might also come from the hand of Jacob.

2.8 Maclise's men: An imaginary confraternity?

We've now seen a lot, yet Maclise's focus on male genitalia, rectum, and the erotics of skin and touch, are not the whole story. While he refrained from classicizing gestures and conventions, Maclise wasn't indifferent to contemporary ideals of masculine beauty, and surely must have chosen the best and most attractive specimens available to him—likely improving their looks in the rendering. And, at least for the early part of his career, he seems to have had a large number of cadavers from which to choose. We don't know the particulars, but Quain writes that, for the dissections used in *The Anatomy of the Arteries*, "the bodies ... were received during a series of years for the study of anatomy into the School of Medicine in University College" and amounted to either 1,040 or 930. (Quain's two prefaces differ on the exact number, but either way, it's a lot.)[79] For *Surgical Anatomy*, Maclise doesn't total up his cadavers, but states, "in guarantee of their anatomical accuracy," the drawings ...

> have been made by myself, from my own dissections, first planned at the London University College [maybe some of the same specimens used in his collaboration with Quain?] and afterwards realized at the Ecole Pratique and School of Anatomy, adjoining the Hospital La Pitié, Paris, a few years since. Those representing pathological conditions of parts, I have made from *natural specimens* [Maclise's emphasis], recent and preserved, which I had the opportunity of examining at the Hospitals and Museums in Paris, London, and elsewhere.[80]

Paris was then famous for its prodigious numbers of bodies available to dissectors. The cadavers came, with little administrative interference or public protest, mostly from the large state-run charity hospitals, where poor people were treated and died. London, less well endowed with large hospitals, had fewer deceased patients, but North London Hospital (later called London University Hospital) seems to have had adequate numbers for Quain's use, perhaps supplemented with deceased inmates from other institutions. After the end of his collaboration with Quain, Maclise didn't have a steady position that could guarantee him a large supply of "anatomical subjects." Hence, his reliance on source drawings made years earlier—"planned" during his time as a student in London and "realized" in Paris. An ambitious project for a young surgeon, a young artist ...[81]

Still there were limits, and even in the best of circumstances, Maclise was constrained in his selection of subjects. Some plates feature older men; others (probably the majority) are composites (perhaps incorporating those "natural specimens"); and still others may have turned up opportunely with some particular condition that Maclise wanted to illustrate. Given how alive his subjects appear to be, Anthea Callen suggests it's likely that Maclise used live models—"very real, athletic men," to pose—and then made composite drawings, blending the figure of the model with the figure of a dissected cadaver.[82]

I agree—it does seem likely—but whether dead or alive, true-to-life or composites, one doesn't have to work hard to assemble a gallery of handsome young working-class men from Maclise's publications. In fact, Maclise himself used a series of thoracic dissections (Figs. 3.29–33] in *Surgical Anatomy* (plates 11–15, 1851 ed.; plates 21–25, 1856 ed.) as the occasion to make a little grouping of men. In their survey of the European anatomical tradition, K.B. Roberts and J.D.W. Tomlinson remark on how "life-like" Maclise's figures seem, almost "a gallery of portraits, perhaps of visitors to the Great Exhibition of 1851" at the Crystal Palace.[83] So lifelike that Maclise shows irrelevant details like conformations of the penis, each one different, and even a tiny piercing-hole in the ear of a young black man and a scar on his thigh (Figs. 3.33–34, 3.37, 3.39).[84]

Would it be out of place to mention that the faces, musculature and poses have an oddly familiar look? Some faint resemblance to the figures that appear on the covers of gay pornographic paperbacks of the 1950s and

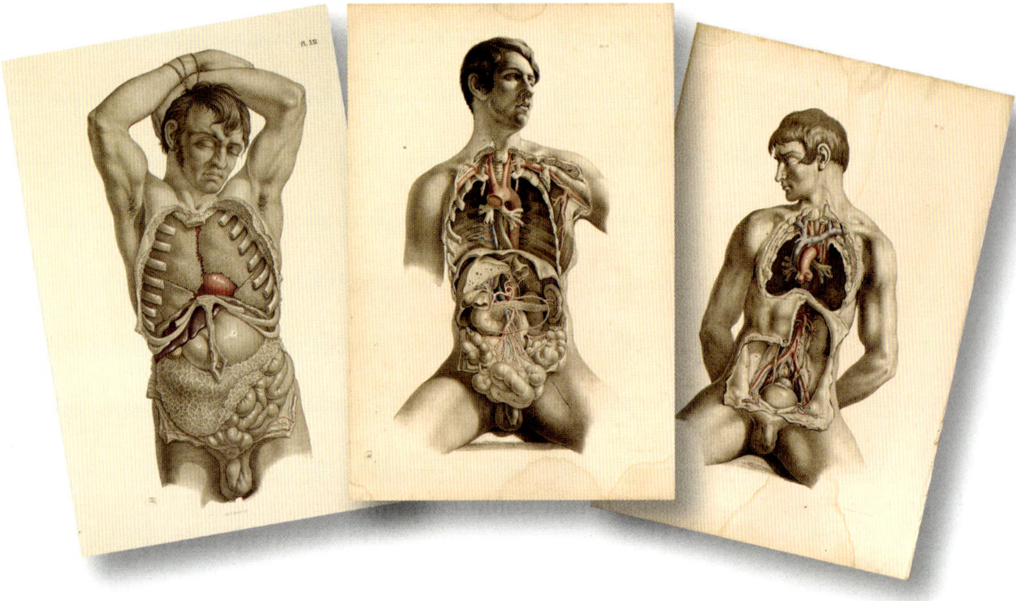

3.29–31 *Joseph Maclise,* Surgical Anatomy *(1st ed. London, 1851; 2d ed. London, 1856). Lithographs. 54 × 38 cm.* LEFT: *pl. 21 (1856, Hagströmer Medico-Historical Library).* CENTER: *pl. 13 (1851, Osler Library, McGill University).* RIGHT: *pl. 15 (1851, Osler Library).*

1960s? (A Google image search for "Maclise anatomy" offers up a link to a vintage gay porn website.) Maybe that's a stretch. But, leaving that aside, we can still put Maclise's men in the same frame as the soft-core homoeroticism of mid-nineteenth-century history and religious painting, all broadly situated in and licensed by the grand aesthetic tradition of masculine nudity. With a signal difference: Maclise's anatomical license to represent the naked body down to the genital and rectum (fading out just below that) …

If, as Callen proposes, Maclise used some combination of anatomized corpses and living men to "perform death," was he thereby participating in the mid-century Romantic eroticization of the dead body? The kind of thing that painter Paul Hippolyte Delaroche was picturing in his over-the-top The Wife of the Artist, Louise Vernet, on her Deathbed *(1845/46) and that Edgar Allan Poe adverted to in his famous remark: "The death of a beautiful woman is, unquestionably, the most poetical topic in the world" (also from 1846).*[85] *The timing's right—the cult of morbid sentimentality was cresting in the 1840s and 1850s—but Maclise's men don't fit the template. That cult mostly scripts the cadaver as a desirable*

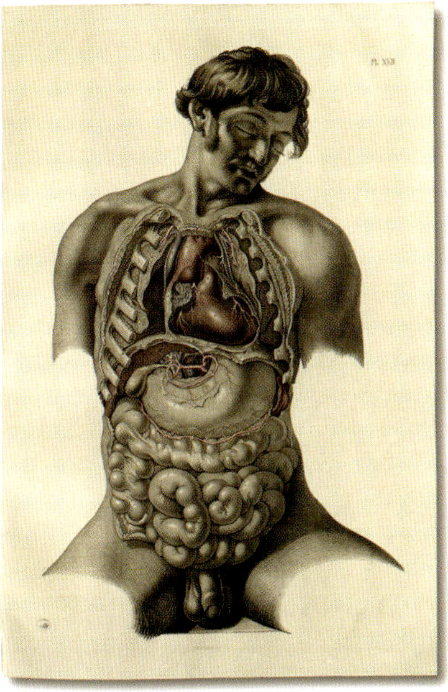

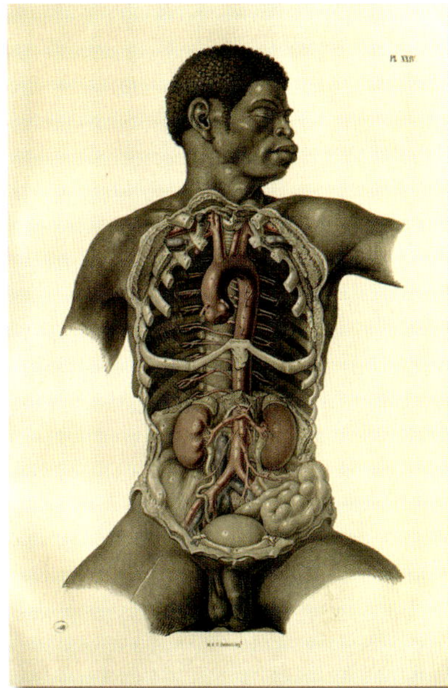

3.32–33 *Joseph Maclise,* Surgical Anatomy *(London, 1856).* LEFT: *pl. 22.* RIGHT: *pl. 24, notice the earpiercing hole and the scar on the right thigh. Lithographs. 54 × 38 cm. Hagströmer Medico-Historical Library.*

woman, naked or shrouded, cold like marble, impassive but intact, without any decomposition or rupture. The dead body, mostly supine, maintains a chaste mostly silent feminine modesty. Given voice, it confines itself to mournful reproaches or sibylline utterances, even as the occasion of death utterly exposes the female form to male contemplation, and sometimes anatomical violation.[86] *In contrast, the men in Maclise's gallery stand upright before the reader. They may be cadaveric objects of desire—but not the ones so often encountered in gothic tales of dissectors, body-snatchers and beautiful dead maidens. Maclise's men come alive on the printed page, are more than generic fairytale figures.*[87]

In Maclise's milieu, open homoerotic expression and relations were disapproved and subject to punishment. If his erotic attachments were principally directed to men—as clearly we have some reason to suspect—his gallery of men could have served him as an imaginary confraternity. Not exactly pin-ups, but a projection of desired objects of affection, imaginary friends, phantom companions. A representational consolation for relations and attachments never realized. Or (another possibility) encoded figurations of the affective life he did enjoy. Maybe Maclise imagined he was breathing life into his cadavers as he sketched them: transporting the men from the dissecting tables back to life, where they once congregated in student rooms, the medical school lecture hall, theatre or pub ... Or maybe, if Callen is correct, it took no imagination at all, and Maclise's anatomical studies afforded him opportunities to intimately associate with healthy living "specimens" of sweaty naked Victorian manhood.

Unlike Cheselden, whose Anatomy of the Human Body *looks outward to a mixed audience of medical men, artists, and the interested public, in Maclise's time, the print marketplace was much enlarged and increasingly sorted into well-defined niches. His atlases face outward to just one segment: medical men. And, inward, only to a single person: Maclise himself. But a divided self: Maclise the anatomist demonstrating his knowledge of the human body to Maclise the surgeon; Maclise the artist exhibiting his command of line, texture and space to Maclise the lover of art (and an imaginary audience of fellow gallery artists and art lovers). And Maclise the man contemplating for his own private pleasure the succession of beautiful young men he has contrived to appear before him.*

2.9 Race and universalist embodiment

No reviewer ever remarked upon the queerness of Maclise's anatomical renderings of handsome young men and their genitalia. But his prose did come in for criticism. Maclise overstuffed his prefaces with rhetorical flourishes (according to one reviewer, in a style "rather labored, and wanting in that transparency which is so particularly desirable in a scientific treatise").[88] Loquacious, argumentative, resentful, peculiar. Here's a chunk, to give you the full sense of it:

> ... this endless search after new anatomical facts has already so exhausted the sinking soul of Science, that she heaves the gorge at thoughts of it. It must be now by the broad clarion sounds of laws and systems, not by the narrow piping notes of isolated particulars and dislocated phenomena, that we can ever hope to wake to attention again her slumbering ear. In what direction ... are we now to search for a new branch of nerve or artery, an unknown muscle, or process of bone? For what number of such facts are we still to rein-in impatience ... for the purpose of summing together the whole encircling and satisfying account of a law—of that Law of *unity in variety* the sum and substance of Nature's living volume, the time and final answer to our *quid est?*—whether we question the difference between two vertebrae, two hearts, or two brains, of any one species, or of all? The womb of anatomical science teems with the true interpretation of this law, but the birth (even though while of no greater bulk than a pamphlet, it would outweigh in

> worth all the dissectors' guide-books fossilized in the library strata of past time) is delayed, owing to the parent mind having become altogether "practical." The present state of knowledge proclaims that the unborn form of this transcendent law awaits some future Newton to help it into life. This is the subject for scalpels of the mind! The iron scalpel has already made acquaintance with not only the greater parts, but even with the infinitesimals of the human body, and Reason, confined to this narrow range of the subject, perceives herself to be imprisoned, and quenches her guiding light in despair. Originality has here outlived itself; discovery is here a fruitless enterprise; nor even though we pursue it in the microcosm on the field of the microscope, can we draw forth demonstrations of other objects than such as are ... as little in respect to "practical" importance as they are in regard to physical dimensions ... It is not a list of new and disjointed facts that Science at present thirsts for, but ... the creation of a new and truthful theory ...[89]

Like Dickens's Mr. Micawber, Maclise "had a relish in this formal piling up of words."[90] His speechifying texts say what they mean and mean what they say, but also say and mean much more than that. The verbose introductions to the first and second editions of *Surgical Anatomy* bristle with digs at unnamed adversaries, fortified by fulsome quote- and name-dropping: Fontenelle (in French, untranslated), Shakespeare (*Coriolanus* Act II, Scene III, unattributed), Goethe (untranslated and unattributed), and Bacon (*Novum Organum*, in Latin, also untranslated).[91] And each plate was paired with a "commentary," sometimes lengthy, sometimes argumentative, in which Maclise discoursed upon "philosophical," "transcendental" principles and "the comparative method." Those concepts weren't Maclise's invention—he wrote under the spell of Lorenz Oken and Geoffroy Saint-Hilaire and their followers. But in *their* writings, the arguments mostly figure in discussions of comparative anatomy and embryology and debates over transformism (speciation and evolution).[92] Maclise's philosophizing contentions look glaringly out of place in practical atlases of surgical anatomy. He knew it was impolitic, unseemly, but just couldn't help it: "I have indulged in such a consideration of the facts ... as may seem to many to have but a very remote tendency towards developing the requirements of a work with that title."[93]

Transcendental anatomy's foundational axiom, according to historian Philip Rehbock, was that "a single Ideal Plan or Type ... lay behind the great multiplicity of visible structures of the animal and plant kingdoms," a simple symmetrical template that "acted as a force for the maintenance of anatomical uniformity, in opposition to the diversity-inducing" or "degenerating ... forces of the physical environment."[94] Maclise didn't concern himself much with degeneration, except as something for surgeons to fix. Instead he emphasized anatomical and aesthetic unity—and configurations of symmetrical order within or overlaying the human body, or between bodies.

That *idée fixe* had ideological and social valences. Maclise was the son of a Scottish Presbyterian regimental soldier who settled in County Cork,

Ireland—occupied territory to the native Irish—to work and live as a tanner and shoemaker. Presbyterians ranked below members of the Churches of England and Ireland. They were a lower caste, adjacent to but not included in the Protestant Ascendancy. Maclise came to London as an outsider, with a bit of a chip on his shoulder, a burning need to show that he was much more than just a "mechanic" of the body, and that anatomy (and therefore surgery) had depths that went beyond dutiful description and instrumental utility. According to historian Adrian Desmond, the anatomical philosophy espoused by Maclise was:

> a form of "crisis knowledge" for a radical dissenting intelligentsia locked out of the corridors of power. Democratization did come—in 1843 at the College of Surgeons and with the opening of the hospitals to new bourgeois blood—and it was followed by a gradual decline in radical agitation and ... interest in Geoffroy's philosophical anatomy. As late as 1846 the [London University-] and Paris-trained Joseph Maclise might still doubt "whether absolute differences of form have any real existence, except as forms under metamorphosis" ... But by now the standard was passing to [Richard] Owen in an age of Peelite compromise, and a more conservative archetypal anatomy was already in the making.[95]

Frustrated in his efforts to secure any high hospital or university appointment, Maclise was a perfect example of a self-made dissident intellectual locked out of power. And while he made some feeble attempts to temper his rhetoric (for example, by dropping the word "transcendental" from the second edition of *Surgical Anatomy*), he was a diehard, and kept the Geoffroyist faith well into the 1850s.[96] And was therefore not only out of place, but also out of date. And also out of class: the rhetorical excesses and literary pretensions of his prose were a form of overcompensation for lack of social standing, Maclise laying it on thick. (Did anyone buy it?)

His drawings were more persuasive, at least as a bid for inclusion in the order of high aesthetics. But they also visually argued for his philosophical convictions, if anyone cared to notice. (Maybe he was emancipated by the fact that hardly anyone did.) Take, for example, his triangular, tripartite rectum figure (Fig. 3.26). A device to show where the surgeon should make his cut. But, for Maclise, symmetry is an overarching principle. It universalizes organic creation, gives humanity and the rest of the natural world a common "unity of plan" that attenuates distinctions like sexual and racial difference. And, of course, undermines the logic of the British class system, with its finely graded ranks of privilege lording over everything. Which, in the 1840s and 1850s, was the principal target of the radical critique.

And so *Surgical Anatomy* features a dissection of a young black man (Figs. 3.33–34, 3.37, 3.39). Yet Maclise makes no reference at all to racial difference, abstains entirely from the proliferating discourse of race and its (now infamous) taxonomies of cranial morphology.[97] From the man's pierced right ear, evident in plate 5 (London, 1851) (Fig. 3.34) and plate 4 (London, 1856) (Fig. 3.39), we can surmise that he had likely been a sailor,

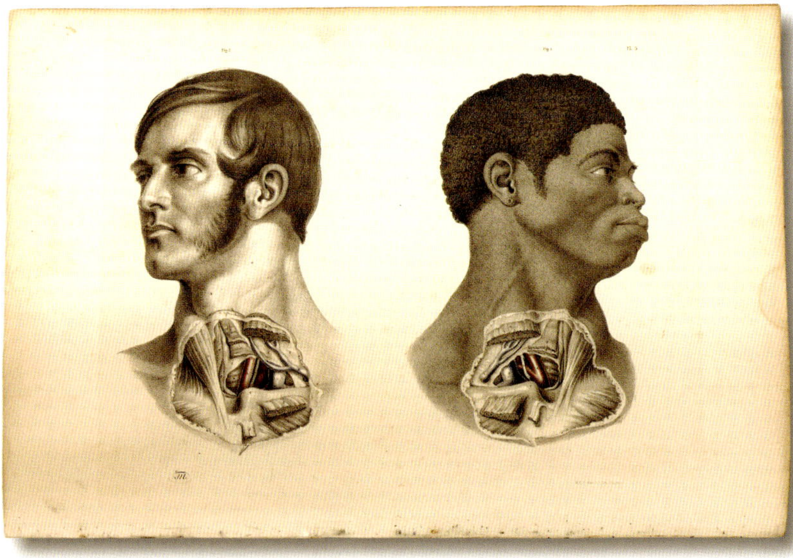

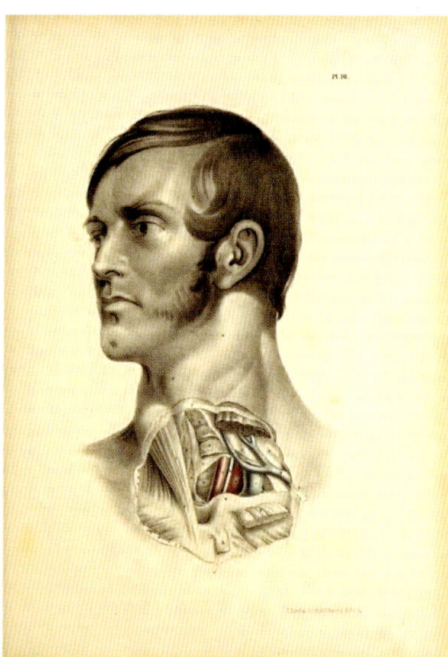

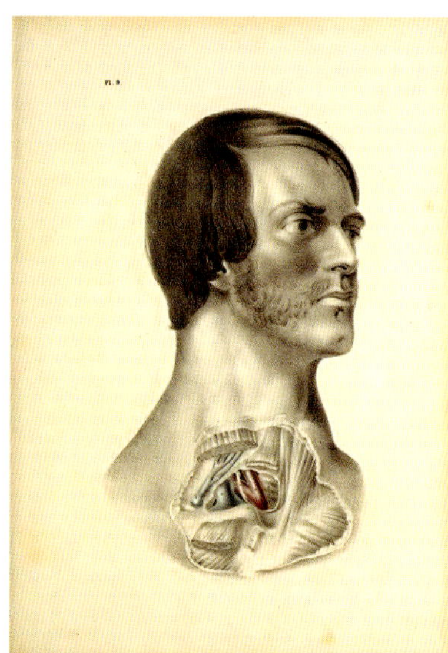

3.34–36 *Before and after. Maclise's 1851 London edition (pl. 5) shows two men on one page, open-eyed and looking away from each other (as if alive and alert). The redrawn smaller format 1851 Philadelphia edition (38 cm.) puts the two figures on opposite pages (pls. 9–10), but re-"colors" the figure on the right, and replacing the black man's face with the face and racial identity of the white man (the figure on the left).* TOP: *Joseph Maclise,* Surgical Anatomy *(London, 1851). Lithograph. Osler Library, McGill University.* BOTTOM: *Joseph Maclise,* Surgical Anatomy *(Philadelphia, 1851). Lithograph. Wellcome Collection.*

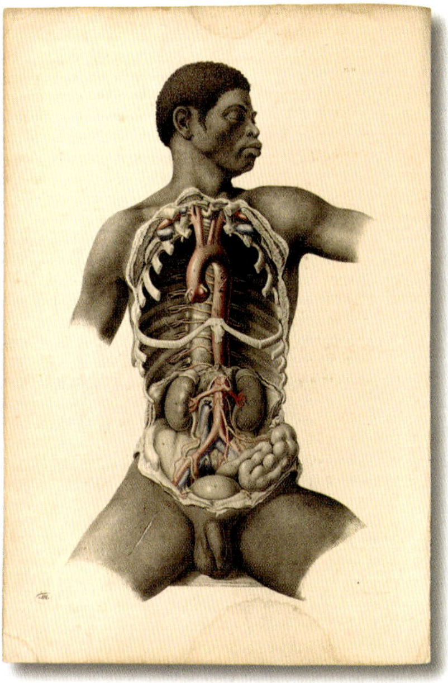

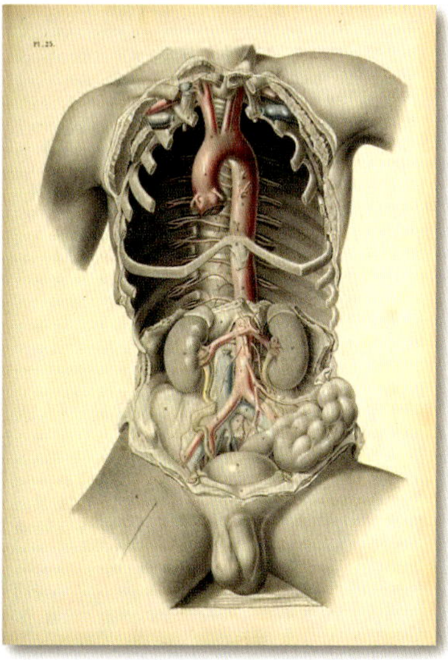

3.37–38 *Another before and after. In Maclise's 1851 London edition, pl. 14, a black figure demonstrates the "relation of the principal blood vessels of the thorax and abdomen to the osseous skeleton," with no reference to any racial difference. The 1851 Philadelphia edition, pl. 25, with smaller page-size (38 cm.), re-"colors" the figure and removes the head so that no identifying features appear. The subject's blackness is whitewashed.* LEFT: *Joseph Maclise,* Surgical Anatomy *(London, 1851). Lithograph. 54 × 38 cm. Osler Library, McGill University.* RIGHT: *Joseph Maclise,* Surgical Anatomy *(Philadelphia, 1851). Lithograph. Wellcome Collection.*

maybe at some time in his life a slave. Sailors and enslaved people often wore earrings. And, as any reader of Herman Melville knows, the nineteenth-century sailing ship was an ethnically and racially diverse workplace.

London, of course, was the center of a vast maritime empire. Small numbers of people of color were established there even in the middle decades of the 1830s and 1840s, and the dissection of a person of African descent could not have been in itself so unusual. A London anatomist like Maclise, who dissected thousands of bodies, mostly taken from poor houses and charity hospitals, would have occasionally gotten opportunities to dissect a black cadaver. But the *depiction* of a black subject in a published anatomical atlas was unusual. (Apart from Maclise's atlas, I know of only two other instances: a black man appears in the 1811 and 1824 editions of Charles Bell's *Engravings of the Arteries*.)[98]

Maclise the artist ably delineates the particularities of the undissected "superficial" parts of his naked subject: the non-European facial features, dark skin, kinky hair, and in addition to the pierced earlobe, an irrelevant scar or cut on the right thigh (Figs. 3.33, 3.37, 3.39)—all attesting to his commitment to true representation. And maybe his affection for this particular subject (who, remember, may have been a living model, perhaps even a friend.) But, again, Maclise abstains from any comment on the man's racial features. His purpose, he tells us, is to show "the form of the abdomen and the relative position of its contained organs in health and disease." He does take the opportunity to point out some idiosyncratic variations ("peculiarities") manifested in the cadaver's aortic arch and elsewhere.[99] And this could be the place to discourse upon the morphological peculiarities of the "African" body. But he doesn't. (Instead, he smuggles in an unlikely dig against homeopaths, "those pathologists of the infinitesimals who would essay to diagnose by the pulse between inflammation of either of the three costas of the bowel and thereupon ply their pharmacy.")

That approach accords with the principle of anatomical "unity in variety." The figure illustrates human, and not "African," anatomy, and appears alongside four white men, as one of a gallery of young good-looking physically-fit anatomical specimens (in the 2d London edition, plates 21 through 25). Maclise diligently renders each and every one of them according each his individual particularities: these are portraits of identifiable people. But his commentary refers to them collectively as representatives of "the human

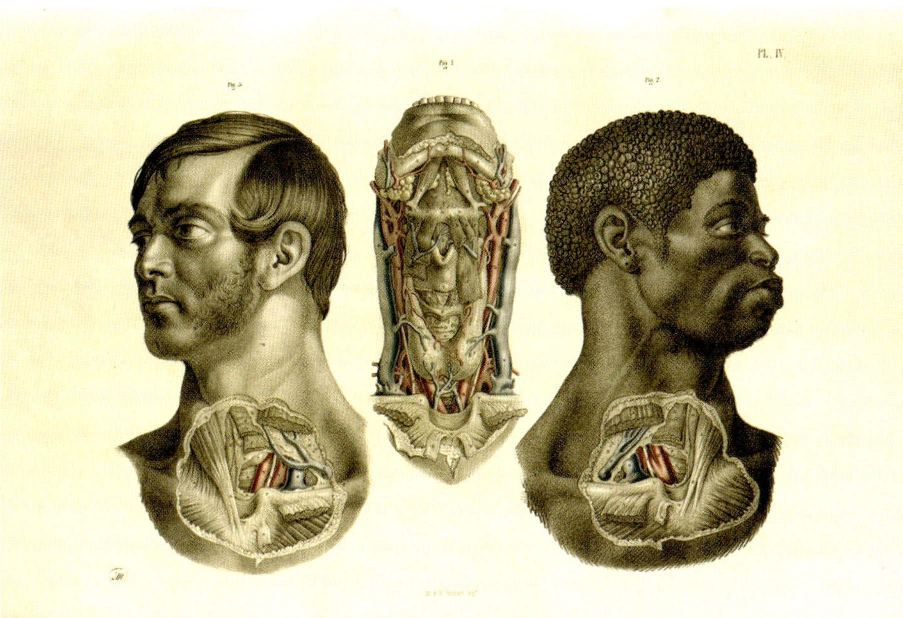

3.39 *"The surgical dissection of the thorax and the episternal region. Deligation of the primary aortic branches. Penetrating wounds, paracentesis. Tracheotomy. Laryngotomy." Joseph Maclise,* Surgical Anatomy *(London, 1856), pl. 4. Colored lithograph. 54 × 38 cm. Hagströmer Medico-Historical Library.*

species" and "man": "all species of vertebrata ... [and] their multitudinous designs, result by the same simple mode of creation."

Differences among species and individual members of a species, even fairly substantial ones, Maclise emphasizes, are "simply that of plus and minus."[100] The portrait sequence visually affirms that argument. But no pluses or minuses are assessed. The men perform anatomical unity—universalism—in their equivalent poses, and in their display of male genitalia. Yet ... Maclise must have been aware of the fact that his readership of white British doctors and surgeons would have noticed, and appreciated, the racial novelty of the figure on anatomical display.

And at home maybe that was a minor selling point. But not in the United States. Discomfort with the image of a black man consorting, on an equal basis, with white counterparts in the pages of an anatomical atlas undoubtedly led his Philadelphia publisher to revise the 1851 American edition of *Surgical Anatomy*, as art historians Keren Rosa Hammerschlag and Naomi Slipp have shown in articles that examine those revisions.[101] In 1850s America, racism was at a boil. Perhaps because of the logistical difficulties in transporting plates or lithographic stones across the Atlantic, and because Blanchard & Lea, his Philadelphia publisher, printed *Surgical Anatomy* in a slightly smaller format, the American edition was entirely redrawn: "a strikingly faithful copy of the original," according to one reviewer.[102] But slightly inferior in artistry to Maclise's original lithographs. And with one substantive (but unacknowledged) difference: the blackness of the black body was erased, "whitewashed." Maclise's black anatomical subject was redrawn and recolored—and transformed into a white man (Figs. 3.34–38).

That change was not carried over into the redrawn 1856 London edition. Maclise kept the figure of the black man, and still refrained from racial commentary in the text. But did make one significant revision (Fig. 3.39): the insertion of a peculiar compound anatomical object—a dissected lower jaw and surrounding and connecting features, covering most of the trachea, going all the way down to the collarbone. Maclise placed it dead center between the black man and the white (Maclise's figure 1 in plate 4, 1856). It's hard to know how much to read into that. Maybe the change was motivated purely on anatomical grounds. Or maybe Maclise was erecting a barrier of separation, silently bowing to racial prejudice. (That would be disappointing.)

But a close reading of the accompanying commentary (another one of those tangled thickets of Maclisean prose) suggests rather the opposite. The intention is improvement, both anatomical and philosophical. Maclise goes on at tedious length about the shared symmetries and universal principles instantiated in the anatomical object, a monstrous almost phallic apparition (topped with teeth). Symmetry is typically associated with beauty. Here it's ugly, the horrific inner core customarily concealed beneath the skin of the two men—really all of us. Uncanny, inhuman. Yet a signifier of our common humanity, as queer as that might be (queer in several senses). And Maclise inscribes that philosophical argument visually, in a composition of balance and symmetry. The anatomical-surgical Beast, flanked by two opposing models of masculine Beauty.

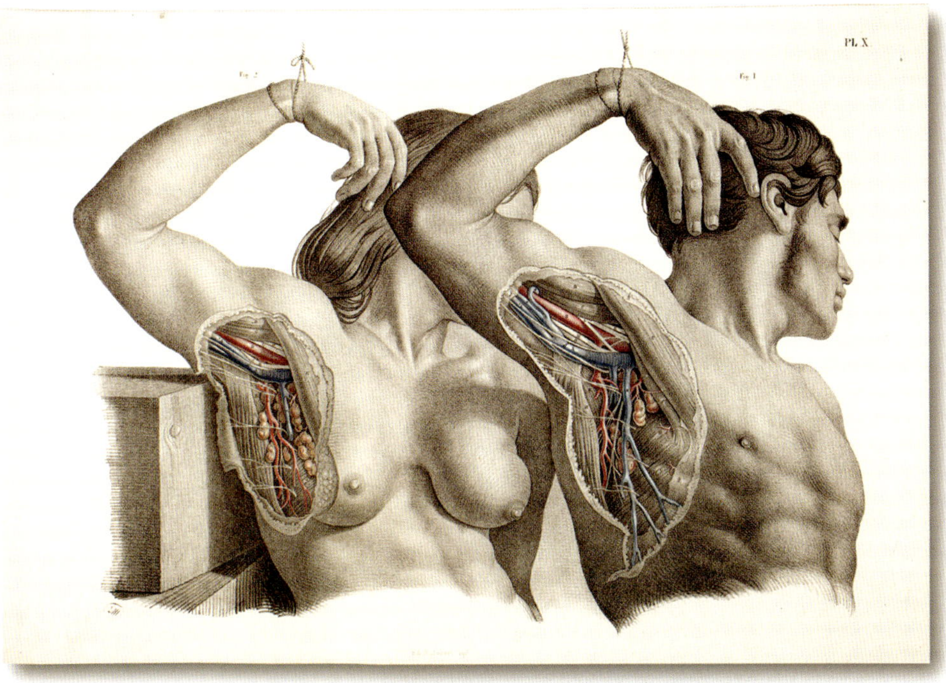

3.40 *"The Male and Female Axillae Compared," Joseph Maclise,* Surgical Anatomy *(London, 1856), pl. 10. Colored lithograph. 54 × 38 cm. Hagströmer Medico-Historical Library.*

2.10 Heteronormative queer

Only one female figure appears in Maclise's *Surgical Anatomy* (pl. 7 in the 1851 London edition, pl. 10 in 1856) (Figs. 3.40–41). Not unaccompanied, but as half of a buff cadaveric couple. Hands dangling, the paired bodies are arranged like marionettes. It's a striking composition: a scene of what appears to be synchronized sleep or entranced dancing. A beautiful naked female anatomical subject shares the space of the page with a beautiful male counterpart—a sharing shared by Maclise with his male readers, who have the option of taking pleasure in either figure, or both. It's a serious lesson in comparative anatomy, on a topic of theoretical interest. Scientific, but mesmeric. Dreamy. Sexy. But is it "queer"?

You could take it to be "heteronormative," an Adam-and-Eve pairing, but remember, the custom at the time was to present images of the dissected female body only when the topic is reproductive anatomy.[103] That isn't the main topic here. Maclise mostly keeps the female reproductive system out of *Surgical Anatomy*.[104] He features this one identifiable female, for the sake of comparison, next to a male figure, to make a politically radical (and sexually perverse) point. In the 1840s and 1850s, European discourse and representation tended to play up the essential psychological and moral differences between male and female, and justify them on anatomical grounds.[105] Maclise's *pas-de-deux* sails against that current. Looked at scientifically, he argues in the accompanying commentary, differences between the sexes "are for the most part superficial": "When we submit those regions to anatomical comparison, we find them to be composed of parts similar." Once again, beneath the skin, we are all variations on a single theme. Homologous. So decrees "the uniformity of the law of nature," the single most important (radical, queer) guiding principle of Maclise's contrarian "philosophical anatomy."[106]

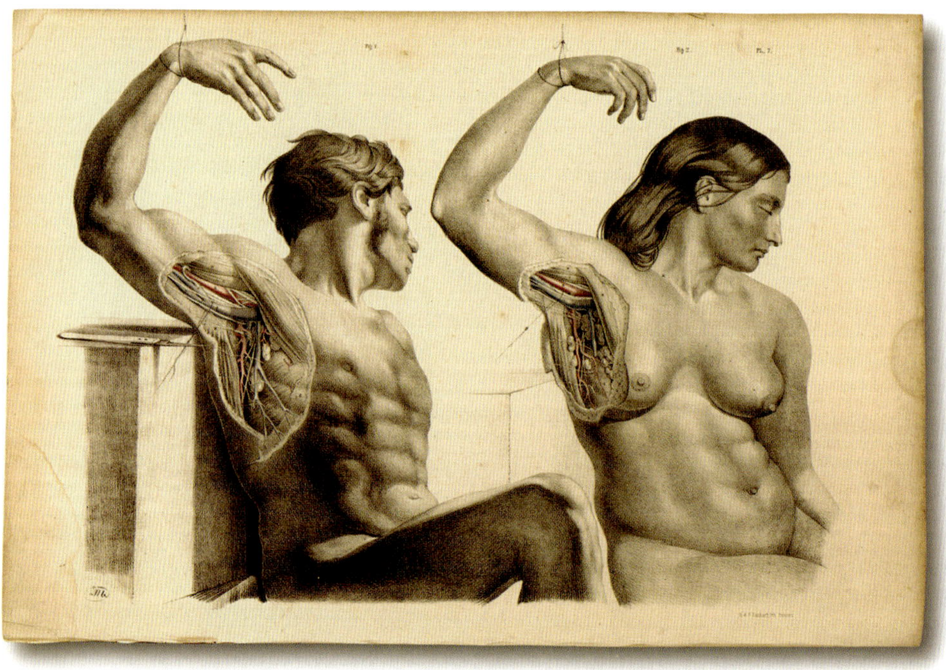

3.41 *"The Surgical Forms of the Male and Female Axillae Compared," Joseph Maclise,* Surgical Anatomy *(1st ed.; London, 1851), pl. 7. Lithograph. 54 × 38 cm. Osler Library, McGill University.*

Note as well the bicep and abdominal muscles of the female subject. Although less well defined than the muscles on her male counterpart, Maclise shows a bit of the muscular structure that lays beneath the skin, to emphasize the similarities between male and female musculature. And declines to play up a commonly observed anatomical difference in the male and female nude: the layer of "adipose tissue" that in living or undissected human beings so often obscures the muscles of the female abdomen.[107]

The 1856 version (Fig. 3.40) shows the couple touching. The man is on the woman's left, slightly in the foreground, his elbow covering her face, which works to emphasize her bare breasts, but masks her identity. In the 1851 version (Fig. 3.41), the two figures echo each other a bit less closely and don't touch and the man is placed on the woman's right.[108] The scene appears to be made of two scenes pasted together; the man and woman are not really in the same room. Maclise leaves a small space between them, which allows him to show the woman's face—plausibly the face of an identifiable person—another attestation to the truthfulness of his depiction. We can also see her entire abdomen, the musculature a bit more defined than in the 1856 plate. Maclise redrew and revised the plates for the second edition to make larger and better images of the anatomical cuts (again, it was an article of faith that the larger, and closer to life-size, the truer the image was to nature), and added a splash of color for highlighting. But the revision also offered him an opportunity to redesign and rethink the plate as a singular scene (the man casts a shadow on the woman): Was he deliberately trying to make the couple more homologous? Did he obscure the woman's face to protect her female modesty, or to focus attention on the handsome male figure (whose face is now a bit more visible), or just to play with a new compositional variation? All three possibilities could be true.

Finally, there's the sumptuous skin, which glistens in the 1851 edition. Maclise's atlas was promoted as a practical aid to students of surgery and anatomy and working surgeons—it served as a standard work for a generation or two—but goes far beyond its remit. The overall effect is pleasurable, sexy, artful, authoritative. And a poke in the eye to the conventional discourse of sexual difference. So not hetero-normative after all. Maclise, who devoted most of his career to representing the anatomy of the male body, is once again coloring outside the lines.

As we have seen, in anatomical illustration over many centuries the male gaze was mostly directed to the male body. While the bulk of Maclise's surgical practice was likely devoted to operations on men (hernias and amputations being quite common), he surely must have also performed surgeries on female patients. And, if he had deemed it important, could have included some dissections of women in his anatomical and surgical atlases. Instead, he featured good-looking, physically fit young men. Apart from the "male and female axillae compared", no other identifiable female face appears in *Surgical Anatomy*, and very few female-sexed body-parts. Maclise never addresses the disparity. Neither did the reviewers.

Maclise's omission of female figures—in keeping with the anatomical tradition of treating the female as a special case, with Man serving as the universal anatomical human—supported his Principle of Unity *idée fixe*. No need to show the female body if male and female are fundamentally just variations on a universal "archetype." Of course, there could have been

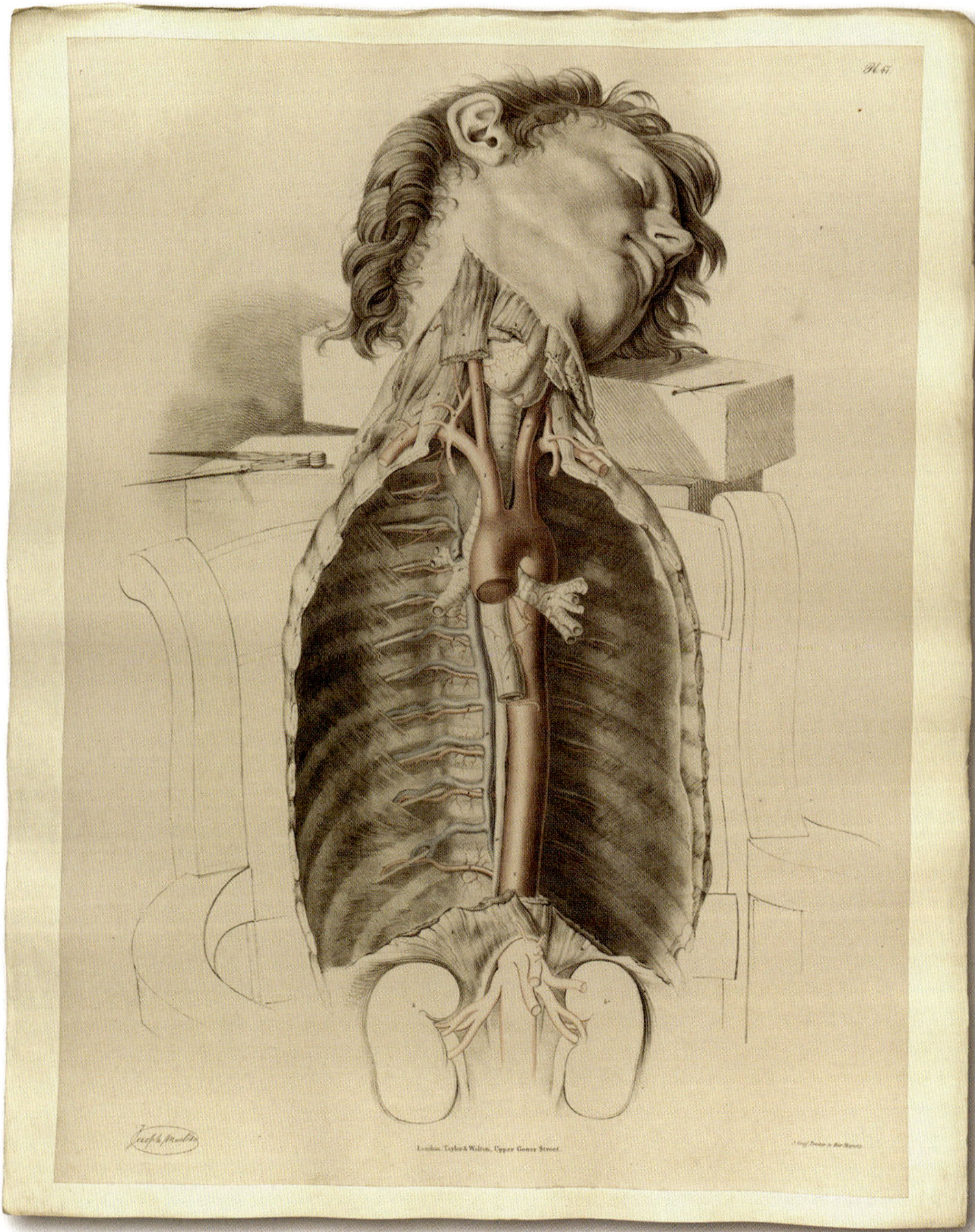

3.42 *"The Thoracic Aorta and the Intercostal arteries, with the Intercostal Veins, Vena Azygos, the Thoracic duct, &c., seen in connexion with the parietes of the thorax,"* *Richard Quain,* The Anatomy of the Arteries of the Human Body *(1844), pl. 47. Art: Joseph Maclise. Lithograph. 68 × 55 cm. Hagströmer Medico-Historical Library.*

another motive behind his omission: maybe Maclise had an erotic preference for male bodies. And if that was the case, in a society that marked the difference between male and female as essential and ineradicable—and which policed that difference socially and juridically—his insistence on the essential oneness of male and female would have been yet another way to join egalitarian radicalism to closeted queerness, without attracting too much attention.

2.11 A crucifixion

Toggling between *Surgical Anatomy* and *Anatomy of the Arteries*, we've looked at a gallery of young men, an anatomical *pas-de-deux*, headless cadavers with sensate hands, anatomical bondage, and male genitalia. Now consider plate 47 of *Anatomy of the Arteries*, another figure study (Fig. 3.42), and another queer scene: the nearly bodiless head of a handsome young man, with flawless skin, flowing hair—but no hands, arms, or genitalia. Seemingly asleep, his head rests on a horizontal block of wood, artfully lit (slightly from below, the left side). But that beautiful face is irrelevant to the demonstration of "the thoracic or descending aorta with the intercostal arteries," as irrelevant as the many penises on display in other plates.[109] As in so many of his eye-catching illustrations, Maclise's hunger to depict—contemplate—masculine beauty (or just Beauty) converges with his eagerness to flaunt his artistic gifts and aesthetic sensibility.

There is of course also anatomy to attend to: an inverted vee-cut incision at the neck leads down to the heavily dissected aortic cavity. Maclise leaves off at the bottom with a *non finito* sketch of the kidneys. What's left of the body, after the radical paring away of parts, is framed by a *non finito* wooden armchair, the staves of the chair echoing the ribs of the thoracic cage, an allusion to their architectural/structural function. Maclise is doubling and redoubling, embellishing the image with a kind of ghost geometry, in step with the dualism that was then coursing through British and continental fiction, philosophy and fine art—capital B Beauty and refined abstraction combined with perspectival realism and getting-it-right detail. (Think of the dualism of real and ideal beauty in the art criticism of William Hazlitt and John Ruskin.)

And, here again, that open-ended, ramifying synthesis dovetails neatly with an anatomical dualism: on the one hand Geoffroy Saint-Hilaire's preachings on the organic "unity of composition"; on the other, Maclise's love of representational and anatomical detail (but utter rejection of descriptive anatomy and materialist empiricism). *Comparative Osteology* (1847), Maclise's most Geoffroyist and philosophical work, published only three years after the collaboration with Quain, emphasizes bodily symmetry within the human body and its parts, throughout, along with

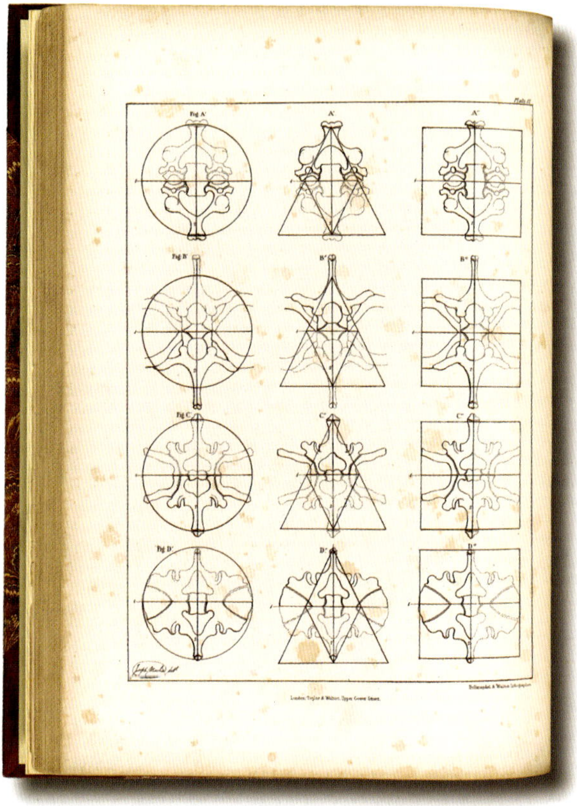

3.43 *"The Duplication of a Vertebra Creates a Figure of Bilateral and Antero-Posterior Symmetry," Joseph Maclise,* Comparative Osteology *(London, 1847), pl. 12. Lithograph. 46 cm. Wellcome Collection.*

skeletal homologies among different organisms (Fig. 3.43).[110] Again argued in crystal-clear illustration, but convoluted word tangles ...

> The law of form is the process of gradation, or the subtraction of parts from plus serial quantities; and directly as this metamorphosis takes place, directly special variety holds that place. The shadow reigns over that region always where the beam of light has ceased to exercise its dominion; and what is shadow but a state of negation, consequent upon the absence of the positive entity of light? Is shadow an ens?[111]—It cannot be regarded as such, while we have reason to interpret it as a mere state of negation, or the absence of something; for to regard shadow as a palpable entity would be no less absurd than to set down the dark void of ignorance as being a presential substance, while experience proves that the God of day, like the torch of knowledge, dispels the phantom nothingness of ignorance and shade. If we will follow the progress of the law of form, by the subtraction of quantity from plus uniformity, we shall plainly discover that the condition

> of what we name special variety is a mere state of the absence of some form or quantity proper to plus uniformity, and hence that species is like darkness, or like ignorance, a non-existence or absence of a something ...[112]

That kind of talk really didn't go down well. The same critics who lauded his artistry and surgical acumen utterly rejected his "transcendental anatomy," and treated his windy prose with a condescension bordering on insult.[113] Which may have initially set him back on his heels, but Maclise remained steadfast. The second edition of *Surgical Anatomy* (London, 1856) adds an illustration—a view of a dissected torso flanked by two diagrams to emphasize corporeal symmetry and unity. (The figure is also a bit Christ-like in its admixture of death, sleep and surrender, the pose of the head ...) Maclise gives it priority, makes it plate number 1, as if to wave the Geoffroyist flag in the face of his critics (Fig. 3.44).

Maclise's supervening philosophical principles, love of diagrammatic geometry, and rejection of empiricism don't sit comfortably with the immersive sensual embodiedness of his dissections and drawings. His stagings of the fleshy, boney, fragile yet obdurate matter of the human body seem like an assault on the centuries-long hegemony of "expressions of mind ... over manipulations of matter." In eighteenth- and nineteenth-century fiction and discourse, the anatomist typically figures as the personification of materialism, its most visible exponent, sometimes in the guise of the village atheist, sometimes as a necrophilic libertine. Yet Maclise, elbow-deep in the manipulation of fleshy matter, and demonstrably enchanted with the material, loudly declines to play the role of materialist in his textual commentaries.[114]

Quain does all the talking in *Anatomy of the Arteries*, and the commentary on plate 47 states simply that "The body was in the sitting posture," in a wooden armchair probably, "while the drawing was being made." But in depicting the thoracic artery, Maclise takes the liberty to fool around with pictorial elements and visually encode transcendental anatomical precepts—principles that Quain might not have fully endorsed, maybe wasn't even fully cognizant of. One reviewer commented that "Mr. Quain has allowed himself to be completely overshadowed by the artist."[115] You get the feeling that Maclise hijacked the project. From Maclise's later account, the two men agreed on "the Law of a 'unity of organization'"—Quain is included in a list of scientific men Maclise credits with teaching him that "Law"—but Quain's text omits any mention of such principles.[116] If that disappointed Maclise, perhaps he compensated by speaking loudly through his artwork.

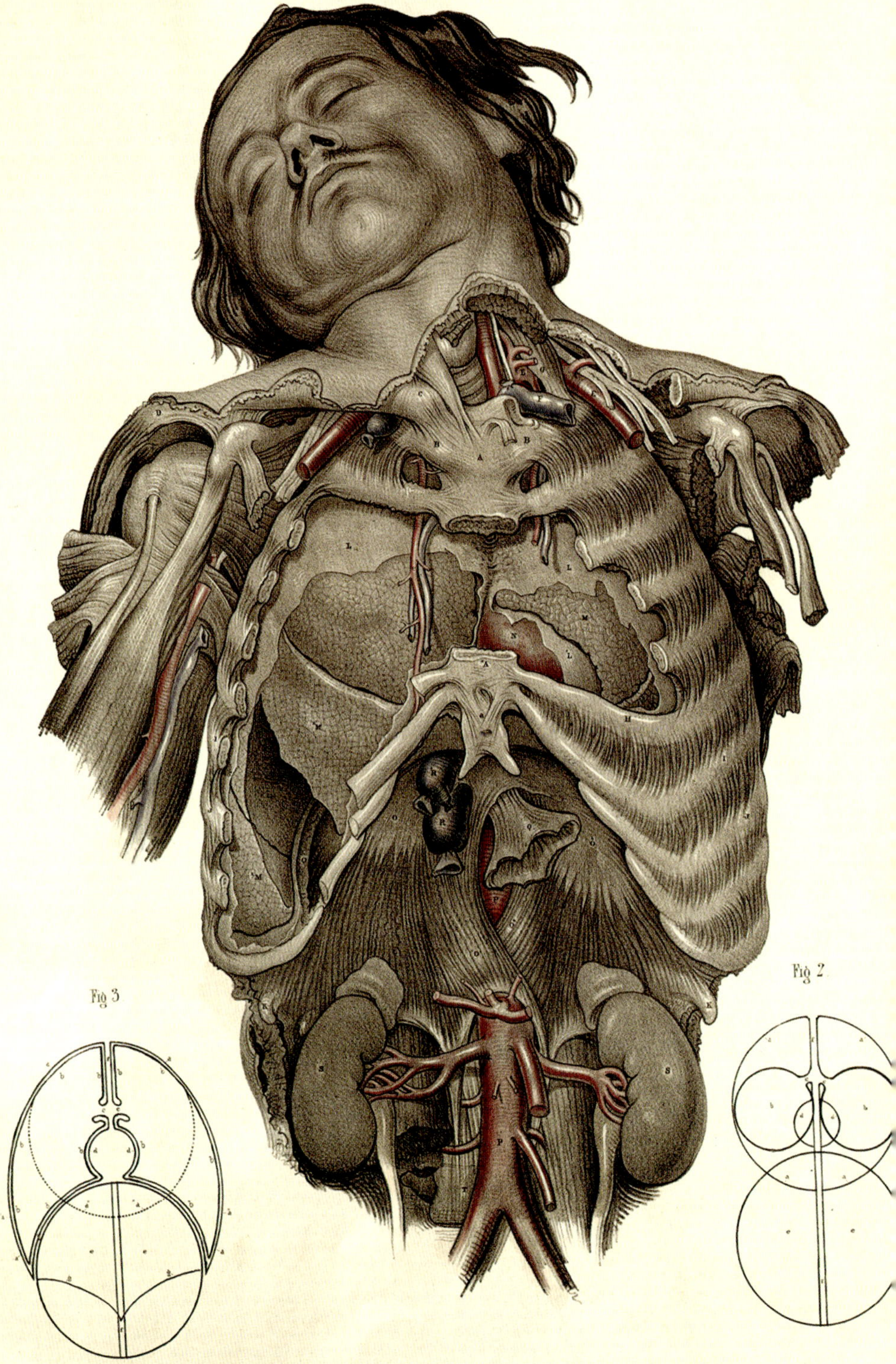

3.44 *"The Form of the Thorax, and the Relative Position of the Lungs, Heart and Primary Bloodvessels…" Joseph Maclise,* Surgical Anatomy *(London, 1856), pl. 1. Colored lithograph. 54 × 38 cm. Hagströmer Medico-Historical Library.*

2.12 How did Quain and Maclise get on?

Which raises more questions. You've got to wonder: how did Quain and Maclise get on? What was the character and trajectory of their connection? Was it strictly business or a friendship? Neither man was married during the years of their collaboration. (Some 15 years after the publication of the *Anatomy of the Arteries*, Quain entered into a late and childless marriage, at age 59, to a viscount's widow. Maclise never married.) We have no sources on Maclise's character (apart from his own published words), but we do on Quain. They mock him as short "and rather stout," an "unamiable colleague," irritable and prone to grudges, "constantly involved in disputes." (There were acrimonious struggles over preferment and appointments for positions at the University and North London Hospital.) As a surgeon, he was said to be risibly "cautious, even to timidity."[117] His obituaries mention his feud with the charismatic, famously incautious Robert Liston (also one of Maclise's teachers) and with other members of the medical faculty. Liston was one of two men to whom Maclise dedicated his *Surgical Anatomy*.[118] Quain can't have liked that. (Maclise only allots Quain a few passing citations in the commentaries on the plates.) Did the two men have a falling out? From the peevish tone of his writings, it's evident that Maclise carried a sizeable chip on his shoulder. It's not hard to imagine the two men clashing on philosophical anatomy, politics, money, or something else.

Maclise never addresses Quain or any contemporary anatomist by name in *Surgical Anatomy*, but does bestir himself to lay out strongly held opinions. "Descriptive human anatomy" is described as something "so cold, poor and sterile in its own nature, and so barren of product," it would "be impossible for even the genius of Promethean fire to warm it." Quain, professor of "descriptive anatomy" at the University of London, can't have liked that either (and, an additional sting, was never lauded by anyone as a genius). So there may have well been a rift between the two men.[119]

But if there were personal issues between Quain and Maclise, the larger differences were matters of principles and commitment: Quain championed nothing. Maclise championed transcendental anatomy, "unity," "symmetry," "homology," the "guiding light of the comparative method," and vehemently opposed laboratory science and new programs of empirical research.[120] He argued that dissections and skeletal specimens reveal how the body instantiates geometrical forms. Life forms have a shadowy mathematical Beauty, which can be discerned via "an expansive gaze," that ranges over and compares different species, and also the different sexes, different stages of development, and different structures.[121] Maclise, in *Surgical Anatomy*, refers to "ideal and real facts."[122]

There were, it seems, two kinds of facts for Maclise to deploy as the elements of a visual dialogue. (And maybe two kinds of beauty?) And so plate 47 (Fig. 3.42) stages the principle of symmetry in two registers. The body is positioned in the center of the page, as an axis, framed by a symmetrical ribs and arms of the chair, and underneath, almost as an after-thought, Maclise sketches in a symmetrical pair of kidneys. On the anatomical subject's "right shoulder," he places a compass, a symmetrical instrument used by artists, anatomists, mariners, mathematicians, architects to plot distance and figure symmetry—an iconic emblem of the principle of symmetry and aesthetic unity (and, along with the square rule, an emblem of Scottish Rite Freemasonry). (Maclise was of Scottish ancestry. Was he a freemason?) On the "left shoulder," the compass is balanced by a pin, an implement used in the dissecting room to hold open flaps of cadaveric skin and tissue. The two tools stand for the artist's commitment to truthful witness and accurate rendering, and a kind of epistemological balancing act, which holds in suspension "real facts" (the pin) and "ideal facts" (the compass). We get to see the anatomized body as actually dissected; and larger anatomical principles as thereby revealed.

At the center of the composition is the young man's head. Again, Maclise's pleasure in the depiction of the cadaver's face, with all of its homoerotic valences, overlaps his pleasure in showing off his own bravura aesthetic

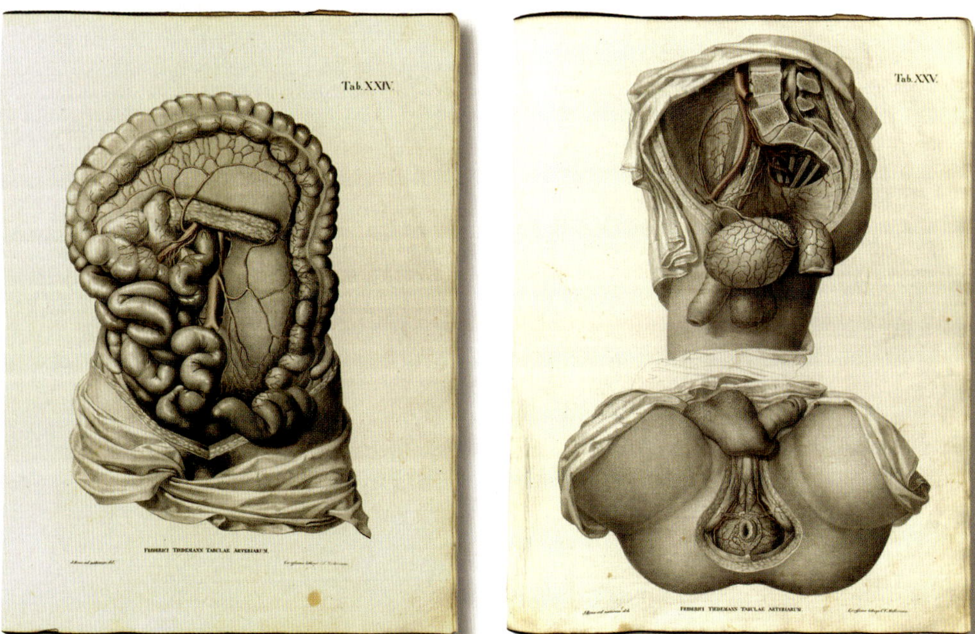

3.45–46 *Friedrich Tiedemann,* Tabulae Arteriarum... *(Karlsruhe, 1822), pls. 24–25. Art: Jakob Wilhelm Christian Roux. Lithographs. 72 × 53 cm. Hagströmer Medico-Historical Library. Tiedemann and Roux mostly conceal genitals with strategic wrappings of cloth (as in pl. 24) and only show them when necessary (as in pl. 25).*

style. The figure could almost be taken as a preparatory drawing for the passion of Christ. The tilt of the head, horizontal bar, and vertical aortic tube, combine to echo the form of a crucifixion. One imagines Maclise—living in the shadow of his famous older brother—as eager to show what he can do beyond mere medical illustration.[123] But an aspiration only to be demonstrated in medical publication: Maclise remained otherwise closeted in his artistic ambitions. We have no non-medical illustrations from his hand, not one. Was he was acquainted with the pre-Raphaelites or John Ruskin's *Modern Painters* (1843)? Who knows? There's not a shred of evidence to indicate any engagement with contemporary art criticism or artists (other than his Parisian studies and his intimate and ongoing connection with brother Daniel).

As a crucifixion, his plate 47 is entirely irregular. The instantiation of God's divinity in a human body is a central feature of Christian theology and iconography—especially in the late medieval and early modern era. And the most instantiated figure of all is the figure of Christ on the cross.[124] Christ's body, with its wounds and blood and genitals and pain and free-flowing feelings of sorrow and ecstasy, is the epitome of the scriptural narrative, a synoptic figure that contains all the elements of the story. Spirit redeems Flesh in all its fleshiness. Transfiguration. Set that against the traditions of anatomical iconography, where the no-longer-living dissected cadaver is drained of blood, and more than anything embodies matter shorn of spirit. In plate 47, the body is so thoroughly dissected, so pared down, as to be a residue, a reduction. Yet, somehow alive, in the rendering. Flesh become spirit, a transfigured transfiguration. We're tempted to identify the head of the young man with the head of Christ but take it one step further and it's the aorta that's standing in for Christ on the cross, functioning as an amalgam of elements. The passion of Christ—the Cross—is refigured as the axis of the body's circulatory system. A formalist abstraction (data compression?), effecting something like what happens in Christian iconography where the story of the crucifixion becomes an emblem, compressed, abstracted into, the sign of the Cross.

2.13 Comparative anatomies: Predecessors, contemporaries

Maclise's packing of signals, gestures, allusions, metaphors, details into hyper-realistic what-the-eye-sees anatomy wasn't unprecedented—historians of anatomy will be reminded of Gerard De Lairesse's drawings for Govard Bidloo's *Anatomia Humani Corporis* (1685). But over 150 years separate De Lairesse and Bidloo from Maclise. The plates of *Anatomy of the Arteries of the Human Body* and the London editions of *Surgical Anatomy* are utterly unlike anything to be found in the atlases of Maclise's Victorian contemporaries and immediate predecessors.

To take the measure of that difference, compare *Anatomy of the Arteries* (1844) to the canonical work Quain says that he aims to supersede, Friedrich Tiedemann's *Tabulae arteriarum corporis humani* (1822) (Figs. 3.45–46).[125] Tiedemann's atlas is spectacular; there are many lessons to be learned, many pleasures to be had. The drawings and dissections are artfully executed and presented, beautifully printed, in a large format. Artist Jakob Wilhelm Christian Roux has an exceptional command of line, texture and composition. But sticks to anatomical business.

The delineation is exceptionally crisp—no mistaking where some anatomical region begins or ends. Anything irrelevant to the topic demonstrated is covered up or omitted. Tiedemann and Roux don't bring readers into the anatomy room. There is almost no undissected skin. No "bedroom scenes," echolalic crucifixions, dissecting-room tables, or *non finito* chairs: no scenes or settings whatsoever. No comely faces or fine physiques. No human figures at all, except for a generic face in the introductory plate. No incidental genitalia: genitals only appear when absolutely necessary, as the main event. And equal treatment for the male and female apparatus.

Roux poses his dissections, mostly torsos, to stand vertically against the white of the page, as if carved in stone. The dissections are tightly wrapped in cloth at one or both ends. And the clothfolds, while beautifully rendered, are stiff, almost sculptural.[126] (Maclise's wraps are looser, freer.) Roux's plates objectify—the anatomist's gaze on the dissected subject is frozen, isolated from any distracting webs of meaning, separated from both the scene of dissection and the viewer. Maclise's plates subjectify—we see the anatomical scene through the anatomist's eyes, gazing upon a sensate anatomical subject, alive with meaning and affective agency. To see the difference just compare Tiedemann's pared-down mesenteric artery (Fig. 3.45), with Maclise's (Fig. 3.5) and Tiedemann's much less sensual dissected rectum and male genital (Fig. 3.46) versus Maclise's take on that pairing (Figs. 3.7, 3.10, 3.26).

Tiedemann's atlas is brilliant, hard to top—Quain acknowledges that "the modern student of anatomy is almost exclusively indebted" to "this valuable work ... for representations of the arterial system." But Maclise tops it. Gives more detail, inside and outside the dissection, more information, relevant and extraneous.[127] Maclise makes scenes which open-endedly refer to both the canon of medical anatomy and non-medical figure drawing. When critics singled out his artwork for its aesthetic virtue, they always paired that with epistemological virtue: "Very beautiful and life-like"; "exceedingly beautiful specimens of art, as well as faithful copies of nature"; "so faithful they will terrify."[128] An advertisement for the Quain-Maclise atlas takes it further: the plates are "Works of Art"

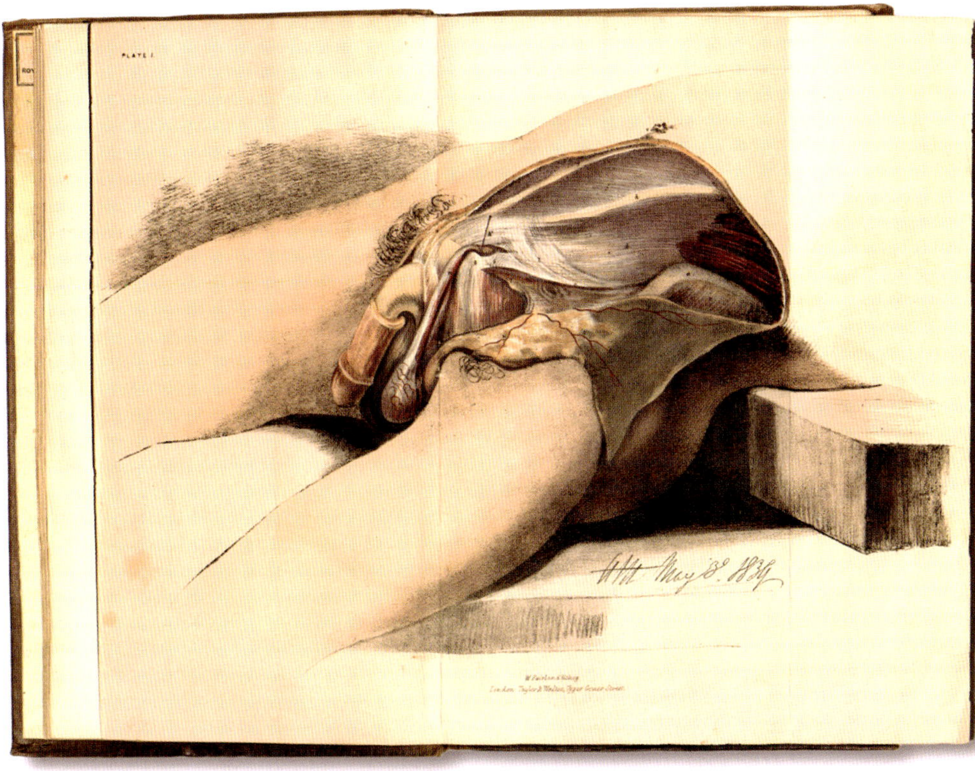

3.47 *Thomas Morton,* The Surgical Anatomy of Inguinal Herniae, the Testis and its Coverings *(London, 1844). Art: Andrew Morton. Chromolithograph. 27 × 16 cm. Hagströmer Medico-Historical Library.*

which are "of intrinsic merit"—not just useful for surgical pedagogy or reference.[129] When Maclise shows the viewer what his eye sees and hand accomplishes, that work is a command performance in two domains.

For another telling comparison, contrast Maclise's plates with those of his near contemporary and colleague, University College Hospital surgeon Thomas Morton (another former student of Richard Quain). Like Maclise, the lithographs (by Morton's elder brother, Andrew) were intended to serve as a guide to surgery on patients with hernias, stones, and fistulas—Morton's specialty—and show male genitals aplenty (Fig. 3.47).[130] And like Maclise, Morton's illustrations have a certain beauty. But an entirely different aesthetic: less controlled, less volumetrically sculptural, a freer hand. Morton's plates have the look of pastels or watercolors, almost a floral color palette. Maybe they incite the visual imagination. But not desire. Morton focuses on the field of surgical operation—regions and body parts—and not the young men and women they are attached to. As in Tiedemann, no comely faces or fine physiques appear.

2.14 The queer figure study

The comparisons are telling, but the epistemological problem remains. We have a kind of queer intensity in his images but we certainly can't say that Maclise had any sort of homosexual love-life or identity (and can't say he didn't). As for the nature of Quain's and Maclise's relations with each other: you have to wonder. But there's no evidence to support any conjecture. Nothing to suggest that they had intimate relations or homosexual inclinations, or shared anything of that sort with each other or anyone else. And we certainly don't know much about conditions in 1840s, 1850s and 1860s Britain. Was there even an inchoate "social context in which homosexual desire might congeal into a personal identity"? (John D'Emilio's question about the twentieth-century formation of "a homosexual minority in the United States.")[131] Scholarship on same-sex desire in mid-century Britain is thin compared to the late nineteenth century.

Maclise's biographical details are especially skimpy. We know he was a bachelor, well-educated and professionally skilled, but what was he like? Thin or thick? Plain or dapper? Shy or outgoing? We have no picture of the man in words or any medium. No photograph, engraving, painted portrait or silhouette. What we know comes almost entirely from his published *oeuvre*, a few references in John Churchill's papers, and the biography of his much better-known brother Daniel. We know he was close to Daniel (who also never married), and for some periods of time the two men lived together in Chelsea and Bloomsbury, and traveled the Continent. That's it.

And we know that, for a few seasons, Maclise was a critics' darling. First for *Anatomy of the Arteries*, then *Surgical Anatomy*, which sold well, went into several editions, and stayed in print for decades. Reviewers singled it out for its usefulness as a practical guide to difficult surgeries and for "the great truth and beauty of illustration": the way it met the cultural goal of combining, conflating, Beauty and Truth.[132] They also marveled at its "moderate cost," only five shillings per installment of the second London edition, "the cheapest illustrated publication on surgical anatomy which has ever appeared."[133] Humble working surgeons and country practitioners could finally afford access to a work of high scientific and aesthetic value, something heretofore only available in the libraries of the great medical schools, and wealthy medical men. The low price, a shrewd marketing decision, was also connected to a democratizing impulse, shared by Maclise and publisher John Churchill. But what no reviewer commented on, could

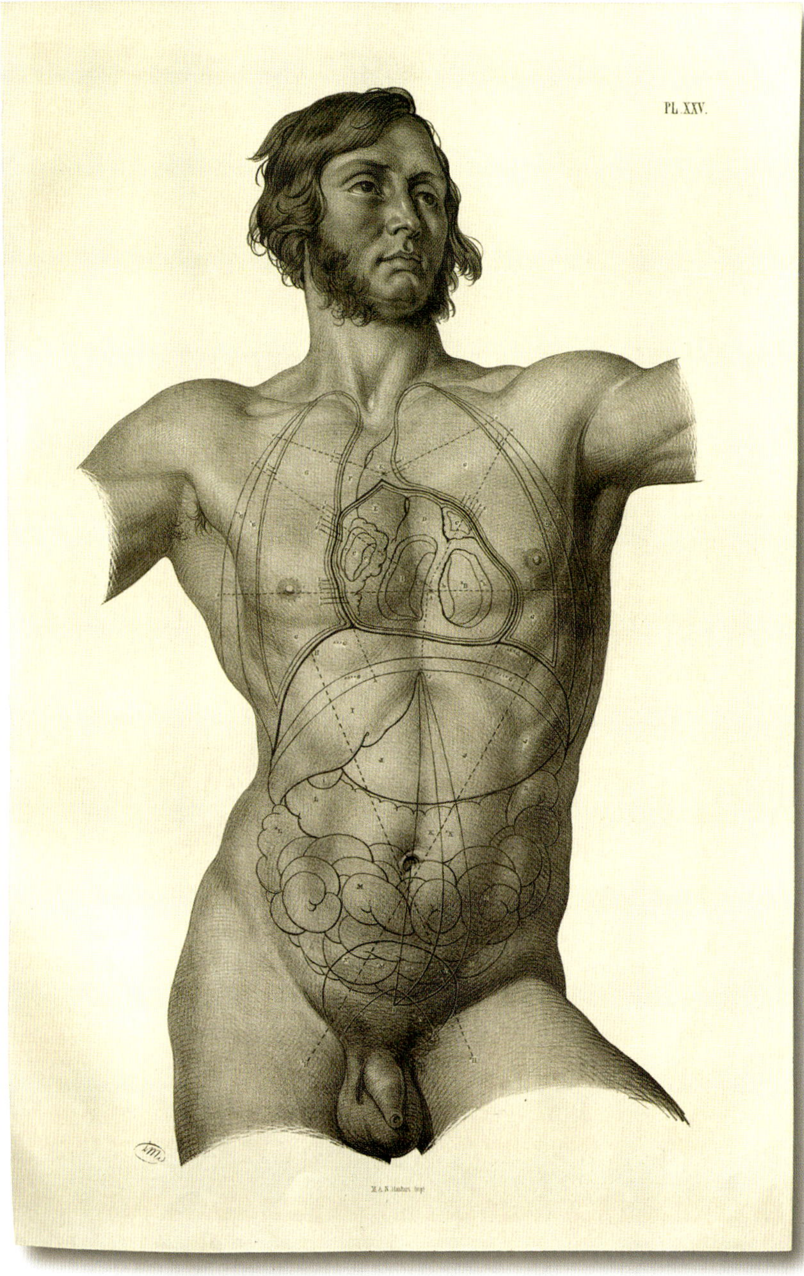

3.48 *The inner view that a surgeon should envision when confronted with a body. (Or the desirable body the artist might conjure when contemplating the anatomical interior.) Joseph Maclise,* Surgical Anatomy *(London, 1856), pl. 25. Lithograph. 54 × 38 cm. Hagströmer Medico-Historical Library.*

ever comment on, is what seems so apparent to us: the encoded homoerotic valence of Maclise's illustrations. Queerness.

So, lots of unknowns. The reviews and commentaries, and even the images, can't help us answer questions of sexual identity or proclivities. Which are simply the wrong questions. Our habit of casting sexual practices in terms of identity leads us astray. Maclise had a proclivity for making pictures of men and masculine body parts—galleries of pictures (Fig. 3.48). The last third of this book is an exercise in interpreting them.

What remains? Genre. Maclise's drawings are a fancy, aestheticized kind of anatomical illustration. Which overlaps another genre that has a long tradition of erotic investment in the male nude—the figure study. Indeed, considered historically, the figure study originated, and has been practiced, as a kind of anatomical study. And vice versa. A knowledge of muscular and skeletal anatomy was the prerequisite for advanced figure study, or rather the very thing that was to be acquired in the iterative practice of making representational studies of the human figure on paper—a pedagogical method, a way to study and learn with hand and eye and mind all operating in concert.

And at the epicenter of the figure study was the artist "drawing from life" mostly naked men—the artist making images, with pen and pencil, charcoal, crayon, etc., of live naked models.[134] Off center, though not far off, were cadavers and écorchés and skeletal remains. The figure study originated as a type of practice drawing—learning by doing—student work, self-study—and also as system of preliminary sketching, preparatory drawing, reference drawing, for an end product—the finished painting or sculpture or engraving.[135] It began with a characteristic sketchiness, an emancipating freeness of hand. As art pedagogy and connoisseurship matured and expanded, that freeness became a valued characteristic even for finished paintings, etchings, and sculptures.[136] And eventually even a method of analysis—a kind of anatomical heuristic.

The hand-drawn sketch could be an artfully crafted end-product, maybe highly polished but often retaining an intimate and beautiful roughness. As a preparatory drawing for a finished painting or sculpture, the sensuality of the drawing method and the representation of nudes could be amply justified by a moral purpose (say a historical, mythological or religious theme) which licensed the artist to craft, and viewer to see, a beautifully made image of a sexy human figure. But once made into a genre, the figure study needed no moral purpose at all: it could just be for pleasure. The pleasure of artist and model. And, as the cult of connoisseurship developed, the pleasure of the collector and knowing aesthete: pleasure in the skill and expressiveness of the artist, pleasure in the buying, owning, showing and seeing, pleasure in knowledgeable assessment and description. And, given the centrality of the male nude in figure drawing—the figure of Man—pleasure in the homoerotic valences.

Those circles of art appreciators were continually enlarged by a growing secondary market in collectable copperplate prints, in profusely illustrated books, and unbound folios and single sheets. And then along came lithography—printing using stone rather than copperplates or wood engravings—invented by Alois Senefelder in 1796 and perfected in France and Germany in the decades that followed the Napoleonic Wars. Lithography made it possible and economical to reproduce and publish images that looked almost exactly like a drawing. The lithograph could reproduce the fine lines and textures of fine pencil and crayon work, and, by the 1840s, even the intense colors of oil painting. "Drawing directly on stone," as Maclise did, there could be a deliberate sketchiness, a feeling of carefree unfinishedness—or carefully enameled finish.

And so in his medical illustrations, N.-H. Jacob, once a student of Jacques-Louis David, was able to demonstrate the same perfectionist mastery of aesthetically tricked-out realism (what Diderot called the *beau réel*) and the precisely delineated "outline style" associated with Ingres and David, who both famously painted luscious images of beautiful naked and semi-naked people with beautiful skin (and sumptuous attire and textiles, if clothed or draped).[137] Maclise was less painterly, though evidently influenced by Jacob, and perhaps Pierre-Nicolas Gerdy (as Anthea Callen suggests) and other artists he might have encountered in Paris.[138] He conjured up images of dissected male nudes with immaculate cross-hatching, sometimes embellished with *non finito* elements. Where color does appear in his plates it is reticent, restrained, a highlighting device, unlike Jacob's illustrations for Bourgery which have a bright painterly clarity—even in their depiction of dire conditions and surgeries—a day-lit joyfulness. Maclise's art refers more to the Renaissance tradition of master draughtsmanship, as carried forward in the great art academies of the day.

That tradition was formulated and reformulated in centuries of connoisseurial discourse, art pedagogy and practice, in treatises, parlors, studios, and galleries. Its most influential eighteenth-century exponent was art historian Johann Joachim Winckelmann. In his writings, the human figure (whether painted, drawn or sculpted) was full of sensuality and erotic valences, infused with his pleasure in Greco-Roman pleasures in, and desire for, idealized hairless, white marbled, naked masculine beauty, along with less idealized, more fleshy variations on the theme. As Whitney Davis and others have argued: queer erotics were at the center, not the periphery.[139] Unspeakable yet obvious, those erotic valences somehow evaded the religious and secular policiers of the intervening centuries. Fine art and the figure study continued to function as domains in which the artist could freely show and play with objects of desire.

Well not entirely free. Certain conventions of modesty governed even sexy Italian and French Empire and post-Empire neoclassical art, say the paintings of Anne-Louis Girodet de Trioson (1767–1824) and Méry-Joseph Blondel (1781–1853), and the sculptures of Antonio Canova (1757–1822).

Sensual pleasure received ample expression, but always licensed by some underlying or attached moral frame, a mythological or historical or religious or philosophical reference, or some stylistic reference to classicism.[140] But, until the provocations of Courbet and later the Decadents (which implicitly asserted that the very category of "art" could simultaneously serve as a moral frame, an honest avowal of desire, and a critique of bourgeois morality and classicist aesthetics)—and until the advent of photographic pornography (which asserted nothing at all)—the connoisseurial gaze had to content itself with the male figure in its entirety. Artists knew to obscure genitalia with a pose, fig leaf or some other device. If male genitalia were to receive representation within the figure (even to titillate or scandalize), there could be no special focus. There had to be some reference to classicism, and following classical precedents, male genitalia were rendered as disproportionately small, juvenilized, "ephebic." Until that also became a bit too much. The space for erotic representation of the male nude was reduced: the female nude became the default vehicle for erotic desire.[141]

As for the erect penis, after antiquity that could only receive polite representation in a medical or scholarly context, and even then only when a particular medical or antiquarian study warranted it, and only for an exclusive, privileged audience.[142] Which is why in the middle decades of the nineteenth century the image of the erect penis discussed earlier in this book would have exerted such a powerful force on those members of the public who could finally get their eyes (hands) on it. The prerogatives of medical publication allowed for a measure of freedom in the representation of parts. In that dedicated space, the impossible was possible.[143]

And so Maclise, uniquely licensed and committed to illustrating the male genitalia—and with a sense of himself as an artist in the grand tradition—and *anatomist* in the grand tradition—was able to make books of figure studies of what was scanted in the academic genre of illusionistic perspectival figure study. And scanted in British anatomical and surgical illustration: naturalistic, sensual, highly aestheticized, proportionate renderings of nude and semi-nude men with genitalia. Which could be hidden in the pages of the anatomical book, among the volumes on the shelves of a medical library, or tacked up for collective but sequestered viewing on the walls of a dissecting room or classroom or lecture hall. Shared among men in the homosocial clubs of professional medicine. While hidden away from view. The anatomical closet.

Maclise was protected by the fact that his transactions with male genitalia were in printed representation, in medical books with a presumably male readership (made even safer still, by the fact that subjects of representation were dead young, presumably working-class men)—and not by any contact with the genitalia of living breathing persons. Contrast that with the storm that erupted in 1886 when newspapers reported that painter Thomas Eakins had removed the loincloth of a living male model while lecturing on anatomy to a mixed drawing class of young men and women at the Philadelphia Academy of the Fine Arts. Eakins was forced to resign his professorship. The outrage over the genital exposure mostly focused on the impropriety of Eakins's failure to protect his female students (and his history of infringing on genital decorum). Eakins had uncovered what ought to be covered. The male genital was a hot zone.[144] *(And contrast that with the delicacy with which Quadal treated the male genital (Fig. 3.4) in his depiction of the drawing class in Vienna, a hundred years earlier.)*

Medical aims provided cover. *Surgical Anatomy* was celebrated as a work of scientific accuracy, surgical acumen and usefulness, and an aesthetic achievement of the highest order. It was the sort of fine publication that previously would have only been found in the libraries of well-to-do medical institutions and elite medical gentlemen—but now was made affordable to hard-working country, urban and military surgeons. It gestured to the world of fine art and high aesthetics, but wasn't just for rich aficionados. It was a useable anatomical-surgical reference *and* a book of delicious beauty, high artistic merit and erudition. And so was inoculated against the charge that it might endanger readers and society by giving vent to "unregulated pleasure," "the explicit articulation of desire."[145] And not just any desire: perverse desire.

2.15 The locked atlas and locked closet

Should such a book—widely distributed and of practical use—be locked away, forced into the closet? Somebody thought so. Columbia University's copy of the London 1851 edition of *Surgical Anatomy* sports a robust brass lock (the key is missing) (Fig. 3.49). We don't know who affixed or installed it: the publisher didn't market *Surgical Anatomy* with a lock. (And we don't know the full provenance, only that the book was previously owned by the anatomy department at Cambridge University, and must have had at least one prior or subsequent owner.)

The question then: why lock up this particular book? We're accustomed to seeing locks on diaries and bound volumes of confidential records or letters, but not on a surgical atlas. A lock can keep secrets safe from prying eyes and moral judgments. Or keep innocent eyes away from a morally corrupting or traumatizing picture or text. A locked book may closet secret knowledge, hidden thoughts, forbidden pleasures, and keep them safe for personal use. A lock may prevent a book from being opened by those who would misuse the contents for illegitimate pleasure, personal gratification.

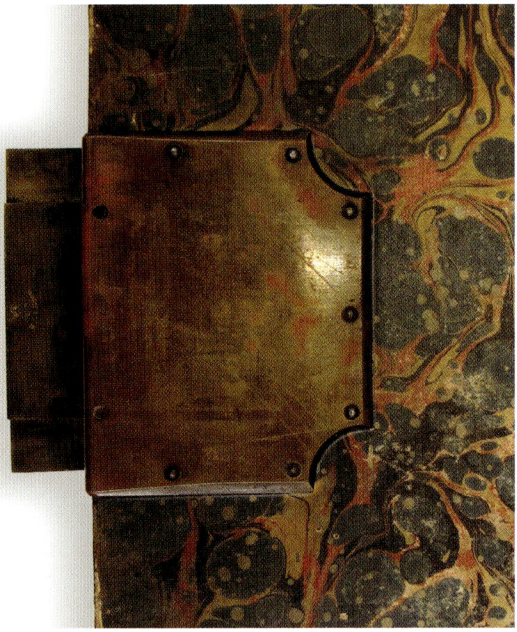

3.49 *Brass lock (close-up), Joseph Maclise,* Surgical Anatomy *(London, 1851), cover. Photograph: Stephen E. Novak. Archives & Special Collections, Columbia University Health Sciences Library.*

All of which indicates some discomfort attached to the contents of a book: the kind of panic that simultaneously fuels homophobia *and* erotic obsession, the panic that instigates and constructs the closet.

In a bibliographic note, Roger Gaskell, the antiquarian bookseller who sold the book to Columbia University's Health Sciences Library, comments that he had never before seen "an anatomy atlas with lock and key," which suggests to him:

> that dissection, like sex, moved the naked body away from the possibility of general viewing into the realm of the specialist. At the same time it demonstrates a domestic location for this copy, the surgeon's house in which a large folio atlas of anatomy might, if it were not locked, be viewed by non-specialists: is this a book you would want your wife or your servants [or children] to look at?[146]

But a lock is not merely a security device. It has meanings and effects. Placed on a book, or cabinet of books, a lock might activate, intensify, the erotic frisson to be enjoyed by potential readers. And so the titlepage of a turn-of-the-century catalogue of pornographic and sexological books leads with this admonition:

> *To be kept under Lock-and-Key* ...: BEING A ROUGH LIST OF Rare, Curious and Uncommon Books, Pamphlets, Prints and Engravings That have been Privately Printed, Prohibited by Law, Seized, Anathematized, Burnt or Bowdlerised; more particularly those relating to the Mysteries of Human Affinities, or dealing with the Attractions and Aversions—Vices and Virtues—Loves and Longings—Hates and Failings—Passions and Peculiarities of Live, Moving Men and Women—and throwing light upon the PSYCHOLOGY OF SEX. (emphasis added)

The offerings of nineteenth-century booksellers and the collections of some wealthy bibliophiles, historian Sarah Bull tells us, commingled pornography with works on medicine, anthropology, psychology, fine art, and Greco-Roman antiquity, all of which could be mobilized for erotic contemplation:

> [C]atalogues such as *Bibliotheca Arcana* (1899), *Choice English Books* (1904), and *Catalogue of Rare and Curious English Books* (*c.*1900) suggest the eroticism and rarity of the sexual-scientific books ... they advertise by listing them side by side with expensive pornography [and] ... imply generic continuity between them.[147]

Such had already been the case back at mid-century, when Maclise was working up *Anatomy of the Arteries* and *Surgical Anatomy.* Bull again:

> In the late 1850s, the Metropolitan Police conducted a series of high-profile raids in Holywell Street—the narrow London lane that was virtually synonymous with obscenity in the Victorian imagination—and seized medical books alongside erotica in the establishments of numerous smut dealers ... When these men ... appeared in court, some argued that their medical books were perfectly respectable professional textbooks and represented the bulk of their trade ... Others ... protested that the "point at which the line could be drawn" between a medical work and an erotic one was so unclear that they could not recognize it and thus could not legitimately be held accountable for tracking obscenity.[148]

Four or five decades after Maclise's debut, that undrawable line was not just a legal defense but also a marketing strategy, well-worn but still successful, on both sides of the publishing divide—pornographic and medical. On the medical side, the Western Publishing House of Chicago, Bong et Cie of Paris, and other publishers, began issuing brightly colored, anatomically explicit "manikins" bound into books or larger-format stand-alones (Figs. 3.50–52) which made no claims to be works of artistic or scientific distinction. These "flap anatomies" exposed in various states of diagrammatic dissection: cut-out (not quite pop-up) "organs of generation": vaginas and penises—some flaccid, others outstandingly erect. And to protect the innocent—and give cover to the prurient—Western Publishing and Bong equipped the editions with locks.[149]

Maclise didn't do that, but take the point: an anatomy book can be a closet or a private club. Open to some readers, closed to others. Coded for

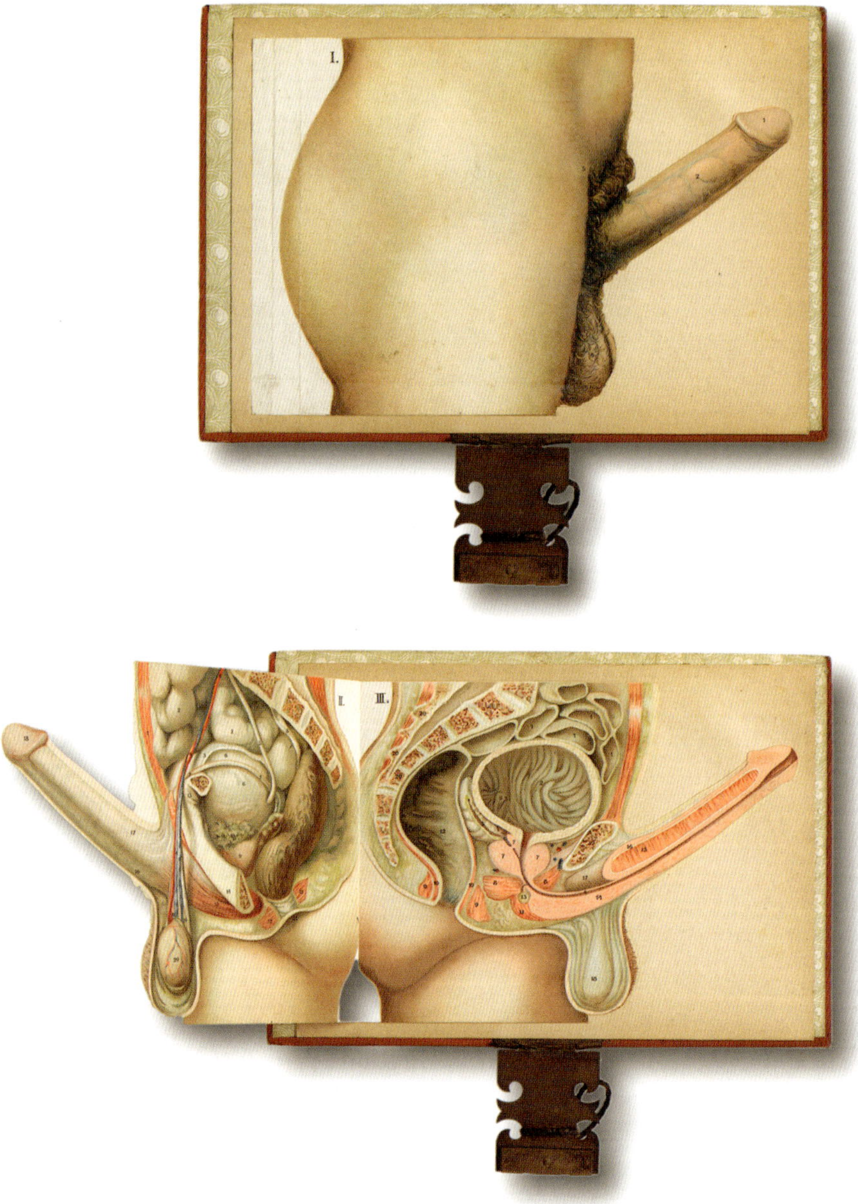

3.50–51 *Erect penises unlocked. M. Platen,* Livre d'Or, *vol. 3 (Paris,* c.*1900).* TOP: *Flap closed, body undissected.* BOTTOM: *Flap open, showing two dissections. Photographs: Laurie Auchterlonie. Wellcome Collection.*

different kinds of reading. Top shelf or easily accessible. Gazed on: with subtle appreciation, or clinical detachment, or intellectual curiosity, or avid sensation-seeking ... Privately viewed or shared in a gated homosocial community. Not in any way a typical contribution to the mid-Victorian "political economy of the closet," whatever else might have been stored there, but suitable for use.[150]

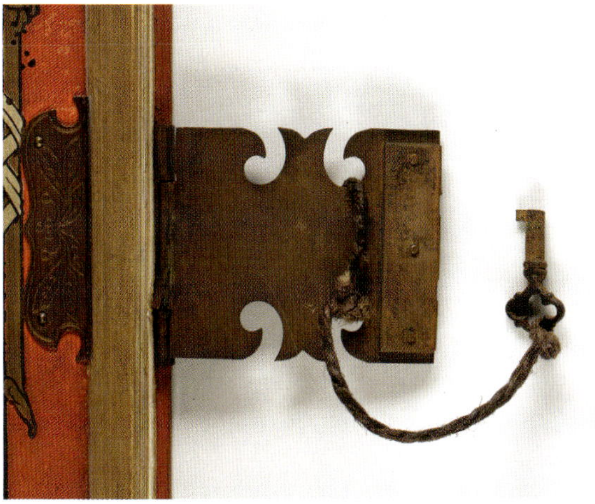

3.52 *Brass lock with key, M. Platen,* Livre d'Or, *vol. 3 (Paris, c.1900), close-up. Photograph: Laurie Auchterlonie. Wellcome Collection.*

2.16 Joseph Maclise's long goodbye

Well then: Slender reeds on which to build an argument. That's all we have, so we have to make do.

Which still leaves us with loose ends dangling. Maclise insisted that "An anatomical illustration enters the understanding straight-forward in a direct passage."[151] Yet a straight-forward reading of his images is not so easily accomplished. Maybe, if we read them in conjunction with other sources, they can be made to say something more about his social and professional performance, and his erotic attachments. We know that in the 1840s and 1850s Maclise attracts notice as a firebrand transformist and receives laudatory mentions in *The Lancet* (then still an oppositional journal, a champion of political and medical radicalism).[152] (Maclise and editor Thomas Wakley likely had a personal acquaintance, maybe a friendship: both studied surgery under Quain and Liston.)[153] As he settles into a career as practicing surgeon, medical author and illustrator, Maclise's drawings are acclaimed and he is raised up to the status of Fellow of the Royal College of Surgeons.[154]

But maybe the dust never settles. Maclise's Geoffroyist ideas on the unity of species, and taste for Lamarckianism, mark him as politically suspect, with "materialist" (atheist) and republican tendencies.[155] Given the brilliance of his artwork, reviewers mostly set aside his transgressive politics. But outside the journals? ... In the spring of 1852, Maclise is passed over for a hospital appointment. A less qualified, less distinguished, man is named instead. An editorial in *The Lancet*—penned by Wakley himself?—vociferously protests on his behalf.[156]

Then, in 1858, at the height of his publishing success, Maclise enters into a pointless two-year-long controversy in the pages of *The Lancet*. Which he brings upon himself by inserting a cranky, disparaging diatribe against William Harvey's account of the action of the heart into *On Dislocations and Fractures*, a book on an entirely unrelated topic. It was a peculiar off-kilter provocation. Harvey was a beloved icon of British medical science, celebrated in lectures, paintings, engravings and sculptures. The convoluted literary tone of Maclise's rant, and convoluted defense of his position in several rounds of letters to *The Lancet*, work to discredit him.[157] (Was he losing his mind?) In 1861 Maclise turns up as a candidate for the position of conservator at the Hunterian Museum. The committee ranks the five applicants; Maclise somehow comes in dead last.[158] As the 1860s unfold, he produces no new publications and drops out of the pages of *The Lancet* and every other medical journal. Maybe he falls from grace when Thomas Wakley dies in 1862 and proprietorship of *The Lancet* passes to Thomas Henry Wakley (Wakley's oldest son), and younger son James takes the post of editor.[159] Maybe Quain doesn't use his pull for Maclise, or doesn't have pull to use. Or maybe Maclise is shunned as politically suspect and temperamentally unserviceable or just plain queer. (A lot is at stake in such matters: Thomas Morton, another Quain student, and the author of a flurry of surgical guides, commits suicide at age 36 when he fails to obtain a hospital appointment.)

During this period, Joseph, in his 40s, lives with brother Daniel. (An unmarried sister, Isabella, "keeps house" for them until her untimely death in 1865.) Perhaps he decides to recuse himself from medical publication and controversy, and concentrate on his surgical practice. Or retires to live off his savings and royalties (if those amount to anything) or his brother's fortune (if he received an inheritance). Or, when Daniel dies in 1870, becomes morbidly despondent over the loss of his beloved siblings. (Another brother, William, had died in the late 1850s.)[160] Or something.

There was also this: Despite "exhortations" in the *British & Foreign Medico-Chirurgical Review* to exercise restraint—the hidden hand of his publisher John Churchill? (who was also publisher of *BFMCR* and *The Lancet*)—Maclise continues to wave the flag for philosophical anatomy. It's a perilous stand, given the nasty tenor of the debate over "creation" "transmutation" and "development."[161] Which puts Maclise at odds with potential benefactors, members of socially and politically powerful circles.[162] And which increasingly invites mockery and, one imagines, eye-rolling condescension. And, in the 1860s, after Darwin comes out with *On the Origin of Species by Means of Natural Selection*, and the controversy shifts from *transformism* to *evolution*, it's a stance that consigns philosophical anatomy to utter irrelevance. Was that turn of events also something that worked to silence Maclise? (He never publicly shares his thoughts on Darwin and evolutionary theory.)[163]

Maclise courts further disfavor by condemning empirical research—in an "age of progress," when research programs are abundantly productive with new findings, and receiving acclaim in scientific journals and the press.[164] It's as if Maclise is declaring the end of history, full stop. In the preface to *Surgical Anatomy*, he fulminates:

> All the sum of facts are long since gathered, sown, and known. We have been seekers after those from the days of Aristotle. And what is ... now remaining to be done, if it be not to arrange the facts in hand, with a view to their proper interpretation? Are we to put off the day of attempting this interpretation for three thousand years more, in order to allow these dissectors time for knife-grinding, for hair-splitting, for sawing, chopping, and hammering this pauper *corpus mortuum* ... ? How long are they to lead us on this dull road, weed-gathering, tracking out bloodvessels, tricking out nerves, and slicing the brain into still more delicate atoms ... in order to coin new names and swell the dictionary?[165]

No subtleties there. It's not the only passage in which Maclise bludgeons the opposition, lays out grievances and expounds on disagreements amounting almost to hatred. If he lays it on thick in his drawings, he lays it on thicker in his prose. To reviewers who called him on his textual excesses, he replies in the "Notice to the second edition" of *Surgical Anatomy*: "I have at times left the beaten march but to seek recreation," then obscurely breaks off into four not very revelatory sentences on science and nature, in Latin, from Bacon's *Novum Organum*. And finishes with this: "I have throughout ... recorded ideal and real facts ... for the seemingly exhausted subject of Anthropotomy [human anatomy] which have not hitherto been either written, spoken, or known ...."[166]

Even with the brilliance of his illustrations, rhetoric like that could scuttle a career. To critics it was crazy talk. (One imagines readers skipping Maclise's prefaces and commentaries and going directly to the plates.) But let's also entertain the possibility that Maclise might be alluding (consciously or not) to other things when musing over recreation-seeking off "the beaten march" and "facts ... not hitherto ... written, spoken, or known ..."

Was there anything? We know that Maclise was in Paris in the 1830s and 40s with Daniel and the two men traveled "over the Continent" (Lyon, Florence, Munich, Naples, Milan, Rome). It's tempting to speculate about what went on in those places: The "Continent" was notoriously an occluded zone where British men, especially artists, went to let their hair down, explore aspects of hetero- *and* homosexual desire that were less rigorously policed there than in their homelands.[167] If such was the case with the brothers Maclise, who shared lodgings in Paris, we might have gotten clues from Daniel's letters to his great friend Charles Dickens. But Dickens, who delivered the eulogy at Daniel's funeral, wrote that he destroyed that "immense correspondence ... because I could not answer for its privacy being respected when I should be dead."[168] No letters from Joseph to Daniel or anyone else have thus far turned up, and no letters to Joseph either. Likely also destroyed, as so often happened in nineteenth-century Britain. So a big blind spot.

Then darkness. Quain dies in 1887 and receives chatty (though not entirely laudatory) obituaries in *The Lancet* and *The British Medical Journal.*[169] Maclise receives no obituary, not in *The Lancet* or any other journal. So what happened? We haven't a clue. His name drops out of the *Medical Directory* in 1879 (the year most catalogs and references give as his death date). Maybe he retired that year but there was no printed announcement. And there was no announcement or remembrance upon his death from "bronchitis" and "syncope" in 1891. Which also seems odd, considering his distinguished record of publication and distinguished brother.[170] (The death certificate describes him as a "retired army surgeon." That was likely a mistake, but if at some point he had entered the service in his 40s or 50s, that would add another twist to his life-story.)

So consider the possibilities: Maybe Maclise had a rich professional, social and erotic life, lots of patients and friends, one or more lovers. Nothing in the record suggests he did or didn't ... Or imagine the opposite: Maclise as a loner, thwarted in sociability, career aspirations, and love, a man who lives in the shadow of a famous and gregarious brother. Imagine him as an extraordinarily sensitive, even oversensitive, man of highly cultivated senses—medical and artistic, and let's say erotic—gripped by same-sex desire, which in his homophobic milieu gives rise to another kind of sensitivity: a sensitivity to hidden erotic valences in people and things, slight cues, little gestures, subtle tones and textures, camouflaged symbols, nuances—"Gay-dar"?—which others may be entirely blind to (a motif that would later be given voice in late nineteenth-century Aestheticist and Decadent narratives).[171] Yet also a man easily wounded, touchy, prickly, with a talent for alienating people and undermining himself. A practitioner of "the queer art of failure" (the piquant title of a seminal work of queer theory by Jack Halberstam).[172] A poor candidate for homosociality or any other kind of sociality. But who, consciously or not, compensates by concocting an expressive circle of imaginary friends, a cast of naked masculine figures—cadavers, yes, yet somehow alive in the drawn image. And a man who, consciously or not, places emphatic marks of erotic feeling in those drawings. While suppressing them in his public persona as a practicing surgeon and medical author. And also in his social persona?

We don't know ... And can't know. Because Maclise declined to say anything at all about his affective life. When he writes that pictures "enter the understanding straightforward in a direct passage," he is also saying that words don't. A limitation of language itself. But perhaps, less grandly, more personally, a stricture on words, *his* words. A stricture on Maclise the speaker, the writer, the social actor.[173]

Pictures communicate things—strongly, directly—a "more vivid reality" (Maclise insists)—that words don't.[174] And maybe Maclise is signaling two things at the same time, in words as well as images: Words can't adequately describe the functions and structures of the body. And words can't be permitted to declare erotic investments in masculine bodies.

Pl. 28.

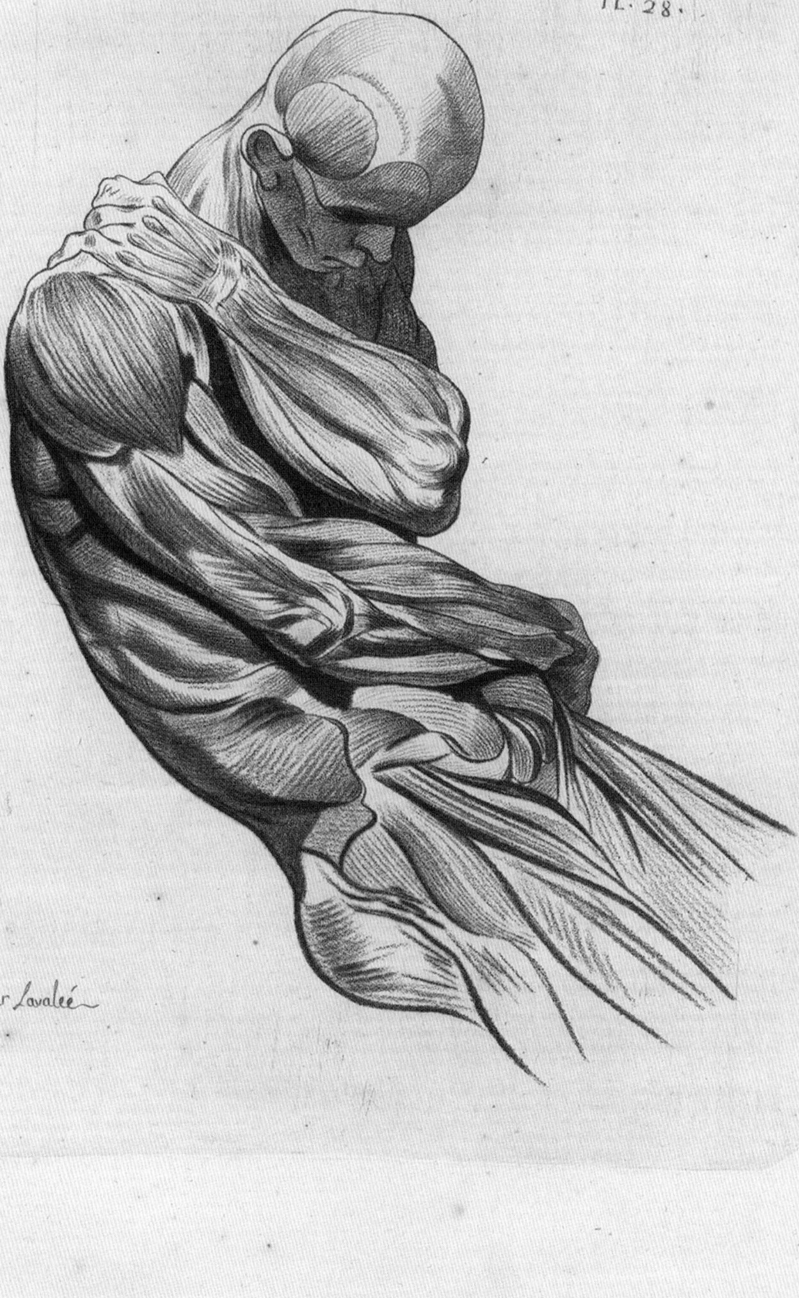

Gravé par Lavalée

PART FOUR

Conclusion

1.1 The ontology of the anatomical closet

A generation or two after his zenith, Maclise's image-work and reputation began to fade from memory.[1] Works like *The Anatomy of the Arteries of the Human Body* and *Surgical Anatomy*, though still valued by collectors, no longer seemed modern, and the arty illustrated super-sized anatomical folio no longer stood atop the hierarchy of medical publication. The old medical order was coming undone. As medical specialties proliferated, the very idea of such a hierarchy was losing currency. And the market in anatomical publication was coming to be dominated by the many affordable (and continually updated) editions of *Gray's Anatomy* (Fig. 4.2) and similar works, with their many thousands of small, emphatically legible, line-art diagrams and wood engravings.

Even had *Surgical Anatomy* somehow retained its usefulness as a practical guide, its visual holism, high aesthetics, cranky politics, literary allusions, and glowing sensuality would still have looked old fashioned—and maybe a bit *queer*. The *tour de force* plates, the extraordinary sensitivity to touch, the provocative commentaries, had an over-the-top intensity which exceeded the conventions of medical and professional comportment. And which encoded something. Thwarted desire for recognition as an artist? Thwarted desire for recognition (as a master surgeon and dissector and misunderstood genius)? Or thwarted desire to openly touch and be touched? (Thwarted desire.) Some or all of the above.

As advances in medical and surgical technique, theory, and instrumentation piled on top of each other, there was an increasing sense

4.1 *Jacques Gamelin,* Nouveau recueil d'ostéologie et de myologie, dessiné, d'après nature… *(Toulouse, 1779), pl. 28. Copperplate soft-ground etching: Jacques Lavalée. 54 × 40 cm. Waller Collection, Uppsala University Libraries.*

that modern times required modern texts and modern approaches and modern attitudes, and continual updating. A certain kind of modernizing professional and scientific decorum increasingly took hold in medical publication (and in dissecting rooms and anatomy labs, where in centuries past decorum had often been hard to come by).[2] Which did not include value-added encoding and thwarted desire.

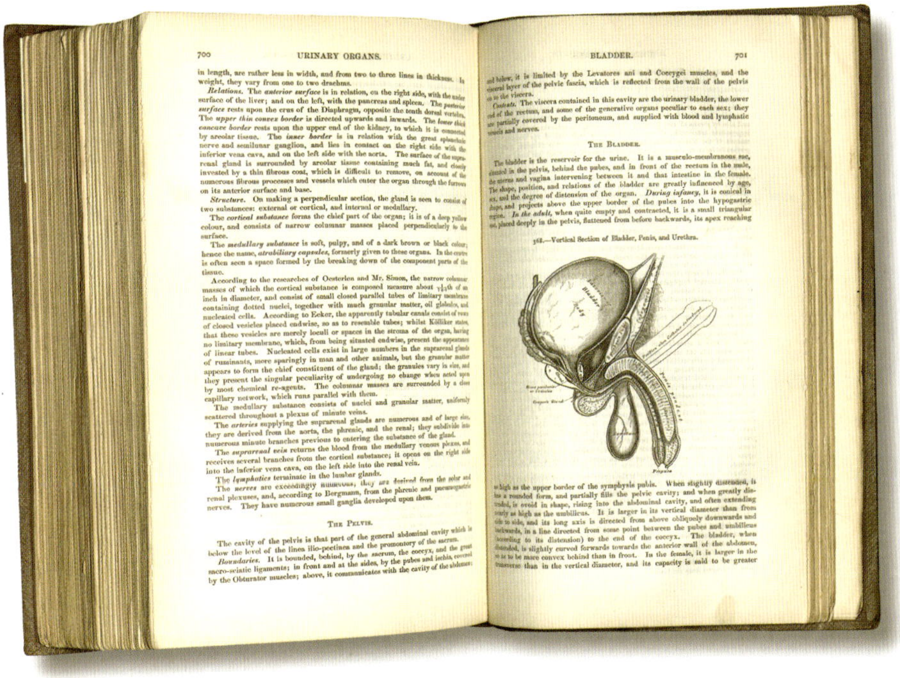

4.2 *Anatomy democratized and practical, with emphasis on parts. "Vertical Section of Bladder, Penis, and Urethra," Henry Gray,* Anatomy Descriptive and Surgical *(1858; London, 1864), 701. The figure illustrates the mechanics of an erection, but with no erotic pleasure added. Art: Henry Vandyke Carter. Wood engraving. 26 × 16 cm. Hagströmer Medico-Historical Library.*

Anatomical publication was rationalized and democratized. Greater professional specialization, and an ever-expanding curriculum of medical knowledge, brought a new focus on parts and regions of the body. Irrelevant material was excised from the anatomical image, expressive style tamped down, deemed unscientific, behind the times. This was not exactly the kind of "crisis of representation" that beset neoclassicism in the 1830s and 1840s (in which sensual, gender-ambiguous naked young "ephebic" men were switched out for sensual young female nudes as paragons of representational beauty, and women began to supplant men as models in life-drawing classes).[3] But certainly a sea-change. Heading into the twentieth century, "Art" and "Science" were taken to be antithetical categories. In the new age, as Lorraine Daston and Peter Galison show, the beautiful and the ideal type were repositioned to stand as the enemy of objectivity.[4] And if beauty was an enemy, sexy beauty was even more so.

Fine art's truth claims in realist depiction were increasingly unsustainable. The order of independently verifiable objectivity gradually gave way to hard-to-define oppositional truths (ramped-up aestheticism, symbolism, impressionism, primitivism, cubism, surrealism, formalism, even engagé

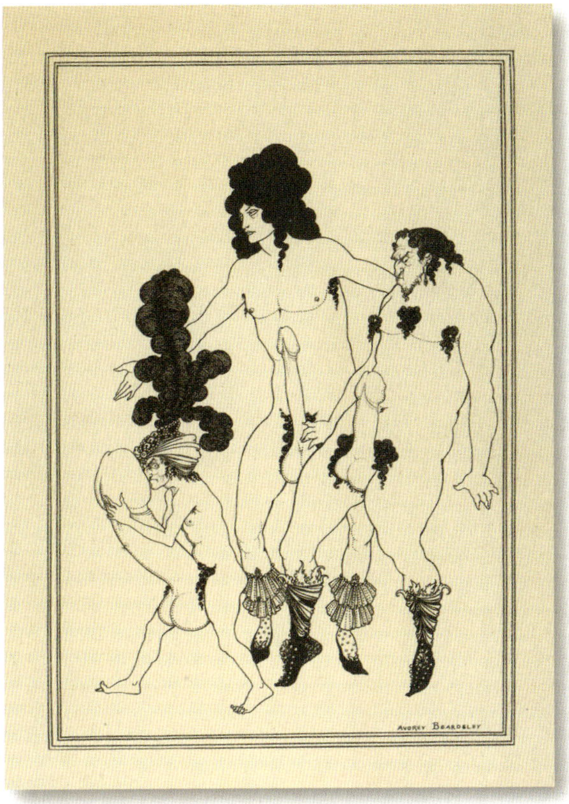

4.3 *Aubrey Beardsley, "The Lacedaemonian Ambassadors,"* Lysistrata *(1896; c.1926). Collotype print. Image: 26 × 18 cm. Sheet: 35 × 25 cm. Metropolitan Museum of Art.*

social reportage).[5] As anatomist *and* artist, Maclise's aim was to conjure up the two traditional kinds of truth-telling: the real and the beautiful. But by century's end that commingling of truths no longer had rhetorical salience. In a world where Art and Science were increasingly consigned to separate spheres, the two poles of scientific illustration were legibility and unblinking truth-to-nature, and the dominant tone was disinterested, unfeeling sobriety. Maclise's coded sensuous multivalent aestheticization queered that, put an idiosyncratic artistic personal stamp on his drawings. When he insisted that "An anatomical illustration enters the understanding straightforward in a direct passage, and is almost independent of written language," did he ever pause to consider how his own drawings complicated that precept?[6]

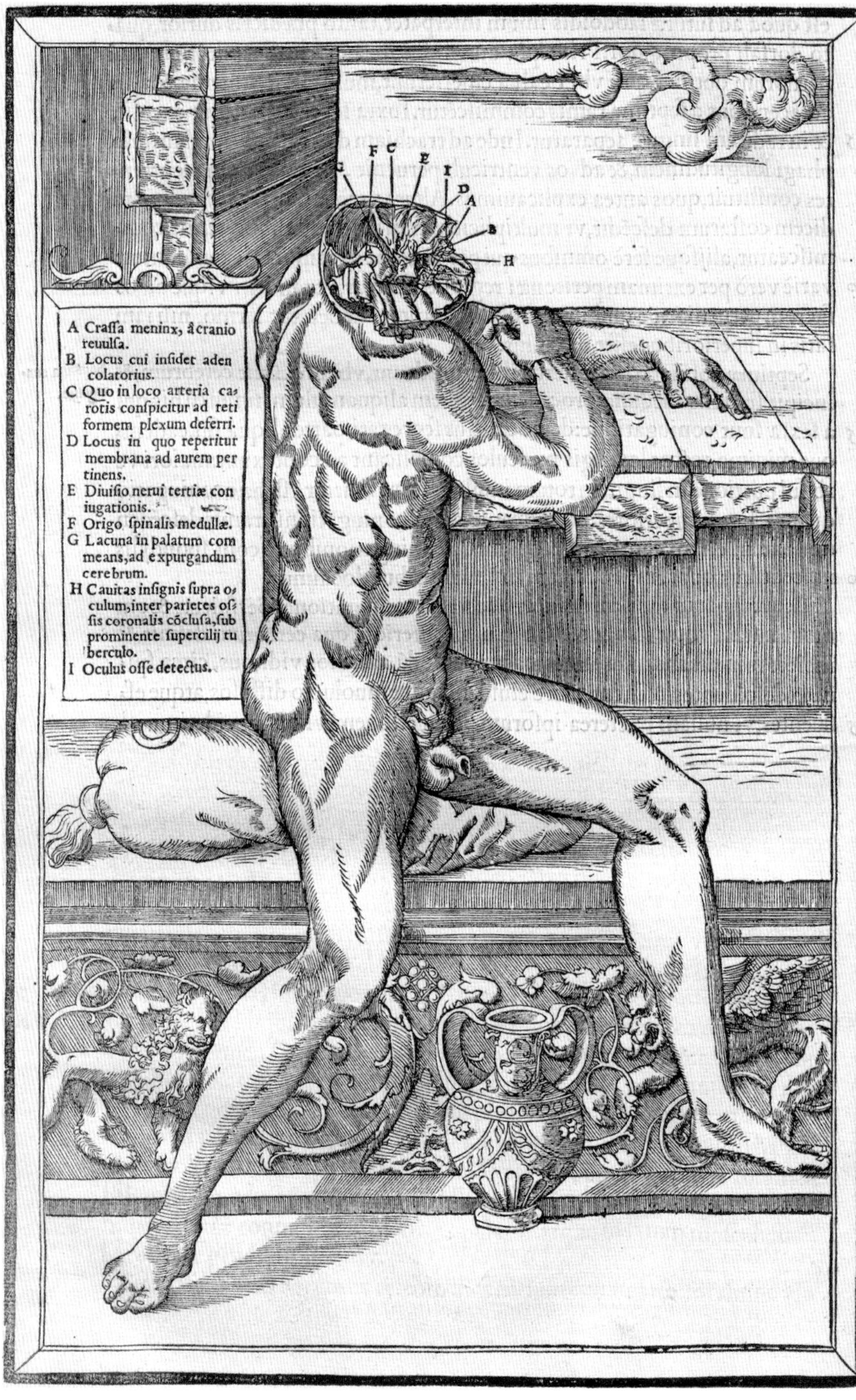

4.4 *Paper doll classicism, riotous filigree, carnivalesque travesty. Charles Estienne,* De dissectione partium corporis humani libri tres *(Paris, 1545), 250. Art: Étienne La Rivière. Woodcut: Jean "Mercure" Jollat. 36 × 23 cm. National Library of Medicine.*

Beyond that, with the rise of the Decadents, Aesthetes and pornographic photography—and advertising graphics, burlesque, and then silent film—the signs and meanings and venues of erotic beauty began to transmutate … Artists like Aubrey Beardsley, Walter Sickert and Franz von Stuck were perversely, daringly, staging themselves *in* their artwork as the apotheosis of connoisseurial sophistication and sensitivity and/or apostacy, scandalously collapsing the distinction between pornography and art, representing unrepresentables: sexual intercourse, fetishism, homoeroticism, even the erect penis (Fig. 4.3).[7] Erotic connoisseurship no longer needed anatomical plates to supply representational objects of desire.

All of that happened a long time ago. And now in the twenty-first century we arrive at a new season of returns and reappraisals. The anatomical illustrations of Joseph Maclise come down to us unlocked, emancipated from the closet and private club, the secret museum and medical library. And right behind them, flaunting their wares, Casserius, Spigelius and Fialetti, Cheselden, Gautier Dagoty, Bourgery and Jacob, Sappey and Léveillé, and the rest. All relics of a lost (I think queer) civilization, where same-sex engagements and perverse desires were very common, maybe more common than in our time, but entirely unmentionable. Yet asserted nonetheless by anatomical hands in pencil and crayon and ink on paper.

Now released to us, those queer images freely circulate in a much enlarged and diversified public domain of appreciative viewers: male, female, non-binary; white, off-white, black, people of color; homo, hetero, bi, queer, trans, kinky, cultural theorists, art historians, historians of medicine, collectors, postcolonialists, gender and queer studyists, and hipsters. Health professionals and the laity. Anyone who has eyes to see what was once "hiding in plain sight": images that previous generations of scholars were conditioned to ignore or politely refrain from remarking on.[8]

And yet, we also have blinders. We tend to sort the world into "cultures": dominant, subaltern, Indigenous and queer. Which surely makes sense in one way: Marginalized and self-marginalizing people develop particularities of place and time and preference, and seek each other out in any space that they can occupy. Our/their histories are overlooked or suppressed, left out of the hegemonic narrative. So we/they want to write us/them back in.

But look at the relationality of it. Only some of us are born into or grow up in those "subcultures." We form or join them (and are changed by them), yet even fewer of us live in them exclusively. Instead, we divide ourselves between abnormative and normative culture(s). Where we play out, tweak, suffer and push back against the contradictions and traumas—and exploit potentialities and opportunities (*aka* "affordances"). Queer effects and persons grow from that fertile or toxic soil … Male effeminacy and female masculinity (and non-binarity) grow out of the male/female gender binary, and so do male hyper-masculinity and female hyper-femininity: our butches, femmes and drag kings and queens depend upon it. D/s and BDSM are chained to the unattainable ideal of the sovereign self-reliant self-possessed individual in a world of racialized, classed, gendered and propertied relations of power and dependency. Teacher/student, boss/employee, parent/child, cop/civilian, landlord/tenant. Unequal, lopsided, relations of power super-charge the erotics of kink.

And so on, going through all the particulars of our civilization's major themes and fragmented byways ... People of color, kink, queer and deviant communities have a special claim and a special role, a special awareness, but everyone partakes in some way (willingly or unwillingly, willingly *and* unwillingly) in the categories and power relations that enact and re-enact perverse desire, illegibility, resistance, queerness. No one is pure. Everyone is complicit.

And maybe that's the trajectory of this book. With the invention of the printed illustration, the body and its parts were transformed into the sequenced pages of an encyclopedic scientific treatise, where the flimsy, perspectivally-challenged anatomical "theater" of early modern and Enlightenment delighted readers with its carnivalesque travesties. Anatomy gave the world a rich new visual vocabulary of the human, an epistemically privileged template of the ideal body—Man—that also served as the venue for all sorts of perverse performances: cadaverous flirtation, muscle-beach classicism, danse macabre, jokey scenes of dissected horror, riotous filigree, unmitigated grotesquery (Figs. 4.4–5). Which could provoke wayward desire or just wink it away.

But when you get to Govard Bidloo (Fig. 4.6), William Hunter, Albrecht von Haller and John Bell, you cross a threshold. The anatomist transforms himself (and by extension the viewer) into a scope, empties himself of affect as he enters the human body. And uses visual provocation, shock treatment, to persuade the viewer (and himself) that he's not kidding (or takes the opposite tack: overwhelms the reader with fulsome, sometimes boring, technical detail). Anatomical representation alienates the viewer from embodied experience. The anatomist and surgeon claim the body as their technical property. Then along comes Maclise who gives it an additional turn of the screw: he's present at both ends of the scope, staring at his dissected men but also surrendering to them, inhabiting them, and staring back. There's a collapse between viewer and representation.

How should we account for that? Foucault taught us that there are "orders of things," a historical succession of orders, each with its distinctive vocabulary, hierarchies, metaphors, technologies and operating instructions. And each attended by its own particular configurations of disorder. The contradictions, edges, inconsistencies, pile up. It takes a lot of work to keep order in the order of things, a lot of policing, a lot of institutional resources, often a lot of violence. And eventually the order breaks down or transforms, and a new order comes into being, a new world.

"Nothing"—no person, no object—"comes without its world" (says eco-feminist philosopher Donna Haraway).[9] So what of Spigelius's world?

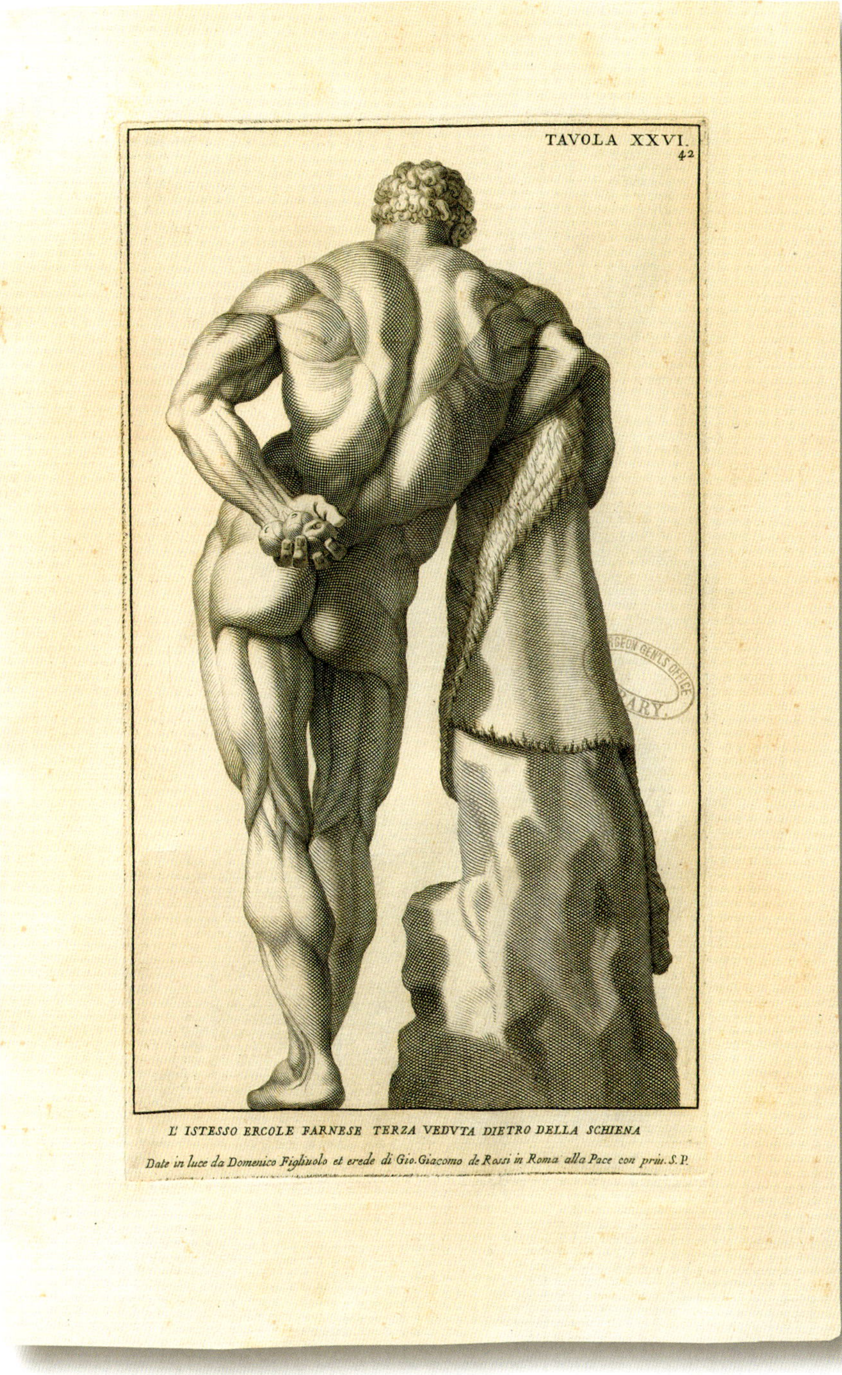

4.5 *Bernardino Genga,* Anatomia per uso et intelligenza del disegno ricercata non solo su gl'ossi, e muscoli del corpo humano *(Rome, 1691), pl. 42. Copperplate engraving. 48 × 36 cm. National Library of Medicine. A beefed-up representation of the (already beefy) Farnese Hercules, an ancient statue unearthed in Rome in 1546. That celebrated discovery inspired a new wave of enthusiasm for the figure of Hercules as the personification of marbled (rock-hard, muscular) masculine strength.*

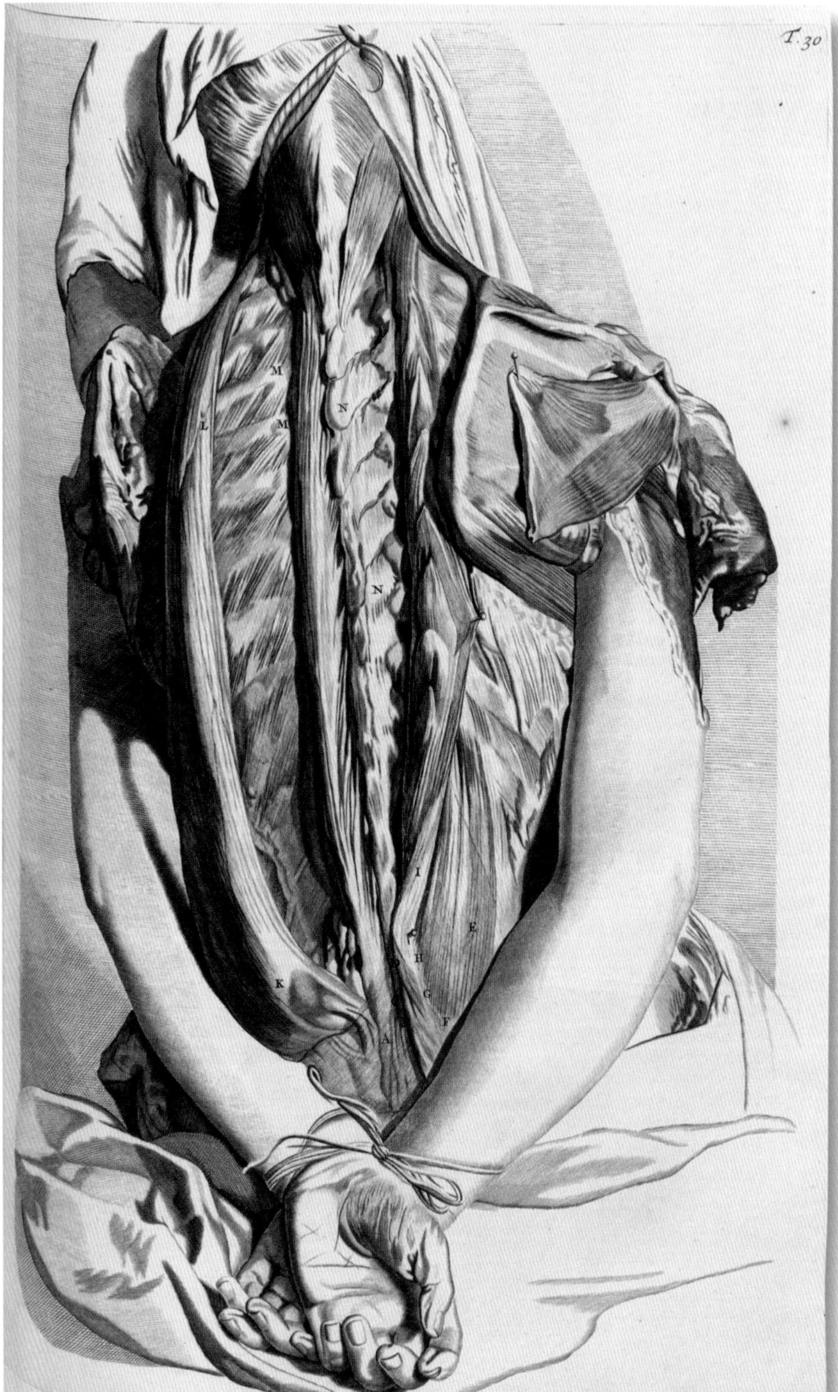

4.6 *Visual provocation, horror, in the mode of Netherlandish illusionistic trompe l'oeil realism. Govard Bidloo,* Ontleding des menschelyken lichaams *(Amsterdam, 1690), pl. 30. Art: Gerard De Lairesse. Copperplate engraving. 51 × 36 cm. National Library of Medicine.*

Cheselden's. Maclise's. Ours. It's no easy task to name and explicate worlds (in Foucault-speak, *epistemes*). Take, for example, the visual tactics of early modern illustrated anatomies, with their unstable mixture of classicism, pictorial conventions of framing and entertaining, and commitments to truthful visual depiction. Do they correspond to an erotics and a menu of types of personhood, a system? If so, what could that be?

When we conjure up the masculine world of the Restoration and Enlightenment elite, we conjure up a culture of connoisseurship, sensibility, discernment, rhetoric, great wealth amid great poverty. And a publicly visible erotics, performatively extravagant, full of drunken excess and homosocial revelry. We envision clubs of libertines acting out their masculine upper-class prerogatives, while sneering at middle-class propriety and the slatternly unwashed lower classes. In both Britain and France, men of privilege were governed by codes of masculine honor that tolerated, even celebrated, whoring and sodomitical relations as long as there was some plausible public deniability. A life of the senses and sensual gratification, full of intellectual interest for some, but attended by an almost compulsory playfulness, violence and militarism, and a certain superficiality. A flatness that was saturated in hierarchy. None of which was connected to any cult of deep feeling, or transcendence or "metaphysics of presence." (Let's call that a rough sketch of an eighteenth-century flat ontology—not to be confused with the more thorough-going anti-hierarchical, anti-essentialist version that makes the rounds in the works of Manuel DeLanda and Bruno Latour.)[10]

Set all that against the history of anatomical representation in early modernity and the Enlightenment. Since Vesalius and his successors placed the dissected body at the center of anatomical knowledge production, way back in the sixteenth century, anatomy has always oscillated between the flat two-dimensionality of the printed illustration (often in the mode of classicism) and the messy, smelly, hard-to-manage three-dimensional presence of organic life and death. And mediating between: techniques that evoked three-dimensional depth and volume in two-dimensional representation. Such as Netherlandish illusionistic perspective (the brilliant renderings of De Lairesse and Van Rymsdyk), flap anatomy (*Dr. Franke's Phantom*), the stereograph, the layered anatomical transparency, and, nowadays, digital and holographic anatomy. Those authoritative anatomical images, crafted within an uneven blend of aesthetic styles—and sometimes including male and female genitalia—had cognitive effects. Under the influence of anatomy, the literate elite, medical professionals, and later a growing readership of middling persons, came to see themselves as anatomical bodies corresponding to the illustrations they looked at in printed books. And so do we. (A longwinded answer to the question: Why should we care about the history of anatomical representation?)

But what of same-sex desire? The literary historian Regina Janes locates a hinge in the mid-1700s, a transition in what was permitted to elite masculinity. Writing on John Wilkes's *An Essay on Woman* (1763), his utterly obscene parody of Alexander Pope's *An Essay on Man* (1733), she argues that, "for the Restoration wits of the previous century":

> ... boys were proper objects for the libertine aristocratic yard, an occasional debate being "Whether the boy fucked you, or I the boy" (Rochester, "The Disabled Debauchee" [*c*.1675]). In *The Country Wife* [1675], William Wycherley's rake hero Horner French kisses Margery dressed in a boy's clothes, but thinks he's kissing a boy. By the mid-18th century, however, "Woman" limits the legitimate excursions even of libertinism. The boys are gone, and the men are ... simultaneously acknowledged and disallowed as objects of desire.

What was left for wanton rakery was the brandishing of phalluses and phallic potency, as a kind of naughty, impish celebration, which was evident in both Wilkes's suppressed poem and in the Society of Dilettanti's willful attachment to priapic antiquities and survivals. The libertine, always gesturing to his homosocial clubmates, now pointed to his collection to boastfully affirm his manhood among pals, but with a hard limit: a ban on self-avowed homoerotic expression. Which was a big change from the graded hierarchy of the Restoration and early Georgian era, "in which women and boys (or fools)," that is to say weak men, "were taken to be equally inferior" and "equally proper as sexual objects": equally fuckable.

Janes (apparently following Thomas Laqueur) explains the transition as the consequence of a "new gendering" that insisted on "biological difference and incommensurability."[11] And therefore: "boys belong with men, while sodomites belong with 'woman'." But across the Channel, the Marquis de Sade certainly wasn't insisting on biological difference, he was trying to universalize, de-Christianize and sensorialize the old order of fuck-anyone-or-anything aristocratic male privilege. And "new gendering" doesn't satisfy as an explanation. "Gendering" isn't an agent: the term can't be anything other than a synoptic label for a trend made up of people, organized into groups and systems and political agendas. And you don't have to accept Laqueur's "one-sex" thesis (which has been shot full of holes over the decades) to get that there was a reconfiguration of erotics, a shift from openly permitted expression of sodomitical interest to a new culture of discretion, one that still allowed wide scope for "libertine play," maybe even "greater personal freedom" to play (according to Janes)—but which came packaged with a new sacralization of "true" womanhood and a heightened vilification of male effeminacy—and a dire new carceral regime of sodomy laws and prosecutions.[12]

But what caused that? Clearly, a bunch of things changed toward the end of the eighteenth century: The rise of wealthy mercantile and industrial elites and bourgeois (or is that middle-class?) morality; the cult of sentimentality; Romanticism and the valorization of deep feeling; temperance and reform; the spread of literacy, journalism and the rise of the novel with its wish fulfillments and braided moral tales; the puritanical moralism of the French Revolution (in France, a reaction against aristocratic libertinism) or (in Britain) the puritanical reaction against the French Revolution and

Frenchness, and then Napoleon. Jason Kelly, arguing along some of the same lines as Janes, notes that, in the last decades of the eighteenth century:

> A public predisposed to respect middling values of gentility and knowledge increasingly encouraged men to cloak their liaisons, discussing them only within limited peer groups. Self-control and manly duty to the maintenance of a virtuous household were essential features in the developing "cult of domesticity" which demanded that men pursue sexual encounters privately ... Masculine communities [became] ... private realms within the public world in which men could indulge their sexual appetites ... [W]hat began in the 1780s was the creation of a private space for male libertinage.[13]

Libertinage was forced to become more discreet and justify its clubby revels with moral or scientific purpose. (That sounds familiar.) There was an increase of policing of erotic behavior up and down the social hierarchy: an increasingly powerful state in which police and judicial systems were being established and expanded. Let's also take "private space" as an indispensable location for the closet, and the formation of closeted homoeroticism. But we still don't get much of *why* it happened. Like Janes, Kelly's *Society of Dilettanti* gets fuzzy when it comes to accounting for the details and reasons for that broad transformation in the order of things. (Same thing with Solomon-Godeau's big transition.) It's hard to know when it comes to causation.

So we end with questions, just like we started. What configuration of forces and trends (institutions, architecture, social hierarchy, political realignments, wars, technologies, economies, and associations) led from Cheselden to Hunter (with Bidloo, presciently anticipating the shift, messing up the chronology, by almost a century)? And what configuration then gave rise to the multi-layered multi-textured illusionistic perspective of mid-nineteenth-century anatomy (Jacob and Maclise), with all of its erotic valences? And how did that correspond or contribute to (or even chafe against) the dynamically transforming deep-mind, deep-body self of deep-feeling essentialist Victorian personhood (*aka* Romanticism)?

During the writing of this book, I kept "the epistemology of the anatomical closet" top of mind as a title or subtitle. But maybe "the ontology of the anatomical closet" is just as good. *Queer Anatomies* doesn't argue that Casserius or Gautier or Cheselden or Holmes were closeted, only that their anatomical illustrations were a vehicle ("affordances") for homoerotic, connoisseurial and libertine attachments. The anatomical image was full of representational queerness, open and easily decoded, for the clubs of men who looked upon them in medical and private libraries. By the 1830s and 1840s, that had coalesced into an archive of visual and epistemic tactics that made Joseph Maclise and a different kind of queerness possible (but not inevitable). The shadowy unproveable anatomical closet.

This book is an extended argument, in words and (especially) images, for *queer* as a vital category of analysis for historians of anatomical representation. *Queer* has all sorts of special virtues for scholars trained in

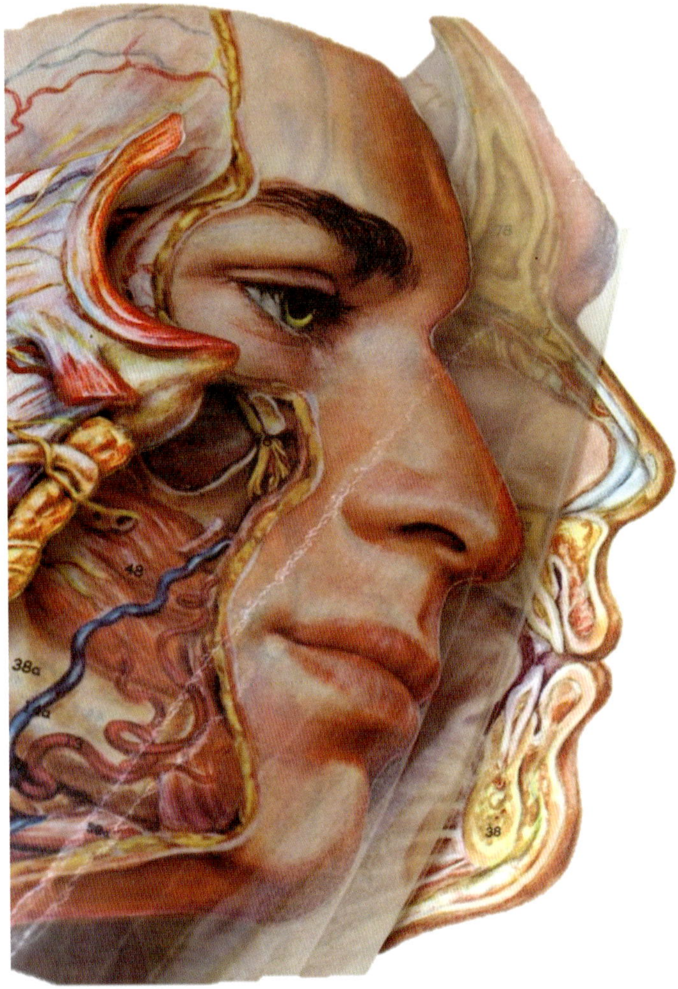

4.7 *Gladys McHugh, P.C. Kronfeld & S.L. Polyak,* The Human Eye in Anatomical Transparencies *(Rochester, NY: Bausch & Lomb, 1943). Art: Gladys McHugh. Plastic overlay transparency. 29 × 23 cm. National Library of Medicine. Photograph: Mark Kessell.*

art history and scholars trained in the history of medicine and science (who haven't done much talking to each other until recently). But *queer* has its own history. A lot of queer studies scholarship is undertaken as a rescue mission, to uncover and then memorialize the lost and erased histories of marginalized queers and queer communities. Worthy, important work, but *Queer Anatomies*, even if it does excavate a "lost archive," has a different agenda. It conceives of *queer* as a built-in feature. Orthodoxy generates queerness. Normativity needs queerness (whatever that might be) to define itself in opposition to.[14] And that makes *queer* vital and necessary for cultural history, analysis and critique.

All good. But once *queer* is everywhere and everything, maybe it's nowhere and nothing. Does putting *queer* in the very center of "normative" anatomical representation, and normativity writ large, queer the concept of queerness? Queer theorists have recurrently, brilliantly, attended to that question for several decades now.[15] *Queer Anatomies* won't. It's enough to show here that, over the centuries, anatomy was a genre that allowed, encouraged, the depiction of objects of perverse desire—objects that outside of anatomy were suppressed as morally objectionable or just plain illegible.

Perverse objects, perverse desire. Attentive readers will have noticed that throughout this book *perverse desire* and *queer desire* stand as close proxies for each other. *Queer* is especially useful because it comes with a finely articulated theory and descriptive vocabulary. But perversity, while not as closely identified with homosexuality, covers a lot of the same ground: same-sex desire, necrophilic enthusiasm for the dissected body, libidinal investments in aesthetic and medical objects, compulsions to possess, relations of dominance/submission, body modification and transformation, role reversal, bondage, voyeuristic pleasure in the viewing of anatomical scenes that are otherwise unseeable in polite company. Rage, abjection, travesty, heat.

Yet I'm aware that some readers will take *perverse* to be a derogatory term and may be offended. Or take it as a negative and put the term entirely under the sign of patriarchal violence, rape, and abuse. Or just don't want to associate queerness (which has gained a measure of acceptance) with perversity (which hasn't). For those readers, the word is ruined by its association with the mostly discarded psychological/sociological term *sexual perversion*, with all of the normative judgmentalism that goes along with it. And by association with *pervert*, a word which continues to be tossed around as an insult—even though many people in queer and kink communities use it as a term of endearment (and embrace *perversity* and *deviance* without any negatives attached, in the same way that *queer* has been elevated from insult to cherished identity). I don't have any issues with *perverse desire*. But, to allay concerns that readers might be dissuaded from giving *Queer Anatomies* a chance, I've removed it from the subtitle, though not the text.

A final thought: if same-sex pleasure and desire have for centuries stood in plain view at the very center of medical publication, they can also lurk in the margins and shadows, in color, texture and line, even negative space. A partial unveiling. A spoken silence … Which is as much in the eye of the beholder as the eye of the artist. So, to end, here's a 1943 plastic overlay (Fig. 4.7) by medical illustrator Gladys McHugh. Which we can take as an emblem of veiled queer interiority, double and triple identity—longing belonging estrangement—even if there's nothing to suggest that McHugh ever did.

Michael Sappol
Stockholm
30 January 2024

NOTES

Part One The unbearable queerness of anatomy [pages 1–45]

1 The lecture, "Scholastic and Bedside Teaching," appeared thereafter as a pamphlet and then was included in Holmes's much loved and oft-reprinted *Medical Essays 1842–1882*, and also included in *The Works of Oliver Wendell Holmes* (Boston: Houghton Mifflin, 1893) [*WOH*], 273–311. All quotes in this section are from *WOH*, 1893. The quote here is from 277. For Holmes as lecturer, see Wilson Sullivan, *New England Men of Letters* (New York: Macmillan, 1972), 235. (To avoid confusion, note: our Holmes is Holmes Sr., *father* of the now more famous Supreme Court Justice, Oliver Wendell Holmes Jr.)

2 *Medical Essays* includes "The Contagiousness of Puerperal Fever" (103–72), which argued for a new evidence-based version of contagion theory, based on the research of Ignaz Semmelweiss. In 1847 Semmelweiss, a physician at the Vienna General Hospital, observed that doctors who examined and dissected cadavers, and then attended women in childbirth, were transmitting infectious matter that caused puerperal fever. He then persuaded the doctors to wash their hands in a solution of chlorinated lime after leaving the dissecting table. By that expedient, incidence of the often fatal fever was reduced by over 90 percent in the hospital clinic.

3 John Ward Dean, *A Brief Memoir of Rev. Giles Firmin, one of the ejected ministers of 1662* (Boston: David Clapp & Son, 1866), lists 15 publications by Firmin, and tells us that Firmin's father came to Massachusetts with his son at the behest of the "Apostle" John Eliot. Published a year before Holmes's lecture, Dean's pamphlet was likely the source that spurred Holmes to feature Firmin in his lecture. See also Alexander Gordon, "Giles Firmin," *Dictionary of National Biography* (London, 1889), 19: 45–6. Holmes coined the term "Brahmin" in "The Professor's Story: Chapter 1: The Brahmin Caste of New England," *The Atlantic Monthly* 5.27 (1860): 93.

4 Holmes later donated his personal library, some 968 books, including his Spigelius, to the Boston Medical Library (BML), which he helped establish in 1875. (The BML also received the libraries of predecessor professors of anatomy at Harvard, John Warren and John Collins Warren.) Holmes served as BML's first President. The BML collection was later deposited in Harvard's Countway Library of Medicine. Jessica Murphy, a librarian (email, 10 Dec 2021) confirmed that Countway had the Spigelius and Paré, but in 2022

Countway returned the collection to BML. At present writing, Holmes's books appear to be in storage.

5 See Laura M. Walters, "Odoardo Fialetti (1573–*c*.1638): The interrelation of Venetian art and anatomy, and his importance in England" (PhD thesis, University of St. Andrews, 2009).

6 In *One Hundred Days in Europe* (in *WOH*, 146–9), Holmes writes about visiting an English rare-books shop, the rare-book trade in Paris, and contacts with dealers in Boston and New York. In *Over the Teacups* (in *WOH*, 115–16), Holmes muses that his library is "such a curious collection of old and new books, such a mosaic of learning and fancies and follies …," including some "curious books": "A library of a few thousand volumes ought always to have some books in it which the owner almost never opens, yet with whose backs he is so well acquainted that he feels as if he knew something of their contents. They are like those persons whom we meet in our daily walks, with whose faces and figures, whose summer and winter garments, whose walking-sticks and umbrellas even, we feel acquainted, and yet whose names, whose business, whose residences, we know nothing about. Some of these books are so formidable in their dimensions, so rusty and crabbed in their aspect, that it takes a considerable amount of courage to attack them. I will ask Delilah to bring down from my library a very thick, stout volume, bound in parchment, and standing on the lower shelf, next the fireplace. The pretty handmaid knows my books almost as if she were my librarian, and I don't doubt she would have found it if I had given only the name on the back. Delilah returned presently, with the heavy quarto in her arms. It was a pleasing sight—the old book in the embrace of the fresh young damsel …" And so Holmes connects the desires and pleasures of book ownership and collection to the desirable body of his young female servant.

7 Was Holmes just day-dreaming, or did he know for a fact that Firmin owned works by Vesalius, Paré, Fallopius and Spigelius, perhaps the very copies that Holmes owned?

8 Susan Sontag, "Against Interpretation," in *Against Interpretation and Other Essays* (New York: Farrar, Straus & Giroux, 1966), 104.

9 Patricia Lockwood, "I hate Nadia beyond reason," *London Review of Books* (18 February 2021): 22; Lockwood is channeling the voice and perspective of Elena Ferrante and her characters, Lila and Lenu. Embodied reading is a corollary of "embodied seeing"; James Elkins, *Pictures of the Body* (Stanford: Stanford University Press, 1999, rev. 2021), preface.

10 Eve Kosofsky Sedgwick, *The Epistemology of the Closet* (1990; Berkeley: University of California Press, 2008). See also David M. Halperin, *Saint Foucault: Toward a Gay Hagiography* (New York: Oxford University Press, 1997), esp. 24–48.

11 Annamarie Jagose, *Queer Theory: An Introduction* (New York: New York University Press, 1996), 3. See Judith Butler, *Gender Trouble: Feminism and the Subversion of Identity* (New York: Routledge, 1990) and *Bodies That Matter: On the Discursive Limits of Sex* (New York: Routledge, 1993); and Halperin, *Saint Foucault*, 112–15.

12 Throughout this book, the term "performance" takes on some of the same functions as Judith Butler's *performativity*, Erving Goffman's *social performance* and Pierre Bourdieu's *habitus*. See Butler, *Gender Trouble* and *Bodies That Matter*; Erving Goffman, *The Presentation of Self in Everyday Life* (New York: Doubleday, 1959); and Pierre Bourdieu, *Distinction: A Social Critique of the Judgment of Taste* (1979; New York: Routledge, 1984).

13 Kosofsky Sedgwick, *Epistemology of the Closet*, 2.

14 Pamela Paul, "Let's Say Gay" (*New York Times*, 23 Oct 2022), https://www.nytimes.com/2022/10/23/opinion/queer-gay-identity.html?smid=nytcoreios-share&referringSource=articleShare. Paul argues that *queer* is also now succumbing to domestication, cooptation, and diminishing critical utility and that, in the moment of "don't say gay" culture war, *gay* is the term with more critical salience.

15 Rosemary Hennessy, *Profit and Pleasure: Sexual Identities in Late Capitalism* (2d ed., London: Routledge, 2018), 52–3.

16 David M. Halperin, "How to Do the History of Male Homosexuality," in Donald E. Hall et al., *The Routledge Queer Studies Reader* (New York: Routledge, 2013), 262–86, devises a five-part taxonomy consisting of male effeminacy, same-sex love, inversion, and sodomy (in two positions: "passive" and "active") as categories that are fused in the current meaning of the term "homosexual," and argues that, in other times and places, any one of the five categories could be taken to be normative or queer.

17 José Esteban Muñoz, *Cruising Utopia: The Then and There of Queer Futurity* (New York: New York University Press, 2009), 1; Peggy Phelan, *Mourning Sex: Performing Public Memories* (New York: Routledge, 1997), 3. My argument here is partly prompted by Jocelyn E. Marshall's call for papers for a Society for Cinema & Media Studies panel on "Queer Ruptures: Alternative Narrative Praxis as Un/Recovering Histories", H-Sex, 7 Aug 2019.

18 Whitney Davis, *Queer Beauty: Sexuality and Aesthetics from Winckelmann to Freud and Beyond* (New York: Columbia University Press, 2010), 40.

19 George Kubler, *The Shape of Time: Remarks on the History of Things* (New Haven: Yale University Press, 1962), 17.

20 Arnold I. Davidson, "Sex and the Emergence of Sexuality," *Critical Inquiry* 14.1 (1987): 18, 26–7. Notice how Davidson's adjectives enact an odd subtext: Coarseness, disability, disfigurement! Davidson doesn't play nice.

21 For a critique of incommensurability and untranslatability, see Seyla Benhabib, *The Claims of Culture: Equality and Diversity in the Global Era* (Princeton: Princeton University Press, 2002), chap. 2.

22 Gary Ferguson, *Same-Sex Marriage in Renaissance Rome: Sexuality, Identity, and Community in Early Modern Europe* (Ithaca: Cornell University Press, 2016), 158.

23 L.P. Hartley, *The Go-Between* (1953; New York: New York Review of Books, 2002), 1.

24 Davidson, "Sex and the Emergence of Sexuality," 27, referring to critics of Leo Steinberg, *The Sexuality of Christ in Renaissance Art and in Modern Oblivion* (Chicago: University of Chicago Press, 1997).

25 Rosemarie Garland-Thomson, *Staring: How We Look* (Oxford: Oxford University Press, 2009), 9, argues from a similar premise: "the gaze … has been extensively defined as an oppressive act of disciplinary looking that subordinates its victim."

26 Michel Foucault, *The Birth of the Clinic* (1963; trans. Alan Sheridan Smith, 1973; New York: Routledge, 2003), 204. Smith's translation of *le regard* as "the gaze" (*le regard medicale* = the medical gaze) bequeathed the stronger word to multiple strands of Anglophone scholarship.

27 James Elkins, *The Object Stares Back: On the Nature of Seeing* (New York: Harcourt Brace, 1996). Cf. Walter Benjamin's notion of "aura" in "The Work of Art in the Age of Mechanical Reproduction" (1936), which also describes investment in objects and the effects such objects have on the viewer, not just in viewing an object but in structuring perception and making hierarchies; Benjamin, *Illuminations*, ed. Hannah Arendt (New York: Schocken/Random House, 1969). See also John Berger, *Ways of Seeing* (London: Penguin, 1973).

28 Michel Foucault, *The Order of Things: An Archaeology of the Human Sciences* (1966; New York: Vintage, 1973), 4–5 (translation slightly modified).

29 Scholarship on the agency of images is vast. Among other works, this discussion is influenced by: David Freedberg, *The Power of Images: Studies in the History and Theory of Response* (Chicago: University of Chicago Press, 1991); Horst Bredekamp, *Der Bildakt* (Berlin: Wagenbach Klaus, 2015); many works by W.J.T. Mitchell, including *What Do Pictures Want?* (Chicago: University of Chicago Press, 2005). For the social and cognitive effects of anatomical performance, see Michael Sappol, *A Traffic of Dead Bodies: Anatomy and Embodied Social Identity in 19th-Century America* (Princeton: Princeton University Press, 2002).

30 John Berger is credited with introducing the term "male gaze," first in the BBC documentary series *Ways of Seeing* (1972). Laura Mulvey developed the concept in a much-reprinted essay, "Visual Pleasure and Narrative Cinema," *Screen* 16.3 (1975): 6–18; see also Mulvey, "Afterthoughts on 'Visual Pleasure and Narrative Cinema,' Inspired by 'Duel in the Sun' (King Vidor, 1946)," *Framework* 15/17 (1981): 12–15. For a review of gaze theory, see Caroline Evans & Lorraine Gamman, "The Gaze Revisited, or Reviewing Queer Viewing," in *A Queer Romance: Lesbianism, Gay Men and Popular Culture*, ed. Paul Burston & Colin Richardson (London: Routledge, 1995), 13–56, quote 14. Gamman and Evans call for a relational, historical approach to the gaze against essentialist reductionist, and reflexively pejorative, approaches.

31 But female gazes emerge nonetheless, countering suppression and independently of it. See Mulvey, op. cit.; Linda Nochlin, *Representing Women* (London: Thames & Hudson, 1999) and "Why have there been no great women artists," *Art News* (January 1971).

32 To further complicate matters, practices of gendered gazing are shaped by uneven policing, local custom, idiosyncratic performances of social class, national identity, religion, etc.

33 A strong current of contemporary feminist art history and cultural criticism has arisen to examine the male gaze on male bodies. See for example Abigail Solomon-Godeau, *Male Trouble: A Crisis in Representation* (London: Thames

& Hudson, 1997); Anthea Callen, *Looking at Men: Art, Anatomy and the Modern Male Body* (New Haven and London: Yale University Press, 2018); and Tanya Augsburg, "Some Starting Points, Theories, and Themes," in Augsburg, ed., *Man as Object: Reversing the Gaze* (New York: Women's Caucus for the Arts, 2011), 13–31. For homoeroticism and the gaze, see Solomon-Godeau, *Male Trouble*; Michael Hatt, "The Male Body in Another Frame: Thomas Eakins' *The Swimming Hole* as a Homoerotic Image," in *Journal of Philosophy and the Visual Arts: The Body*, ed. Andrew Benjamin (London: Academy Group, 1993), 9–21, esp. 11–16; and "Physical Culture: The male nude and sculpture in late Victorian Britain," in *After the Pre-Raphaelites: Art and Aestheticism in Victorian England*, ed. E. Prettejohn (New Brunswick: Rutgers University Press, 1999).

34 Foucault, *Birth of the Clinic*, 204.

35 Much of gaze scholarship pairs acts of group or collective gazing with the representation/performance of gazing in motion pictures. For technologies of intensive looking, my starting point is Jonathan Crary, *Techniques of the Observer* (Cambridge: MIT Press, 1990) and *Suspensions of Perception: Attention, Spectacle and Modern Culture* (Cambridge: MIT Press, 2000).

36 Callen, *Looking at Men*, 15–16. Callen's "plurisensoriality" includes smell.

37 Stereography was introduced to the British public at the Crystal Palace exhibition of 1851; Holmes invented the hand-held stereographic viewer in 1859.

38 Steven Shapin & Simon Schaffer, *Leviathan and the Air-Pump: Hobbes, Boyle, and the Experimental Life* (Princeton: Princeton University Press, 1985), 25, 60–5.

39 Anita Guerrini, "Anatomists and Entrepreneurs in Early Eighteenth-Century London," *Journal of the History of Medicine and Allied Sciences* 59.2 (2004): 238.

40 William Hazlitt, "On Genius and Common Sense," *The Complete Works of William Hazlitt*, ed. P.P. Howe, 21 vols. (London, 1930–4), 18:46; quoted in William C. Wright, "Hazlitt, Ruskin, and Nineteenth-Century Art," *Journal of Aesthetics and Art Criticism* 32.4 (1974): 511. The article from which the quote is taken originally appeared in an 1824 *Encyclopaedia Britannica* entry.

41 Ralph Waldo Emerson, *Nature* (Boston: James Munroe & Co., 1836): "I become a transparent eye-ball; I am nothing; I see all; the currents of the Universal Being circulate through me; I am part or particle of God."

42 Honoré de Balzac, "The Atheist's Mass" [trans. Clara Bell], in *Scènes de la vie privée* (*La Comédie humaine*) (Paris, 1836) (Project Gutenberg https://www.gutenberg.org/files/1220/1220-h/1220-h.htm). There was a backlash against this version of the gaze in medicine and science, and also to some degree in fine art. Claims of genius and gaze intensity were attacked as innately subjective, corrupting and self-interested, and scopic devices and tactics and technologies of "mechanical objectivity" were elevated. See Lorraine Daston & Peter Galison, *Objectivity* (New York: Zone Books, 2007) for a sweeping overview.

43 Joseph Maclise, *Surgical Anatomy* (Philadelphia, 1859), preface.

44 Foucault, *Birth of the Clinic*, xi; and *La volonté de savoir* (*Histoire de la sexualité* I) (Paris: Gallimard, 1976); *The History of Sexuality, Vol. 1: An Introduction*, trans. Robert Hurley (New York: Vintage, 1990).

45 Discussion with Jenny Sundén, 2 February 2022, Stockholm.

46 Solomon-Godeau, *Male Trouble*.

47 Blair Worden, "Novel and Naughty," *London Review of Books* (26 September 2019): 19. For example, Solomon-Godeau, *Male Trouble*, argues for a "crisis of representation," even if none of her historical actors used the term "crisis" to describe the changes she marks.

48 Some parts of this section are recycled from Michael Sappol, "The Phantom of the Anatomy Lesson," in Sappol, ed., *Hidden Treasure* (New York: Blast Books, 2012), 58–9.

49 Mechthild Fend, *Fleshing Out Surfaces: Skin in French Art and Medicine* (Manchester: University of Manchester Press, 2017), 246: "anatomists and art theorists agreed that women's skin and what they called 'adipose membrane' served to hide [women's] anatomy ... This is why the critic Landon considered the female model inapt for the academic study of the nude, the main purpose of which was, in his eyes, to 'make the science of anatomy shine'." See also Solomon-Godeau, *Male Trouble*, 50, 52, 186–90. Callen, *Looking at Men*, 7, reports that in her art school drawing classes in the 1980s, male models were used exclusively, because "surface anatomy is clearest on a well-toned male body with little subcutaneous fat."

50 Nineteenth-century artists defended themselves with fig leaves and artfully posed twists and turns to avoid genital display. See Hatt, "The Male Body in Another Frame," 15.

51 See Darren N. Wagner, "A Bit Exposed: Displays of Male Genitals," in Raymond Stephanson & D.N. Wagner, eds., *The Secrets of Generation: Reproduction in the Long Eighteenth Century* (Toronto: University of Toronto Press, 2015), 386–414.

52 William Hunter, *Anatomia uteri humani gravidi tabulis illustrata* [*Anatomy of the Human Gravid Uterus, exhibited in Figures*] (London: Baskerville, 1774). The artist, Jan Van Rymsdyk, was a master of hyper-realistic anatomical illustration. He also illustrated obstetrical studies by William Smellie and Nicholas Jenty. For "truth to nature," see Daston & Galison, *Objectivity*.

53 According to Alicia Hughes, "Authorship, Image-Making, and Excess: William Hunter's *Anatomia uteri humani gravidi tabulis illustrata* (1774)," *Journal for Eighteenth-Century Studies* 20.1 (2022) https://doi.org/10.1111/1754-0208.12859, Hunter deleted two plates from the final publication, worried that his study would appear to be "overcharged," excessive, not because of the affective impact of its subject matter but rather because of its large size, numerous plates and fulsome detail.

54 There was of course no exact equivalence: manifold problems were connected to pregnancy and childbirth. The erect penis had a different valence. It was both a scientific problem—what were its mechanics?—and a moral, representational, symbolic problem. Unlike women in labor, men didn't die from the process of getting hard and then become available for anatomical dissection.

55 But not just that. Matthew Craske, "'Unwholesome' and 'pornographic': A reassessment of the place of Rackstrow's Museum in the story of eighteenth-century anatomical collection and exhibition," *Journal of the History of*

Collections 23.1 (2011): 75–99, shows that Rackstrow's served sex-segregated audiences of both men and women, and had much in common with (and some connections to) John and William Hunter and their well-respected anatomical museums. Popular museums that catered to a ticket-buying clientele, Craske argues, have been disparaged by scholars as purely pornographic, voyeuristic and exploitative on the basis of no evidence. Rackstrow's, for a good part of its run, was owned by a woman. While it did engage in sensationalist showmanship in some wax displays, it also made what appear to be sincere efforts to tastefully educate the public, perform female virtue, and even offered anatomical instruction to midwives, using models. For anatomical (or "Florentine," or "Medici," or "Demountable") Venuses, see Kathryn Hoffmann, "Sleeping Beauties in the Fairground: The Spitzner, Pedley, and Chemisé Exhibits," *Early Popular Visual Culture* 4.2 (2006): 139–59 and Joanna Ebenstein, *The Anatomical Venus* (London: Thames & Hudson, 2016).

56 Annette Wickham, "Strike a Pose: 250 Years of Life Drawing at the RA," *RA Blog* (6 Feb 2018), https://www.royalacademy.org.uk/article/from-life-history-of-life-drawing-annette-wickham. According to Wickham, "continental academic tradition … focused exclusively on the male figure," but the Royal Academy used models of both sexes, while excluding female artists (until Lucy Herford broke the barrier in the 1860s). See also Jane Macnaughton, "Flesh Revealed: Medicine, Art and Anatomy," in Corinne Saunders et al., eds., *The Body and the Arts* (London: Palgrave Macmillan, 2009), 72–102.

57 For the conventions of anatomical representation, see Rebecca Messbarger, *The Lady Anatomist: The Work of Anna Morandi Manzolini* (Chicago: University of Chicago Press, 2010), 136–62. One more caveat: the female body was the main event in works on anatomy aimed at midwives and women with scientific, educational interests, a segregated genre which became a genre within the market for popular medical publication in the course of the nineteenth century.

58 Philip Van Buskirk's diaries are a key source for understanding same-sex interactions in nineteenth-century maritime culture. See Philip C. Van Buskirk Diaries, 1851–1902, University of Washington Libraries Special Collections. Transcription, *Philip C. Van Buskirk Archive* on the *CUNY Academic Commons*, https://vanbuskirk.commons.gc.cuny.edu/; Matthew Knip, "Melville's Queer Hauntology: Selections from the Erotic Journals of Marine Drummer Philip C. Van Buskirk," *Leviathan* 22.1 (2020): 28–54; B.R. Burg, *An American Seafarer in the Age of Sail: The Erotic Diaries of Philip C. Van Buskirk 1851–1870* (New Haven: Yale University Press, 1994). Knip and Burg emphasize that much of the sex was intergenerational; a good portion of the maritime workforce consisted of teenagers and boys as young as eight or nine.

59 Rictor Norton, ed., "A Few Words about Margeries, c.1855," *Homosexuality in Nineteenth-Century England: A Sourcebook* (29 October 2017), http://rictornorton.co.uk/eighteen/yokel.htm, from *The Yokel's Preceptor: Or, More Sprees in London!, Being a … Show-up of All the Rigs and Doings of the Flash Cribs in this Great Metropolis* (London: H. Smith, 37 Holywell Street, Strand, [*c.*1855]).

60 See Charles Upchurch, *Before Wilde: Sex Between Men in Britain's Age of Reform* (Berkeley: University of California Press, 2009), perhaps the best currrent study of this still understudied topic. Capital punishment for sodomy was abolished in France in 1791 by the revolutionary Assembly.

61 The 1885 White Slave Traffic Bill, among its many provisions, criminalized homosexuality. A 1912 Act of Parliament, known as the Criminal Law Amendment Act (White Slave Traffic Bill) singled out "ponces" as one of its targets and increased penalties to include the flogging of male offenders; *Hansard* (19 Feb 1912), v. 39: https://hansard.parliament.uk/commons/1912-02-19/debates/57e63059-0975-4676-98c5-76a9bff23a72/CriminalLawAmendment(WhiteSlaveTraffic)Bill.

62 Jeffrey Weeks, *Coming Out: Homosexual Politics in Britain from the 19th Century to the Present* (London: Quartet Books, 1977), 14–16; Charles Upchurch, *"Beyond the Law": The Politics of Ending the Death Penalty for Sodomy in Britain* (Philadelphia: Temple University Press, 2022). For an online sourcebook of press and court reports of incidents, persons and cases at law regarding sodomy and cross-dressing, see Norton, *Homosexuality in 19th-Century England*. Some cases of sodomy would nowadays be categorized as rape or statutory rape, but much of the jurisprudence is vague on this point: if the very act was illegal and immoral, consent was irrelevant. Other nations had comparable laws, customs and dynamics.

63 Tom Crewe, "Short Cuts," *London Review of Books* (12 August 2021): 27.

64 As Foucault famously argued in *History of Sexuality, Vol. 1*, parts 1 & 2, especially 44–9.

65 The closet ≠ grave reference is an allusion to Leo Bersani, "Is the Rectum a Grave?" *October* 43 (Winter 1987): 197–222.

66 Jenny Sundén, "Digital Kink Obscurity: A Sexual Politics Beyond Visibility and Comprehension," *Sexualities* (2023) https://doi.org/10.1177/13634607221124401; Édouard Glissant, *Poetics of Relation* (Ann Arbor: University of Michigan Press, 1990); Nicholas de Villiers, *Opacity and the Closet: Tactics in Foucault, Barthes and Warhol* (Minneapolis: University of Minnesota Press, 2012).

67 The *closet* couldn't be activated as a metaphor until closets became a common feature of the built environment, which was not always the case until the mid- and late nineteenth century. Poor people, people living in inadequate or older housing, lacked closets, and the domestic private spaces that the closet became a metonym for.

68 Matthew Bevis, "On Rachael Allen," *London Review of Books* (5 March 2020): 30. The quote refers to tropes of watching and watching others watch in the poetry of Rachael Allen.

69 Wittgenstein, *Tractatus* 7; Kosofsky Sedgwick, *Epistemology of the Closet*, 3.

70 Cheryl Misak, "Philosophy Must Be Useful," *Aeon* (23 Jan 2019), https://aeon.co/essays/what-is-truth-on-ramsey-wittgenstein-and-the-vienna-circle; Nikhil Krishnan, "How Queer was Ludwig Wittgenstein?" *The New Yorker* (16 May 2022), https://www.newyorker.com/magazine/2022/05/16/how-queer-was-ludwig-wittgenstein.

71 Rowan Williams, *Dostoyevsky: Language, Faith and Fiction* (New York: Continuum, 2008), 51.

72 Carlo Ginzburg, *Clues, Myths and the Historical Method* (Baltimore: Johns Hopkins University Press, 1989), 124.

73 *Anatomia Universa* ... (Pisa: Niccolò Capurro, 1823–30) was acclaimed as a masterpiece of dissection, analysis, illustration. A massive "double-elephant folio" (life-size), it was only accessible to those who could afford the extravagant price of 2,520 gold francs (according to Christie's, equivalent to about 750 grams of gold or about $20,000). For the homoerotics of the buttocks in early modern Europe, see Patricia Lee Rubin, *Seen from Behind: Perspectives on the Male Body and Renaissance Art* (New Haven: Yale University Press, 2018).

74 Perhaps it was a distant echo of the Counter-Reformation response to Protestant discomfort with images, formulated in the Council of Trent's 1563 decree that "all lasciviousness" be avoided in sacred art, "in such wise that figures shall not be painted or adorned with a beauty exciting to lust"; Lauren Kilroy-Ewbank, "The Council of Trent and the Call to Reform Art," *Smart History* (20 May 2021), https://smarthistory.org/the-council-of-trent-and-the-call-to-reform-art/.

75 Michael Sappol, *Dream Anatomy* (Washington, DC: GPO, 2003). For a late eighteenth-century art anatomy full of macabre fantasy and play, see Jacques Gamelin, *Nouveau recueil d'ostéologie et de myologie, dessiné, d'après nature* ... (Toulouse: J.F. Desclassan, 1779). But, over the course of the nineteenth century, art anatomy was increasingly also winnowed down to the basics: figures posed in the nude, ecorché, or as skeleton, without grand gesture, affect or scenography.

76 Hunter, *Anatomy of the Gravid Uterus*, preface; John Bell, *Engravings of the Bones, Muscles, and Joints*, illustrating the first volume of the *Anatomy of the Human Body* (Edinburgh and London: Printed for Longman, 1794; 2d ed. 1804). Yet, even with their advocacy of anatomical sobriety, Hunter and Bell choreographed and orchestrated their illustrations, engaged in a kind of provocative image play.

77 Therapeutic nihilism, a powerful thread of European medicine in the 1840s and 1850s (brought to America by Oliver Wendell Holmes), reappraised traditional medical therapeutics as scientifically unproven, mostly ineffective, and often harmful. It was a hard sell. No patient goes to a doctor to hear that nothing can be done; no doctor gains a clientele by acknowledging that nothing can be done. As for interpretive nihilism: Susan Sontag, who early in her career wrote "against interpretation" (1966), nevertheless produced an *oeuvre* full of productive interpretations. (What she mostly deplored in *Against Interpretation* was hubristic Freudian and sociological overinterpretation.)

78 Maria Stepanova, *In Memory of Memory: A Romance*, trans. Sasha Dugdale (New York: New Directions, 2021), 56.

79 Kosofsky Sedgwick, *Epistemology of the Closet*, 2–3.

80 Jones Quain, *The Muscles of the Human Body* ... (London: Taylor & Walton, 1836). Art: J. Walsh. Lithography: J. Walsh and William Fairland. The figure

is closely based on Jules Cloquet, *Anatomie de l'homme ou descriptions et figures lithografiées de toutes les parties du corps humain* (Paris, 1822), v. 2, pl. 83. Nearly all of the plates in Quain's atlas are copied roughly or closely from other anatomies; most of volume 2 is from Cloquet. Quain's prospectus acknowledges the borrowing: "This Publication will consist of a Series of the most approved Anatomical Drawings, selected from monograph treatises or from systematic works. The highest place in the former class is deservedly conceded to the works of Scarpa and Tiedemann, and in the latter, to those of Mascagni and Caldani; but from their size and ... style ... the expence of publication is necessarily such as to confine their usefulness to comparatively few persons ... [T]he collections of Cloquet and Loder, though not of equal pretension, are no less valuable ... As ... the works ... are inaccessible to some, and to others from the descriptions and references being given in a foreign language, the want of a similar publication in an English garb has been for some time complained of."

81 The figure is based on Giuseppe Perini's copperplate titlepage engraving in Gavin Hamilton, *Schola Italica picturae* ... (Rome: [G. Hamilton], 1773). The titlepage, like Michelangelo's fresco, shows acorns.

82 Cloquet, *Anatomie de l'homme* ... vol. 2 (1822), pl. 82. Quain's plate 48 appears to be an illustration of two specimens freshly made by Quain, based on Cloquet's plate. But Quain's plate 47, also a freshly made specimen, shows a demurely folded-over penis, and not the two fully extended penises shown in Cloquet's plate 81.

83 For a brief guide to penile anatomy, see Louise Morales-Brown, "What to know about the anatomy and function of the penis," *Medical News Today* (13 June 2021), https://www.medicalnewstoday.com/articles/penis-anatomy.

84 The only information that appears on the page is the discreet identification of the printer as "Martin" and lithographer as "Langlumé". Pierre Langlumé (1790–1830) began working as a lithographer in 1818, opened a shop in Paris in 1820 under the sponsorship of Alois Senefelder and François-Séraphin Delpech. He died in the summer of 1830. In August 1840 his son enters the trade but signs his work as "Langlumé, fil". If the print under discussion was by Langlumé père, it would likely have been prepared sometime between 1820 and summer 1830. Langlumé did work of the highest quality for the highest rank of medical and non-medical authors, including illustrations for Jean Cruveilhier, *Anatomie pathologique du corps humain* (Paris: Baillière, 1829–42) and Georges Cuvier & Geoffroy Saint-Hilaire, *Histoire naturelle des mammifères*, 5 vols. (Paris, 1824). See "Pierre Langlumé," École Nationale des Chartes, *Dictionnaire des imprimeurs-lithographes du XIX*[e] *siècle* and "Pierre Langlumé", *Wikipedia*, https://fr.wikipedia.org/wiki/Pierre_Langlum%C3%A9.

85 For a roughly contemporary description of the procedure for introducing the catheter for lithotomy, along with a somewhat similar (but less artful) illustration of an inflated bladder, see Thomas Morton, *The Surgical Anatomy of the Perinaeum* (London: Taylor & Walton, 1838), 63–6.

86 Sometime later, possibly years after the physician's death, his medical library would have been sold off. The volume, perhaps seldom or never opened,

eventually came to reside in the National Library of Medicine (how or when is unknown), along with another copy (which has of course no illustration). The NLM cataloguer noted the copy with the single illustration, but not that the plate was smaller than the book dimensions, didn't fit with the rest of the content, and was loose (i.e. not bound with the rest of the book). When the book was later rebound, the illustration was bound in.

87 Darren N. Wagner, "Arousing Applications: Syringes and Anatomical: Preparations of Genital Organs in the Long Eighteenth Century," *Bulletin of the Scientific Instrument Society* 113 (2012): 4–9, quotes from 7–8.

88 Antique figures with disproportionately large erections (like those found at Pompeii in the 1790s) were also displayed in books for scholars and connoisseurs, as objects of "scientific" art historical connoisseurship. Those books were expensive and artfully illustrated, and only accessible to an exclusive audience. But the reaction against the French Revolution led to a closing down of the cultural space for such publications in Britain; see Davis, *Queer Beauty*, 51–81. For politeness and bawdiness, see Kate Davison, "Occasional Politeness and Gentlemen's Laughter in Eighteenth-century England," *The Historical Journal* 57.4 (2014): 921–45. For regulation of images of the phallus in America, see Judith Giesberg, *Sex and the Civil War: Soldiers, Pornography and the Making of American Morality* (Chapel Hill: University of North Carolina Press, 2017).

89 One wonders, in a society where impolite public urination by men and boys must have been a commonly observed occurrence, how this structured the meaning of polite printed representation.

90 See Helen Lefkowitz Horowitz, *Rereading Sex: Battles over Sexual Knowledge and Suppression in Nineteenth-century America* (New York: Alfred Knopf, 2002), 218.

91 R. & L. Perry & Co. [R.J. Jordan], *The Silent Friend* ... (London, 1847). See also R.J. Culverwell ["Fellow of the London Royal College of Surgeons and licentiated practitioner of medicine"], *The Green Book: The modern treatment of syphilis, urethral affections, and all diseases of the urinary and sexual organs* ... (London, 1841) which shows engraved medical diagrams of penises of somewhat higher quality, mostly detached from bodies, including one of a penis with a catheter inserted. See Sarah Bull, "Managing the 'Obscene M.D.': Medical Publishing, the Medical Profession, and the Changing Definition of Obscenity in mid-Victorian England," *Bulletin of the History of Medicine* 91.4 (2017): 713–43. Bull notes: "In the 1840s," books and pamphlets on reproductive and sexual topics, "sold for a median three shillings, putting most within easy reach of middle-class consumers. By the 1860s, these works were also widely accessible to working-class readers: median prices dropped below one shilling, and many commercial medical dealers gave their publications away for free ... as advertisements for their authors' more expensive proprietary medicines and personal consultations ... in-person and by post." See also Lefkowitz Horowitz, *Rereading Sex*. Other popular health books used similar diagrams: e.g. works by O.S. Fowler, E.B. Foote, James Ashton, R.L. Trall.

92 Donna Dennis, *Licentious Gotham: Erotic Publishing and Its Prosecution in Nineteenth-Century New York* (Cambridge: Harvard University Press,

2009), 118–23; April Haynes, "The Trials of Frederick Hollick: Obscenity, Sex Education, and Medical Democracy in the Antebellum United States," *Journal of the History of Sexuality* 12.4 (2003): 543–74; Sappol, *A Traffic of Dead Bodies*, chaps. 6 & 8; Michael Sappol, "The Odd Case of Charles Knowlton: Anatomical Performance, Medical Narrative and Professional Identity in Antebellum America," *Bulletin of the History of Medicine* 83.3 (2009): 460–98; Janice Ruth Wood, *The Struggle for Free Speech in the United States, 1872–1915: Edward Bliss Foote, Edward Bond Foote, and Anti-Comstock Operations* (New York: Routledge, 2012).

93 Philip Van Buskirk Diary, August 1855, qtd. in Burg, *American Seafarer in the Age of Sail*, xi. The Philip C. Van Buskirk Archive is currently digitizing all of the journals, amounting to more than three dozen.

94 Offered as a substitute for cock, balls, twat, cunt, etc., "penis," "testes," "clitoris," and "vagina" almost from the outset were quickly relegated to the status of unmentionables in "mixed" polite company. In the twentieth century, as psychological, medical and sociological discourse circulated more widely, the latinate terms became more acceptable at the dinner table.

95 E.B. Foote, *Science in Story: Sammy Tubbs, the Boy Doctor, and "Sponsie," the Troublesome Monkey* (New York: Murray Hill Publishing Co., 1874–5), v. 5, "The Gymnast Tubbs: Elimination and Reproduction, a Book for Private Reading," 113.

96 Burg, *American Seafarer in the Age of Sail*, 88–9: "Literature, medicine and science ignored homoerotic acts ... [B]ooks, pamphlets and tracts ... on physiological and sexual matters left exclusively male relations, obscure, ill defined, and indistinct ... Sexual relations between males ... involved no biological, psychological or social predisposition, nor did they imply membership in a discrete category. [T]he widespread neglect of the subject by legal authorities, physicians, writers and clerics suggest a profound willingness to disbelieve that such practices occurred." Writers like Melville, "kept ... references discreet and sufficiently obscure that their meaning was inaccessible to most readers. When [Melville] stepped through the opaque curtain ... the publisher quickly deleted it."

97 The "secret museum" alludes to Walter Kendrick's classic, *The Secret Museum: Pornography in Modern Culture* (Berkeley: University of California Press, 1987) and Sarah Bull, "Reading, Writing, and Publishing an Obscene Canon: The Archival Logic of the Secret Museum, *c.*1860–*c.*1900," *Book History* 20 (2017): 226–57.

Part Two Connoisseurship, taste and "the beauty of the plate" [pages 46–95]

1 Zakir Paul, rev. Hannah Freed-Thall, *Spoiled Distinctions: Aesthetics and the Ordinary in French Modernism* (2015) in *Critical Inquiry* 43.4 (2017): 910.

2 Bull, "Reading, Writing, and Publishing an Obscene Canon," 226: "Works falling into each of these generic categories ... were subject to accusations of obscenity in the nineteenth century, and discussed alongside pornographic

fiction within public, governmental, and judicial debates about how to regulate the rapidly expanding print marketplace."

3 Thanks to Ad Stijnman, email, June 2021, for helping me on Gautier; also Sarah Lowengard, Elizabeth Savage and Anita Guerrini.

4 For French economic expansion and the vast increase in publications printed and sold, see William H. Sewell Jr., *Capitalism and the Emergence of Civic Equality in Eighteenth-Century France* (Chicago: University of Chicago Press, 2021).

5 Monique Kornell, *Flesh and Bones: The Art of Anatomy* (Los Angeles: Getty Publications, 2022), 176.

6 Corinne Le Bitouzé & Morwena Joly-Parvex, "Cadavre Exquis: L'Ange anatomique de Jacques Fabien Gautier d'Agoty," *Revue de BNF* 52.1 (2016): 106–18. Gautier's images often appear in coffee-table books, websites and on book covers, but the scholarship is surprisingly thin and mainly comes out of the history of print technology and antiquarian book collection, not the history of medicine. See Sarah Lowengard, *The Creation of Color in Eighteenth-Century Europe* (New York: Columbia University Press, 2006), chap. 12 (http://www.gutenberg-e.org/lowengard/C_Chap12.html), and Christine André Hahn & Paul Dumaitre, "Le livre d'anatomie en couleurs au XVIIIe siècle, de J.C. Le Blon à J. Gautier-d'Agoty," *Médecine de France: panorama de la pensée médicale littéraire et artistique française* 40 (1962): 10–13. Much of what we know comes from scholarship focused on Jacob Christoff Le Blon, the inventor of multi-color mezzotint technology. See Florian Rodari, "Mélanges anatomiques," in *Anatomie de la couleur: l'invention de l'estampe en couleurs*, exh. cat., ed. Rodari (Paris: Bibliothèque Nationale de France; Lausanne: Musée Olympique, 1996), 106–32; Ad Stijnman et al., *Jacob Christoff Le Blon and Trichromatic Printing*, 2 vols. (Ouderkerk aan den IJssel: Sound & Vision; Amsterdam: Rijksmuseum: 2020), xxvi, xxx, xli, xlvi–xlvii, lii, lv, lxiv–lxv, lxvii–lxviii, lxx–lxxvi, lxxviii–lxxxi, lxxxiii, lxxxix–xc, xciv, xcvii, xcix–c, cii. According to Anne L. Schroder, review of "Colorful Impressions: The Print-making Revolution in Eighteenth-century France" and "The Age of Watteau ...", *Eighteenth-Century Studies* 37.3 (2004): 455–63, Gautier competed with other printmakers who specialized in color prints for an upscale market of collectors.

7 But less expensive than works of original art. See Schroder, "Colorful Impressions": "Color prints made as facsimiles of drawing became an important part of the art market ... Writers at the time argued that prints offered collectors the opportunity to own an image after a famous artist at a fraction of the cost of the original. [461] ... Yet "their exquisite craftsmanship and the highly competitive print market," gave prints "their own aura of preciosity .... [T]here was an intentional delight in a print that could deceive a beholder into believing that it was a drawing. Once the work was framed and mounted on the wall, the ability to discern a print from an original drawing [or painting] was exceedingly difficult." [462]

8 That journal was succeeded by *Observations physiques* (1750–3); *Observations sur la peinture* (1753–4); and *Journal de Monsieur* (1776–7); Lowengard, *Creation of Color*, chap. 12.

9 Jacques-Fabien Gautier [Dagoty], *Chroa-Génésie ou génération des couleurs, contre le systeme de Newton* (Paris: Antoine Boudet, 1750–1); *Bulletin of the Royal College of Surgeons* (18 Sept 2015), https://www.rcseng.ac.uk/library-and-publications/library/blog/jacques-fabien-gautier-dagoty-exposition/. Anti-Newtonianism was respectable enough and not uncommon, but ultimately the losing side.

10 Lowengard, *Creation of Color*, chap. 12.

11 Jacques-Fabien Gautier Dagoty, *Anatomie des parties de la génération de l'homme et de la femme* (Paris: J.B. Brunet & Demonville, 1773), 1: "Anatomists who taught at the Royal Garden, & of whom I say I was a student, with good reason, having dissected for several years with Mr. Duverney, with whom I first undertook to give my first Anatomy Course; but he only saw … the first part of this work, the Myology, and some parts of the brain. After his death, I followed his plan & his intentions; and even the additions that I am giving today, without his help, nevertheless depend on this general plan, which he had so skillfully imagined, and about which he had often spoken to me. The Public will not have difficulty in believing that for the execution, it was necessary for me to employ several years in research necessary since my first publication …" [my translation]; Toby Gelfand, "The 'Paris Manner' of Dissection: Student Anatomical Dissection in Early Eighteenth-Century Paris," *Bulletin of the History of Medicine* 46.2 (1972): 99–130.

12 [Jacques-François-Marie] Duverney & Jacques-Fabien Gautier [Dagoty], *Myologie complette en couleur et grandeur naturelle* (Paris: Gautier, 1746); and *Anatomie de la tête, en tableaux imprimés qui représentent au naturel le cerveau sous différentes coupes, la distribution des vaisseaux dans toutes les parties de la tête, les organes des sens et une partie de la névrologie …* (Paris: Gautier, 1748). Some bibliographic listings wrongly credit these works to J.-F.-M. Duverney's more renowned brother Joseph-Guichard Duverney, who died in 1730.

13 J.-F. Gautier [Dagoty], *Hermaphrodite. Dissertation au sujet de la fameuse Hermaphrodite, qui a paru aux yeux du public depuis environ trois mois, faite par le sieur METRUD, Chirurgien ordinaire du Roi … Laquelle Hermaphrodite a été peinte & gravée par le sieur GAUTIER …* (Paris: Berryer, 1749) and *Observations sur l'histoire naturelle, sur la physique et sur la peinture …* 1.1 (Paris: Delaguette, 1752).

14 Kornell, *Flesh and Bones*, 176.

15 Scholarship on libertinage is vast. For a recent treatment, see Benedetta Craveri, *The Last Libertines*, trans. Aaron Kerner (New York: NYRB, 2020).

16 Joseph D. Bryan, "Dazzled, Blinded, & Numb: The Body and Society in Eighteenth-Century France" (PhD dissertation, Duke University, 2016).

17 Marquis [Donatien Alphonse François] de Sade, *120 Days of Sodom and Other Writings*, trans. Richard Seaver & Austryn Wainhouse (1785; New York: Grove Press, 1966), Day 11; cited in Le Bitouzé & Joly-Parvex, "Cadavre Exquis," 117. Sade's descriptions of elaborate tortures, part-by-anatomical-part, parallel the procedures of anatomical dissection. See, for example, Day 24.

18 Claude-Nicolas Le Cat, *Traité du sens* (Paris, 1742; Amsterdam: J. Wetstein, 1744).

19 Jacques-Fabien Gautier Dagoty, *Exposition anatomique des organes des sens, jointe la névrologie entière du corps humain …* (Paris: Demonville, 1775).

20 Gautier Dagoty, *Anatomie des parties de la génération de l'homme et de la femme*, 1.

21 Qtd. in Ebenstein, *Anatomical Venus*, 45, from A.-É. Gautier D'Agoty & Nicolas Jadelot, *Cours complet d'anatomie peint et gravé en couleurs naturelles par M. A.E. Gautier d'Agoty, second fils; et expliqué par M. Jadelot, Professeur d'Anatomie à la Faculté de Médecine de Nancy, & de l'Académie des Sciences & Belles-Lettres de la même Ville* (Nancy: LeClerc, 1773). Arnaud-Éloi (also Arnauld and Arnault) was Gautier's second son.

22 Gautier treated all of these subjects in his scientific journals, pamphlets, and other publications.

23 Shroder, "Colorful Impressions."

24 Take for example Jacques Benigne Winslow's well-regarded *Exposition anatomique de la structure du corps humain* (Paris, 1732). In anatomy, accuracy of depiction was the prime consideration, before any consideration of aesthetic merits. Gautier's accuracy got mixed reviews.

25 The non-French anatomists collaborated with exceptionally talented artists: Bidloo/Cowper – Gerard De Lairesse, Albinus – Jan Wandelaar, Hunter – Jan Van Riemsdyk, Haller – C.J. Rollinus.

26 Torsten Weimarck, *Akademi och anatomi: Några aspekter på människokroppens historia i nya tides konstnärsutbildning och ateljépraktik, med särskild tonvikt på anatomiundervisningen vid konstakademierna i Stockholm oh Köpenhamn fram till 1800-talets början* (Stockholm: Brutus Östlings Bokförlag Symposion, 1996), 213. By way of contrast, Floding (214) approved Haller's *Icones anatomicae*, as well as William Cheselden and Bidloo (but allowed that Bidloo, who published in the late 1600s, was long out of date).

27 Two Gautier items in Hagströmer Medico-Historical Library, Stockholm, come from Hallman's library.

28 While most anatomical circles and locations routinely excluded women, some women of talent and learning did manage to participate in the study of anatomy as artist-artisans, students and patrons. Marie Marguerite Biheron (1719–95), roughly contemporaneous with Gautier, was an anatomist and wax modeler who was approved and befriended in the highest intellectual circles—Diderot, d'Alembert, Vic d'Azyr and Benjamin Franklin were supporters—circles which kept Gautier at arms-length. Biheron gave anatomy lessons to women in conjunction with exhibitions of her waxes in both Paris and London, and eventually got the patronage of the French court. In some ways her career forms a striking parallel to, and contrast with, Gautier's. While her circle was heterosocial, she also catered to a partly sequestered circle of enlightened women and their daughters and was admitted to circles of homosocial men as an exceptional talent, almost a freak of nature. See Lucia

Dacome, "Intimate Connections: Marie Marguerite Biheron and her 'Little Boudoir'," *Bulletin of the History of Medicine* 95.3 (2021): 315–49.

29 Jennifer Tsien & Jacques Morizot, "Eighteenth-Century French Aesthetics," in E.N. Zalta, ed., *The Stanford Encyclopedia of Philosophy* (Winter 2021), https://plato.stanford.edu/archives/win2021/entries/aesthetics-18th-french/.

30 Le Bitouzé & Joly-Parvex, "Cadavre Exquis," 118, citing Louis Petit de Bachaumont.

31 See Jonathan Richardson, *Two Discourses: I. An Essay on the whole Art of Criticism as it Relates to Painting; II. An Argument in Behalf of the Science of a Connoisseur, Wherein is shewn the Dignity, Certainty, Pleasure, and Advantage of it* (London: Printed for W. Churchill at Black Swan ... 1719).

32 The first edition of *The Anatomy of the Humane* [later *Human*] *Body* was printed in 1713; the 13th in 1792. There were also supplements, American editions (1795, 1806), and a German translation (1790). The book's popularity was partly due to its plain-speaking rhetorical style, affordable price, and the fact that it had little competition in its price range. The preface to the fifth edition (1740) explains that Cheselden has raised the price to defray the expense of newly added plates, which are "larger, better designed, and better executed."

33 Domenico Bertoloni Meli, *Visualizing Disease: The Art and History of Pathological Illustrations* (Chicago: University of Chicago Press, 2017), 55, 70, 79, mentions several instances where authors of treatises on pathology suppressed the numbers on selected plates or entire volumes of plates, using almost the same language as Cheselden.

34 Zachary Cope, *William Cheselden 1688–1752* (Edinburgh–London: E. & S. Livingstone, 1953), 1–6.

35 Elizabeth Prettejohn, "Surplusage!" *London Review of Books* (6 February 2020): 33, in a review of Walter Pater's Platonism, gives a good synopsis: "It is visible beauty, the kind that inspires erotic love, which provides the direct route to the idea of Beauty, which is of highest value in Plato's philosophy."

36 The conception of Beauty as the embodiment of an ideal "Form" was pervasive in eighteenth-century English print and visual culture. Cheselden and his contemporaries received it from multiple literary and theatrical sources: via Plato's *Symposium* (especially the "ladder of love" discussion) in Greek, Latin translation and Louis Le Roy's mid sixteenth-century French translation (translated into English in the seventeenth century); via other Latin and Greek works from antiquity and translations thereof; via contemporary and near contemporary poetry, drama and philosophy influenced by neoplatonist discourse. More importantly: Beauty wasn't just theorized and imagined, it was visually enacted in the personification of Beauty in painting, drawing, sculpture and on stage.

37 Edmund Burke, "Of Beauty," *A Philosophical Inquiry into the Origin of Our Ideas of the Sublime and Beautiful; With an Introductory Discourse Concerning Taste* (London, 1757), III.1.

38 Romana Byrne, *Aesthetic Sexuality: A Literary History of Sadomasochism* (New York and London: Bloomsbury Academic, 2013), 12, citing Baumgarten,

Shaftesbury and Burke for the eighteenth century and then Pater and Nietzsche for the nineteenth: "One of the ideological functions of 18th-century aesthetics is to discourage sexual indulgence ... Yet these injunctions [of Baumgarten, Shaftesbury and Burke] did little to prevent sexuality from lacing ... aesthetics." Benjamin Morgan, *The Outward Mind: Materialist Aesthetics in Victorian Science and Literature* (Chicago: University of Chicago Press, 2017), 7–8, argues that Kant distinguished his concept of beauty from Burke and other eighteenth-century British philosophers of "taste" by rejecting "usefulness, sensuous gratification, and moral or formal perfection" in favor of a disinterested, disembodied immanent aesthetic. If so, this was still not very different *functionally* from Richardson and Burke, who located true aesthetic judgment in the distinterested expertise of the manly independent connoisseur (functionally in dialogue with other such men).

39 Jason M. Kelly, *The Society of Dilettanti* (New Haven and London: Paul Mellon Centre for Studies in British Art, Yale University Press, 2009), 4.

40 David Hume, "Of the Standards of Taste" (*c.*1745), originally published in *Four Dissertations* (London: A. Millar in the Strand, 1757), qtd. in Umberto Eco, *On Beauty: A History of a Western Idea*, trans. Alastair McEwen (London: Secker & Warburg, 2018), 276.

41 Thomas S. Kuhn, *The Structure of Scientific Revolutions* (Chicago: University of Chicago Press, 1962). For social epistemology, see Martin Kusch, "Social Epistemology" https://www.hps.cam.ac.uk/students/research-guide/social-epistemology; F.F. Schmitt, ed., *Socializing Epistemology: The Social Dimensions of Knowledge* (Lanham, MD: Rowman & Littlefield, 1994).

42 Kelly, *Society of Dilettanti*, chap. 1. According to Brian Cowan, "An Open Elite: The Peculiarities of Connoisseurship in Early Modern England," *Modern Intellectual History* 1.2 (2004): 151–2, Richardson probably took the term from Bernard Mandeville's *Fable of the Bees* (1714), the earliest documented use in printed English. The term gained currency in late seventeenth-century France. Cowan suggests that the culture of connoisseurship, and a widespread feeling that French culture was more advanced, was developing within the seventeenth-century British *virtuosi*, well before Mandeville and Richardson.

43 Richardson, *Two Discourses,* 2:200, 205. For the politics of eighteenth-century British connoisseurship, see Harry Mount, "The Monkey with the Magnifying Glass: Constructions of the Connoisseur in Eighteenth-Century Britain," *Oxford Art Journal* 29.2 (2006): 167–83. Mount discusses the critique of connoisseurship by Hogarth and others. I am using connoisseurship here more generally, to denote a burgeoning culture and social praxis of knowledgeable collectorship and discerning viewership. The debates over beauty, the quality of paintings, and the genius of particular artists that Mount so brilliantly analyzes were part and parcel of that burgeoning connoisseurial culture.

44 Carol Gibson-Wood, "Picture Consumption in London at the End of the Seventeenth Century," *Art Bulletin* 84.3 (2002): 491–9.

45 Anthony Ashley Cooper, 3d Earl of Shaftesbury, *A Notion of the Historical Draught or Tablature of the Judgment of Hercules* (London, 1713), conclusion, point 4, qtd in Gibson-Wood, "Picture Consumption in London at the End of the Seventeenth Century," 491.

46 Abigail Zitin, "Wantonness: Milton, Hogarth, and *The Analysis of Beauty*," *differences* 27.1 (2016): 25–46. Davis, *Queer Beauty*, chap. 1 and "Homoerotic Art Collection from 1750 to 1920," *Art History* 24.2 (2001): 247–77, argues that this disembodying cleavage of corporeality from beauty has been regarded as a defining principle of Kantian aesthetics. But, as Zitin shows in her analysis of Hogarth's *Analysis of Beauty*, Kant was giving voice to an already ongoing, and ambivalent, thematic of aesthetic discourse and practice as well as neoplatonist discourse.

47 Kristel Sementek, *Mariette and the Science of the Connoisseur in Eighteenth-Century Europe* (Farnham and Burlington: Ashgate, 2014), 2–3.

48 Cope, *William Cheselden*, 6, 8, citing some ambiguous remarks in the *Anatomy of the Human Body* (1713), asserts that Cheselden was "an excellent draughtsman" and the illustrator of his own works. Carol Gibson-Wood, *Jonathan Richardson: Art Theorist of the English Enlightenment* (New Haven: Yale University Press, 2000), 78, says that Cheselden, "a skilled draughtsman ... [did] the anatomical drawings for ... *The Anatomy of the Human Body* of 1713 and *Osteographia* of 1733," but also gives no source for that claim. Museo Bargello, Florence, has two tabletop-sized bronzes of Maderno's Hercules and Antaeus (along with models of Hercules and Antaeus by other sculptors). A painting by Cornelis de Bailleur (Studio of Rubens) in the Palazzo Pitti, Florence, shows Maderno's Hercules and Antaeus as a small plaster model on a credenza, alongside other models of well-known sculptures.

49 Jenny Uglow, *William Hogarth: A Life and a World* (1998; New York: Farrar Straus & Giroux, 2002), 722, fn12, says that Joseph Highmore (1692–1780) was the artist for the plates of the second edition of *The Anatomy of the Human Body* (1722), but what about the crude plates credited to someone named "Brown"? The plates of the improved fifth edition of 1740 are uncredited to any artist; the engraver is identified as Gerard Vandergucht.

50 Maderno's sculpture is influenced by Antonio del Pollaiuolo's playful bronze (*c.*1475–98; now in Museo Nazionale del Bargello, Florence). The homoerotic valence of that older Hercules and Antaeus was too overt for the (openly homosexual) Victorian art critic John Addington Symonds who disapproved of its "brutal" passions and "eccentric energy" (quoted in Davis, *Queer Beauty*, 125–6).

51 Even if some of Cheselden's readers might not have known the Maderno sculpture, the mere showing of two entirely naked figures from Greek mythology, in and of itself, referenced classical antiquity and the refined appreciation of such things.

52 Nicholas Penny, "At the Royal Academy" [rev. of *The Renaissance Nude* exhibition, London, 2019], *London Review of Books* (23 May 2019): 18; Anita Guerrini, "The Whiteness of Bones: Sceletopoeia and the Human Body in Early Modern Europe," *Bulletin of the History of Medicine* 96.1 (2022): 34–70, esp. 60–9.

53 William Gilpin, *An Essay Upon Prints: Remarks upon the Principles of picturesque Beauty, the Different Kinds of Prints, and the Characters of the most noted Masters; illustrated by Criticisms upon particular Pieces; to which are added, Some Cautions that may be useful in collecting Prints* (London: J. Robson, 1768).

54 Karel Du Jardin (or Dujardin) (1622–78), a Dutch Golden Age painter.

55 Raymond La Fage (or Lafage) (1656–84), a French Baroque artist.

56 Matthew Craske, *Joseph Wright of Derby: Painter of Darkness* (London: Paul Mellon Centre for Studies in British Art, 2020), 95: "Hunter, more than any other surgeon of his day, saw the value of the art of drawing to anatomy and vice versa."

57 *Lectures on Sculpture as Delivered Before the President and the Members of the Royal Academy by John Flaxman* (London: Henry G. Bohn, 1838). The art of medieval Christianity, and the loss of the anatomical knowledge of antiquity, was hard to account for in Flaxman's narrative of progress.

58 Benjamin Robert Haydon, "Table Talk," in B.R. Haydon & F.W. Haydon, *The Life, Letters and Table Talk of Benjamin Robert Haydon* (New York: Scribner, 1876), 261. According to William Michael Rosetti, "Benjamin Robert Haydon," *Encyclopaedia Britannica* vol. 13 (11th ed., 1991), 11–12, early exposure to Albinus's anatomical atlas sparked the painter's lifelong love of anatomy.

59 Craig Ashley Hanson, *The English Virtuoso: Art, Medicine and Antiquarianism in the Age of Empiricism* (Chicago: University of Chicago Press, 2009) shows that this emphasis on careful observation and description, in words and image, was entangled with the new science that was taking root in the Royal Society.

60 *Anatomy of the Humane Body* (1st ed., London, 1713); in later editions, "the human body."

61 See Anita Guerrini, "Anatomists and Entrepreneurs in Early Eighteenth-Century London," *Journal of the History of Medicine and Allied Sciences* 59.2 (2004): 219–39, esp. 234; quoted material appears on 235.

62 See introductory pages to various editions of *Anatomy of the Human Body*. Class identity was not entirely fixed. Education in science, literature and aesthetics was a vehicle of social mobility, redefinition and pleasure. Artisans and working people, interested in anatomy and other scientific topics, went to popular lectures and anatomical museums (in London, Rackstrow's). At the same time, there were women who didn't accept exclusion from anatomical study, and there were "anatomical prodigies" like Anna Morandi Manzolini (1714–74) and Mme Biheron (1719–95). See Rebecca Messbarger, *The Lady Anatomist: The Work of Anna Morandi Manzolini* (Chicago: University of Chicago Press, 2010); Dacome, "Intimate Connections," 315–49.

63 Cheselden, *Anatomy of the Human Body* (5th ed., London, 1740), 59.

64 Cheselden, *Osteographia, or The Anatomy of the Bones* (London: [William Bowyer for the author], 1733). The high artistic merit claimed for *Osteographia* is in part indicated by omission of call-out numbers throughout. For a discussion of *Osteographia*'s aesthetic aims, see Monique Kornell, "Accuracy and Elegance in Cheselden's *Osteographia* (1733)," *Public Domain Review* (22 Aug 2011), https://publicdomainreview.org/2011/08/22/accuracy-and-elegance-in-cheseldens-osteographia-1733/.

65 Carin Berkowitz, "The Illustrious Anatomist: Authorship, Patronage and Illustrative Style in Anatomy Folios, 1700–1840," *Bulletin of the History of Medicine* 89.2 (2015): 203–4.

66 Cope, *William Cheselden*, chaps. 1–2; Richard H. Meade, *In the Sunshine of Life: A Biography of Richard Meade 1673–1754* (Philadelphia: Dorrance & Co., 1974), 37–40, 48–50.

67 Meade, *In the Sunshine*, 39, quotes a quatrain from Pope: "Weak though I am of limb, and short of sight, / Far from a Lynx, and not a giant quite, / I'll do what Mead and Cheselden advise, / To keep these limbs, and to preserve these eyes" (*Epistle* I, bk. 1).

68 Terry F. Robinson, "Connoisseurship and the Female Body," *Oxford Handbooks Online* (May 2017; update August 2017) DOI: 10.1093/oxfordhb/9780199935338.013.139; Elizabeth Eger, ed., *Bluestockings Displayed: Portraiture, Performance and Patronage, 1730–1830* (Cambridge: Cambridge University Press, 2013).

69 Cope, *William Cheselden*, 94: "Cheselden was undoubtedly the outstanding man of his surgical generation." Joseph Frank Payne, "William Cheselden," *Dictionary of National Biography* (1885–1900), 10: 192–4; John Kirkup, "William Cheselden," *Oxford Dictionary of National Biography* (2006), https://doi-org.ezproxy.its.uu.se/10.1093/ref:odnb/5226; Carol Gibson-Wood, *Jonathan Richardson: Art Theorist of the English Enlightenment* (New Haven: Yale University Press, 2000).

70 Payne, "William Cheselden," 192–4; quote is from 194. Thanks to Anita Guerrini, email 9 June 2020, for pointing out the snobbish tone of Payne's biographical entry.

71 Richardson, *Two Discourses*. For connoisseurship and aesthetics, see also Francis Hutcheson, *An Inquiry into the Original of our Ideas of Beauty and Virtue* (London, 1725). Gibson-Wood, *Jonathan Richardson*, 78–80, gives a bit of the flavor of Cheselden's position and intellectual sociability in his network, quoting a 1722 letter from Alexander Pope to Jonathan Richardson: "'ask your friend Mr Chiseldon' [*sic*] for some ideas about a passage of Shakespeare ... mentioned to Dr Arbuthnot" (78).

72 For a partly itemized list of the holdings of Richardson's collection, see [Christopher] Cock, *A Catalogue of the Genuine and Entire Collection of Italian and Other Drawings, Prints, Models, and Casts, of the Late Eminent Mr. Jonathan Richardson, Painter, Deceas'd. Which Will Be Sold by Auction* (London, 1747). Richardson owned more than 1000 items by major artists (Michelangelo, Rembrandt, Carracci, Leonardo da Vinci, Rubens and Raphael among them), including drawings and prints of classical and Renaissance sculptures. The catalogue doesn't list any drawing or print of Maderno's Hercules and Antaeus, but some items are only identified by the artist. If Richardson owned a drawing or engraving of it, or drew one himself, he might have shared it with Cheselden. Cheselden's papers, quite limited in scope, provide no answers.

73 Richardson, *Two Discourses* (1719), 2d discourse: 7–8.

74 On connoisseurship and Cheselden, see Alexander Wragge-Morley, "Connoisseurship and the Communication of Anatomical Knowledge: The Case of William Cheselden's *Osteographia* (1733)," in A. Craciun & S. Schaffer, eds., *The Material Cultures of Enlightenment* (London: Palgrave Macmillan, 2016), 271–89; and M. Terrall, "Natural Philosophy for Fashionable Readers," in M. Frasca-Spada & N. Jardine, eds., *Books and the Sciences in History* (Cambridge: Cambridge University Press, 2000), 239–54.

75 According to Kornell, "Accuracy and Elegance," the illustrations were originally commissioned for another work, by Cheselden's friend anatomist James Douglas, but instead debuted in Cheselden's 1713 *Anatomy of the Humane Body*.

76 Wragge-Morley, "Connoisseurship"; Cope, *William Cheselden*, 67–8; Rica Jones, "The Artist's Training and Technique," *Manners and Morals* (London: Tate Gallery, 1987), 19–24; "John Vanderbank," *Wikipedia* https://en.wikipedia.org/wiki/John_Vanderbank; "St. Martin's Lane Academy," *Wikipedia* https://en.wikipedia.org/wiki/St_Martin%27s_Lane_Academy. William Hogarth also studied with Vanderbank.

77 Cheselden, *Osteographia* (London, 1733), preface.

78 Richard Payne Knight, *An Analytical Inquiry into the Principles of Taste* (London, 1806): "Taste is a subject upon which it might be naturally supposed that all mankind would agree ... This is, however ... far from the case ... there is scarcely any subject upon which men differ more ..." (1); "[Y]et there are certain standards of excellence, which every generation of civilized man ... has uniformly recognized ... Such are the precious remains of Grecian sculpture; which afford standards of real beauty, grace, and elegance in human form ..." (4–5).

79 Advertisement, *Anatomy of the Human Body* (5th ed.; London, 1740). Cheselden explains the differences in content and price and offers various deals for new purchasers and current owners of previous editions.

80 *Anatomy of the Human Body* (5th ed., 1740), "The Case of Samuel Wood," 321, tab. 38; the genitals of two "Hermaphrodites", 315, tab. 33; Anita Guerrini, "The Hermaphrodite of Charing Cross," in Erika Dyck & Larry Stewart, eds., *The Uses of Humans in Experiment: Perspectives from the 17th to the 20th Century* (Leiden and Boston: Brill, Rodopi, 2016), 28–51 and Guerrini, "Anatomists and Entrepreneurs," 234–5. The case of the hermaphrodites was carried over from the fourth ed., 1730, but the case of Samuel Wood, and the plate, was a new addition to the fifth ed.

81 My discussion here is informed by the discussion of the history of taste in Allison Pease, *Modernism, Mass Culture and the Aesthetics of Obscenity* (Cambridge: Cambridge University Press, 2000), esp. xii, 1–3, 6, 11–14, 20–2; Karen Harvey, *Reading Sex in the Eighteenth Century: Bodies and Gender in English Erotic Culture* (Cambridge: Cambridge University Press, 2004), esp. 68–9; Lyle Massey, "Against the 'Statue Anatomized': The 'Art' of Eighteenth-century Anatomy on Trial," *Art History* 40.1 (2017): 68–103; and Abigail Zitin, "Wantonness: Milton, Hogarth, and *The Analysis of Beauty*," *differences* 27.1 (2016): 25–46. For the sociology of taste, see Bourdieu, *Distinction* (1987).

82 William Hogarth, *The Analysis of Beauty: Written with a View of Fixing the Fluctuating Ideas of Taste* (London: J. Reeves, 1753), viii.

83 Alexander Wragge-Morley, "Connoisseurship and the Communication of Anatomical Knowledge," discussing John Douglas, *Animadversions on a Late Pompous Book, Intituled, Osteographia: or, The Anatomy of the Bones ...* (London, 1735). Douglas sneers at Cheselden's "florid" language on page 4 and at the "supposed beauty" of the plates on page 24 and elsewhere.

84 Hutcheson, *An Inquiry into the Original of our Ideas of Beauty and Virtue* (1726), xvi.

85 Wadd, *Memorabilia* (1824), quoted in Cope, *William Cheselden*, 101.

86 Eve Kosofsky Sedgwick, *Between Men: English Literature and Male Homosocial Desire* (New York: Columbia University Press, 1985). See also Zitin, "Wantonness, 25–46, for a smart discussion of how erotics played out as a kind of boundary of aesthetic pleasure.

87 For the social aims of high medical publication, and the way in which knowledge production affirmed claims of authority and the search for patronage and prestige, see Berkowitz, "The Illustrious Anatomist," 171–208. Anatomy occupied a unique place of privilege in medical knowledge production because: (1) it occasioned the production of works of collectable fine illustration in a subject which had a dynamic relation to fine art; (2) it had a "higher purpose", was both a field and a method of natural philosophy, and more than just a guide to the practice of medicine and surgery; and, (3) the subject of anatomy had a mystique due to its association with dissection of the dead, and the assertion of medical privilege over the dead.

88 Fiona Stafford, "What Are Books for? Darcy's Library, Crabbe's *The Library*, and Shillito's *The Country Book-Club*," in Alice Crawford & Robert Crawford, eds., *Libraries in Literature* (Oxford: Oxford University Press, 2022), 72–75.

89 Viccy Coltman, *Fabricating the Antique: Neoclassicism in Britain, 1760–1800* (Chicago: University of Chicago Press, 2006), 196.

90 Bernardino Genga, *Anatomia per uso et intelligenza del disegno ricercata non solo su gl'ossi, e muscoli del corpo humano* (Rome, 1691).

91 According to Hanson, *The English Virtuoso*, 9, "physicians constituted the largest and most active occupational membership group" in the Royal Society "during its early history, and many members who were not doctors cultivated a keen interest in medical matters." Throughout his study, Hanson shows that British (and Italian, French and Dutch) medical men from the late sixteenth century well into the eighteenth century cultivated interests in art, aesthetics and connoisseurship, and drew vital connections between medicine, the human body, antiquarian classicism in the humanist mode of Renaissance Italy, and issues of representation in painting, drawing and sculpture.

92 Stafford, "What Are Books for?", 75.

93 Email, Michael North to Sappol (14 July 2022). North continues: "Many of his books ... were third or fourth editions, some ... published in Dublin, etc. He did not want to pay top dollar—he wanted the text, not an *objet d'art*. His bindings were also cheap ... easily damaged when we try to scan them, and therefore many of his books are not yet available online."

94 *Jefferson's Catalogue of Paintings &c.*, Accession #2958-b, Thomas Jefferson Papers, Special Collections, University of Virginia Library, https://www.monticello.org/site/research-and-collections/catalogue-paintings (transcription from Seymour Howard, "Thomas Jefferson's Art Gallery for Monticello," *The Art Bulletin* 59.4 (1977): 597–600). Thanks to Michael North, Head Reference & Readers Services, Rare Book & Special Collections Division, Library of Congress, for locating Jefferson's copy of Cheselden and sharing his insights into Jefferson as collector.

95 *The Anatomy of the Human Body* (8th ed.; London: H. Woodfall, 1763) [now LC QM21.C5 1763 or Sowerby 996]. Jefferson quoted Herodotus, in Greek, in the margins. He also wrote in corrections for two typos. Michael North, "Thomas Jefferson Library Collection: A Research Guide," https://guides.loc.gov/thomas-jefferson-library (6 May 2022); Gerard Gawalt, curator, *Thomas Jefferson*, "Jefferson's Library," "Thomas Jefferson offers his library to Congress after the British burn the Capitol in 1814" (Library of Congress), https://www.loc.gov/exhibits/jefferson/jefflib.html; E. Millicent Sowerby, *Catalogue of the Library of Thomas Jefferson* (Washington, DC: Library of Congress, 1952–55) 1: 450–5.

96 For Jefferson's Richardson and Gilpin, see Sowerby, *Catalogue of the Library of Thomas Jefferson* 4: 391 (#12). Sowerby, 389–99, lists 15 works on painting, sculpture, antiquities, and "beauty", including a first edition of an Italian translation of Winckelmann (*Storia delle Arti del Disegno*) and a 1648–63 edition of Vasari's *Lives*. Jefferson also owned Gilpin's book on the gardens of Stowe.

97 Davison, "Occasional Politeness," 929.

98 Andrew Graciano, "Observation, Imitation and Emulation in *An Academy by Lamplight* by Joseph Wright of Derby (1734–97)," *British Art Journal* 14.3 (2013–14): 40: "Eighteenth-century caricatures of connoisseurs—both subtle and overt—frequently depict their subjects' profession as a thin veil for the entertainment of lustful, lingering eyes. Many also hint at the folly of connoisseurship …"

99 Thanks to Alexander Wragge-Morley for alerting me to this detail.

100 Cosway, although eventually made a fellow of the Royal Academy, was himself the object of considerable mockery. See Philippe Bordes, "Richard and Maria Cosway, Edinburgh," *The Burlington Magazine* 137.1111 (1995): 700–2; Robinson, "Connoisseurship and the Female Body."

101 Tony Kitto, "Group of Connoisseurs by Richard Cosway," *Towneley from A to Z* (Oct 2018), www.atoz.myzen.co.uk/atoz/cosway.html, citing "Catalogue of the Portraits and Paintings at Towneley Lancashire" (ms. Sept 1844, on loan at Towneley Hall Art Gallery, from family descendants); Charles Townley, Account Book, 14 Oct 1775: "To Mr. Cosway for his picture with 6 portraits £100."

102 Warwick William Wroth, "Charles Towneley or Townley," *Dictionary of National Biography* 57 (London: Smith, Elder & Co., 1899), 97–8.

103 Kelly, *Society of Dilettanti*, 251.

104 Richard Payne Knight, *An Account of the Remains of the Worship of Priapus, Lately Existing at Isernia in the Kingdom of Naples: In Two Letters*

(London, 1786); a few years after publication, Knight was pressured into buying back most of the edition and destroying it. Only a few copies remain. See Kelly, *Society of Dilettanti,* 243–57; Bruce Redford, *Dilettanti: The Antic and the Antique in Eighteenth-Century England* (Los Angeles: Getty Publications, 2008); and Davis, *Queer Beauty*, esp. 51–81. Hamilton's wax votive objects were of more recent origin but regarded as atavistic survivals of Greco-Roman antiquity. They now reside in the British Museum.

105 Gibson-Wood, "Picture Consumption," 491, citing Anthony Ashley Cooper, third earl of Shaftesbury, *A Notion of the Historical Draught or Tablature of the Judgment of Hercules* (London, 1713), conclusion, point 4; Cooper, *Characteristicks of Men, Manners, Opinions, Times, Vol. 1* (1732), 11 ["A Letter Concerning Enthusiasm"], 339 ["Advice to an Author"].

106 Cooper, *Characteristicks*, 333–5 ["Advice to an Author"]. Yet "The Vulgar ... may swallow any sordid Jest, any mere Drollery or Buffoonery; ... it must be a finer and truer Wit which takes with the Men of Sense and Breeding," 11 ["A Letter Concerning Enthusiasm"].

107 Cooper, "Advice to Authors," 135.

108 William Godwin, *Things as They are: or, The Adventures of Caleb Williams* (1794; 4th ed., London, 1816), 1:70.

109 See Godwin, *The Adventures of Caleb Williams* (London: Richard Bentley, 1849), 72, 154, 423 et passim. The character Emily Melville (a stand-in for Mary Wollstonecraft) is the bearer of all these noble traits.

110 As the figure of the connoisseur became more visible, the word "connoisseur" was already acquiring a mixed reputation, and was in some eyes a debased coinage. There wasn't any high connoisseurship in *The Connoisseur, by Mr. Town, Critic and Censor General*, a London weekly newspaper of 1754–6, just mockery; see for example, *The Connoisseur* 1.2 (1754): 7–11. Boswell's *The Life of Johnson* links connoisseurship to crude prurient interest: "Mr. [John] Wilkes held a candle to shew a fine print of a beautiful female figure which hung in the room, and pointed out the elegant contour of the bosom with the finger of an arch connoisseur."

111 Vicesimus Knox, *An Essay on Education* (London, 1802) 2:80; quoted in Marcus Tomalin, *The French Language and British Literature 1756–1830* (London and New York: Routledge, 2016), 62–6. The same words appear in Knox's 1785 *An Essay on Liberal Education.*

112 In concentrating on homosociality, my account omits discussion of the spaces the roles that women played in the culture of connoisseurship; see Ann Bermingham, "The Aesthetics of Ignorance: The Accomplished Woman in the Culture of Connoisseurship," *Oxford Art Journal* 16.2 (1993): 3–20.

113 Thanks to Alexander Wragge-Morley for directing my attention to "Three men." For more on the painting and Wright, see Craske, *Joseph Wright of Derby*, 89–100 and Graciano, "Observation," 40–1. According to Craske, 96–7, the scene records a moment after one of the men has just finished drawing the statuette. Drawing being a means of deep study of both the artfulness of the statue and the gladiator's exemplification of masculine muscular anatomy, proportion and beauty. Craske, 98–100,

pairs "Three men" with Wright's later painting, "An academy by lamplight" (1769), in which an adolescent boy is captivated by a classical statue of a beautiful nymph, as other boys draw and study it. In the background is the Borghese gladiator, which the boys entirely ignore. The mature homosocial camaraderie depicted in the1765 painting, with its focus on the male nude, vividly contrasts with the 1769 painting where the gaze upon the female nude is connected to adolescent sexuality and doesn't bind the boys together as a group.

114 The plaster figure was commercially sold as a study object and for home decoration. It was likely manufactured in multiples in the workshop of Benjamin Rackstrow, who was later the proprietor of a London museum which exhibited anatomical models. See Craske, "Unwholesome and Pornographic," 79.

115 Graciano, "Observation," 39–41.

116 "Three Men Viewing the Gladiator by Candlelight" (1769); sheet: 48.9 × 56.7 cm. Engraver: William Pether.

117 Townley sometimes also spelled his name as the more elegant "Towneley" (which has been adopted as the name of the estate and manor museum in Burnley). His friends shown here are: Pierre-François Hugues, Baron d'Hancarville (1719–1805), a French art historian and amateur art dealer (and author of two pornographic works); Thomas Astle (1735–1803), an English antiquary and paleographer; Charles Francis Greville (1749–1809), an English politician and collector of art, antiquities and gems and minerals, and also a member of the Society of Dilettanti.

118 The book is open to pl. 42 of *Le Antichità di Ercolano esposte* (Naples: Reale Accademia Ercolanese di Archeologia, 1757–92), v. 6 (1771); Coltman, *Fabricating the Antique*, 54–5.

119 Mary Webster, "Zoffany's Painting of Charles Towneley's Library in Park St. Westminster," *Burlington Magazine* 56 (July 1964): 316–23 and *Johan Zoffany 1733–1810* (New Haven: Yale University Press, 2011). See also Chris Haffenden, *Every Man His Own Monument: Self-Monumentalizing in Romantic Britain* (Uppsala: Acta Universitatis Upsaliensis, 2018), 116–19; Wolfgang Ernst, "Frames at Work: Museological Imagination and Historical Discourse in Neoclassical Britain," *Art Bulletin* 75.3 (1993): 481–98, esp. 488–90, emphasizes that the scene is an imaginary, aestheticized, ideal "museal" space. Townley's collection is now owned by the British Museum, where most of it sits in storage.

120 Kelly, *Society of Dilettanti*, 246–8.

121 Bordes, "Richard and Maria Cosway," 700.

122 Kitto, "Group of Connoisseurs by Richard Cosway," identifies them as "Dr Verdun" and "Dr Oliver."

123 Hanson, *The English Virtuoso*, 157–93.

124 Kelly, *Society of Dilettanti*, 28–9, discusses just such a scene depicted in William Hogarth's *Marriage A-la-Mode Scene 4: The Toilette* (*c.*1745).

125 Weeks, *Coming Out*, 6.

126 For the critique of connoisseurship, see Mount, "The Monkey in the Magnifying Glass," and Zitin, "Wantonness."

127 Solomon-Godeau, *Male Trouble*, 84–97. See also Michael Hatt, "Near and Far: Homoeroticism, Labour, and Hamo Thornycroft's *Mower*," *Art History* 26.1 (2003): 26–55. Hatt, discussing late Victorian sculpture of male nudes, distinguishes between homoeroticism and the outright avowal of same-sex desire: "Desire was invoked in order that it be contained." He argues that, where "legitimacy, that very thing which attempts to ward off homosexuality and keep it at a distance, brings it close, enables the experience of desire," the term "homoerotic" is a useful "name for this structure of enablement and disavowal." (51) Such was also the case with anatomical male nudes and anatomical representation of male genitalia, and throughout this book I use "homoerotic" in much the same way, to suggest an erotic potential in medical illustration that could be both enabled and disavowed.

128 Harry Cocks, "Safeguarding Civility: Sodomy, Class and Moral Reform in Early 19th-Century England," *Past & Present* 190 (2006): 121–46, esp. 125.

129 For homosexual practice in eighteenth- and nineteenth-century England, see Weeks, *Coming Out*, 33–44.

130 Cocks, "Safeguarding Civility"; and *Nameless Offences: Speaking of Male Homosexual Desire in Nineteenth-Century England* (London: I.B. Tauris, 2003); Upchurch, *Before Wilde: Sex between Men in Britain's Age of Reform* (2013). For a review of the literature and conceptual difficulties of writing the history of same-sex friendship and desire, see Barry Reay, "Writing the Modern Histories of Homosexual England," *The Historical Journal* 52.1 (2009): 213–33. Following David Halperin (and Foucault), Reay breaks down male same-sex relations in nineteenth-century Britain into five broad categories: "effeminacy, sodomy, friendship, inversion, and homosexuality itself" (the last problematic category denoting something that converges with recognizable modern sexual identity categories) (216).

131 John Bell, *Letters on Professional Character and Manners: on the education of a surgeon, and the duties and qualifications of a physician ...* (Edinburgh, 1810), 543–612. Most of the quotes are from Letter XIV.

132 Bell, *Letters*, 603.

133 Michael Brown, "Surgery, Identity and Embodied Emotion: John Bell, James Gregory and the Edinburgh 'Medical War'," *History* 104 (2018): 19–41; thanks again to Anita Guerrini, email 9 June 2020, for emphasizing the point.

134 Michael Brown, "Surgery, Identity and Embodied Emotion" and "Surgery and Emotion: The Era before Anaesthesia," conference paper, Society for the Social History of Medicine annual meeting, University of Kent, UK, July 2016.

135 In America, there was less of a professional distinction, surgeons tended to also be doctors of medicine. In Britain, physicians were addressed as "doctor", surgeons as "mister."

136 A.C. Braddock, "'Jeff College Boys': Thomas Eakins, Dr. Forbes, and Anatomical Fraternity in Postbellum Philadelphia," *American Quarterly* 57.2 (2005): 355–83, esp. 358–60; Sappol, *A Traffic of Dead Bodies*, chap. 1.

137 See Lauren Young, "Bibliomania, the Dark Desire for Books that Infected Europe in the 1800s," *Atlas Obscura* (2 Dec 2016), https://www.atlasobscura.com/articles/bibliomania-the-dark-desire-for-books-that-infected-europe-in-the-1800s; and Victoria Mills, "Men and Books: Narratives of Desire" (28 June 2014), https://www.cam.ac.uk/research/features/men-and-books-narratives-of-desire. Mills and Young discuss "book madness", and passionate book collecting, but similar forms of madness were attached to the collecting of art and historical objects.

138 William C. Wright, "Hazlitt, Ruskin, and Nineteenth-Century Art Criticism," *Journal of Aesthetics and Art Criticism* 32.4 (1974): 509–23.

139 Oscar Wilde, "The Critic as Artist," *Intentions* (London, 1891). For late nineteenth-century aestheticism, see Getsy, Shirland, Corbett, Hatt, Stephenson, and Edwards.

Part Three "Overshadowed by the artist": Mr Joseph Maclise's queer anatomy [pages 96–169]

1 Jean-Baptiste-Marc Bourgery and Nicolas-Henri Jacob, *Traité complet de l'anatomie de l'homme: comprenant la médecine opératoire, avec planches lithographiées d'après nature*, 8 vols. (Paris: C.A. Delaunay, 1831–54; 2d ed., Guerin et Cie, 1866–71). Bourgery died in 1849, five years before the initial set of volumes was completed. The second edition, completed in 1871, adds Claude Bernard as co-author, but according to Melissa Lo, "Ideal Pathologies: Jean-Marc Bourgery's *Traité complet de l'anatomie de l'homme* (1831–54)," M.S. thesis (Massachusetts Institute of Technology, 2008), 25, Bernard added little to the production and was only credited to exploit his growing prestige as France's preeminent advocate of experimental physiology. The first edition was sold in two versions: monochrome and hand- and stencil-colored. The second edition was fully chromolithographic.

2 Natalie J. Lauer, *Der Kontrakt des Zeichners mit der Medizin: Ästhetik und Wissenschaft im Bildatlas Bourgery & Jacob* (Würzburg: Königshausen & Neumann, 2013), 13. Jacob's collaborators and assistants were gifted illustrators in their own right (Ludwig Hirschfeld, Jean-Baptiste Léveillé, Charlotte Hublier (who later married Jacob), and several others), but the work is unified, a *gesamtkunstwerk;* Lo, "Ideal Pathologies," 25.

3 Dorothy Johnson, *Jacques-Louis David: The Art of Metamorphosis* (Princeton: Princeton University Press, 1993); see also Melissa Lo, "The wounded ideal goes anatomical," in Michael Sappol, ed., *Hidden Treasure* (New York: Blast Books, 2011), 44–9.

4 For the trope of disembodied medical hands on a passive subject, and indexicality, elided tactility, and their erotic frisson, see Elizabeth Stephens, "Touching Bodies: Tact/ility in Nineteenth-Century Medical Photographs and Models," in Kate Fisher & Sarah Toulalan, eds., *Bodies, Sex and Desire from the Renaissance to the Present* (London: Palgrave Macmillan, 2011), 87–101. Stephens focuses on the use of disembodied hands to exhibit

patients in pathological photographs, and illustrations, but her argument is also applicable to surgical anatomies and handbooks. See also Hoffmann, "Sleeping Beauties" and Ebenstein, *Anatomical Venus.*

5 *Traité complet* was initially sold to subscribers in installments, which could be collected to make up chapters of a bound volume. From 1831–40, seventy installments were issued, "each containing eight panels of illustrations and eight sheets accompanying the text." In monochrome the cost was about 800 francs, in color 1600 francs: the "high price obviously was an obstacle for the spread of the work" (according to "Jean-Baptiste-Marc Bourgery," *Wikipedia*, https://en.wikipedia.org/wiki/Jean-Baptiste_Marc_Bourgery). See also Lauer, *Der Kontrakt,* 14 and Naomi Slipp, "International Anatomies: Teaching Visual Literacy in the Harvard Lecture Hall," in Kaat Wils, Raf de Bont, & Sokhieng Au, eds., *Bodies Beyond Borders: Moving Anatomies, 1750–1950* (Leuven: Leuven University Press, 2017), 228, n40.

6 For more on the *Traité*, see Lauer, *Der Kontrakt*; Cindy Stelmackowich, "Bodies of Knowledge: The 19th-Century Anatomical Atlas in the Spaces of Art and Science," *RACAR: revue d'art canadienne / Canadian Art Review* 33.1/2 (2008): 75–86; and Lo, "Ideal Pathologies."

7 Stefan Hirschauer, "The Manufacture of Bodies in Surgery," *Social Studies of Science* 21.2 (1991): 279–319, esp. 284–6, argues that the hand as instrument of the willful subject is explicitly operationalized in modern surgery. An older rhetorical formation that goes back thousands of years figures the hand as mediator between spirit and matter; see Emily Jane Cohen, "Enlightenment and the Dirty Philosopher," *Configurations* 5 (1997): 369–424.

8 Stephens, "Touching Bodies," 89, 96, and 98–9.

9 Stephens, "Touching Bodies," 89.

10 For the erotics of book collecting in the late nineteenth century, see Mills, "Men and Books" and Young, "Bibliomania."

11 For socializing and shared readings and viewings in scientific societies for the elite, see James Secord, *Victorian Sensation* (Chicago: University of Chicago Press, 2000), 410–36.

12 The subject matter of medical illustration was more corporeal and extreme, but "fine art" and "religious art" enjoyed exemptions that could legitimate pleasurable or provocative scenes and figures.

13 Vanessa R. Schwartz, *Spectacular Realities: Early Mass Culture in Fin-de-Siècle Paris* (Berkeley: University of California Press, 1999), 45–88; and John Edmondson, "Death and the Tourist: Dark Encounters in Mid-Nineteenth-Century London via the Paris Morgue," in Philip R. Stone et al., eds., *The Palgrave Handbook of Dark Tourism Studies* (London: Palgrave, 2017), 77–101.

14 Leo Steinberg, "The Sexuality of Christ in Renaissance Art and in Modern Oblivion," *October* 25 (1983): 82.

15 See, for example, Anne-Louis de Roussy Girodet-Trioson, "The Death of Phaedra" (black chalk, 26.5 × 35.5 cm, Paris, the Louvre), which is a preparatory design with all four figures in the nude, for an engraving for Pierre Didot, *Oeuvres completes de Jean Racine*, 1801 [act 5, scene 7], in

which the four figures are clad in Greek robes. Thanks to Stephen John Campbell, Facebook post, 11 Aug 2020, for the reference. Campbell comments: "Painters learned as much anatomy as most trained physicians and their 'first drafts' had to show it. In retrospect it does look like an improbable TV production where the rehearsals were all-nude and the screened version was full-dress."

16 For anatomy in art pedagogy, see Helen McCormack, *William Hunter and his Eighteenth-Century Cultural Worlds: The Anatomist and the Fine Arts* (London: Routledge, 2017), 146–9.

17 There were, of course, erotically pleasurable scenes, lots of nudity, in finished fine art, ostensibly legitimated by religious, historical and moral purposes. But the penis was a sensitive area. Jacob's teacher, Jacques-Louis David, did exactly the same thing, rendered the male genital in his preparatory drawing of *Cupid and Psyche*, but covered it with a folded towel in the finished 1817 painting. See David, "Cupid and Psyche" (1813), pen and black ink, brush and gray wash, heightened with white gouache, over black chalk (Cleveland Museum of Art [2002.91]); "Cupid and Psyche" (1817), oil on canvas (Cleveland Museum of Art [1962.37]). Psyche, the female figure, gets a different treatment. Her pubic region, covered by Cupid's knee in the drawing, is exposed but shorn of pubic hair in the painting, with legs pressed tightly together to suppress any view of labia or genitalia. (Female pubic hair, a taboo erogenous feature, was only depicted in pornography.) See also Perrin Stein, ed., *Jacques Louis David: Radical Draftsman* (New York: Metropolitan Museum of Art, 2022), 244–5.

18 See, also for example, Johan Zoffany, "A Life Class at St Martin's Lane Academy" (London, 1761–2), in which the genitals of a nude male model are ambiguously wrapped, and Wilhelm Bendz, "The Life Class at the Royal Academy of Fine Arts" (Copenhagen, 1826), in which the male genital is obscured by the model's leg. "The Life Class of the Vienna Academy" also circulated as a mezzotint print and engraved "outline drawing." How representative is Quadal's depiction? While local practices did vary, art pedagogy was pan-European and Vienna was one of the main centers. Quadal studied in Paris, Italy and Vienna, before embarking on a career as painter and teacher which took him from St Petersburg, Russia to London and Dublin.

19 Joseph Maclise, *Surgical Anatomy* (London: John Churchill, 1851), preface, reports that he studied at University College, London, and then in Paris at the "Ecole Pratique, and School of Anatomy adjoining the Hospital La Pitié."

20 *Surgical Anatomy* (1851 and succeeding editions). Compare Maclise's dream of unmediated reception with Susan Sontag, "Against Interpretation," 102: "Ideally, it is possible to elude the interpreters ... by making works of art whose surface is so unified and clean, whose momentum is so rapid, whose address is so direct that the work can be ... just what it is." [First ellipse, my deletion; second ellipse, Sontag's emphasis.]

21 But there was a tension in Maclise's philosophy between directly witnessed, true-to-nature representation, and his use of ideal or composite anatomical constructions. According to *Surgical Anatomy* (London, 1856), preface, his illustrations, "in guarantee of their anatomical accuracy ... have been made

myself, from my own dissections," that is without the distortions introduced by artists or other anatomists, "first planned at London University College, and afterwards realized at the Ecole Pratique and School of Anatomy, the Hospital La Pitié, Paris ... Those representing pathological conditions of parts, I have made from *natural specimens* [Maclise's emphasis], recent and preserved, which I had the opportunity of examining ..." This suggests that, while the witnessing of actual dissected bodies is a foundational epistemology, some of Maclise's illustrations are composites, and not a transcription of directly witnessed (and performed) dissection, as the plates visually suggest.

22 The existence of unconscious signaling, and complex fragmented personhood, is almost universally accepted in our cultural milieu. Not so in Maclise's time. But it wasn't long in coming. In the 1880s John Addington Symonds argued that unconscious homoerotic expression could be discerned in works of art, marks that even the artist might be unaware of, unintended, and then of course came Freud. See David Getsy, "Recognizing the Homoerotic: The Uses of Intersubjectivity in John Addington Symonds' 1887 Essays," *Visual Culture in Britain* 8.1 (2007): 37–57.

23 *The Anatomy of the Arteries of the Human Body* "with ... applications to pathology and operative surgery" (London: Taylor & Walton, 1844) began as a series of installments, beginning in 1840. The first edition measures 50 × 66 cm.

24 For the history and modes of representation described as "from nature," see Thomas Balfe, Joanna Woodall, Claus Zittel, eds., *Ad vivum? Visual Materials and the Vocabulary of Life-Likeness in Europe before 1800* (Leiden: Brill, 2019); and Daston & Galison, *Objectivity*.

25 Anonymous, review of Quain, *Anatomy of the Arteries* ... Pts. 1& 2 (1840), in *Provincial Medical & Surgical Journal* 1.12 (19 Dec 1840): 203. An anonymous reviewer in *British & Foreign Medico-Chirurgical Review* 3 (Jan.–Apr. 1849): 205 makes a similar point, with a nationalist twist: "Mr. Maclise's work bids fair to redeem our country from the stigma of possessing no original work on surgical anatomy, that could take rank in regard to completeness and beauty of execution with many continental productions that might be named." See also the rave review in *London Medical Gazette* 27 (1841): 580–2.

26 Roland Barthes, "The Reality Effect" (1969), in François Wahl, ed., *The Rustle of Language*, trans. Richard Howard (Berkeley: University of California Press, 1989): 141–8. Mary Hunter, *The Face of Medicine: Visualizing Medical Masculinities in Late 19th-Century Paris* (Manchester: Manchester University Press, 2016), discusses competing versions of realism circulating in nineteenth-century art and medicine.

27 Daston & Galison, *Objectivity*, 86, 95, 98, et passim.

28 Today, in major surgical operations and gross anatomy class, it's customary to cover up parts not directly relevant to the operation or lesson; Hirschauer, "The Manufacture of Bodies in Surgery," 288–97 ("the patient-body is visually reduced to the field of operation," 297). It's an open question as to whether that was the case in Maclise's time. Images in Jacob and Bourgery, which is in many respects a how-to guide, are inconsistent on this point.

29 Maclise was an exponent of the idea, espoused most prominently by Geoffroy Saint-Hilaire, that individual organic bodies and species instantiate archetypal forms.

30 We don't know who did the dissections for each plate: Richard Quain, Joseph Maclise, or someone else. *Bravura* is not just an adjective but also a sixteenth- and seventeenth-century style associated with artists who ostentatiously flaunted the brilliance of their mimesis. See Nicola Suthor, *Bravura: Virtuosity and Ambition in Early Modern European Painting* (Princeton: Princeton University Press, 2021).

31 W.F. Bynum, "Richard Quain," *Oxford Dictionary of National Biography* (2004), https://doi-org.ezproxy.its.uu.se/10.1093/ref:odnb/22940; *Plarr's Lives of the Fellows* [of the Royal College of Surgeons] *Online*; [obituary], *Address of George David Pollock, F.R.C.S., President of the Royal Medical and Chirurgical Society of London at the annual meeting, March 1st, 1888* (London, 1888), 20–2; [obituary], *British Medical Journal* 2.1395 (24 Sept 1887): 694–5; J.F. Clarke, *Autobiographical Recollections of the Medical Profession* (London: Churchill, 1874), 145–6. Quain's Hunterian Oration argued that medical men and the general public would be much improved if they customarily received an education in the liberal arts; Richard Quain, *On Some Defects in General Education: Being the Hunterian Oration of the Royal College of Surgeons for 1869* (London: Macmillan, 1870). Quain appears on the list of contributors in volume 1 of R.B. Todd et al., *Cyclopaedia of Anatomy & Physiology* (London: Sherwood, Gilbert & Piper, 1836), but didn't write any articles. (Maclise wrote the article on "Skeleton" in volume 4.) Quain took up the co-editorship of Jones Quain's widely-used *Elements of Anatomy* for the revised 5th edition (London: Taylor & Walton, 1843), roughly coincident with the appearance of *Anatomy of the Arteries*. Richard Quain (1800–87) is not to be confused with his cousin, also named Richard Quain (1816–98) (later Sir Richard), a prominent physician who was also a Fellow of the Royal Society and who is said to have assisted in the writing of the text of *Anatomy of the Arteries* (or have written it in its entirety).

32 *Daily News* (London), 14 November 1846. To salvage the project, Taylor & Walton came up with a subscription scheme: they reduced the price and promised to destroy the lithographic stones after printing 500 more copies, and thereby creating a limited edition for collector-subscribers.

33 Quain, *Anatomy of the Arteries*, vi–vii. Quain names Tiedemann's *Tabulae Arteriarum* (Karlsrühe, 1822), Haller's *Icones Anatomicae* (Göttingen, 1804) and Scarpa's *Sull'Aneurisma Reflessioni ed Osservazioni Anatomico-chirurgiche* (Pavia, 1804), all venerated large-size works.

34 Haffenden, *Every Man His Own Monument*, 11–12, places the creation of "self-monumentalizing," "self-historicizing" works and collections in a larger culture of great-man historicism that generated all sorts of real and potential pantheons and "strategies for posthumous recognition" and the capturing of "future commemorative attention." This agenda of historical place-seeking was widespread among ambitious men of accomplishment in anatomy, and every other field. (Berkowitz, "The Illustrious Anatomist," 201, notes that William Hunter wrote of "securing a sort of immortality," in lavishing immense sums on the publication of his *Anatomy of the Gravid Uterus* (1775).)

35 Jones Quain & Erasmus Wilson, *A Series of Anatomical Plates in Lithography*, 3 vols. (London: Taylor & Walton, 1836–42); Bynum, "Richard Quain," *ODNB* (2004). But, one wonders, if relations between the brothers were sour, how was it that Richard was chosen to succeed his brother as co-editor of *Elements of Anatomy*.

36 Quain, *Anatomy of the Arteries*, preface, vi.

37 "Joseph Maclise," *Plarr's Lives of the Fellows of the Royal College of Surgeons*, 2 vols. (London, 1930), https://livesonline.rcseng.ac.uk/client/en_GB/lives/search/detailnonmodal/ent:$002f$002fSD_ASSET$002f0$002fSD_ASSET:374796/one?qu=%22rcs%3A+E002613%22&rt=false%7C%7C%7CIDENTIFIER%7C%7C%7CResource+Identifier; see also John Turpin, "Daniel Maclise," *ODNB* (2004).

38 Eoin Lettice, "'Drink deeply of the nectared cup of science': Woodroffe and the Cork anatomists" (13 Sept 2011), http://www.communicatescience.eu/2011/09/drink-deeply-of-nectared-cup-of-science.html. Daniel Maclise also preceded his brother Joseph in the move to London. Joseph's major contribution to the transformism debates was as author-illustrator of *Comparative Osteology: Being morphological studies to demonstrate the archetype skeleton of vertebrate animals* (London: Taylor & Walton, 1847).

39 "Transformism" wasn't just a synonym for evolution (the word Darwin promoted to displace it), but also took in the morphology of animal forms (including human), adaptation, embryological and postnatal development, and comparative anatomy. For Maclise and transformism, see Adrian Desmond, *The Politics of Evolution: Morphology, Medicine and Reform in Radical London* (Chicago: University of Chicago Press, 1989), 360–4, 368–71, 376, and 425. See also Philip F. Rehbock, "Transcendental Anatomy," in Andrew Cunningham & Nicholas Jardine, eds., *Romanticism and the Sciences* (Cambridge: Cambridge University Press, 1990), 144–60.

40 Quote is from [anonymous], rev. of fasciculus 1, *Surgical Anatomy*, in *New York Journal of Medicine & the Collateral Sciences* 4 (1850): 96; see also *Edinburgh Medical & Surgical Journal* 81 (1854): 580. According to records from Maclise's publisher John Churchill, University of Reading Library, John A. Churchill papers MS 1393, in 1849, as payment for installments of *Surgical Anatomy*, Maclise received £50 (28 Aug), and in 1850 payments of £50 (30 Apr), £15 (1 Oct), £35 (22 Nov) [MS 1393 1_M7 p49–50]. In 1851, Maclise received further payment of £25 (23 Apr), £25 (15 July) [MS 1393 1_M7 p245–6]. The total is £200. The records are incomplete; there is nothing for the years after 1851. In a letter from Churchill to Joseph Maclise, 31 May 1849 (London) [MS 1393 1_M3 p159–60], the publisher explains that while Maclise originally offered his drawings (and text?) to Churchill free of charge, in order to promote his career (which, Churchill assured him, it would), Churchill declined the offer and instead offered to pay Maclise some kind of royalty. Shortly thereafter, Maclise asked for money (indicating he was in need?). Churchill replied that, although the publication was costlier than originally estimated—and would likely take a while to earn a profit—he would advance Maclise an unspecified amount of money, probably those payments listed in Churchill's records. As it happens, the 1851 edition of *Surgical Anatomy* made a good profit for Churchill: his final calculation was

£397 17s 11p; 8429 copies were sold and 300 were given out gratis. The American edition of *Surgical Anatomy* also sold well, going into three editions, but we don't have any record of Maclise's earnings from Blanchard & Lea, the publisher; Kornell, *Flesh and Blood*, 200.

41 For a sample of acclaim, see *BMJ* (14 April 1852): 202. The evidence is thin on Maclise's surgical career and practice and financial condition. Anthea Callen, "Bloodlines: Circulating the Male Body Across Borders in Art and Anatomy 1780–1860," *British Art Studies* 20 (July 2021), fn47 https://www.britishartstudies.ac.uk/issues/issue-index/issue-20/bell-brothers, notes that Maclise was elected Assistant-Surgeon at University College Hospital in April 1852, upon the resignation of William Cadge; see "Miscellaneous: Medical Intelligence: Appointments," *PMSJ* 16 (1852): 202 and *The Lancet* (25 March 1852): 347. But "University College and Mr Maclise," *The Lancet* (1 May 1852): 427 explains that Maclise was in fact passed over, due to "the undisguised antipathy of one of the professors,...whose noxious influence has been felt..."

42 Honoré de Balzac, "The Atheist's Mass" [trans. Clara Bell], in *Scènes de la vie privée* (*La Comédie humaine*) (Paris, 1836) (Project Gutenberg https://www.gutenberg.org/files/1220/1220-h/1220-h.htm). Balzac is said to have based the figure of the famous but soon-to-be-forgotten surgeon on Guillaume Dupuytren. But Dupuytren was (is) hardly forgotten. He authored works that received wide attention in his lifetime and posthumously, and left behind the eponymous Musée Dupuytren. Unlike Maclise, his name is attached to several medical eponyms and regularly appears in histories of nineteenth-century French medicine.

43 Maclise, *Surgical Anatomy* (London, 1851), preface.

44 In the mid-nineteenth century, the "lithotomy position" became the obstetrical term for a commonly used position for pelvic examination of women in pregnancy and childbirth. The term is still used today.

45 John Bell, *Principles of Surgery* (3 vols., Edinburgh: Cadel & Davies & Longman, 1801–8; London: Longman, Hurst, Rees et al., 1815), vol. 2, Fig. 1, facing p. 200. Maclise might have been familiar with any one of the three editions of *Principles*.

46 John Bell, *Engravings of the Bones, Muscles, and Joints, illustrating the first volume of the Anatomy of the Human Body* (London, 1794; 2d ed. 1804), vi; Carin Berkowitz, "Systems of Display: The Making of Anatomical Knowledge in Enlightenment Britain," *British Journal for the History of Science* 46.3 (2013): 359–87.

47 John Bell, *Engravings* (1804). Bell's strongly held attachment to etching and sketchiness is an implicit rebuke to the polish of artful but inaccurate anatomical illustrations. But in the preface to *Engravings* he praises the polished naturalist accuracy of Hunter's and Haller's plates (also Bidloo, who he says is true but disorganized). As for "taste," he offers no critique of it, rather he aspires to a "higher taste," and praises the dedication of artists who study anatomy for art's sake, especially Leonardo and Michelangelo, who he argues know more about anatomy than some anatomists. The diaphragm stuck on the wall is a visual quotation from Vesalius.

48 Keren Rosa Hammerschlag, *Frederic Leighton: Death, Mortality, Resurrection* (Surrey and Burlington: Ashgate, 2015), 165–6, sees mirroring in another Maclise plate from *Anatomy of the Arteries*.

49 Such as Maclise, *Surgical Anatomy* (London, 1856), pl. 26.

50 Daston & Galison, *Objectivity*. According to Carolyn Hannaway and Ann La Berge, "Paris Medicine: Perspectives Past and Present", in *Constructing Paris Medicine* [*Clio Medica* 50], ed. Hannaway & La Berge (Amsterdam: Editions Rodopi, 1998), 23, in the mid-1860s, Charles Daremberg contrasted realism in pathological anatomical illustration *against* beautifying art. For Daremberg, pathological anatomy was the hardest case for "brutal exactitude" in medical illustration, as the field made its passage into the age of photography. But similar concerns arose in gross and surgical anatomy. See Daremberg, *La médecine: Histoire et doctrines* (Paris: Didier et cie, 1865), 290–304; Jacalyn Duffin, "Imaging Disease: The Illustration and Non-Illustration of Medical Texts, 1650–1850," *Queens Quarterly* (1994): 79–108; M. Sappol, "Anatomy's Photography: Objectivity, Showmanship and the Reinvention of the Anatomical Image, 1860–1950," *REMEDIA*, January 2017 (rev. 2018), https://www.academia.edu/31049714/Anatomy_s_photography_Objectivity_showmanship_and_the_reinvention_of_the_anatomical_image_1860_1950_Introduction.

51 Fend, *Fleshing Out Surfaces*, 250–1.

52 Maclise's anatomized male nudes seem to live on the page (even when placed in poses of rest or sleep). Similar issues are at stake in mid-nineteenth-century sculpture. See Michael Hatt, "Near and Far, 45–50.

53 Michael Hatt, "Space, Surface, Self: Homosexuality and the Aesthetic Interior," *Visual Culture in Britain* 8 (2007): 105–28; quoted on 113.

54 Fend, *Fleshing Out Surfaces*, 5.

55 Carracci was a key figure in the development of the figure study as a genre in its own right; Thomas Buser, *A History of Drawing*, ch. 4 http://historyofdrawing.com/seventeenth_century_i/. Homoeroticism was there at the origin: many of Carracci's sketches were of naked boys and young men.

56 Plate 59, the arteries of the female pelvic organs (page 372 in the 1844 bound edition).

57 Francis Sibson, *Medical Anatomy, or, Illustrations of the relative position and movements of the internal organs* (London: John Churchill, 1869), art: William Fairland; George Viner Ellis & G.H. Ford [artist], *Illustrations of dissections: in a series of original colored plates the size of life, representing the dissection of the human body reduced on a uniform scale …* (London: Walton & Maberly [1861?]).

58 Leo Steinberg, "The Sexuality of Christ in Renaissance Art and in Modern Oblivion," *October* 25 (1983): 1–217; first quote is from 1, the second from 67; later enlarged and published as a book of the same name (2d rev. ed.; Chicago: University of Chicago Press, 1996). Steinberg's take on the theological meaning of the presentation of Christ's penis has been disputed (see, for example, Caroline Walker Bynum, "The Body of Christ in the Later Middle Ages: A Reply to Leo Steinberg," *Renaissance Quarterly* 39.3 (1986): 399–439), but what is unquestionable is that paintings and sculptures that showed

the penis were often later altered to cover it up. Which betrays considerable anxiety about the moral effects and propriety of showing the penis in art, in general and Christ's penis in particular. Steinberg remarks (*et passim*, but esp. 176–83) that these cover-ups are hard to date and research, but tend to be overlooked in the scholarship, because scholars, granting authorities and publishers are infected with that same anxiety. Which is why, he concludes, "We are not yet ready to produce a reliable periodization of Western prudery." (180)

59 Steinberg, "Sexuality of Christ," 109: "Readers in their skeptical phase will think half a hundred instances [showing Christ's penis] still too few. And once conviction has taken hold, more than six is too much. But the glut of evidence is essential."

60 For the dialogics of touch in relation to Victorian sculpture, see Michael Hatt, "Near and Far," 45–50; for touch in painting, see Fend, *Fleshing Out Surfaces,* 7, 74–5, 77.

61 Maclise, *Surgical Anatomy* (London, 1851), preface.

62 Fend, *Fleshing Out Surfaces*, 7.

63 The discussion here is heavily indebted to Fend, *Fleshing Out Surfaces*, 42, 65–6, 74–5, 77, on the caressing brushstrokes in Fragonard's *portraits de fantasie*, and eighteenth- and nineteenth-century commentary on the expressive, sensual *touche* of the painter's hand. See also Messbarger, *The Lady Anatomist*, 128–33, on the evocation of touch in the work of Anna Morandi Manzolini as anatomist and wax modeler.

64 Maclise, "Commentary on Plate 9: The surgical dissection of the wrist and hand," *Surgical Anatomy* (London, 1851); "Commentary on Plates 12 & 13," *Surgical Anatomy* (London, 1856). Maclise here is in dialogue with Charles Bell's Bridgewater Treatise, *The Hand, Its Mechanism and Vital Endowments as Evincing Design* (London: William Pickering, 1833).

65 [Anonymous], rev. *Surgical Anatomy* (London, 1849), fascicule 1–3, in *EMSJ* 71.180 (1849): 224–6.

66 Review of Joseph Maclise, *Surgical Anatomy*, fasc. 9 (1851) in *BFMCR* 8 (July–Oct., 1851): 529–30, a decidedly mixed review, tough criticism softened with real and faint praise. We unfortunately don't know a great deal about Joseph Maclise, *Surgical Anatomy* (Philadelphia: "T. Sinclair's lith. 101 Chestnut St Phila", 1851).

67 Fend, *Fleshing Out Surfaces*, 42 and 60, quoting and citing Louis Tocqué, "Reflexions sur la peinture et particulièrement sur le genre du portrait" [1750], in Arnauld Doria, ed., *Le discours de Tocqué sur le genre du portrait* (Paris: Jean Schemit, 1930), 1–40 (p. 22); see also Fend, 193–5.

68 Callen, *Looking at Men*, 16.

69 Victor Stoichita, *The Self-Aware Image: An Insight into Early-Modern Meta-Painting*, trans. Anne-Marie Glasheen (Cambridge: Cambridge University Press, 1997).

70 Elkins, *The Object Stares Back*.

71 For extra grandness, the firm of Taylor & Walton puts the legend "lithographic printer to her Majesty" in small letters at the bottom of each plate. For performative aspects of grand atlas-making, see Carin Berkowitz, "Systems of

Display: The Making of Anatomical Knowledge in Enlightenment Britain," *British Journal for the History of Science* 46.3 (2013): 359–87, which faults Daston & Galison, *Objectivity* for decontextualizing the anatomical atlas and its place in the ensemble of materials mobilized in medical knowledge production and pedagogy.

72 Daston & Galison, *Objectivity*, 84–98; Berkowitz, "The Illustrious Anatomist," 183–97, using the case of Van Rymsdyk, the artist who drew the obstetrical illustrations for William Smellie, William Hunter and Charles Nicholas Jenty, argues that in each case the anatomist made sure that the illustrations of his particular atlas would bear his own distinctive stylistic signature, rather than the stylistic signature of the artist under his employ. That anatomists attempted to do so may be the case, but I would argue that Van Rymsdyk's distinctive style nevertheless shines through, and the same holds true for other anatomical artists. And there was another party to reckon with: the engraver (or, later, the lithographer).

73 Bell, *Engravings*, Hunter, *Gravid Uterus*; Berkowitz, "The Illustrious Anatomist," and Daston & Galison, *Objectivity,* op cit.

74 Bell, *Engravings*, vi. Berkowitz, "Systems of Display," so insightful in her analysis of the Bells and William Hunter, mostly overlooks the performative harshness of their naturalism, their oppositional visual rhetoric (addresses it only in captions on 381–2).

75 In *Surgical Anatomy* (London, 1851), preface, Maclise situates himself within a small lineage of surgeon-anatomists who drew their own illustrations: "Every surgical anatomist will … perceive that, previously to undertaking the performance of an operation upon the living body, he stands reassured and self-reliant in that degree in which he is capable of conjuring up before his mental vision a distinct picture of his subject. Mr. [Robert] Liston (one of Maclise's teachers) could draw the same anatomical picture mentally which Sir Charles Bell's handicraft could draw … [Antonio] Scarpa was his own draughtsman." Surgical practice, reliant on this kind of picturing, is taken to be the foundation of surgical representation. *Surgical Anatomy* (London, 1856), preface, adds Camper, Cuvier and Carus to the list.

76 The literature on this is large. See, for example, Samuel Alberti, *Morbid Curiosities: Medical Museums in Nineteenth-Century Britain* (Oxford: Oxford University Press, 2011); Dániel Margócsy, "A Museum of Wonders or a Cemetery of Corpses? The Commercial Exchange of Anatomical Collections in Early Modern Netherlands," in Sven Dupré & Christoph Lüthy, eds., *Silent Messengers: The Circulation of Material Objects of Knowledge in the Early Modern Low Countries* (Berlin: LIT, 2011), 185–216, and "A Philosophy of Wax: The Anatomy of Frederik Ruysch," in Joanna Ebenstein & Colin Dickey, eds., *The Morbid Anatomy Anthology* (New York: Morbid Anatomy Press, 2014), 82–99; Messbarger, *The Lady Anatomist*; Sappol, *A Traffic of Dead Bodies*, esp. chap. 9, and for an overview, Sappol, *Dream Anatomy*.

77 There was a practical benefit. Arrangements of anatomical material were a kind of data compression, a way to pack a lot of related visual information into a single image or page (or museum display).

78 Guillaume Dupuytren, *Mémoire sur une Manière nouvelle de pratique l'Opération de la Pierre …* (Paris: J.B. Bailliere, 1836). Art: N.-H. Jacob. Lithography: [Pierre] Langlumé. Also published in English in Paris and London, and in German in Leipzig. Dupuytren died in 1835. The folio was posthumously completed by L.J. Sanson and L.J. Begin.

79 Richard Quain, *The Anatomy of the Arteries of the Human Body …* (London: Taylor & Walton, 1844), v [book of captions printed separately from the lithographic folio], gives the number of bodies as 1,040. The lithographic folio's preface gives the number as 930.

80 Maclise, *Surgical Anatomy* (1851, 1856), preface, all London editions.

81 While we have some of Jacob's preparatory drawings, no drawings by Maclise have ever surfaced.

82 Callen, "Bloodlines," introduces it as a likelihood and then takes it as fact: "the difference between Joseph Maclise's work … and that of previous anatomical illustrators is that he fused his dissection drawings with his studies after living 'life models', superimposing onto, *incorporating* these beautifully 'airbrushed' innards into the superbly drawn bodies of his life figures: these are not … those truly dead corpses with muscles tensed in rigor mortis found in anatomy dissection rooms … Where in Vesalius or Valverde, … deathly figures act out *life* (albeit classically, mythologically inspired and often as *memento mori*), Maclise's very real, athletic men perform *death*. Not only do his (almost exclusively) male models hold themselves in ways impossible to rope up or secure dead bodies, but also their flesh and muscle retain the full vigour and synergy of life."

83 K.B. Roberts & J.D.W. Tomlinson, *The Fabric of the Human Body: European Traditions of Anatomical Illustration* (Oxford: Clarendon Press, 1992), 564.

84 Callen, "Bloodlines."

85 E.A. Poe, "The Philosophy of Composition", *Graham's American Monthly Magazine of Literature & Art* (Philadelphia, April 1846).

86 Most of these death productions were the work of men. In her death poetry of the 1840s, 1850s and 1860s, Christina Rossetti gives eloquent, anguished voice to the figure of the dead or dying female.

87 The literature on the erotics of anatomy mostly focuses on the female body. For erotic elements and tropes in anatomical narrative and representation, see Ludmilla Jordanova, *Sexual Visions: Images of Gender in Science and Medicine from the 18th to the 20th Century* (Madison: University of Wisconsin Press, 1989); Jonathan Sawday, *The Body Emblazon'd: Dissection and the Human Body in Renaissance Culture* (London: Routledge, 1995); and Sappol, *A Traffic of Dead Bodies.*

88 F.W.S., "Art. XVIII.—*Surgical Anatomy*, by Joseph Maclise …" [review], *American Journal of the Medical Sciences* 16.39 (July 1850): 123.

89 Maclise, *Surgical Anatomy* (London, 1856), preface. Maclise's over-the-top high style is a very Shakespeare-inflected idiom: "heave the gorge," for example, comes from *Othello*, Act 2, scene 1. But Maclise draws upon a variety of sources: "sinking soul" comes from a late eighteenth-century Protestant hymn.

90 Charles Dickens, *David Copperfield* (1850; London: Penguin, 2004), 758.

91 Maclise, *Surgical Anatomy* (London, 1851, 1856), preface.

92 See also Ilse Jahn, "On the Origin of Romantic Biology and its Further Development at the University of Jena between 1790 and 1850," in Stefano Poggi & Maurizio Bossi, eds., *Romanticism in Science: Science in Europe 1790–1840* (Dordrecht: Kluwer Academic, 1994), 75–89. The scholarship on transcendental anatomy is mostly folded into the history of comparative anatomy and evolutionary theory, and therefore tends to overlook Maclise, who only wrote one book entirely devoted to the subject (*Comparative Osteology*), but carried on the debate in his surgical anatomical publications.

93 Maclise, *Surgical Anatomy* (London, 1856), preface.

94 Rehbock, "Transcendental Anatomy," 144–5.

95 Adrian Desmond, "Lamarckism and Democracy: Corporations, Corruption and Comparative Anatomy in the 1830s," in James Richard Moore, ed., *History, Humanity and Evolution: Essays for John C. Greene* (Cambridge: Cambridge University Press, 2002), 124, 130; quoting Joseph Maclise, "On the nomenclature of anatomy," *Lancet* 1 (1846): 299.

96 While "philosophical anatomy" and "transcendental anatomy" were often taken to be roughly synonymous terms, as political lines sharpened, there were attempts to make a distinction. See, for example, Thomas Dwight, "Report on Anatomy," *Boston Medical & Surgical Journal* n.s. 10.10 (5 Sept 1872): 165–6, who says "philosophical anatomy" is perfectly acceptable, but dismisses "the study of transcendental anatomy," which he "believe[s] and hope[s] is on the decline."

97 For much of this section, I am indebted to discussions with Keren Rosa Hammerschlag. For a fuller exploration of the topic, see her "Black Apollo: Aesthetics, Dissection, and Race in Joseph Maclise's *Surgical Anatomy*," *British Art Studies* 20 (July 2021), https://doi.org/10.17658/issn.2058-5462/issue-20/khammerschlag and "Drawing Racial Comparisons in Nineteenth-Century British and American Anatomical Atlases," in Nancy Rose Marshall, ed., *Victorian Science and Imagery: Representation and Knowledge in Nineteenth-Century Visual Culture* (Pittsburgh: University of Pittsburgh Press, 2021), 167–88.

98 Charles Bell, *Engravings of the Arteries* (3d ed., London: Longman, Hurst, Rees, Orme, & Brown, 1811; 4th ed., 1824), pl. 4 uses a black man to show the dissection of "the arteries of the head." (Given Bell's status as a great surgical-anatomical author, artist and writer, Maclise would have undoubtedly been aware of the illustration.) Like Maclise, Bell's subject was human anatomy and not racial difference: Bell comments (11, 3d ed.) that he finds in the head "the most common and regular distribution of the branches" (i.e., without any racial difference). But unlike Maclise, Bell mentions that his subject is "black." (In plate 5, a further dissection of the head, the only visible racial characteristic is a tuft of kinky hair.) The plate was later revised: the first (1801) and second edition (1806) show a different head (plates 3–4), entirely stripped of flesh and hair, so that no racial identification is possible. In the original 1797(?) manuscript of (colored) illustrations (owned by the National

Library of Medicine), Bell depicts the black man used in the 1811 and 1824 editions. Bell also uses a black subject to demonstrate "the Operation of Trepan" in his *Illustrations of the Great Operations of Surgery: Trepan, hernia, amputation, aneurism, and lithotomy* (London: Longman et al., 1820–1), pl. 2. In that surgical textbook, the subject's race goes unmentioned.

99 "Commentary on plate 14," Maclise, *Surgical Anatomy* (London, 1851).

100 "Commentary on plates 21, 22, 23, 24 & 25," Maclise, *Surgical Anatomy* (London, 1856).

101 Naomi Slipp, "'It Should Be on Every Surgeon's Table': The Reception and Adoption of Joseph Maclise's *Surgical Anatomy* (1851) in the United States," https://doi.org/10.17658/issn.2058-5462/issue-20/nslipp; and Hammerschlag, "Black Apollo" and "Drawing Racial Comparisons in Nineteenth-Century."

102 F.W.S., "*Surgical Anatomy.* By Joseph Maclise ...," *AJMS* 37.1 (January 1850): 151.

103 The one place where an "Adam and Eve" might appear in anatomical atlases (sometimes as a direct biblical reference): in an introductory plate or pair.

104 In *Surgical Anatomy* (London, 1851), Maclise shows the female body only in plate 7 and plate 23, "the dissection of femoral herniae" (two dissected vulvae side by side, corresponding to, but much less fulsomely treated than, male genitalia and hernias). In the text, he makes brief mention of, but does not illustrate, "differences" and "corresponding varieties" in the commentaries to plates 1, 3, 15 and 19.

105 Londa Schiebinger, *The Mind Has No Sex? Women in the Origins of Modern Science* (Cambridge: Harvard University Press, 1989), esp. chaps. 6–7.

106 "Commentary on plates 10 & 11: The male and female axillae compared ...," Maclise, *Surgical Anatomy* (London, 1856). Maclise exemplifies his abstract principles via the rendering of actual dissected bodies, selected for physical characteristics showing some pleasurable proximity to the *beau idéal* of academic art (as was the customary practice in the selection of models for figure-drawing in the art academies of the day), but idiosyncratic enough to be plausible exemplars of the "real" (a *beau réel,* not the harsh reality of brutal realism). For models and ideals of beauty, see Susan S. Waller, *The Invention of the Model: Artists and Models in Paris, 1830–1870* (Aldershot and Burlington: Ashgate, 2006), xiii, 4–5.

107 For the female nude and the politics of the "adipose membrane," see Fend, *Fleshing Out Surfaces*, 246.

108 In the smaller format Philadelphia version of *Surgical Anatomy* (Blanchard & Lea, 1851), the two appear on different pages (plates 13–14).

109 Quain, *Anatomy of the Arteries* [text for the folio plates], 338.

110 For Geoffroy Saint-Hilaire, see Toby A. Appel, *The Cuvier-Geoffroy Debate: French Biology in the Decades before Darwin* (Oxford: Oxford University Press, 1987); Desmond, *Politics of Evolution*; Valerie Racine, "Etienne Geoffroy Saint-Hilaire (1772–1844)," *Embryo Project Encyclopedia* (5 Aug 2013), http://embryo.asu.edu/handle/10776/6045; Secord, *Victorian Sensation*, 61–7, 353. Scholarship on idealism and platonism in Victorian

Britain mostly focuses on the late nineteenth century. Scholarship on the mid-century is thinner, but see Richard Thomas Eldridge, "Idealism in Nineteenth-Century British and American Literature," *Aesthetics and Literature* 3 (2013): 121–44 and Rachel Kravetz, "The Art of Cognition: British Empiricism and Victorian Aesthetics" (PhD dissertation, City University of New York, 2017).

111 Showing off his erudition, Maclise uses the term *ens*, meaning material substance, imported from medieval ontology (perhaps by way of Descartes or some more recent source). It probably would not have been familiar to many of his readers.

112 "Remarks on the Figures of Plate 44," Maclise, *Comparative Osteology*, 2.

113 See for example, [Review], *Surgical Anatomy*, in *BFMCR* 3 (1849): 205: "We are heartily glad to welcome Mr. Maclise back to his own field of labour [i.e., back to surgical anatomy from his previous publication, *Comparative Osteology*]. Of his claims as a philosophical anatomist, we felt compelled to express an opinion which was far from flattering. As a surgical anatomist he has probably no superior. As a philosophical writer we found him obscure, sometimes almost incomprehensible, labouring to express ideas which probably had a definite form in his own mind, but which he wanted power to convey to others. But *substitute the pencil for the pen*, the drawing-board for the writing-desk, the real dissection for the abstract archetype; and Mr. Maclise then displays the graphic power of the accomplished artist, united with the truthful exposition of the pains-taking demonstrator." [emphasis added]

114 Quotes are from Susan Tallman, "Knowing How," *New York Review of Books* (19 August 2021): 4. In Maclise's time, anatomical materialism typically carried the suggestion of atheism, a socially and politically dangerous position that most anatomists, physicians and surgeons were quick to disavow.

115 Review of Quain and Maclise, *Anatomy of the Arteries ... Pts. 1& 2 (1840)*, in *PMSJ* 1.12 (19 Dec 1840): 203. Note the reviewer's treatment of Quain: it's not just that the artwork outshines the text, it's that the anatomist "allowed" the artist (his social and medical inferior) to do so (unlike Hunter and Cheselden who controlled their artist-collaborators).

116 Maclise, *Comparative Osteology*, iv: "While believing ... the subject of Anatomical Unity forms the goal of all comparative research, I sought also the opinions of ... Cuvier, Goethe, Geoffroy, Oken, Spix, Carus and ... Dr. Sharpey, Mr. Quain, and Mr. Owen ... and from these I learned that the Law of a 'unity of organization' ... [is] admitted now-a-day of as little dispute as a mathematical axiom" (in the next sentence, Maclise adds Grant Jones and Rymer Jones to his list of supporters of "Philosophical Unity"). While it may be that for a season or two, Maclise could claim Quain as an ideological ally, one telling indicator of their differing levels of commitment: the keyword *symmetry* (and permutations thereon) appears three times in the text of Quain's *Anatomy of the Arteries* (and then in innocent description), but 37 times in Maclise's *Surgical Anatomy* (1856), often in contentious argument.

117 Quotes are from obituary, "Richard Quain", *BMJ* 2.1395 (24 September 1887): 694–5; see also obituary, "Richard Quain", *The Lancet* (1 October 1887): 687–8. Quain's *BMJ* obituary mentions Maclise: "Without exaggeration, it may be said that Richard Quain's life would have been well spent had he lived only to produce the *Anatomy of the Arteries.*" The obituary goes on to credit "the artistic powers of Mr. Joseph Maclise, F.R.C.S., author of a *Surgical Anatomy*, and an almost forgotten work on the homologies of the skeleton" [*Comparative Osteology*].

118 The other dedicatee was Samuel Cooper, also one of Maclise's teachers. For Liston, see Michael Brown, *Emotions and Surgery in Britain, 1793–1912* (Cambridge: Cambridge University Press, 2023), 51–64.

119 Maclise, *Surgical Anatomy* (Philadelphia: Blanchard & Lea, 1859), preface.

120 Maclise, *Surgical Anatomy* (London: Churchill, 1856), preface.

121 See, for example, *Comparative Osteology* (1847), but even in practical works, such as *Surgical Anatomy* and *On Dislocations and Fractures* (1859), Maclise championed the comparative method: "Comparison [is] ... the nurse of reason"; "Contrast is our pioneer to truth" [*Surgical Anatomy* (1856), preface].

122 *Surgical Anatomy* (1856), second quote from "Notice to the Second Edition."

123 *Plarr's Lives of the Fellows of the Royal College of Surgeons* (London, 1912–40), treats Joseph's *oeuvre* as a footnote to Daniel's: "The whole interest [of Joseph's illustrations] is the relation of Joseph's drawings to those of Daniel, as to how far the two brothers may be said to have viewed the human figure from the same point of view." That polarity is reversed in *Queer Anatomies*, which discusses Daniel only in relation to Joseph. In my opinion, while Daniel is the far more historically significant figure, Joseph is the much more gifted artist.

124 The point is treated at length in Leo Steinberg, *The Sexuality of Christ in Renaissance Art and in Modern Oblivion* (2d rev. ed.; Chicago: University of Chicago Press, 1996); and Caroline Walker Bynum, "The Body of Christ in the Later Middle Ages: A Reply to Leo Steinberg," *Renaissance Quarterly* 39.3 (1986): 399–439.

125 Quain, *Anatomy of the Arteries*, vii, cites Friedrich Tiedemann, *Tabulae arteriarum corporis humani* (Karlsruhe: C.F. Müller, 1822) which also circulated in an inferior British edition: Friedrich Tiedemann, *Plates of the Arteries of the Human Body*, ed. Thomas Wharton Jones and Robert Knox (Edinburgh: Maclachlan & Stewart, 1829–36). Quain also cites Albrecht von Haller, *Icones anatomicae quibus praecipuae aliquae partes corporis humani delineatae proponuntur et arteriarum potissimum historia continetur* (Göttingen: Vandenhoeck, 1743–56; many editions thereafter); and Antonio Scarpa, *Sull'aneurisma riflessioni ed osservazioni anatomico-chirurgiche* (Pavia, 1804)—all venerated works. Maclise, in the preface to *Surgical Anatomy* (London, 1851, 1856), namedrops Haller, Hunter, Astley Cooper, Robert Liston, Charles Bell, Scarpa, Cowper, Soemmerring, Cruveilhier, Magendie, Burdach, Carus, Meckel, and Camper, who we can take as members of Maclise's pantheon of anatomical, physiological, and surgical greats. Maclise

also praises anatomists who brilliantly illustrated their own works: Charles Bell, Petrus Camper, and Antonio Scarpa, a pantheon within a pantheon.

126 Roux's lithographs look like high-quality copperplate engravings: 1822 was the early days of anatomical lithography, and Roux was using lithography as a cheaper way to do what engravers do. The unique capabilities of lithographic depiction were still to be explored.

127 Tiedemann, *Tabulae arteriarum* (1822). Compare also Astley Cooper's influential studies of diseases of the breast, testicles and hernias. They concentrate solely and dispassionately on affected diseased parts, and give no pleasurable views of the male and female body and genitalia. See Cooper, *The Testis* (London, 1830); *Diseases of the Breast* (London, 1829); *The Anatomy and Surgical Treatment of Abdominal Hernia* (London, 1827).

128 Review, Maclise, *Surgical Anatomy*, in *Dublin Quarterly Journal of Medical Science* 13.1 (Feb 1852): 193–4; review, Maclise, *Surgical Anatomy*, in *PMSJ* 15.14 (9 July 1851): 375–6.

129 Advertisement for Quain-Maclise "Imperial" folio, back matter, in Thomas Morton, *The Surgical Anatomy of the Principal Regions of the Human Body* (London: Taylor & Walton, 1850): "The Plates considered only as *Works of Art* are, for their large size and *intrinsic merit*, worth at least Ten Shillings each."

130 Thomas Morton, *Surgical Anatomy of the Principal Regions of the Human Body; Surgical Anatomy of the Perinaeum; The Surgical Anatomy of the Groin, the Femoral, and Popliteal Regions* (London: Taylor & Walton, 1839); *The Surgical Anatomy of Inguinal Herniae, the Testis and its Coverings* (London: Taylor & Walton, 1844). Art for all of the above-cited Morton works by Andrew Morton. See D'A. Power, revised by Patrick Wallis, "Thomas Morton," *ODNB* (2008) https://doi-org.ezproxy.its.uu.se/10.1093/ref:odnb/19376. Andrew Morton was, by trade, a portrait painter.

131 John D'Emilio, *Sexual Politics, Sexual Communities: The Making of a Homosexual Minority in the United States, 1940–1970* (Chicago: University of Chicago Press, 1983), 22.

132 For favorable reviews, see F.W.S., review, Maclise, *Surgical Anatomy*, in *AJMS* 37.1 (Jan 1850): 151–4; review, Maclise, *Surgical Anatomy*, in *PMSJ* 13 (7 March 1849): 129–30. One exception was an unsigned mixed review of *Surgical Anatomy,* fasciculus 3, in *BFMCR* 8 (Oct 1851): 529–31. That reviewer praised Maclise's plates for their style, accuracy, usefulness, and reasonable cost, but faulted "Philosophical Anatomy" as "out of place" in "a work on Surgical Anatomy" (530–1).

133 Review, *Surgical Anatomy*, in *DQJMS* 13.1 (Feb 1852): 193–4; review, *Surgical Anatomy*, in *PMSJ* 15.14 (9 July 1851): 375–6; review, *Surgical Anatomy*, in *LMG* n.s. 65 (July 1850): 769.

134 T. Buser, *A History of Drawing*, ch. 4 http://historyofdrawing.com/seventeenth_century_i/, describes Annibale Carracci as a leader in the "reform of art," and a key figure in the development of the figure study as

a genre for its own sake (many of them sketches of naked boys and young men), rather than just as a preparatory sketch for painting or sculpture.

135 Caroline O. Fowler, "*Res papirea*: Mantegna's Paper Things," *Art Bulletin* 99.1 (2017): 9–35. "With important exceptions ... fifteenth-century drawings are rarely autonomous works. Artists kept their drawings as models ... In turn, artists depended on drawings to retain forms and *invenzione* ... storing them in model books and sketchbooks for future use." (16)

136 For a brief history, see Wickham, "Strike a pose," op.cit.

137 Johnson, *Jacques-Louis David* (1993); Diderot qtd. in Frederick Burwick, *Illusion and the Drama: Critical Theory of the Enlightenment and Romantic Era* (Harrisburg: Penn State Press, 2010), 46, 56–7.

138 Gerdy's École d'Anatomie was attached to the Hôpital de la Pitié, where Maclise studied; Callen, "Blood Lines."

139 Davis, *Queer Beauty*. Gerdy's canonical male nude (with a fig-leaf over the penis) is reproduced in Todd, ed., *Cyclopaedia of Anatomy and Physiology* (London, 1836), 1:3, a work to which Maclise contributed.

140 For overviews, see James Smalls, *Homosexuality in Art* (New York: Parkstone Press, 2015); James M. Saslow, *Pictures and Passions: A History of Homosexuality in the Visual Arts* (New York and London: Viking, 1999).

141 Solomon-Godeau, *Male Trouble*, 177–85, shows that a gradient of meanings accrued to male nudity and the representation of male genitalia. Masculine power could be represented by displacement: phallic objects, especially the sword. (In antiquity the disproportionately large and erect penis was only assigned to satyrs, priapic comic half-human figures.)

142 Davis, *Queer Beauty*, 51–81. Until the reaction that attended the French Revolution, British antiquarians openly commissioned and collected engravings that showed classical sculpture in which satyrs and the god Priapus appeared; afterwards it went underground.

143 There was, of course, an irrepressible industry in *impolite* representation: works of pornography and comedically bawdy prints.

144 See Braddock, "'Jeff College Boys'," 355–83, esp. 361. Eakins, a notably enthusiastic painter and photographer of male nudity (and to a somewhat lesser degree female), was dismissed from another teaching position in 1895 for a similar offense: presenting female students with a male model who left his genitals uncovered.

145 Hatt, "The Male Body in Another Frame," 9–21, quotes from 16.

146 Roger Gaskell, book description [2001] accompanying the sale of *Surgical Anatomy* (London, 1851) to Columbia University.

147 Sarah Bull, "A Purveyor of Garbage? Charles Carrington and the marketing of sexual science in late-Victorian Britain," *Victorian Review* 38.1 (2012): 55–76; quote on 71.

148 Bull, ibid., 59, quoting "Seizure of Indecent Publications," *Morning Chronicle* (London, 27 Nov 1857).

149 J.S. Knox et al., *Physicians' Anatomical Aid: A Manikin of Superimposed Diagrammatic Plates* (Chicago: Western Publishing House, 1884), multiple editions thereafter; also published as *Embalmers' Anatomical Aid* (some editions come equipped with a lock on the section of plates dealing with "organs of generation," others have a lock on the entire folio); M[oritz] Platen, *Livre d'Or de la Santé*, 3 vols. (2d ed.; Paris: Bong et Cie, *c.*1900); multiple editions thereafter into the 1920s. The "special" vol. 3, on the "organs of generation," reproduction and sexual disease, pathologies and inversions, comes with a lock on the fore-edge. *Livre d'Or* is a French translation of *Die neue Heilmethode* (1896). The same books also came in sanitized editions that omit the organs of generation and the lock. In those versions, male manikins are fig-leaved and the female manikins have blank flesh in the genital region. Thanks to Deborah Coltham for sharing information on Platen.

150 Jeffrey Escoffier, "The Political Economy of the Closet," in *American Homo: Community and Perversity* (Berkeley: University of California Press, 1998), 66, lists components of that political economy in pre-Stonewall America: "bars ... adult bookstores, bathhouses, and mail-order services—most of which operated on the margins of legality."

151 Maclise, *Surgical Anatomy* (Philadelphia: Blanchard & Lea, 1859), vi.

152 *Transformism* was not just an early term for what became "evolution"; it also included adaptation, embryological and post-natal development, and comparative anatomy. See Desmond, *Politics of Evolution*, 360–3, 368–71, 376, 425, 453.

153 Henry Patrick Chomeley, "Thomas Henry Wakley," *DNB* (1912), supplement, 572.

154 How much weight should we put on Maclise's promotion from Member to Fellow? Maybe not much. According to "Gray's Anatomy: The First Hundred Years," *BMJ* (6 Sept 1958): 610, when Henry Gray was made a Fellow of the Royal College of Surgeons in 1848, it was "a distinction much less notable than it is to-day."

155 For the negative social consequences that attended Lamarckianism and Geoffroyism, see Adrian Desmond, "Robert E. Grant: The Social Predicament of a Pre-Darwinian Transmutationist," *Journal of the History of Biology* 17.2 (1984): 189–223. Maclise cites Lamarck as an authority with evident enthusiasm nine times in *Comparative Osteology*, "Nomenclature," 5, 7; "Introduction," 14; "Remarks on the figures of plate" 21, 22, 26, and 38.

156 *Lancet* (25 March 1852): 347 and (1 May 1852): 426–8. Stelmackowich, "Bodies of Knowledge," 75, claims that, in the nineteenth century, good reviews of deluxe illustrated anatomical treatises "frequently secured for their authors lucrative and prestigious positions." The point is debatable: some authors of prestigious treatise already had high positions, but Bourgery, Maclise, and Thomas Morton, failed to secure high position despite positive notices.

157 Joseph Maclise, *On Dislocations and Fractures* (London: Churchill, 1859), dedication: "... I have founded my Thoracic Theory of Circulation [on] ... Animal Mechanics. Modern Science is constrained to acknowledge that the doctrine of Harvey does not answer all important Anatomical facts and Physiological and Pathological phenomena." The argument against Harvey is mounted in "Commentary on Plates 5, 6, 7 and 8, The form and mechanism of the thorax as an ingestive apparatus—Fractures and Dislocations of the Ribs, Sternum, and Clavicle": "In the beginning, when Harvey and originality (imitating that immortal fiat in Genesis which made Harvey 'after its own image') looked upon the Chaos of Animal Physiology, and saw that it was without form and void ...." Maclise connected his critique of Harvey to a defense of "philosophical," "transcendental," and "comparative" anatomy and analysis of "homologies." Critics in turn mocked him for fancy philosophizing and overblown speechifying. *Lancet* (20 March 1858): 292; (5 May 1858): 470; (29 May 1858): 4; (September 1858): 258; (28 July 1860): 95–6; (4 August 1860): 120–2; (11 August 1860): 146; (18 August 1860): 172.

158 Jessie Dobson, *Conservators of the Hunterian Museum* (London: Jackson, Ruston & Keeton, 1975), 25–6.

159 Chomeley, "Thomas Henry Wakley," *DNB* (1912), supplement, 572.

160 Joseph and Daniel lived together from at least the 1850s and perhaps earlier. William Schupbach, "Joseph Maclise, Taylor & Walton, and Publishing on Gower Street in the 1840s," *British Art Studies* 20 (July 2021): https://www.britishartstudies.ac.uk/issues/issue-index/issue-20/publishing-on-gower-street; see also Roberts & Tomlinson, *Fabric of the Body*, 56–65; and John Turpin, "Daniel Maclise and Cork Society," *Journal of the Cork Historical and Archaeological Society* 85 (1985): 66–88. We don't know about Joseph, but Daniel Maclise was said to have been distressed by his sister's death. A third brother, William Maclise, was an army surgeon, whose health is said to have been destroyed in the Crimean War and who died upon his return to England or Ireland. So another sibling to mourn? There were two other siblings, Anna, who was married, and Alexander, "a leather sales-man" (*London Gazette*, 1836, pt. 2, 2204), who is listed as residing at 14 Russell Place, Fitzroy Square, the same address as Daniel (and in the 1850s, Joseph). As for leather sales, remember, back in County Cork, Maclise *père* was a tanner and shoemaker.

161 See Secord, *Victorian Sensation*.

162 Two reviews of instalments of *Surgical Anatomy*, by an anonymous reviewer, discuss the problem in *BFMCR* 3 (Jan.–Apr. 1849): 205–7 and 4 (July–Oct. 1849): 242–3. Both praise Maclise's artwork and anatomical erudition highly; both worry over his text. The first review goes on at length: "As a philosophical writer we found him obscure, sometimes almost incomprehensible ... When he tries to edge in a bit of philosophical anatomy ... his language becomes obscure, transcendental, and un-English ... confused ...." The second review concludes: "The plates are all excellent; and we are happy to find that our exhortations have been so well taken by Mr. Maclise,

that there is not a single line in their accompanying commentary to which we can object as transcendental," which suggests that Maclise—heeding Churchill?—may have backed off a bit in later commentaries. One sign of that is the substitution of the term "philosophical" for "transcendental," a move perhaps intended to mollify critics. Whatever the case, the fascicules, collected together and published in 1851 as a book, carried forward Maclise's opinionated discourse, as did the second edition of 1856.

163 Darwin lists Maclise's *Comparative Osteology* (1847) in his first reading diary [1839–51, DAR *119: 22v.], *Darwin's Reading Notebooks*, https://www.darwinproject.ac.uk/people/about-darwin/what-darwin-read/darwin-s-reading-notebooks. He notes that Maclise's atlas is "good for woodcuts," but probably wouldn't have liked the text. See for example, Darwin to J.D. Hooker, 29 March 1863 (Darwin Correspondence Project): "Who would have ever thought of the old stupid *Athenæum* [a scientific journal] taking to Oken-like transcendental philosophy written in Owenian style! It will be some time before we see 'slime, snot or protoplasm' (what an elegant writer) generating a new animal. But I have long regretted that I truckled to public opinion & used [the] Pentateuchal term of creation, by which I really meant 'appeared' by some wholly unknown process—It is mere rubbish thinking, at present, of origin of life; one might as well think of origin of matter." Yet Darwin maintained good relations with Geoffroy, who offered to translate *Origin of the Species* into French.

164 For more on transcendental anatomy, see Secord, *Victorian Sensation*, 61–7.

165 Maclise, *Surgical Anatomy* (London, 1856), preface. Maclise's dislike of contemporary science is maybe an echo of Robert Chambers's expressed "disappointment" with the British Association for the Advancement of Science, because it presented "many valuable isolated facts, but … never … a comprehensive view of nature … It is all very well to decry rash generalization, but while science professes to show merely a collection of bricks … it will never get any credit as an architect" ("The Scientific Meeting at Cambridge," *Chamber's Journal* (2 Aug 1845): 65–9, qtd. in *Victorian Sensation*, 384). Chambers regarded enthusiasm for empirical data gathering and discovery as antithetical to larger and possibly subversive principles. As far as I know, Maclise never quoted or cited Chambers's controversial but wildly popular *Vestiges of the Natural History of Creation* (London: Churchill, 1844 and many editions thereafter), even though the two men's views were to some degree aligned and Churchill also published *Surgical Anatomy*.

166 Maclise, *Surgical Anatomy* (London, 1856), second quote from "Notice to the Second Edition."

167 Solomon-Godeau, *Male Trouble*, 93.

168 Dickens died a year after penning that remark. W. Justin O'Donnell, *A Memoir of Daniel Maclise, R.A.* (London: Longmans, Green & Co., 1871), vi. Daniel Maclise illustrated a number of Dickens's books and the two men were close friends, although they eventually drifted apart. Some of Dickens's letters to Maclise survive; see John Turpin, "Daniel Maclise and Charles

Dickens: A Study of Their Friendship," *Studies: An Irish Quarterly Review* 73.289 (Spring 1984): 47–66.

169 Obituary, "Richard Quain," *Lancet* (1 Oct 1887): 687–8; Obituary, "Richard Quain," *BMJ* 2.1395 (24 Sept 1887): 694–5. Quain's *BMJ* obituary mentions Maclise: "Without exaggeration, it may be said that Richard Quain's life would have been well spent had he lived only to produce the *Anatomy of the Arteries.*" The obituary goes on to credit "the artistic powers of Mr. Joseph Maclise, F.R.C.S, author of a *Surgical Anatomy*, and an almost forgotten work on the homologies of the skeleton" [*Comparative Osteology*].

170 O'Donnell, *Memoir of Daniel Maclise*, 117–20.

171 For homoeroticism, homosociality, social performance, aesthetics and aestheticism in late Victorian Britain, see Jason Edwards, "'Anxious Flirtations': Homoeroticism, Art and Aestheticism in Late-Victorian Britain," *Visual Culture in Britain* 8.1 (2007): 1–14; Getsy, "Recognizing the Homoerotic," 37–57; and Andrew Stephenson, "Precarious Poses: The Problem of Artistic Visibility and its Homosocial Performances in Late Nineteenth-century London," *Visual Culture in Britain* 8.1 (2007): 73–103.

172 Jack Halberstam, *The Queer Art of Failure* (Durham: Duke University Press, 2011), esp. chap. 3.

173 Maclise, *Surgical Anatomy* (London, 1851), preface.

174 Maclise, *Surgical Anatomy* (London, 1856), preface.

Part Four Conclusion [pages 170–83]

1 In this period, serious medical bibliophiles were mostly concerned with old manuscripts and early printed works. Large atlases from the 1840s and 1850s, and works connected to recent contributions to medical progress, received less attention. See T.M. Boggs, "Osler as Bibliophile," *Bulletin of the Johns Hopkins Hospital* 30.341 (1919): 216; Edward C. Streeter, "Osler as Bibliophile," *BMSJ* (1 Apr 1920): 335–8. Osler, the dean of medical bibliophilia in his period, was far from typical, but shared with his colleagues a broader bibliophilia that went far beyond medical topics.

2 Oddly, as scientization and professionalization of anatomy advanced, high-spirited homosocial fellowship was increasingly institutionalized in medical school fraternities, yearbooks, and publications devoted to medical humor. Which became the venue for students to photograph themselves fooling around with skeletons and cadavers and perform strong assertions of masculinity, from which women were generally excluded—although we know a parallel student culture developed in some women's medical colleges. See James Edmondson & John Harley Warner, *Dissection: Photographs of a Rite of Passage in American Medicine 1880–1930* (New York: Blast Books, 2009); Sappol, *A Traffic of Dead Bodies,* chaps. 2–4.

3 Solomon-Godeau, *Male Trouble.*

4 Daston & Galison, *Objectivity*. The beginnings of the binary opposition go back at least a century earlier. See Massey, "Against the 'statue' anatomized."

5 At mid-century, literary and artistic circles increasingly took up a rhetoric of objectivity and scientization. "Realists" sought to make an activist "scientific" art devoted to (often fictionalized) documentary social reportage on social "problems" (e.g. Zola) which challenged the notion that beauty inheres in truth and truth in beauty. *Realisme* eventually came to have a marked impact on medical illustration. See Hunter, *Face of Medicine*, 12, 16, 19–20, 24, 123 et passim.

6 Maclise, *Surgical Anatomy* (London, 1851), preface.

7 For *fin de siècle* British culture, see David Peters Corbett, "Oedipus and the Sphinx: Visual Knowledge and Homosociality in the Ricketts Circle," *Visual Culture in Britain* 8.1 (2007): 59–71. One wonders if Oscar Wilde (the son of a doctor), Walter Sickert and Aubrey Beardsley ever encountered Maclise's work and, if so, what they would have made of it.

8 To take another example, according to art historians Arthur Lubow, Adrian Hyman and Walter Melion, the blatant homoeroticism of late sixteenth-century artist Cornelis Cornelisz van Haarlem—his brazen drawings and painting of groups of naked muscular men—especially their buttocks—has been systematically overlooked in the scholarship, even while it stands "hidden in plain sight" (Hyman); Lubow, "The Lusty Creativity of Cornelis Cornelisz van Haarlem," *New York Times* (13 Jan 2021), https://www.nytimes.com/2021/01/13/t-magazine/art-cornelis-cornelisz-van-haarlem.html.

9 Foucault, *The Order of Things*; Donna J. Haraway, with Thyrza Goodeve, *Modest_Witness@Second_Millennium. FemaleMan_Meets_OncoMouse* (1997; New York: Routledge, 2018).

10 For flat ontology, see Manuel DeLanda, *Intensive Science and Virtual Philosophy* (London: Bloomsbury, 2013); and Bruno Latour, "On Interobjectivity," *Mind, Culture and Activity* 3.4 (1996): 228–45.

11 Thomas Laqueur, *Making Sex: Bodies and Gender from the Greeks to Freud* (Cambridge: Harvard University Press, 1992) was, and remains, enormously influential, despite severe criticism. For a recent critique which reviews its influence and critics, see Katharine Park, "The Myth of the 'One-Sex' Body," *Isis* 114.1 (2023): 150–75.

12 Regina Janes, "The Salacious Sorrows of Scholarship, Or 'The Gentleman in Lace'," *Salmagundi* 143 (2004): 221–36, quotes from 226, 231; Cocks, "Safeguarding Civility," 121–3.

13 Kelly, *Society of Dilettanti*, 252.

14 More than that, the lines continually blur, are drawn and redrawn. The categories are chained together: dominance-and-submission, bondage-and-discipline, sadomasochism, homosociality and homoerotics, fetishism, transgenderism and cosplay, are everyone's norm, whether the normies know it or not. So naturalized and pervasive as to be invisible. (But not

at all invisible to "queers" and "perverts".) And history tells us that "out" queerness doesn't necessarily recruit anyone into an oppositional emancipatory politics of transformation. Sadly, it can even give rise to trollish reactionary nihilism (e.g. Peter Thiel and Milo Yiannopoulos). See Halberstam, *Queer Art of Failure*, chap. 5 ("The Killer in Me is the Killer in You: Homosexuality and Fascism"), which uses examples taken from Nazi Germany.

15 See, for example, David L. Eng, Jack Halberstam and José Esteban Muñoz, eds., "What's Queer about Queer Studies Now?" [special issue], *Social Text* 23.3–4 (2005), https://www.dukeupress.edu/whats-queer-about-queer-studies-now-1 (84–5); Lisa Duggan, "The New Homonormativity: The Sexual Politics of Neoliberalism," in *Materializing Democracy*, ed. Russ Castronovo & Dana D. Nelson (Durham: Duke University Press, 2002); Judith Butler, "Is Kinship Always Already Heterosexual?", *differences* 13.1 (2002): 14–44, and *Undoing Gender* (London: Routledge, 2005), 2–3. Thanks again to Jenny Sundén for schooling me on queer theory debates.

BIBLIOGRAPHY

Sources

[Anonymous], *The Life and Adventures of Cicily Martin* (New York, 1846).
[Anonymous], "Clorion" manuscript, *c.*1844, National Library of Medicine.
Honoré de Balzac, "The Atheist's Mass" [trans. Clara Bell], in *Scènes de la vie privée* (*La Comédie humaine*) (Paris, 1836). Project Gutenberg https://www.gutenberg.org/files/1220/1220-h/1220-h.htm.
Aubrey Beardsley, "The Laecedaemonian Ambassadors," *Lysistrata* (1896).
Charles Bell, [drawings of arteries, *c.* 1797], manuscript. National Library of Medicine.
Charles Bell, *Engravings of the Arteries* (3d ed.; London: Longman, Hurst, Rees, Orme, and Brown, 1811; 4th ed. 1824).
Charles Bell, *Illustrations of the Great Operations of Surgery: Trepan, Hernia, Amputation, Aneurism, and Lithotomy* (London: Longman, 1820–1).
Charles Bell, *The Hand, Its Mechanism and Vital Endowments as Evincing Design* (London: William Pickering, 1833).
John Bell, *Engravings of the Bones, Muscles, and Joints, illustrating the first volume of the Anatomy of the Human Body* (London, 1794; 2d ed. 1804).
John Bell, *Principles of Surgery*, 3 vols. (Edinburgh, 1801–8; London, 1815); 4 vols. (London, 1825).
John Bell, *Letters on Professional Character and Manners: On the education of a surgeon, and the duties and qualifications of a physician …* (Edinburgh, 1810).
Pietro da Cortona Berrettini, *Tabulae Anatomicae …* (1618; Rome, 1741).
Govard Bidloo, *Onleding des menschelyken lichaams* (Amsterdam, 1690). Art: Gerard De Lairesse.
J.-B.-M. Bourgery & N.-H. Jacob, *Traité complet de l'anatomie de l'homme: comprenant la médecine opératoire, avec planches lithographiées d'après nature* (Paris: C. Delaunay, 1831–54; 2d ed. 1866–71, with Claude Bernard).
Casimir Broussais, *Atlas historique et bibliographique de la médecine …* (Paris, 1834).
Edmund Burke, "Of Beauty," *A Philosophical Inquiry into the Origin of Our Ideas of the Sublime and Beautiful; With An Introductory Discourse Concerning Taste* (London, 1757).
William Cheselden, *Anatomy of the Humane Body* (1st ed.; London, 1713; later editions: *Anatomy of the Human Body*).
William Cheselden, *Osteographia, or The Anatomy of the Bones* (London: [William Bowyer for the author], 1733).
J.F. Clarke, *Autobiographical Recollections of the Medical Profession* (London: J. & A. Churchill, 1874).

[Christopher] Cock, *A Catalogue of the Genuine and Entire Collection of Italian and Other Drawings, Prints, Models, and Casts, of the Late Eminent Mr. Jonathan Richardson, Painter, Deceas'd. Which Will Be Sold by Auction … by Mr. Cock, at his House in the Great Piazza, Covent-Garden, on Thursday the 22d of January, 1746–7, and the Seventeen following Nights (Sunday excepted)* … (London, 1747).

Astley Cooper, *The Anatomy and Surgical Treatment of Abdominal Hernia* (London, 1827).

Astley Cooper, *Diseases of the Breast* (London, 1829).

Astley Cooper, *The Testis* (London, 1830).

R.J. Culverwell ["Fellow of the London Royal College of Surgeons and licentiated practitioner of medicine"], *The Green Book: The modern treatment of syphilis, urethral affections, and all diseases of the urinary and sexual organs* … (London: Published for the author, 1841).

Charles Daremberg, *La Médecine: Histoire et doctrines* (Paris: Didier et cie, 1865).

Charles Darwin, *Darwin's Reading Notebooks* [*c.*1847, DAR *119: 22v.] https://www.darwinproject.ac.uk/people/about-darwin/what-darwin-read/darwin-s-reading-notebooks

Charles Darwin to J.D. Hooker (29 March 1863), *Darwin Correspondence Project* https://www.darwinproject.ac.uk/letter/?docId=letters/DCP-LETT-4065.xml&query=J.%20D.%20Hooker

John Ward Dean, *A Brief Memoir of Rev. Giles Firmin, one of the ejected ministers of 1662* (Boston: David Clapp & Son, 1866).

Charles Dickens, *David Copperfield* (1850; London: Penguin, 2004).

Dr. Franke's Phantom (Berlin, 1891).

Guillaume Dupuytren, *Mémoire sur une maniere nouvelle de pratiquer l'operation de la pierre* (Paris and London: J.B. Bailliére, 1836).

Guillaume Dupuytren (completed by L.J. Sanson & L.J. Begin), *Abhandlung über die Steinoperation nach einer neuen Methode* … [German trans. *Mémoire sur une Manière nouvelle de pratique l'Opération de la Pierre*] (Paris: J.B. Bailliére, 1836)]. Art: N.-H. Jacob; trans. F. Reichmeister (Leipzig: Hochhausen & Fournes, 1837).

Thomas Dwight, "Report on Anatomy," *Boston Medical & Surgical Journal* n.s. 10.10 (5 Sept 1872): 165–6.

George Viner Ellis & G.H. Ford, *Illustrations of Dissections: in a series of original colored plates the size of life, representing the dissection of the human body reduced on a uniform scale* … (London: Walton & Maberly [1861?]).

Ralph Waldo Emerson, *Nature* (Boston: James Munroe & Co., 1836).

Charles Estienne, *De dissectione partium corporis humani libri tres* (Paris, 1545). Art: Étienne La Rivière.

Jacques Gamelin, *Nouveau recueil d'ostéologie et de myologie, dessiné, d'après nature … pour l'utilité, des sciences et des arts* (Toulouse: J.F. Desclassan, 1779).

Arnaud-Éloi Gautier D'Agoty & Nicolas Jadelot, *Cours complet d'anatomie peint et gravé en couleurs naturelles* … (Nancy: LeClerc, 1773).

Jacques-Fabien Gautier [Dagoty] & [Jacques-François-Marie] Duverney, *Myologie complette en couleur et grandeur naturelle* (Paris: Gautier, 1746).

Jacques-Fabien Gautier, *Anatomie de la tête, en tableaux imprimés qui représentent au naturel le cerveau sous différentes coupes, la distribution des vaisseaux dans toutes les parties de la tête, les organes des sens et une partie de la névrologie* …

en 8 grandes planches dessinées, peintes, gravées et imprimées en couleur et grandeur naturelle … (Paris: Gautier, 1748).

Jacques-Fabien Gautier, *Hermaphrodite. Dissertation au sujet de la fameuse Hermaphrodite, qui a paru aux yeux du public depuis environ trois mois, faite par le sieur METRUD, Chirurgien ordinaire du Roi … Laquelle Hermaphrodite a été peinte & gravée par le sieur GAUTIER …* (Paris: Berryer, 1749).

Jacques-Fabien Gautier, *Chroa-Génésie ou génération des couleurs, contre le systeme de Newton* (Paris: Antoine Boudet, 1750–1).

Jacques-Fabien Gautier, *Anatomie des parties de la génération de l'homme et de la femme* (Paris: J.B. Brunet & Demonville, 1773).

Bernardino Genga, *Anatomia per uso et intelligenza del disegno ricercata non solo su gl'ossi, e muscoli del corpo humano* (Rome, 1691).

William Godwin, *Things as They are: or, The Adventures of Caleb Williams* (1794; 4th ed., London, 1816).

Alexander Gordon, "Giles Firmin," *Dictionary of National Biography* (London, 1889), 19: 45–6.

Henry Gray, *Anatomy Descriptive and Surgical* (London, 1864). Art: Henry Vandyke Carter.

Albrecht von Haller, *Icones anatomicae quibus praecipuae aliquae partes corporis humani delineatae proponuntur et arteriarum potissimum historia continetur* (Göttingen: Vandenhoeck, 1743–56; many editions thereafter).

William Hazlitt, "On Genius and Common Sense," in *The Complete Works of William Hazlitt*, ed. P.P. Howe, 21 vols. (London, 1930–4), vol. 18.

William Hogarth, *The Analysis of Beauty: Written with a view of fixing the fluctuating Ideas of Taste* (London, 1753).

Frederick C. Hollick, *The Male Generative Organs in Health and Disease …* (New York: T.W. Strong, 1853).

Oliver Wendell Holmes, "The Professor's Story: Chapter 1: The Brahmin Caste of New England," *The Atlantic Monthly* 5.27 (1860): 93.

Oliver Wendell Holmes, "Scholastic and Bedside Teaching" and "The Contagiousness of Puerperal Fever," in *Medical Essays 1842–1882*, in *The Works of Oliver Wendell Holmes* (Boston: Houghton Mifflin, 1893), 273–311.

Oliver Wendell Holmes, *One Hundred Days in Europe*, in *The Works of Oliver Wendell Holmes* (Boston: Houghton Mifflin, 1892).

Oliver Wendell Holmes, *Over the Teacups*, in *The Works of Oliver Wendell Holmes* (1891; Boston: Houghton Mifflin, 1892).

David Hume, "Of the Standards of Taste" (*c.*1745), originally published in *Four Dissertations* (London: A. Millar in the Strand, 1757).

William Hunter, *The Anatomy of the Gravid Uterus* (Birmingham: John Baskerville, 1774). Art: Jan Van Rymsdyk.

Francis Hutcheson, *An Inquiry into the Original of our Ideas of Beauty and Virtue* (London, 1725).

Richard Payne Knight, *An Account of the Remains of the Worship of Priapus, Lately Existing at Isernia in the Kingdom of Naples: In Two Letters* (London, 1786).

Richard Payne Knight, *An Analytical Inquiry into the Principles of Taste* (London, 1806).

J. Suydam Knox et al., *Physicians' Anatomical Aid: A Manikin of Superimposed Diagrammatic Plates* (Chicago: Western Publishing House, 1884, multiple editions thereafter; also published as *Embalmers' Anatomical Aid*).

Vicesimus Knox, *An Essay on Education*, 2 vols. (London, 1802).

Claude-Nicolas Le Cat, *Traité du sens* (1742; Amsterdam: J. Wetstein, 1744).
Joseph Maclise, *Comparative Osteology: Being morphological studies to demonstrate the archetype skeleton of vertebrated animals* (London: Taylor & Walton, 1847).
Joseph Maclise, *Surgical Anatomy* (1st English ed., London: John Churchill, 1851; 2d ed., 1856).
Joseph Maclise, *Surgical Anatomy* (1st American ed., Philadelphia: Blanchard & Lea, 1851; 2d American ed., 1859).
Joseph Maclise, *On Dislocations and Fractures* (London: John Churchill, 1859).
Paolo Mascagni, *Anatomia Universa or Grande Anatomia del Corpo Umano* (Pisa, 1823–30). Art: Antonio Serrantoni.
Thomas Morton, *The Surgical Anatomy of the Perineum* (London: Taylor & Walton, 1836; 2d ed. 1846). Art: Andrew Morton.
Thomas Morton, *The Surgical Anatomy of Inguinal Herniae, the Testis and its Coverings* (London: Taylor & Walton, 1844). Art: Andrew Morton.
Thomas Morton, *The Surgical Anatomy of the Principal Regions of the Human Body* (London: Taylor & Walton, 1850). Art: Andrew Morton.
W. Justin O'Donnell, *A Memoir of Daniel Maclise, R.A.* (London: Longmans, Green & Co., 1871).
R. & L. Perry & Co. ["consulting surgeons"] [R.J. Jordan], *The Silent Friend …* (London: Published by the authors, 1847).
Victor Plarr, *Plarr's Lives of the Fellows of the Royal College of Surgeons*, 2 vols. (London, 1930).
Moritz Platen, *Livre d'Or de la Santé*, 3 vols. (2d ed.; Paris: Bong et Cie, *c.*1900). [French translation of Platen, *Die neue Heilmethode* (1896).]
Edgar Allan Poe, "The Philosophy of Composition," *Graham's American Monthly Magazine of Literature & Art* (Philadelphia), Apr 1846.
George David Pollock, "Richard Quain," *Address of George David Pollock, F.R.C.S., President of the Royal Medical and Chirurgical Society of London at the annual meeting, March 1st, 1888* (London, 1888), 20–2.
D'A. Power, rerevised By Patrick Wallis, "Thomas Morton," *Oxford Dictionary of National Biography* (2008) https://doi-org.ezproxy.its.uu.se/10.1093/ref:odnb/19376
Jones Quain, *Elements of Anatomy*, eds. Richard Quain & William Sharpey (5th ed., London: Taylor & Walton, 1843).
Jones Quain, *A Series of Anatomical Plates in Lithography*, 3 vols. (London: Taylor & Walton, 1836–42).
Richard Quain, *The Anatomy of the Arteries of the Human Body, with its applications to pathology and operative surgery: in lithographic drawings with practical commentaries* (London: Taylor & Walton, 1844). Art: Joseph Maclise.
Richard Quain, *On Some Defects in General Education: Being the Hunterian Oration of the Royal College of Surgeons for 1869* (London: Macmillan, 1870).
Jonathan Richardson, *Two Discourses: I. An Essay on the whole Art of Criticism as it Relates to Painting; II. An Argument in Behalf of the Science of a Connoisseur, Wherein is shewn the Dignity, Certainty, Pleasure, and Advantage of it* (London: Printed for W. Churchill at Black Swan … 1719).
Marquis [Donatien Alphonse François] de Sade, *120 Days of Sodom and Other Writings*, trans. Richard Seaver & Austryn Wainhouse (1785; New York: Grove Press, 1966).

Marie Philibert Constant Sappey, *Anatomie, Physiologie, Pathologie des Vaisseaux Lymphatiques ...* (Paris: A. Delahaye & E. Lacrosnier, 1874). Art: Jean-Baptiste Léveillé.
Antonio Scarpa, *Sull'Aneurisma Riflessioni ed Osservazioni Anatomico-chirurgiche* (Pavia, 1804).
Francis Sibson, *Medical Anatomy, or, Illustrations of the relative position and movements of the internal organs* (London: John Churchill, 1869). Art: William Fairland.
Adrianus Spigelius, *De humani corporis fabrica libri ...* [from Giulio Casseri] (Amsterdam, 1627). Art: Odoardo Fialetti.
Adrianus Spigelius, *De formato foetu liber singularis aeneis figuris exornatus* (Padua: Martini, Giovanni Battista, 1612–31 & Lorenzo Pasquato, 1626). Art: Odoardo Fialetti.
Friedrich Tiedemann, *Tabulae arteriarum corporis humani* (Karlsruhe: C.F. Müller, 1822). Art: Jakob Wilhelm Christian Roux.
Friedrich Tiedemann, *Plates of the Arteries of the Human Body*, ed. Thos. Wharton Jones, Robert Knox (Edinburgh – Glasgow – London: 1831–35).
Robert B. Todd, ed., *Cyclopædia of Anatomy and Physiology* (London: Sherwood, Gilbert & Piper, 1836).
Philip C. Van Buskirk, Diaries, 1851–1902, University of Washington Libraries Special Collections. Transcription, *Philip C. Van Buskirk Archive* on the *CUNY Academic Commons*, https://vanbuskirk.commons.gc.cuny.edu/.
Oscar Wilde, "The Critic as Artist," *Intentions* (London, 1891).
Jacques Benigne Winslow, *Exposition anatomique de la structure du corps humain* (Paris: Laurent & d'Houry fils, 1732).

Serials

AJMS = *American Journal of the Medical Sciences*, 1850
BFMCR = *British & Foreign Medico-Chirurgical Review*, 1851
BMJ = *British Medical Journal*, 1887, 1958
BMSJ = *Boston Medical & Surgical Journal*, 1872
DNB = *Dictionary of National Biography*, 1912
DQJMS = *Dublin Quarterly Journal of Medical Science*, 1852
EMSJ = *Edinburgh Medical & Surgical Journal*, 1849, 1854
Journal de Monsieur (1776–7) [Jacques-Fabien Gautier Dagoty]
The Lancet 1846, 1852–60, 1887
LMG = *London Medical Gazette*, 1841, 1850
Observations sur l'Histoire Naturelle, sur la Physique et sur la Peinture (1752–55) [Jacques-Fabien Gautier Dagoty]
Observations physiques (1750–3) [Jacques-Fabien Gautier Dagoty]
Observations sur la peinture (1753–4) [Jacques-Fabien Gautier Dagoty]
ODNB = *Oxford Dictionary of National Biography*, 2004; 2008
Plarr's Lives of the Fellows of the Royal College of Surgeons, 1912–40
PMSJ = *Provincial Medical & Surgical Journal*, 1840–51

Scholarship

Samuel Alberti, *Morbid Curiosities: Medical Museums in Nineteenth-Century Britain* (Oxford: Oxford University Press, 2011).

Tanya Augsburg, "Introduction: Some Starting Points, Theories, and Themes," in Augsburg, ed., *Man as Object: Reversing the Gaze* (New York: Women's Caucus for the Arts, 2011), 13–31.

Thomas Balfe, Joanna Woodall, Claus Zittel, eds., *Ad vivum? Visual Materials and the Vocabulary of Life-Likeness in Europe before 1800* (Leiden: Brill, 2019).

Roland Barthes, "The Reality Effect" (1969), in François Wahl, ed., *The Rustle of Language*, trans. Richard Howard (Berkeley: University of California Press, 1989): 141–8.

Seyla Benhabib, *The Claims of Culture: Equality and Diversity in the Global Era* (Princeton: Princeton University Press, 2002).

Walter Benjamin, "The Work of Art in the Age of Mechanical Reproduction" (1936) in *Illuminations*, ed. Hannah Arendt (New York: Schocken/Random House, 1969).

John Berger, *Ways of Seeing* (London: Penguin, 1973).

Carin Berkowitz, "The Beauty of Anatomy: Visual Displays and Surgical Education in Early Nineteenth-Century London," *Bulletin of the History of Medicine* 85.2 (2011): 248–78.

Carin Berkowitz, "Systems of Display: The Making of Anatomical Knowledge in Enlightenment Britain," *British Journal for the History of Science* 46.3 (2013): 359–87.

Carin Berkowitz, "The Illustrious Anatomist: Authorship, Patronage and Illustrative Style in Anatomy Folios, 1700–1840," *Bulletin of the History of Medicine* (2015): 171–208.

Ann Bermingham, "The Aesthetics of Ignorance: The Accomplished Woman in the Culture of Connoisseurship," *Oxford Art Journal* 16.2 (1993): 3–20.

Leo Bersani, "Is the Rectum a Grave?" *October* 43 (Winter 1987): 197–222.

Matthew Bevis, "On Rachael Allen," *London Review of Books* (5 March 2020): 30.

James D. Bloom, *Reading the Male Gaze in Literature and Culture* (London: Palgrave Macmillan, 2017).

T.M. Boggs, "Osler as Bibliophile," *Bulletin of the Johns Hopkins Hospital* 30.341 (1919): 216.

Philippe Bordes, "Richard and Maria Cosway, Edinburgh," *The Burlington Magazine* 137.1111 (1995): 700–2.

Frances Borzello, *The Naked Nude* (London: Thames & Hudson, 2012).

Pierre Bourdieu, *Distinction: A Social Critique of the Judgment of Taste* (1979; trans. Richard Nice, Cambridge: Harvard University Press, 1987).

Alan C. Braddock, "'Jeff College Boys': Thomas Eakins, Dr. Forbes, and Anatomical Fraternity in Postbellum Philadelphia," *American Quarterly* 57.2 (2005): 355–83.

Horst Bredekamp, *Der Bildakt* (Berlin: Wagenbach Klaus, 2015).

Michael Brown, "Surgery and Emotion: The Era Before Anaesthesia," conference paper, Society for the Social History of Medicine annual meeting, University of Kent, UK, July 2016.

Michael Brown, "Surgery, Identity and Embodied Emotion: John Bell, James Gregory and the Edinburgh 'Medical War'," *History* 104 (2018): 19–41.

Michael Brown, *Emotions and Surgery in Britain, 1793–1912* (Cambridge: Cambridge University Press, 2023).

Joseph D. Bryan, "Dazzled, Blinded, & Numb: The Body and Society in Eighteenth-Century France" (PhD dissertation, Duke University, 2016).

Sarah Bull, "A Purveyor of Garbage? Charles Carrington and the Marketing of Sexual Science in Late-Victorian Britain," *Victorian Review* 38.1 (2012): 55–76.

Sarah Bull, "Reading, Writing, and Publishing an Obscene Canon: The Archival Logic of the Secret Museum, *c.*1860–*c.*1900," *Book History* 20 (2017): 226–57.

Sarah Bull, "Managing the 'Obscene M.D.': Medical Publishing, the Medical Profession, and the Changing Definition of Obscenity in mid-Victorian England," *Bulletin of the History of Medicine* 91.4 (2017): 713–43.

B.R. Burg, *An American Seafarer in the Age of Sail: The Erotic Diaries of Philip C. Van Buskirk 1851–1870* (New Haven: Yale University Press, 1994).

Frederick Burwick, *Illusion and the Drama: Critical Theory of the Enlightenment and Romantic Era* (Harrisburg: Penn State Press, 2010).

Thomas Buser, *A History of Drawing*, ch. 4: The Seventeenth Century http://historyofdrawing.com/seventeenth_century_i/.

Judith Butler, *Gender Trouble: Feminism and the Subversion of Identity* (New York: Routledge, 1990).

Judith Butler, *Bodies That Matter: On the Discursive Limits of Sex* (New York: Routledge, 1993).

Judith Butler, "Is Kinship Always Already Heterosexual?," *differences* 13.1 (2002): 14–44.

Judith Butler, *Undoing Gender* (New York: Routledge, 2005).

Caroline Walker Bynum, "The Body of Christ in the Later Middle Ages: A Reply to Leo Steinberg," *Renaissance Quarterly* 39.3 (1986): 399–439.

W.F. Bynum, "Richard Quain," *Oxford Dictionary of National Biography* (2004), https://doi-org.ezproxy.its.uu.se/10.1093/ref:odnb/22940.

Romana Byrne, *Aesthetic Sexuality: A Literary History of Sadomasochism* (New York and London: Bloomsbury, 2013).

Anthea Callen, *Looking at Men: Art, Anatomy and the Modern Male Body* (New Haven and London: Yale University Press, 2018).

Anthea Callen, "Bloodlines: Circulating the Male Body Across Borders in Art and Anatomy 1780–1860," *British Art Studies* 20 (July 2021), https://www.britishartstudies.ac.uk/issues/issue-index/issue-20/bell-brothers.

Henry Patrick Chomeley, "Thomas Henry Wakley," *Dictionary of National Biography* (1912), supplement.

Harry Cocks, "Safeguarding Civility: Sodomy, Class and Moral Reform in Early 19th-Century England," *Past & Present* 190 (2006): 121–46.

Harry Cocks, *Nameless Offences: Speaking of Male Homosexual Desire in Nineteenth-Century England* (London: I.B. Tauris, 2003).

Emily Jane Cohen, "Enlightenment and the Dirty Philosopher," *Configurations* 5 (1997): 369–424.

Viccy Coltman, *Fabricating the Antique: Neoclassicism in Britain, 1760–1800* (Chicago: University of Chicago Press, 2006).

Zachary Cope, *William Cheselden 1688–1752* (Edinburgh and London: E. & S. Livingstone, 1953).

David Peters Corbett, "Oedipus and the Sphinx: Visual Knowledge and Homosociality in the Ricketts Circle," *Visual Culture in Britain* 8.1 (2007): 59–71.

Brian Cowan, "An Open Elite: The Peculiarities of Connoisseurship in Early Modern England," *Modern Intellectual History* 1.2 (2004): 151–83.

Jonathan Crary, *Techniques of the Observer* (Cambridge: MIT Press, 1990).

Jonathan Crary, *Suspensions of Perception: Attention, Spectacle and Modern Culture* (Cambridge: MIT Press, 2000).

Matthew Craske, "'Unwholesome' and 'Pornographic': A Reassessment of the Place of Rackstrow's Museum in the Sory of Eighteenth-century Anatomical Collection and Exhibition," *Journal of the History of Collections* 23.1 (2011): 75–99.

Matthew Craske, *Joseph Wright of Derby: Painter of Darkness* (London: Paul Mellon Centre for Studies in British Art, 2020).

Benedetta Craveri, *The Last Libertines*, trans. Aaron Kerner (New York: NYRB, 2020).

Tom Crewe, "Short Cuts," *London Review of Books* (12 August 2021): 26–7.

Andrew Cunningham & Nicholas Jardine, eds., *Romanticism and the Sciences* (Cambridge: Cambridge University Press, 1990).

Lucia Dacome, "Intimate Connections: Marie Marguerite Biheron and her 'Little Boudoir'," *Bulletin of the History of Medicine* 95.3 (2021): 315–49.

Lorraine Daston & Peter Galison, *Objectivity* (New York: Zone Books, 2007).

Arnold I. Davidson, "Sex and the Emergence of Sexuality," *Critical Inquiry* 14.1 (1987): 16–48 [reprinted as chapter 2 of *The Emergence of Sexuality: Historical Epistemology and the Formation of Concepts* (Cambridge: Harvard University Press, 2001)].

Whitney Davis, *Queer Beauty: Sexuality and Aesthetics from Winckelmann to Freud and Beyond* (New York: Columbia University Press, 2010).

Whitney Davis, "Homoerotic Art Collection from 1750 to 1920," *Art History* 24.2 (2001): 247–77.

Kate Davison, "Occasional Politeness and Gentlemen's Laughter in Eighteenth-Century England," *The Historical Journal* 57.4 (2014): 921–45.

Manuel DeLanda, *Intensive Science and Virtual Philosophy* (London: Bloomsbury, 2013).

Donna Dennis, *Licentious Gotham: Erotic Publishing and Its Prosecution in Nineteenth-Century New York* (Cambridge: Harvard University Press, 2009).

Adrian Desmond, "Robert E. Grant: The Social Predicament of a Pre-Darwinian Transmutationist," *Journal of the History of Biology* 17.2 (1984): 189–223.

Adrian Desmond, *Politics of Evolution* (Chicago: University of Chicago Press, 1989).

Adrian Desmond, "Lamarckism and Democracy: Corporations, Corruption and Comparative Anatomy in the 1830s," in James Richard Moore, ed., *History, Humanity and Evolution: Essays for John C. Greene* (Cambridge: Cambridge University Press, 2002), 99–130.

Jessie Dobson, *Conservators of the Hunterian Museum* (London: Jackson, Ruston & Keeton, 1975).

Jacalyn Duffin, "Imaging Disease ...," in Castel, Leith, Riley, eds., "Muse and Reason: The Relation of Ats and Sciences, 1650–1850," *Queens Quarterly* (1994): 79–108.

Lisa Duggan, "The New Homonormativity: The Sexual Politics of Neoliberalism," in *Materializing Democracy*, ed. Russ Castronovo & Dana D. Nelson (Durham, NC: Duke University Press, 2002).

Joanna Ebenstein, *The Anatomical Venus* (London: Thames & Hudson, 2016).

James Edmondson & John Harley Warner, *Dissection: Photographs of a Rite of Passage in American Medicine 1880–1930* (New York: Blast Books, 2009).

John Edmondson, "Death and the Tourist: Dark Encounters in Mid-Nineteenth-Century London via the Paris Morgue," in *The Palgrave Handbook of Dark Tourism Studies*, ed. Philip R. Stone et al. (London: Palgrave, 2017), 77–101.

Jason Edwards, "'Anxious Flirtations': Homoeroticism, Art and Aestheticism in Late-Victorian Britain," *Visual Culture in Britain* 8.1 (2007): 1–14.

Richard Thomas Eldridge, "Idealism in Nineteenth-Century British and American Literature," *Aesthetics and Literature* 3 (2013): 121–44.

James Elkins, *The Object Stares Back: On the Nature of Seeing* (New York: Harcourt Brace, 1996).

James Elkins, *Pictures of the Body* (1999; Stanford: Stanford University Press, 2021).

David L. Eng; Jack Halberstam; José Esteban Muñoz, eds., "What's Queer about Queer Studies Now?" [special issue], *Social Text* 23.3–4 (2005) https://read.dukeupress.edu/social-text/issue/23/3-4%20(84–5).

Wolfgang Ernst, "Frames at Work: Museological Imagination and Historical Discourse in Neoclassical Britain," *Art Bulletin* 75.3 (1993): 481–98.

Jeffrey Escoffier, "The Political Economy of the Closet," *American Homo: Community and Perversity* (Berkeley: University of California Press, 1998), 66–79.

Mechthild Fend, *Fleshing Out Surfaces: Skin in French Art and Medicine* (Manchester: University of Manchester Press, 2017).

Gary Ferguson, *Same-sex Marriage in Renaissance Rome: Sexuality, Identity, and Community in Early Modern Europe* (Ithaca: Cornell University Press, 2016).

Michel Foucault, *The Birth of the Clinic* (1963; trans. Alan Sheridan Smith, 1973; New York: Routledge, 2003).

Michel Foucault, *The Order of Things: An Archaeology of the Human Sciences* (1966; New York: Vintage, 1973).

Michel Foucault, *La volonté de savoir* (*Histoire de la sexualité* I) (Paris: Gallimard, 1976).

Caroline O. Fowler, "*Res papirea*: Mantegna's Paper Things," *Art Bulletin* 99.1 (2017): 9–35.

David Freedberg, *The Power of Images: Studies in the History and Theory of Response* (Chicago: University of Chicago Press, 1991).

Lorraine Gamman & Caroline Evans, "The Gaze Revisited, or Reviewing Queer Viewing," in *A Queer Romance: Lesbianism, Gay Men and Popular Culture*, ed. Paul Burston & Colin Richardson (London: Routledge, 1995), 13–56.

Rosemarie Garland-Thomson, *Staring: How We Look* (Oxford: Oxford University Press, 2009).

Gerard Gawalt (Library of Congress, USA), "Jefferson's Library: Thomas Jefferson Offers his Library to Congress after the British Burn the Capitol in 1814," *Thomas Jefferson* https://www.loc.gov/exhibits/jefferson/jefflib.html.

Toby Gelfand, "The 'Paris Manner' of Dissection: Student Anatomical Dissection in Early Eighteenth-Century Paris," *Bulletin of the History of Medicine* 46.2 (1972): 99–130.

David Getsy, "Recognizing the Homoerotic: The Uses of Intersubjectivity in John Addington Symonds' 1887 Essays," *Visual Culture in Britain* 8.1 (2007): 37–57.

Carol Gibson-Wood, *Jonathan Richardson: Art Theorist of the English Enlightenment* (New Haven: Yale University Press, 2000).

Carol Gibson-Wood, "Picture Consumption in London at the End of the Seventeenth Century," *Art Bulletin* 84.3 (2002): 491–9.

Judith Giesberg, *Sex and the Civil War: Soldiers, Pornography and the Making of American Morality* (Chapel Hill: University of North Carolina Press, 2017).

Carlo Ginzburg, *Clues, Myths, and the Historical Method* (Baltimore: Johns Hopkins University Press, 1989).

Édouard Glissant, *Poetics of Relation* (Ann Arbor: University of Michigan Press, 1990).

Erving Goffman, *The Presentation of Self in Everyday Life* (New York: Doubleday, 1959).

Alexander Gordon, "Giles Firmin," *Dictionary of National Biography* (London, 1889), 19: 45–6.

Andrew Graciano, "Observation, Imitation and Emulation in *An Academy by Lamplight* by Joseph Wright of Derby (1734–97)," *British Art Journal* 14.3 (2013–14): 36–41.

Anita Guerrini, "Anatomists and Entrepreneurs in Early Eighteenth-Century London," *Journal of the History of Medicine and Allied Sciences* 59.2 (2004): 219–39.

Anita Guerrini, "The Hermaphrodite of Charing Cross," in Erika Dyck & Larry Stewart, eds., *The Uses of Humans in Experiment: Perspectives from the 17th to the 20th Century* (Leiden and Boston: Brill, Rodopi, 2016).

Anita Guerrini, "The Whiteness of Bones: Sceletopoeia and the Human Body in Early Modern Europe," *Bulletin of the History of Medicine* 96.1 (2022): 34–70.

Chris Haffenden, *Every Man His Own Monument: Self-Monumentalizing in Romantic Britain* (Uppsala: Acta Universitatis Upsaliensis, 2018).

André Hahn & Paul Dumaitre, "Le livre d'anatomie en couleurs au XVIIIe siècle, de J.C. Le Blon à J. Gautier-d'Agoty," *Médecine de France: panorama de la pensée médicale littéraire et artistique française* 40 (1962): 10–13.

Jack Halberstam, *The Queer Art of Failure* (Durham, NC: Duke University Press, 2011).

David M. Halperin, *Saint Foucault: Toward a Gay Hagiography* (New York: Oxford University Press, 1997).

David M. Halperin, "How to Do the History of Male Homosexuality," in Donald E. Hall et al., *The Routledge Queer Studies Reader* (New York: Routledge, 2013), 262–86.

Keren Rosa Hammerschlag, *Frederic Leighton: Death, Mortality, Resurrection* (Farnham Surrey and Burlington: Ashgate, 2015).

Keren Rosa Hammerschlag, "Drawing Racial Comparisons in Nineteenth-Century British and American Anatomical Atlases," in Nancy Rose Marshall, ed., *Victorian Science and Imagery: Representation and Knowledge in Nineteenth-Century Visual Culture* (Pittsburgh: University of Pittsburgh Press, 2021), 167–88.

Keren Rosa Hammerschlag, "Black Apollo: Aesthetics, Dissection, and Race in Joseph Maclise's *Surgical Anatomy*," *British Art Studies* 20 (July 2021), https://doi.org/10.17658/issn.2058-5462/issue-20/khammerschlag.

Carolyn Hannaway & Ann La Berge, "Paris Medicine: Perspectives Past and Present," in Hannaway & La Berge, eds., *Constructing Paris Medicine* [*Clio Medica* 50] (Amsterdam: Editions Rodopi, 1998).

Craig Ashley Hanson, *The English Virtuoso: Art, Medicine and Antiquarianism in the Age of Empiricism* (Chicago: University of Chicago Press, 2009).

Karen Harvey, *Reading Sex in the Eighteenth Century: Bodies and Gender in English Erotic Culture* (Cambridge: Cambridge University Press, 2004).

Michael Hatt, "The Male Body in Another Frame: Thomas Eakins' *The Swimming Hole* as a Homoerotic Image," in *Journal of Philosophy & the Visual Arts: The Body*, ed. Andrew Benjamin (London: Academy Group, 1993).

Michael Hatt, "Physical Culture: The Male Nude and Sculpture in Late Victorian Britain," in *After the Pre-Raphaelites: Art and Aestheticism in Victorian England*, ed. E. Prettejohn (New Brunswick: Rutgers University Press, 1999).

Michael Hatt, "Near and Far: Homoeroticism, Labour, and Hamo Thornycroft's *Mower*," *Art History* 26.1 (2003): 26–55.

Michael Hatt, "Space, Surface, Self: Homosexuality and the Aesthetic Interior," *Visual Culture in Britain* 8 (2007): 105–28.

Rosemary Hennessy, "The Material of Sex," in Donald Hall, Annamarie Jagose et al., *The Routledge Queer Studies Reader* (London and New York: Routledge, 2013).

Rosemary Hennessy, *Profit and Pleasure: Sexual Identities in Late Capitalism* (2d ed.; London: Routledge, 2018).

Stefan Hirschauer, "The Manufacture of Bodies in Surgery," *Social Studies of Science* 21.2 (1991): 279–319.

Kathryn Hoffmann, "Sleeping Beauties in the Fairground: The Spitzner, Pedley, and Chemisé Exhibits," *Early Popular Visual Culture* 4.2 (July 2006): 139–59.

Helen Lefkowitz Horowitz, *Rereading Sex: Battles over Sexual Knowledge and Suppression in 19th-Century America* (New York: Knopf, 2002).

Alicia Hughes, "Authorship, Image-Making, and Excess: William Hunter's *Anatomia uteri humani gravidi tabulis illustrata* (1774)," *Journal for Eighteenth-Century Studies* 20.1 (2022), https://doi.org/10.1111/1754-0208.12859.

Mary Hunter, *The Face of Medicine: Visualizing Medical Masculinities in Late 19th-Century Paris* (Manchester: Manchester University Press, 2016).

Annamarie Jagose, *Queer Theory: An Introduction* (New York: New York University Press, 1996).

Ilse Jahn, "On the Origin of Romantic Biology and its Further Development at the University of Jena between 1790 and 1850," in *Romanticism in Science: Science in Europe 1790–1840*, ed. Stefano Poggi & Maurizio Bossi (Dordrecht: Kluwer Academic, 1994).

Regina Janes, "The Salacious Sorrows of Scholarship, Or 'The Gentleman in Lace'," *Salmagundi* 143 (2004): 221–36.

Dorothy Johnson, *Jacques-Louis David: The Art of Metamorphosis* (Princeton: Princeton University Press, 1993).

Rica Jones, "The Artist's Training and Technique," *Manners and Morals* (London: Tate Gallery, 1987).

Ludmilla Jordanova, *Sexual Visions: Images of Gender in Science and Medicine from the Eighteenth to the Twentieth Century* (Madison: University of Wisconsin Press, 1989).

Jason M. Kelly, *The Society of Dilettanti* (New Haven and London: Paul Mellon Centre for Studies in British Art; Yale University Press, 2009).

Walter Kendrick, *The Secret Museum: Pornography in Modern Culture* (Berkeley: University of California Press, 1987).

John Kirkup, "William Cheselden," *Oxford Dictionary of National Biography* (2006), https://doi-org.ezproxy.its.uu.se/10.1093/ref:odnb/5226.

Matthew Knip, "Melville's Queer Hauntology: Selections from the Erotic Journals of Marine Drummer Philip C. Van Buskirk," *Leviathan* 22.1 (2020): 28–54.

Monique Kornell, "Accuracy and Elegance in Cheselden's *Osteographia* (1733)," *Public Domain Review* (22 Aug 2011), https://publicdomainreview.org/2011/08/22/accuracy-and-elegance-in-cheseldens-osteographia-1733/.

Monique Kornell, *Flesh and Bones: The Art of Anatomy* (Los Angeles: Getty Publications, 2022).

Rachel Kravetz, "The Art of Cognition: British Empiricism and Victorian Aesthetics" (PhD dissertation, City University of New York, 2017).

George Kubler, *The Shape of Time: Remarks on the History of Things* (New Haven: Yale University Press, 1962).

Thomas S. Kuhn, *The Structure of Scientific Revolutions* (Chicago: University of Chicago Press, 1962).

Martin Kusch, "Social Epistemology" https://www.hps.cam.ac.uk/students/research-guide/social-epistemology.

Thomas Laqueur, *Making Sex: Bodies and Gender from the Greeks to Freud* (Cambridge: Harvard University Press, 1992).

Bruno Latour, "On Interobjectivity," *Mind, Culture and Activity* 3.4 (1996): 228–45.

Natalie J. Lauer, *Der Kontrakt des Zeichners mit der Medizin: Ästhetik und Wissenschaft im Bildatlas Bourgery & Jacob* (Würzburg: Königshausen & Neumann, 2013).

Corinne Le Bitouzé & Morwena Joly-Parvex, "Cadavre Exquis: L'Ange anatomique de Jacques Fabien Gautier d'Agoty," *Revue de BNF* 52.1 (2016): 106–18.

Eoin Lettice, "'Drink deeply of the nectared cup of science': Woodroffe and the Cork anatomists" (13 Sept 2011), http://www.communicatescience.eu/2011/09/drink-deeply-of-nectared-cup-of-science.html.

Melissa Lo, "Ideal Pathologies: Jean-Marc Bourgery's *Traité complet de l'anatomie de l'homme* (1831–54)," M.S. thesis (Massachusetts Institute of Technology, 2008).

Melissa Lo, "The Wounded Ideal Goes Anatomical," in Michael Sappol, ed., *Hidden Treasure* (New York: Blast Books, 2011), 44–9.

Patricia Lockwood, "I hate Nadia Beyond Reason," *London Review of Books*, (18 February 2021).

Sarah Lowengard, *The Creation of Color in Eighteenth-Century Europe* (New York: Columbia University Press, 2006).

Arthur Lubow, "The Lusty Creativity of Cornelis Cornelisz van Haarlem," *New York Times* (13 January 2021), https://www.nytimes.com/2021/01/13/t-magazine/art-cornelis-cornelisz-van-haarlem.html

Jane Macnaughton, "Flesh Revealed: Medicine, Art and Anatomy," in Corinne Saunders, Ulrika Maude & Jane Macnaughton, eds., *The Body and the Arts* (London: Palgrave Macmillan, 2009).

Dániel Margócsy, "A Museum of Wonders or a Cemetery of Corpses? The Commercial Exchange of Anatomical Collections in Early Modern Netherlands," in Sven Dupré & Christoph Lüthy, eds., *Silent Messengers: The Circulation of Material Objects of Knowledge in the Early Modern Low Countries* (Berlin: LIT, 2011).

Dániel Margócsy, "A Philosophy of Wax: The Anatomy of Frederik Ruysch," in Joanna Ebenstein & Colin Dickey, eds., *The Morbid Anatomy Anthology* (New York: Morbid Anatomy Press, 2014).

Jocelyn E. Marshall, Call for papers for Society for Cinema & Media Studies panel on "Queer Ruptures: Alternative Narrative Praxis as Un/Recovering Histories," H-Sex (7 August 2019).

Lyle Massey, "Against the 'Statue Anatomized': The 'Art' of Eighteenth-Century Anatomy on Trial," *Art History* 40.1 (2017): 68–103.

Rebecca May, "'This shattered prison': Bodily Dissolution, *Wuthering Heights*, and Joseph Maclise's Dissection Manuals," *Nineteenth-Century Contexts* 33.5 (2011): 415–36.

Helen McCormack, *William Hunter and his Eighteenth-Century Cultural Worlds: The Anatomist and the Fine Arts* (London: Routledge, 2017).

Gladys McHugh [art], P.C. Kronfeld & S.L. Polyak [text], *The Human Eye in Anatomical Transparencies* (Rochester, NY: Bausch & Lomb, 1943).

Richard H. Meade, *In the Sunshine of Life: A Biography of Richard Meade 1673–1754* (Philadelphia: Dorrance & Co., 1974).

Domenico Bertoloni Meli, *Visualizing Disease: The Art and History of Pathological Illustrations* (Chicago: University of Chicago Press, 2017).

Rebecca Messbarger, *The Lady Anatomist: The Work of Anna Morandi Manzolini* (Chicago: University of Chicago Press, 2010).

Victoria Mills, "Men and Books: Narratives of Desire," 28 June 2014, https://www.cam.ac.uk/research/features/men-and-books-narratives-of-desire.

W.J.T. Mitchell, *What Do Pictures Want?* (Chicago: University of Chicago Press, 2005).

Benjamin Morgan, *The Outward Mind: Materialist Aesthetics in Victorian Science and Literature* (Chicago: University of Chicago Press, 2017).

Harry Mount, "The Monkey with the Magnifying Glass: Constructions of the Connoisseur in Eighteenth-Century Britain," *Oxford Art Journal* 29.2 (2006): 167–83.

Laura Mulvey, "Visual Pleasure and Narrative Cinema," *Screen* 16.3 (1975): 6–18.

Laura Mulvey, "Afterthoughts on 'Visual Pleasure and Narrative Cinema,' Inspired by 'Duel in the Sun' (King Vidor, 1946)," *Framework* 15/17 (1981): 12–15.

José Esteban Muñoz, *Cruising Utopia: The Then and There of Queer Futurity* (New York: New York University Press, 2009).

Linda Nochlin, *Representing Women* (London: Thames & Hudson, 1999).

Linda Nochlin, "Why Have There Been no Great Women Artists?," *Art News* (January 1971).

Rictor Norton, *Homosexuality in Nineteenth-Century England* https://rictornorton.co.uk/eighteen/nineteen.htm.

Katharine Park, "The Myth of the 'One-Sex' Body," *Isis* 114.1 (2023): 150–75.

Pamela Paul, "Let's Say Gay," *New York Times* (23 October 2023), https://www.nytimes.com/2022/10/23/opinion/queer-gay-identity.html?smid=nytcore-ios-share&referringSource=articleShare.

Zakir Paul, reviewing Hannah Freed-Thall, *Spoiled Distinctions: Aesthetics and the Ordinary in French Modernism* in *Critical Inquiry* 43.4 (2017): 910.

Joseph Frank Payne, "William Cheselden," *Dictionary of National Biography* (1885–1900), 10: 192–4.

Allison Pease, *Modernism, Mass Culture, and the Aesthetics of Obscenity* (Cambridge: Cambridge University Press, 2000).

Nicholas Penny, "At the Royal Academy" [rev. of *The Renaissance Nude* exhibition, London, March-June 2019], *London Review of Books* (23 May 2019): 18.

Jed Perl [rev. of recent editions of books by Leo Steinberg and an exhibition of his prints], "See more, think more," *New York Review of Books* (13 May 2021).

Peggy Phelan, *Mourning Sex: Performing Public Memories* (New York and London: Routledge, 1997).

Elizabeth Prettejohn, "Surplusage!" *London Review of Books* (6 February 2020): 33.

Valerie Racine, "Etienne Geoffroy Saint-Hilaire (1772–1844)," *Embryo Project Encyclopedia* (2013-08-05) http://embryo.asu.edu/handle/10776/6045

Barry Reay, "Writing the Modern Histories of Homosexual England," *The Historical Journal* 52.1 (2009): 213–33.

Philip F. Rehbock, "Transcendental Anatomy," in Andrew Cunningham & Nicholas Jardine, eds., *Romanticism and the Sciences* (Cambridge: Cambridge University Press, 1990), 144–60.

K.B. Roberts & J.D.W. Tomlinson, *The Fabric of the Body: European Traditions of Anatomical Illustration* (Oxford: Clarendon, 1992).

Terry F. Robinson, "Connoisseurship and the Female Body," *Oxford Handbooks Online* (May 2017; update August 2017) DOI: 10.1093/oxfordhb/9780199935338.013.139.

Florian Rodari, "Mélanges anatomiques," in *Anatomie de la couleur: l'invention de l'estampe en couleurs*, Exh. Cat., ed. Florian Rodari (Paris: Bibliothèque nationale de France; Lausanne: Musée Olympique, 1996), 106–32.

Patricia Lee Rubin, *Seen from Behind: Perspectives on the Male Body and Renaissance Art* (New Haven: Yale University Press, 2018).

Michael Sappol, *A Traffic of Dead Bodies: Anatomy and Embodied Social Identity in Nineteenth-Century America* (Princeton: Princeton University Press, 2002).

Michael Sappol, *Dream Anatomy* (Washington: GPO, 2003).

Michael Sappol, "The Odd Case of Charles Knowlton: Anatomical performance, medical narrative and professional Identity in antebellum America," *Bulletin of the History of Medicine* 83.3 (2009): 460–98.

Michael Sappol, "The Phantom of the Anatomy Lesson," in Michael Sappol, ed., *Hidden Treasure* (New York: Blast Books, 2012), 58–9.

Michael Sappol, "Anatomy's Photography: Objectivity, Showmanship and the Reinvention of the Anatomical Image, 1860–1950," *REMEDIA* (January 2017, rev. 2018), https://www.academia.edu/31049714/Anatomy_s_photography_Objectivity_showmanship_and_the_reinvention_of_the_anatomical_image_1860_1950_Introduction.

James M. Saslow, *Pictures and Passions: A History of Homosexuality in the Visual Arts* (New York and London: Viking, 1999).

Jonathan Sawday, *The Body Emblazon'd: Dissection and the Human Body in Renaissance Culture* (London: Routledge, 1995).

Londa Schiebinger, *The Mind Has No Sex? Women in the Origins of Modern Science* (Cambridge: Harvard University Press, 1989).
F.F. Schmitt, ed., *Socializing Epistemology: The Social Dimensions of Knowledge* (Lanham, MD: Rowman & Littlefield, 1994).
Anne L. Schroder, review of "Colorful Impressions: The Print-making Revolution in 18th-century France" and "The Age of Watteau …," *Eighteenth-Century Studies* 37.3 (2004): 455–63.
Vanessa R. Schwartz, *Spectacular Realities: Early Mass Culture in Fin-de-Siècle Paris* (Berkeley: University of California Press, 1999).
Braden Scott, review, Gary Ferguson, *Same-Sex Marriage in Renaissance Rome: Sexuality, Identity, and Community in Early Modern Europe* (Cornell University Press). *H-Histsex, H-Net Reviews* (December 2020), https://www.h-net.org/reviews/showrev.php?id=54849
James Secord, *Victorian Sensation* (Chicago: University of Chicago Press, 2000).
Eve Kosofsky Sedgwick, *The Epistemology of the Closet* (1990; Berkeley: University of California Press, 2008).
Eve Kosofsky Sedgwick, *Between Men: English Literature and Male Homosocial Desire* (New York: Columbia University Press, 1985).
Kristel Sementek, *Mariette and the Science of the Connoisseur in Eighteenth-Century Europe* (Farnham and Burlington: Ashgate, 2014).
William H. Sewell Jr., *Capitalism and the Emergence of Civic Equality in Eighteenth-Century France* (Chicago: University of Chicago Press, 2021).
Steven Shapin & Simon Schaffer, *Leviathan and the Air-Pump: Hobbes, Boyle, and the Experimental Life* (Princeton: Princeton University Press, 1985).
Naomi Slipp, "International Anatomies: Teaching Visual Literacy in the Harvard Lecture Hall," in *Bodies Beyond Borders: Moving Anatomies, 1750–1950*, ed. Kaat Wils, Raf de Bont, and Sokhieng Au (Leuven: Leuven University Press, 2017).
Naomi Slipp, "'It Should Be on Every Surgeon's Table': The Reception and Adoption of Joseph Maclise's *Surgical Anatomy* (1851) in the United States," *British Art Studies* 20 (July 2021), https://doi.org/10.17658/issn.2058-5462/issue-20/nslipp.
James Smalls, *Homosexuality in Art* (New York: Parkstone Press, 2015).
Abigail Solomon-Godeau, *Male Trouble: A Crisis in Representation* (London: Thames & Hudson, 1997).
Susan Sontag, "Against Interpretation," in *Against Interpretation and Other Essays* (New York: Farrar, Straus & Giroux, 1966).
Fiona Stafford, "What Are Books for? Darcy's Library, Crabbe's *The Library*, and Shillito's *The Country Book-Club*," in Alice Crawford & Robert Crawford, eds., *Libraries in Literature* (Oxford: Oxford University Press, 2022), 71–85.
Perrin Stein, ed., *Jacques Louis David: Radical Draftsman* (New York: Metropolitan Museum of Art, 2022).
Leo Steinberg, "The Sexuality of Christ in Renaissance Art and in Modern Oblivion," *October* 25 (1983): 1–217.
Leo Steinberg, *The Sexuality of Christ in Renaissance Art and in Modern Oblivion* (Chicago: University of Chicago Press, 1997).
Cindy Stelmackowich, "Bodies of Knowledge: The Nineteenth-Century Anatomical Atlas in the Spaces of Art and Science," *RACAR: revue d'art canadienne/Canadian Art Review* 33.1/2 (2008) [Medical Tabulae: Visual Arts and Medical

Representation/Tabulae Médicale: Arts Visuels et Représentation Médicale]: 75–86.

Elizabeth Stephens, "Touching Bodies: Tact/ility in Nineteenth-Century Medical Photographs and Models", in *Bodies, Sex and Desire from the Renaissance to the Present*, ed. Kate Fisher & Sarah Toulalan (London: Palgrave Macmillan, 2011), 87–101.

Andrew Stephenson, "Precarious Poses: The Problem of Artistic Visibility and its Homosocial Performances in Late Nineteenth-Century London," *Visual Culture in Britain* 8.1 (2007): 73–103.

Ad Stijnman et al., *Jacob Christoff Le Blon and Trichromatic Printing*, 2 vols. (Ouderkerk aan den IJssel: Sound & Vision; Amsterdam: Rijksmuseum, 2020).

Edward C. Streeter, "Osler as Bibliophile," *Boston Medical & Surgical Journal* 1 Apr 1920: 335–8.

Wilson Sullivan, *New England Men of Letters* (New York: Macmillan, 1972).

Jenny Sundén, "Digital Kink Obscurity: A Sexual Politics Beyond Visibility and Comprehension," *Sexualities* (2023), https://journals.sagepub.com/doi/epub/10.1177/13634607221124401.

Nicola Suthor, *Bravura: Virtuosity and Ambition in Early Modern European Painting* (Princeton: Princeton University Press, 2021).

M. Terrall, "Natural Philosophy for Fashionable Readers," in M. Frasca-Spada & N. Jardine, eds., *Books and the Sciences in History* (Cambridge: Cambridge University Press, 2000), 239–54.

Marcus Tomalin, *The French Language and British Literature 1756–1830* (London – New York: Routledge, 2016).

Jennifer Tsien & Jacques Morizot, "Eighteenth-Century French Aesthetics," in E.N. Zalta, ed., *The Stanford Encyclopedia of Philosophy* (Winter 2021), https://plato.stanford.edu/archives/win2021/entries/aesthetics-18th-french/.

John Turpin, "Daniel Maclise and Charles Dickens: A Study of Their Friendship," *Studies: An Irish Quarterly Review* 73.289 (Spring 1984): 47–66.

John Turpin, "Daniel Maclise and Cork Society," *Journal of the Cork Historical and Archaeological Society* 85 (1985): 66–88.

John Turpin, "Daniel Maclise," *Dictionary of National Biography* (Oxford: Oxford University Press, 2004).

Jenny Uglow, *William Hogarth: A Life and a World* (1998; New York: Farrar Straus & Giroux, 2002).

Charles Upchurch, *Before Wilde: Sex between Men in Britain's Age of Reform* (Berkeley: University of California Press, 2013).

Charles Upchurch, "*Beyond the Law*": *The Politics of Ending the Death Penalty for Sodomy in Britain* (Philadelphia: Temple University Press, 2022).

Nicholas de Villiers, *Opacity and the Closet: Tactics in Foucault, Barthes and Warhol* (Minneapolis: University of Minnesota Press, 2012).

Darren N. Wagner, "Arousing Applications: Syringes and Anatomical: Preparations of Genital Organs in the Long Eighteenth Century," *Bulletin of the Scientific Instrument Society* 113 (2012): 4–9.

Darren N. Wagner, "A Bit Exposed: Displays of Male Genitals," in Raymond Stephanson & Darren N. Wagner, eds., *The Secrets of Generation: Reproduction in the Long Eighteenth Century* (Toronto: University of Toronto Press, 2015), 386–414.

Susan S. Waller, *The Invention of the Model: Artists and Models in Paris, 1830–1870* (Aldershot and Burlington: Ashgate, 2006).

Laura M. Walters, *Odoardo Fialetti (1573–c.1638): The Interrelation of Venetian Art and Anatomy, and his Importance in England* (PhD thesis, art history, University of St. Andrews, 2009).

Mary Webster, "Zoffany's Painting of Charles Towneley's Library in Park St. Westminster," *Burlington Magazine* 56 (July 1964): 316–23.

Mary Webster, *Johan Zoffany 1733–1810* (New Haven: Yale University Press, 2011).

Jeffrey Weeks, *Coming Out: Homosexual Politics in Britain from the Nineteenth Century to the Present* (London: Quartet Books, 1977).

Torsten Weimarck, *Akademi och anatomi: Några aspekter på människokroppens historia i nya tides konstnärsutbildning och ateljépraktik, med särskild tonvikt på anatomiundervisningen vid konstakademierna i Stockholm oh Köpenhamn fram till 1800-talets början* (Stockholm: Brutus Östlings Bokförlag Symposion, 1996).

Annette Wickham, "Strike a Pose: 250 Years of Life Drawing at the RA," *RA Blog* (6 February 2018), https://www.royalacademy.org.uk/article/from-life-history-of-life-drawing-annette-wickham.

Janice Ruth Wood, *The Struggle for Free Speech in the United States, 1872–1915: Edward Bliss Foote, Edward Bond Foote, and Anti-Comstock Operations* (New York: Routledge, 2012).

Blair Worden, "Novel and Naughty," *London Review of Books* (26 September 2019): 19.

Alexander Wragge-Morley, "Connoisseurship and the Communication of Anatomical Knowledge: The Case of William Cheselden's *Osteographia* (1733)," in A. Craciun & S. Schaffer, eds., *The Material Cultures of Enlightenment* (London: Palgrave Macmillan, 2016), 271–89.

William C. Wright, "Hazlitt, Ruskin, and Nineteenth-Century Art," *Journal of Aesthetics and Art Criticism* 32.4 (1974): 509–23.

Lauren Young, "Bibliomania, the Dark Desire For Books That Infected Europe in the 1800s," *Atlas Obscura* (2 December 2016), https://www.atlasobscura.com/articles/bibliomania-the-dark-desire-for-books-that-infected-europe-in-the-1800s.

Abigail Zitin, "Wantonness: Milton, Hogarth, and *The Analysis of Beauty*," *differences* 27.1 (2016): 25–46.

INDEX